PRAISE FOR *CHERRY*

"One of the most haunting adventure tales of all time. . . . Wheeler's retelling of [this] famous ordeal is psychologically astute and deeply felt."
—*Outside*

"[An] extraordinarily fine biography. . . . This is so much the stuff of great biography that it comes as somewhat of a surprise that it had not been undertaken before now. But perhaps Cherry was only waiting for an ideal biographer to discover him."
—*The Boston Globe*

"Beautifully written and deeply felt . . . Wheeler has perfect pitch for this material. . . . She has produced a fully realized portrait of one of the 20th century's great tragic heroes."
—*The Globe and Mail* (Toronto)

"Beautiful . . . written with unfailing eloquence and grace, and great admiration for its subject."
—*The Independent* (London)

"Wheeler accomplishes what only the best biographies can. Drawing on her own experience in the Antarctic, she is able to satisfy the reader's curiosity of how it must have felt to be on that doomed expedition."
—*The Times* (London)

"A lively biography of the adventurer-author. . . . Keeps Cherry-Garrard's story humming along, novel-like, from his lord-of-the-manor childhood to his friendship with neighbor George Bernard Shaw."
—*Entertainment Weekly*

"This is Wheeler's first biography and it is a wonderful match of author to subject. . . . She brilliantly communicates the icy spell that holds her, and held Cherry, in its frozen grip."
—*The Observer* (London)

"This is a supple, chewy book, juggling many features. Vulnerability, ambition, foolishness. It's nuanced, bold, and three-dimensional. Ice-worthy. I pored over and argued with it, and when I finished, felt replete."
—Edward Hoagland, author of *Tigers & Ice*

SARA WHEELER is the author of *Terra Incognita* and *Travels in a Thin Country,* both available as Modern Library trade paperbacks, and was co-editor of *Amazonian: The Penguin Book of Women's New Travel Writing.*

   Terra Incognita, an international best-seller about her travels in Antarctica, was chosen by Beryl Bainbridge as one of the Best Books of the Year; *Travels in a Thin Country,* on Chile, was short-listed for the Thomas Cook Travel Book of the Year Award.

CHERRY

A Life of Apsley Cherry-Garrard

Sara Wheeler

THE MODERN LIBRARY

NEW YORK

2003 Modern Library Paperback Edition

Copyright © 2001 by Sara Wheeler

All rights reserved under International and Pan-American Copyright
Conventions. Published in the United States by Modern Library,
a division of Random House, Inc., New York, and simultaneously
in Canada by Random House of Canada Limited, Toronto.

MODERN LIBRARY and the TORCHBEARER Design are registered
trademarks of Random House, Inc.

This work was originally published in Great Britain
by Jonathan Cape, a division of Random House UK,
London, in 2001.

LIBRARY OF CONGRESS CATALOGING-IN-PUBLICATION DATA
Wheeler, Sara.
Cherry: a life of Apsley Cherry-Garrard/Sara Wheeler.—1st ed.
p.   cm.
Includes bibliographical references (p.).
ISBN 0-375-75454-7
1. Cherry-Garrard, Apsley, 1886–1959.   2. Explorers—England—Biography.
3. Antarctica—Discovery and exploration.   I. Title.
G875.C53 W54 2002
919.8'904—dc21   2001048466

Modern Library website address: www.modernlibrary.com
Printed in the United States of America
2 4 6 8 9 7 5 3 1

To Angela Mathias and Hugh Turner,
with affection

Contents

Illustrations

THE ANTARCTIC CONTINENT

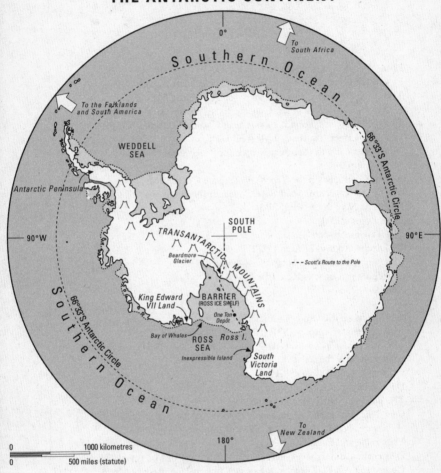

Southern Ocean

To South Africa

To the Falklands
and South America

WEDDELL
SEA

66°33'S Antarctic Circle

Antarctic Peninsula

90°W

90°E

SOUTH
POLE

TRANSANTARCTIC

MOUNTAINS

Scott's Route to the Pole

Beardmore
Glacier

King Edward
VII Land

BARRIER
(ROSS ICE SHELF)

One Ton
Depôt

Bay of Whales

ROSS
SEA

Ross I.

Inexpressible Island

South
Victoria
Land

66°33'S Antarctic Circle

Southern Ocean

180°

To
New Zealand

0   1000 kilometres
0   500 miles (statute)

ROSS ISLAND

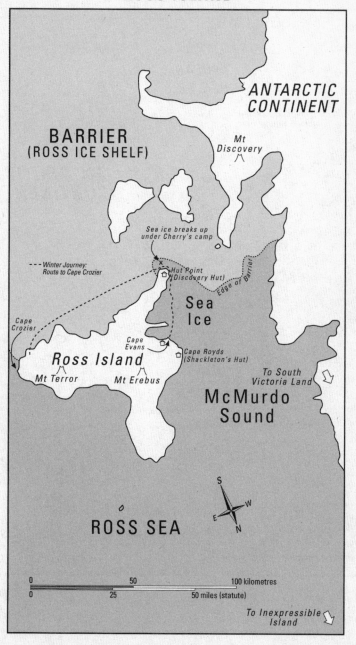

ANTARCTIC
CONTINENT

BARRIER
(ROSS ICE SHELF)

Mt
Discovery

Sea ice breaks up
under Cherry's camp

Winter Journey:
Route to Cape Crozier

X
Hut Point
(Discovery Hut)

Edge of Barrier

Sea
Ice

Cape
Crozier

Cape
Evans

Cape Royds
(Shackleton's Hut)

Ross Island

To South
Victoria Land

Mt Terror

Mt Erebus

McMurdo
Sound

S

E   W

N

ROSS SEA

0   50   100 kilometres
0   25   50 miles (statute)

To Inexpressible
Island

SCOTT'S ROUTE TO THE POLE

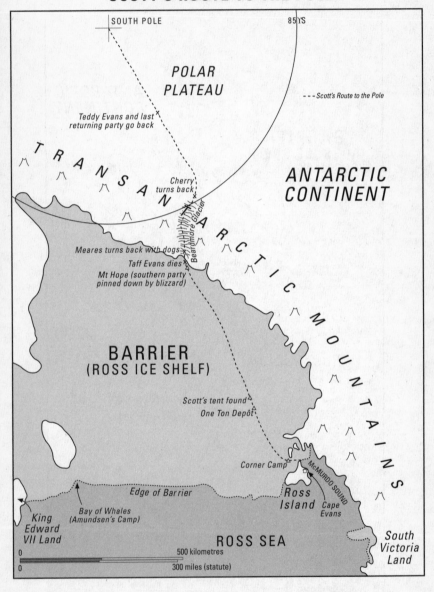

SOUTH POLE   85°S

POLAR
PLATEAU

--- Scott's Route to the Pole

Teddy Evans and last
returning party go back

T R A N S A N

ANTARCTIC
CONTINENT

Cherry
turns back

Beardmore Glacier

Meares turns back with dogs

Taff Evans dies

Mt Hope (southern party
pinned down by blizzard)

A R C T I C

BARRIER
(ROSS ICE SHELF)

M O U N T A I N S

Scott's tent found
One Ton Depôt

Corner Camp

McMURDO SOUND

Ross
Island

Cape
Evans

King
Edward
VII Land

Bay of Whales
(Amundsen's Camp)

Edge of Barrier

ROSS SEA

South
Victoria
Land

0 ———————————— 500 kilometres

0 ———————————— 300 miles (statute)

Introduction

Some years ago, marooned in a small tent close to one of the dynamic ice streams on the west Antarctic ice sheet, I finished reading *The Worst Journey in the World* as a blizzard closed in around our tiny camp. Over the next days I lay in a lonely whiteout and thought about the man who wrote it. I admired his elegant scepticism, the bitter brilliance of his prose and the nimble sleight of hand with which he had transformed his story into a parable. Between the graceful lines I saw, dimly, a vision of a certain kind of Englishness: quizzical detachment, a finely tuned sense of irony, an infinite capacity for gloom tempered with elegiac melancholy. Or that is what I thought I saw.

The story of Captain Scott's doomed expedition to the South Pole, and of Titus Oates' luminous exit from the tent, had been repeated many times. But Cherry-Garrard's story had never been told: there was no biography. It didn't seem right that the author of such a dazzling work should remain a mute and shadowy figure. His book was not the disembodied account of an expedition: it was an intimate reflection of the man behind the authorial mask. I wanted a glimpse of that man.

The journey from that far-off day in the tent has been long and challenging. I had never tackled a biography before. As the months progressed, and then the years, I had to learn to explore the past in the way I had previously explored places. Some parts of Cherry's life were hard to get to, and involved a lot of rough terrain. The amount of material I uncovered varied immensely: a glut of primary material for the Antarctic period; a drought for great stretches of time. For many months I heard little but the sound of trees crashing across my path. Then a cache of letters would turn up, unread since some long-ago recipient folded them back into their flimsy envelopes. A small thing sometimes casts a long light.

Cherry was born in an age as remote as the South Pole: horse-drawn hansom cabs, tribes of indoor servants, a squirearchy sitting comfy in their rural seats, Gladstone and Salisbury battling it out. Yet he died only two years before I was born, when Harold Macmillan was in Downing Street and John Osborne had already written *Look Back in Anger*. He lived to see Sputnik, but his father was born in the reign of William IV. His was a period of huge, unstoppable change. Indeed, so much happened in his seventy-three years that I occasionally wondered in exasperation if anything could possibly have taken place in the world before 1886.

Much has been written about the Edwardian summer that bloomed before the Great War, and about the irreversible changes that war brought to Britain. But for Cherry it was the Antarctic that changed everything. After an upbringing of late-Victorian privilege and a conventional, trussed-up progression through prep school, Winchester and Oxford, he sailed down to the Antarctic at the age of twenty-four. He was away from 1910 to 1913: a crucial period of British history. He came back to a different country. But he was different, too. Like most of the Antarctic veterans he went off to Flanders soon after, but it was his experience in the south that shaped his ideas and determined his private mythology. It lay like a bright, shining band between his youth and the rest of his life.

Meanwhile the legend of Scott quickly hardened. It symbolised a vanished age: one in which Englishmen oiled the engines of imperialism with confidence and quasi-religious zeal. Scott came to embody a set of old-fashioned ideals, especially after the war had given those ideals a good pummelling. He became a kind of Arthurian hero, a mystical Galahad of the snows. As inspirational fuel he was tapped for decades: even after the Second World War crocodiles of schoolboys were marched into cinemas to watch John Mills staggering through fake snow at Ealing Studios. In our own less heroic age the expedition has begun to emerge from the penumbra of proprieties that shrouded public events in those distant days. But its chief chronicler has been left to languish in the historical gloom.

Like many of his peers, before he reached middle age Cherry felt that he had witnessed the collapse of a world that had been ordered and codified by a familiar set of shared values ('God in his Heaven,' as his contemporary Siegfried Sassoon put it, 'and sausages for breakfast.') He had seen the certainties of his youth crumble, and acknowledged bleakly that the world 'was losing its ancient faiths without having much to put in their place'. Soon he was convinced that moral rot had set in, and the conviction relentlessly stoked his personal vision of Spenglerian decline. But through his work, and by dint of his creative impulse, he tried to redeem his losses. I admired that.

It did not save him. Cherry was not a conventional man, and he had never fitted in, even before the great social changes that so vexed him. He was uncomfortable in his father's shoes as head of several large estates, and he had left his own religious faith behind in the nursery. He spent part of his adult life lost in some terrible personal chaos that was infinitely more catastrophic than the upheavals he observed sweeping through middle England. Everyone who has written about Cherry has focused on his periods of debilitating depression, as if those episodes condemned him. I found myself admiring him for not going under. This, surely, was an example of what the human spirit can achieve. Anxiety was one of Cherry's defining characteristics: what could be more human?

He was a mass of contradictions, like most of us, and I have struggled not to gratify the biographer's need to impose coherence. The truth is more complicated than it seems in any biography. I was most interested in Cherry's inner life: the place where the documents stop. A biographer's task is to disengage the essence of a person from the interminable clutter of gas bills and dentist's appointments.

As for the documents: there are almost no published sources. Cherry's Garrard ancestors left boxes of lifeless material which are open to researchers at the Hertfordshire county archives. The family solicitors also recently deposited several boxes of legal documents there, as well as at the Berkshire Record Office. It was interesting material, though largely unusable. Cherry's Antarctic archive, including his journal, resides at the Scott Polar Research Institute in Cambridge, home of much of the unpublished material on the 1910–13 expedition. Most of Scott's officers and some of his seamen left diaries, and their accounts form a rich and sometimes dissonant fugue in many voices. For the later years of Cherry's life I was dependent on the memory, testimony and diaries of his widow Angela Mathias, who has co-operated with this biography far beyond the call of duty. Fragments popped up in other places. But many gaps stubbornly refused to close, and there is a great deal I don't know.

As I moved among the material that does exist, sifting and shaping and selecting the fertile fact, I was not an impartial reporter. All biographers mirror at some unfathomable level their own preoccupations and those of their age. But I hope I have kept myself on the sidelines. I am sure that Cherry will not be imprisoned in this first biography. Others will come and lay their pictures over mine, and other Cherrys will emerge. Biography has no end.

Immersion in his life was a happy experience; I found his company invigorating, most of the time. When he seemed remote I tried to remember that he knew something of loss and failure and sadness; and so did I. It brought him near. Cherry's story, I always believed, was worth telling. I wanted the man who wrote *The Worst Journey* to stand up for a moment. From the start I realised that a glimpse was the most I could hope for; now, at the end, I am even more convinced of the fundamental, immutable isolation of one human being from another. Whom do we really know? But seeing through a glass darkly is still seeing, and the effort brings its own reward, as Cherry might have said. I was encouraged by his own bold approach to biographical writing. Lytton Strachey published *Eminent Victorians* while he was working on *The Worst Journey*, so the idea that biography was more about conjuring flesh and blood than accumulating documents was quite new. Yet alone of the men who produced accounts of the expedition, Cherry insisted on portraying Scott in shades of dark and light.

Towards the end of his life Cherry tried to sum up what he had done in *The Worst Journey*, and why he had done it. 'To me, and perhaps to you, the interest in this story is the men, and it is the spirit of the men, "the response of the spirit", which is interesting rather than what they did or failed to do: except in a superficial sense they never failed.' Nor did he, except in that superficial sense. His words about his book describe his life just as well: 'It is a story about human minds with all kinds of ideas and questions involved, which stretch beyond the furthest horizons.'

1

Ancestral Voices

In the restless years of middle age Cherry used to sit in the bow-window of his library, turning the pages of the journals he had kept in the Antarctic three decades before. Absorbed in those far-off years, he jotted notes in the margins, as if the expedition had not yet reached its conclusion. 'All Scott's orders had been altered,' he wrote crossly. '*Scott should have asked the doctors for their advice.*' Beyond the trimmed lawns outside, the familiar figure of Tilbury, the head gardener, stooped over the rhododendrons. The rooks returned to their nests in the elms, briefly darkening the sky. Cherry leafed through the flimsy notebooks, recalling the rippled glaciers that tumbled down Mount Erebus, their gleaming cliffs casting long blue shadows; the crunching patter of dogs on the march; the pale, shadowless light of the ice shelf and a smudgy sun wreathed in mist. 'Those first days of sledging were wonderful!' he had written. In the quiet of his library he heard again the hiss of the Primus after a long, hard day on the trail, and smelt the homely infusion of tobacco as the night sun sieved through the green cambric of the tent. He tasted the tea flavoured with burnt blubber, and felt the rush of relief as tiny points of light from the kippered hut glimmered faintly in the unforgiving darkness of an Antarctic winter. 'Can we ever forget those days?' he wrote.

Cherry tortured himself over his actions in February 1912, when he had driven a team of dogs 150 miles south to a food depôt to wait for Captain Scott and his four companions; they were expected to return from the Pole at any day. Winter was closing in and Cherry was navigating for the first time in his life, desperately handicapped by short sight, brutal temperatures and diminishing light. He reached the food depôt with his Russian dog-driver, and, following instructions, they stopped, pinned down in a tiny tent in hundreds of miles of opaque, swirling drift. They could not go on: they had no dog food to spare. Cherry remembered straining his eyes in the milky light of the Great Ice Barrier, looking for men who never came. One night he was so sure he could see figures approaching that he had reached for his boots and set out to meet them.

The truth was that he could have gone on. He could have pressed on through the blizzard, killing a dog at a time to feed to the others. He had been ordered to spare the dogs, but, as he had once written, 'In this sort of life orders have to be elastic.' If he had killed the dogs, and if he had journeyed just twelve-and-a-half miles further, there was a tiny chance that he might have stumbled on a small pyramid tent in which three men were dying. One was Captain Scott. The other two were Birdie Bowers and Bill Wilson, the closest friends Cherry had ever had. It was Bill who had got him onto the expedition; Bill who had stood in for his dead father; Bill who had taught him the things he came to think were most important. In death and in life, Bill was never far from Cherry's mind. 'If you knew him,' he wrote of his mentor, 'you could not like him: you simply had to love him.' When, having missed Scott and the others, he got back to the hut that was their Antarctic base, Cherry dreamt that his friends walked in. Almost two decades later he noted in the margin of his polar journal, 'My relief was so intense that I can remember waking up to the disappointment even now.'

Ten months after the journey to the food depôt Cherry and a search party found the tent, piled with snow and weighted to the ice by three mottled corpses. He went through Bill's pockets, collecting the contents for his widow. The body was hard, like stone. After prayers, they left the three men side by side in their sleeping bags, removing the bamboo tent poles and collapsing the cambric over them. The sun was dipping low over the Pole, the Barrier almost in shadow, and the sky was a mass of iridescent cloud, dark against gold and emerald. Cherry said it was a grave which kings must envy.

From that day, he was obsessed by the thought that he might have saved them. 'If we [he and the Russian dog-driver] had travelled on for a day and a half,' he wrote, 'we might have left some food and oil on one of the cairns, hoping that they would see it.' It was a devastating realisation. 'But we never dreamed that they were in great want. It will always to the end of my life be a great sorrow to me that we did not do this.'

When the remnants of the expedition reached New Zealand, Cherry was judged harshly by the press for his decision not to march on from the depôt. But his own psyche was the hardest judge. At the end of the ghastly day on which they uncovered the bodies, he turned again to his journal and wrote, 'I am almost afraid to go to sleep now.' He knew the dreams that were waiting.

Still a bachelor as he approached fifty, he had inherited the seats of both the Cherrys and the Garrards, and prudent investments yielded a generous income, even in the pinched 1930s. He had lived on the Lamer estate in Hertfordshire, the ancestral home of the Garrards, since he was a small child, and after the departure of his mother during the war he had had the handsome Georgian manor to himself. More importantly, for his inner life at least, he had been immensely gratified by the success of *The Worst Journey in the World* following its first publication in 1922. He was thirty-six when it came out, and he said later that it was a sequel to the friendship that had existed between him, Bill and Birdie. The book had taken many years to complete, and as he pored over the pages in the quiet library, his head lowered over his father's desk, he heard again the long-silenced voices calling out across the ice, and glimpsed the familiar smiles he had loved so long ago. As he brooded, he looked back at his vanished self, and when he took up his pen once more his restless reflection seeped into his prose. Much of *The Worst Journey* is infused with a particular, plangent nostalgia.

A winter journey to Cape Crozier lay at the heart of his book, and as he grew older it took on an iconic role in his life. During their first winter on the ice, Cherry, Bill and Birdie had set out to collect the eggs of the Emperor penguin, incubated, alone in the natural world, during the Antarctic darkness. At the time, it was widely believed that if examined at an early stage of development, Emperor embryos would yield a rare Darwinian prize: they would reveal the link between birds and reptiles. The journey to fetch the eggs took five weeks: the temperature fell to minus 75 degrees Fahrenheit, the tent blew away and the men's necks froze the moment they bent to pull their sledges. Then their teeth shattered in the cold. Yet, Cherry wrote, 'We did not forget the Please and Thank you . . . And we kept our tempers, even with God.' Only seven months later Bill and Birdie perished on the Great Ice Barrier with Scott, and when Cherry finally got the precious eggs home the staff at the Natural History Museum made him wait in a corridor, then turned up their noses. The eggs became the central symbol of Cherry's parable. 'If you march your Winter Journeys,' he wrote at the end of his epic, 'you will have your reward, so long as all you want is a penguin's egg.' He had thought his way beyond crampons and rations and snow-blindness, and entered the immortal zone.

For a time it appeared that the process of writing his Antarctic story had quietened his anxieties: a kind of cathartic redemption. There had been happy months and years when the house was filled with the talk of young people. Girlfriends had come and gone; new friendships had been forged. But as the years unravelled, the various editions of *The Worst Journey* lined up on the glazed bookshelves could not assuage Cherry's guilt and self-recrimination. The truths he had captured in his work were more difficult to find off the page.

He was born, on 2 January 1886, at 15 Lansdowne Road, a detached, red-brick house on a tree-lined avenue in deeply respectable Bedford. There was nothing ornate about the houses in the street: they were designed for large, middle-class families with more aspirations than cash. His father, Colonel Apsley Cherry, was fifty-three, the second son of a prosperous family of lawyers and civil servants who had settled in Berkshire a generation before him; his mother, Evelyn Sharpin, was twenty-eight, the daughter of an eminent Bedford doctor.

Colonel Cherry had crinkly brown hair streaked with grey, white sideburns, a high forehead and a strong nose above a neatly waxed handlebar moustache, and he was an upright figure in both the physical and the moral sense. After school at Harrow, which he hated, he proceeded to Christ Church, Oxford, and then, like many younger brothers, went off to fight wars. He joined the 90th Light Infantry as a junior officer, and in 1857, on his way to China with a detachment of his regiment, he was shipwrecked close to Sumatra, not far off the Equator. The soldiers rowed to a small island, and although Apsley Cherry lost most of his gear, his bed floated ashore. The men ate pineapples and coconuts for a week, and then a passing ship brought rescue and news. 'The sepoys have kicked up a row in India,' Apsley wrote to his mother. It turned out to be more than a row: it was the Indian Mutiny. China was forgotten, Apsley Cherry packed up his dried-out bed and the detachment was re-routed to Calcutta on a relief ship. He went on to serve with gallantry in the Mutiny, fighting in the assault, relief and capture of Lucknow, and in the reconquest of Oude. He got a medal with two clasps for all that.

Apsley wrote frequently and affectionately to his family. From Alum-bagh, near Lucknow, he asked his mother, 'Send this please to Amy and Emily, just to shew them, what of course they must know already, that they are never forgotten by their brother Apsley.' He was a natural soldier. 'I don't think,' he wrote to his mother during the siege of Lucknow, when men were falling all around him, 'you need be in much fear for my being hit at this work, for I don't think I was born to be shot.' A cosy domesticity clings to the letters, cheating the miles and the years. Describing an abscess on his hand, he wrote, 'I can fancy you examining into the subject in the brown medicine book!'

After three years' staff service in Bengal, he returned on leave to Denford, the family estate in Berkshire. In his heart he had never really left. What gripped him most keenly was the shooting. 'Mind you give me an account of any good bags,' he wrote to his brother George from Lucknow. George in turn made sure that Apsley was involved in such vital issues as the appointment of a new gamekeeper. It helped diffuse the tension of war. 'It seems to be a great partridge year,' wrote Apsley in the same letter, continuing without even a line break, 'A battlefield is the most awful place you ever saw.' He was a committed correspondent, once dashing off a letter 'during an interval in the firing'. When George wrote asking if he or Mother could help out financially, Apsley replied breezily, 'I thank you exceedingly for thinking of it but truly I have lots here . . . we live on our rations and loot the rest.'

Apsley stayed in India for twenty years. He was promoted to major in 1874, and three years later, still with the 90th Light, he went to southern Africa, where settlers were fighting over their territorial rights. Relations between the first colonists, the Dutch-speaking Boers, and the more recent British immigrants had been tense for decades. That year, 1877, Britain annexed the Boer Republic of the Transvaal as the first step in a campaign to create a South African federation, thereby bringing the whole southern region of the continent under British control. Terrible battles followed, and Apsley Cherry was present at the most gruesome. 'All the morning,' he wrote on 1 May 1878, 'I have been burying men.' He was mentioned in despatches and received a medal with clasp and the brevet (temporary promotion) of lieutenant-colonel, later to be made permanent. The responsibility lay heavily. 'If you have to fight against great odds,' he wrote, 'do so as a subaltern, not as one in command, sleep and rest is better than a brevet.'

As the bodies piled up, he grew disenchanted. 'What a fearful mistake the annexing of the Transvaal now appears,' he wrote in January 1879. 'What on earth we want of millions of square miles of such a country when we have millions of unoccupied land in hand which only, they say, wants scratching to produce anything, I can't imagine. It seems to me that whatever you read about South Africa in books is a falsehood.' The lies printed about the African campaigns in the British newspapers is a leitmotif of his correspondence. In a letter to his friend Alfred Welby from Balte Spruit in Zululand on 29 March 1879, Apsley Cherry explained that he couldn't write to his mother: she would be terrified if she knew how shattering it was there. He wasn't even able to write to his brother, as the women of the house would recognise his handwriting when they saw the envelope on the hall table.

His bitter feelings in Africa never dented his faith in the virtues of imperialism. He remained an exemplary soldier. The one-eyed Field Marshal Lord Wolseley, an outstanding soldier himself, called Apsley Cherry the bravest man he had ever seen. Yet Apsley was not afraid to be human. On Easter Sunday 1879 he confided to Welby from Balte Spruit, 'Between you and me, don't send this on to Denford, the incessant work and anxiety to do the best, etc, etc, is a little beyond what I am able for, as long as what I am responsible for goes straight I am fit enough, but when orders are misunderstood or not carried out and things don't go straight, it is not in me to take it easy, and I get seedy.' It could have been his son writing, when orders were misunderstood in the Antarctic.

Colonel Cherry left Africa at the end of 1879, after two grim years of service, and sailed back to India. The news from home was bad the next spring: his mother had died. She had gone on for thirty-two years longer than her husband. Some time after that Apsley Cherry returned to England, and in July 1883 he was put in charge of the garrison at Kempston Barracks on the outskirts of Bedford, about fifty miles north of London. It was tame work compared with the Zulus and the sepoys and the heat and disease of India and Africa, but perhaps he was grateful. He was fifty years old.

Bedford was a logical home for the old soldier. It was a strong Anglo-Indian centre: a man who went to Bedford Modern School in the 1880s remembered that seventeen of his classmates had been born in India. The retired soldiers, sailors, planters and officials who made up such a large part of the townsfolk were known as Squatters, presumably because they had taken up at Bedford after decamping from the colonies. They were not wealthy – the richer ones probably went to Cheltenham – but they liked to play the Society game. Army officers and the top layer of professionals, which meant mainly doctors and lawyers (no trade!), paraded up and down the High Street every morning from eleven o'clock to half-past twelve in a frenzy of hat-doffing. The regatta at the end of July signalled the end of the Season and a mass exodus to the seaside. It was said that you could fire a cannon down the High Street in August without hitting anyone.

It might have been at the morning walk, or at a meet of Major Carpenter's Harriers, or perhaps at one of the quarterly concerts of the Bedford Musical Society, that Apsley Cherry met Evelyn Sharpin. Dr Henry Wilson Sharpin, her father, was a well-known local figure, ministering to gouty colonels and febrile infants, and he was held in high regard.* Born in India, where his father had served in the 4th Light Dragoons in Bombay, he had been shipped off to attend Great Yarmouth Grammar School, and at sixteen he began studying medicine at Bedford Infirmary. He finished his training at St Bartholomew's in London, where he was a prize-winning student, and after qualifying returned to Bedford Infirmary as House Surgeon. Later he set up in private practice on the ground floor of his home at No. 1, St Paul's Square, a prime site along from the Corn Exchange. Sharpin's wife Edith, baby Apsley's maternal grandmother, was the daughter of John Nicolle of St Helier's, Jersey. She bore Henry six children, the eldest of whom was Evelyn Edith.

Slim and not unattractive, Evelyn wore her brown hair tightly pinned at the back and curled to a gentle froth at the front. Her features were even and well proportioned except for a slightly large mouth; she liked dancing; and she was moderate in all her habits. Her education had been typically sketchy, and she rarely read anything more substantial than *Punch*. She had seldom ventured beyond the south Midlands: her expectations began and ended with marriage and a family. Above all, she was docile and obedient, and her bedroom was hung with an array of biblical scenes that reflected a keenly felt piety.

The rituals of courtship proceeded smoothly, and in 1884 the old soldier determined to ask for Evelyn's hand. She was twenty-five years his junior, but as far as her parents were concerned, it was a good match. The colonel had a solid reputation, and while he was a second son without a fortune, he had a small private income and the prospects of a decent enough military pension. Besides, three younger girls were queuing up behind her.

They were married in St Paul's Church, the largest in Bedford, on 29 January 1885. A row of non-commissioned officers from the regiment formed a guard of honour at the west door and processed in after the bride, who wore a confection of ivory satin, pearls, ostrich feathers and lace with a diamond pendant and bracelet. She was attended by eight bridesmaids wearing, according to a fulsome account in the local paper, 'dresses of braided cream, trimmed with cream Astrakhan, toques of Astrakhan with cream aigrettes, and muffs of silk and lace to match, with sprays of Neapolitan violets in their muffs and at their throats, and gold brooches with the initials "AE" fastened to their toques'. Alfred Welby, the friend who had been such a faithful correspondent during the groom's long years

* When Dr Sharpin died in his eightieth year, the local paper ran a long obituary, noting that, 'In nearly all serious cases in the town in the practice of other medical men, Dr Sharpin was called in when further advice was needed, and many people in his neighbourhood owe their lives to the advice tendered by Dr Sharpin in critical illnesses.'

at the wars, was best man, and one of Evelyn's uncles officiated. The Sharpin progeny had the impressive total of three vicar uncles; the house in St Paul's Square was teeming with churchmen and doctors (by the time Evelyn married, one of her brothers had already qualified as a doctor and the other was at medical school). Perhaps the abundance of ecclesiastical and medical men that crowded his childhood contributed to Apsley junior's subsequent mistrust of both organised religion and the medical profession.

After a lively wedding breakfast the new Mrs Cherry changed into a grey cashmere travelling dress and sealskin jacket, and the couple left in a shower of rice for a night in Oxford on their way to honeymoon in Devon.

Brown-eyed baby Apsley was born at home eleven months later. From the start he was surrounded by loving relations. Large faces smiled in the glow of the crocus-shaped jet of the nursery gaslight, and the most regular of the visitors, Evelyn's doting younger sisters Minnie, Maud and Nellie, became familiar to the infant Apsley as soon as he could focus. When he was six weeks old he was taken down to Denford in Berkshire to be cooed over by his Cherry aunts. On a glacial February morning the family processed into the chapel built on the estate by the baby's long-dead paternal grandfather, and Apsley George Benet was baptised in the same font as his father before him. His Christian names were all plucked from the paternal family tree, and his surname was Cherry: the Garrard was some years ahead.

Like little Lord Fauntleroy,* as a toddler Apsley was dressed for public outings in a black velvet suit with buttoned knickerbockers and a large lace collar; either that or a starched sailor suit. But his reign as little emperor was short. On 21 March 1887 his sister Ida was born in the house on Lansdowne Road. She was only fourteen-and-a-half months younger than her brother, and the pair were soon dubbed 'Lassie' and 'Laddie'. The nicknames stuck for years.

It was a quiet street. The loudest noises were the bell of the butcher's boy's tricycle and the muffled clatter of housemaids polishing brass door knockers. Laddie and Lassie were wheeled out by their nurses while their mother went visiting. But Evelyn was not a remote, matriarchal figure who ascended to the nursery occasionally in a cloud of perfume. She was an attentive and loving mother. She had a strong sense of what was right and proper, and naturally followed her military husband's lead in matters of domestic discipline. Deeply conventional, like most women of her

---

* The book was published the year Apsley was born.

background, she rarely absorbed fresh ideas. Along with everyone she knew, she was a royalist and a Conservative. When there was a mix-up over a visiting political agent at a Cherry estate and it was erroneously implied that the family might support a Liberal candidate, the suggestion brought Evelyn out in a fit of the vapours.

On 12 June 1887 news was brought up from Denford that George Charles, Apsley senior's elder brother, had died after a short illness. The Bedford Cherrys were shocked: George Charles had been an energetic man, and young for his sixty-five years. Evelyn swathed herself in black crêpe, and the whole family went into mourning. A bachelor without issue, George Charles had bequeathed everything bar a couple of small annuities to Apsley, his only brother. Overnight, the colonel and his expanding family acquired a small fortune, land, prestige and responsibility. One-year-old Apsley would never have to follow a profession or struggle to find a red-brick house of his own: he was to be a landed gentleman. Everything had changed.

The colonel decided to move his family to Berkshire. He no longer needed his army salary: he had a large estate, and rents from other land in Berkshire to keep him. The summer of 1887 was taken up with arrangements. On 1 September – his fifty-fifth birthday – Colonel Cherry retired from the regiment, a much-loved and much-admired old soldier with a distinguished campaign record. He was given the rank of honorary major-general.

As for Laddie: he had taken his first tottering steps in Bedford, but before he was two he was led to the carriage and entombed among the sheepskin rugs for the long journey to Denford.

The Cherrys traced their ancestry to the de Chéries of Picardy and Lombardy, lords of Beauval, Liguière and Villencourt. Thomas de Chérie and his son John had settled in Northamptonshire at the beginning of the fifteenth century, and were soon anglicised to Cherrys. By the end of the eighteenth century Cherry men were forging careers in India. George Frederick Cherry, great-grandfather of the subject of this book, joined the Bengal Civil Service in 1778 and was later appointed Resident at Benares on the Ganges, where he was subsequently murdered by the recently deposed Nabob of Oude. His widow took their small son George Henry back to England, and they settled in London. The boy was educated at Harrow and Oxford – he took a double first in Classics – and in 1819 he married Charlotte Drake Garrard of Lamer Park, Hertfordshire. The following year he became a member of parliament. The Cherrys made their home in Gloucester Place in London's Marylebone, and there, in 1822 and 1823, George Charles Cherry and his sister Lucy were born.

At about that time George Henry – baby Apsley's paternal grandfather – decided to put down roots in good English soil. From the back row of an auction at Garaway's Coffee House in London's Cornhill he purchased Denford, an 800-acre estate in the south-west corner of Berkshire, on a trouty part of the River Kennet. It was about two miles from Hungerford and sixty-three from London, roughly half-way between the capital and fashionable Bath. The Berkshire Downs unfurled to the north like a great green wave, and southwards, plainly visible from the bedrooms of the big house, were the north Hampshire Downs. Besides a sand-coloured late-Georgian manor house, the estate included stables, a park bristling with oak and beech, a watermill, two farms, a dozen cottages, plantations and meadows.

George Henry became a justice of the peace, and in 1829 served as High Sheriff of Berkshire. Mechanisation and industrialisation were creeping over the south-west of the county, but the stirrings of progress did not impinge significantly on daily life at Denford. A dozen servants lived in, and many others rented cottages on the estate. More daughters arrived at the big house and were baptised (one buried, too) in the Norman church at Avington, a hamlet on the River Kennet, and finally Charlotte had a second son, whom she called Apsley. He was the Antarctic explorer's father. Besides extending the house, George Henry had commissioned a chapel 150 yards from his front door – it was a minor Gothic extravaganza among the beech trees – and Apsley was the first baby to be baptised in its font.

George Henry died on 6 January 1848. His elder son George Charles, a young barrister, was soon ready to take on his father's mantle. Eight hundred acres did not put him among the top thirty landowners in the county, but his was a respectable holding, and in addition to Denford he owned a large chunk of land his father had bought at the other end of Berkshire. George Charles became a county magistrate and held a range of important judicial positions. Like his father before him, he was High Sheriff for a year. He laid foundation stones, served on a vast number of committees, presented prizes, commanded the 3rd Berks Rifle Corps and contributed handsomely to the Church of England. Strong-featured and infinitely wholesome, he was described in a contemporary memoir as 'one of those men who form the backbone of English provincial life'. He never married. Various sisters had found husbands, and their offspring kept the house young. Emily, the fifth of the Cherry siblings, had wed a barrister called John Smith in 1853, and they frequently sent their children to Denford during school holidays. Reginald Smith, their brilliant second son, was baptised in the estate chapel. He was to play a crucial role in the life of his polar cousin.

The agricultural depression that dragged on from the 1870s to the 1890s bit deeply in south-west Berkshire, and the landscape grew greener as grass replaced tillage. Newbury and Hungerford swelled with desperate workers, farms were left untenanted and so many thousands of acres were switched to dairy pasture that the Great Western Railway was known as the Milky Way. But the Cherrys had plenty of capital. The limitless self-confidence, the moral seriousness, the social vigour: both George Henry and George Charles basked all their lives in the glow of paternalistic Toryism.

When General Cherry moved his family to Berkshire more than seventy people lived on the Denford estate, either working for the Cherrys or subsisting as labourers or small tenant farmers. While the estate was not exactly prospering, the Cherrys were comfortable, and the General had inherited much goodwill in the county. As for Laddie, he toddled fearlessly around the new house pursued by his nurse, pausing to help the cook shell peas or play with his wooden soldiers in the spacious drawing room while Father rustled his newspaper. Occasionally the General received top-hatted visitors from Newbury or London and Laddie was permitted to remain downstairs while Lassie was corralled in the day nursery. The women of the house were almost permanently taken up with babies, and father and son formed a unit of manly isolation. They were often together. The General was a keen trainspotter, and if a new engine was running in the valley or a branch line had been opened, he would take Laddie off in the carriage to have a look. The two Apsleys made a fine sight, one a rotund old soldier pushing sixty with a curling moustache and a thick suit that smelt of cigar smoke, the other a small boy with long hair and a sailor suit.

The General told stories of his Indian and African adventures which thrilled the small boy, especially if they involved one of the exotic souvenirs brought back from those far-off lands. In the upstairs hall at Denford there was a pair of Zulu shields, and Laddie liked to sweep the day nursery with the yak-tail brush stowed in the military chest with the striped cover.

The Denford Cherrys kept in touch with more distant branches of the family, and if news came in that a relation had died, or married, or produced offspring, the fact was recorded in the pages of the family bible. Well-known stories of especially colourful ancestors were aired. And yet, or perhaps because of all this, the grown-up Laddie took no interest in his dead relations, and little more in those who were still alive. He was proud of his distinguished ancestry, but not a man of genealogical piety. His was a theoretical appreciation. In the course of his long life he broke with many traditions, sold the seat and wilfully elected to let the name die.

The arrival of more girls – Elsie in September 1889, and Mildred in May 1891 – meant that Evelyn was permanently preoccupied. When the General was absent, Laddie spent much of his time with the servants. He had his baths by firelight in tepid water ferried in cans by the young nurserymaid, and went to sleep to the small sound of coal falling in the night nursery grate or the orchestrated plumbing in the bathroom. As he grew more independent, the estate gamekeepers and woodmen became his companions. His earliest memories were of the shallows of the spring in Goose Acre Coppice and the cushiony moss of Flaggy Mead. His life followed the rhythm of the seasons, from the millpond freeze to the eruption of the daffodils in the park. He was given rides in the gardener's handcart, and later he was sometimes allowed to play with the estate workers' children, many of whom were baptised in the Denford chapel like the young master.

Evelyn and the General socialised at the local big houses, occasionally even venturing over the border to Hampshire to Lord Carnarvon at Highclere Castle. In the summer of 1891, the year Mildred was born and Laddie turned five, their parents went away to Weymouth. Laddie inscribed the alphabet to send to his mother, with only two reversed letters, and on a separate sheet he wrote: 'LADDIES BEST LOVE BABYS LOVE'. The following year, in November, Evelyn was away again, and once more Laddie showed himself to be a committed correspondent. 'DEAR MAMAR,' he wrote, between lines which his nurse had drawn on the page, 'WE HAVE HAD A VERY WET NIGHT BUT NOW THE SUN AS COME OUT AND WE HAD A NICE ~~WALH~~ WALK WITH LOVE AND KISSES FROM LADDIE.'

The estate was his empire. He was not a natural explorer, and did not dream of discovering great lakes or charting polar wastes, even as an older boy. Instead, he was happy keeping tadpoles and minnows, and picking catkined hazels and primroses. He was shy, and rather an introvert. Laddie did not whack other children unless most severely provoked, nor did he bully his expanding troupe of sisters – at least, no more than any little boy might. Nature was his refuge, and a love of the world he observed in the fields and skies around him stayed with him for the rest of his life.

When the vicar of Hungerford could manage it, the whole family and all the servants, indoor and outdoor, went to a service at Holy Trinity, that sublime piece of Victorian Gothic built by Laddie's grandfather among the beech trees. Constructed from local bricks faced with Bath stone, it seated sixty and featured a bell tower of the elaborately pinnacled variety. Laddie was keen on the pigeons that roosted there, and sometimes, on weekdays, he played on the red tiles with Lassie and his nurse. His paternal grandparents were entombed in the west end, as well as an aunt, and his uncle George Charles. Their chiselled names were not yet worn smooth.

It was a happy time for them all. E. M. Forster, born seven years before Laddie, described his own youth in a phrase that sums up the background against which the General brought up his young family: 'I belong to the fag-end of Victorian liberalism,'[*] wrote Forster, 'and can look back to an age whose challenges were moderate in their tone, and the cloud on whose horizon was no bigger than a man's hand.'

In the summer of 1892 a message arrived from Hertfordshire announcing the death of Honora Drake Garrard, the General's aunt. She was the 78-year-old widow of his mother's brother Charles Benet Drake Garrard, and the General had been her sole heir since his own brother had died. The Cherrys were thrown not so much into mourning (they barely knew Aunt Honora) as confusion: they now owned another fortune and another estate, fifteen times bigger than Denford.

Lamer was only about sixty miles from Denford, but their surroundings were quite different. Thirty-odd miles north of London, Hertfordshire was altogether more benign than Berkshire: it was a gently undulating, loamy expanse of forest and meadow bisected by the River Lea and several great Roman roads. The rise of the railways had brought agricultural prosperity to the region, as the capital was always hungry.

The Cherrys' new acquisition was on the edge of Wheathampstead, a village in the Lea Valley in the heart of the county and only forty-five minutes by train from London. The estate covered about twenty square miles and included numerous farms and cottages, half a dozen Elizabethan manor houses and a park and mansion. Garrards had been there for almost 300 years. They came from Kent, and had migrated to London to make their fortune at the end of the fifteenth century. The founder of the modern family and its considerable wealth was Sir William Garrard of Dorney in Buckinghamshire. He was the son of a grocer, and made his

---

[*] The Cherrys were solid Tories, but the sentiment applies.

money as a haberdasher. By 1555 he had reached the lofty position of Lord Mayor of London. Two other Garrards went on to occupy the position, and a baronetcy was created by James I. When the Tory MP Sir Benet Garrard died without issue in 1767 the baronetcy expired with him, and Lamer was inherited by his distant cousin Charles Drake of Shardeloes, Buckinghamshire. Drake took the name Garrard in addition to his own. His daughter Charlotte married George Henry Cherry, who bought Denford. When Charles's son died without issue, he left his estate to his wife Honora.

The General had not just inherited Lamer Park and its estate. There were Garrard lands in other counties, and the family owned a large house in Watling Street in the City of London which was leased to a firm of cotton traders. The Cherrys had certainly gone up a rung: Charles Benet Drake Garrard's estate was valued at £130,750 gross (well over £6 million in today's terms). There was only one condition attached to their good fortune: under the terms of his uncle's will the General had to assume the name and arms of Garrard. The Drake was abandoned, and, by Royal Licence dated 30 September 1892, the name Cherry-Garrard came into existence.

2

Lamer

Shortly after four o'clock one afternoon in the autumn of 1892, the General, Evelyn and their four small children climbed into a waiting carriage and ascended smartly from Wheathampstead station, trundling past the dog rose and bryony in the hedges, the restharrow on the banks and the furzy brakes on the heath. The horses clopped up the drive to the blocky stone portico of the Lamer mansion. The stuccoed brick of the eighteenth-century house was veined with creepers and gilded in the sunlight, a model of restrained neo-classical elegance. Between the pairs of columns at the entrance, a row of starched servants stood to welcome their new master.

Juggling four small children and two large estates, the General and Evelyn had reluctantly opted to lease Denford and move up to Hertfordshire. Lamer Park needed more looking after, and it was nearer Evelyn's family. But the move was a wrench. As for changing their name: it was an offence to the strong proprietorial sense of a five- and six-year-old, and Laddie and Lassie bitterly resented being Cherry-Garrards.

A Lamer manor had existed since at least the fourteenth century and probably much earlier, and the odd medieval arch had survived. The origins of the name (pronounced to rhyme with 'hammer') were obscure: it may have come from a De La Mare family who held land in the area in the late Middle Ages. The mansion was one of a band of great houses that circled the capital like a ring road: when the first Sir John Garrard decided to live there early in the seventeeth century a gentleman could get to London easily enough – in a day, if he had a good horse. Sir John and his sons and grandsons rebuilt, extended and adorned, but the house the General inherited was an eighteenth-century creation of chaste simplicity, constructed mostly by Sir Benet in the golden age of the country seat. It stood on high ground, and the Garrards and their landscape gardeners – notably the fashionable Humphry Repton in the 1790s – had created a well-stocked park that rolled away from the front windows of the house, the ground sloping upwards slightly in front of the pillared façade. Framing the mansion at the back, stands of mature cedars were threaded with oak. An avenue of lime trees led off in the direction of Ayot St Lawrence, and in front of the library window a manicured path known as the Chain Walk was festooned with immaculate flower beds. The memoir of a mid-nineteenth-century Ayot neighbour noted that, 'the balcony opening out of the saloon on the first floor spoke of syllabubs and shady hats and haymaking'.

Even to children used to Denford, the house was as big as a castle. Immediately inside the front door, the hall gave onto the drawing room on the left and the dining room on the right; they in turn led to the bow-fronted library and the kitchen wing. At the rear of the hall, beyond the staircase, two flanks extended out to the laundry and the old chapel, which now housed the dairy, and from there to the larder, game larder, butchery, brew-house and lamp-room. A warren of rooms at the back and in the attics were occupied by the servants: the housekeeper, a laundress who starched, goffered and ironed, the lady's maid, the cook and kitchen staff, housemaids, footmen, bootboys, hall boys and a newly engaged nurse and nursery maid. Welbourne, the butler, was quartered next to the pantry in a small room where the silver was stored. He slept with a pistol under his pillow. In the upstairs nursery wing the governess, Mrs Bright, presided over the schoolroom, where three cases of stuffed animal heads fought for attention among a profusion of solid mahogany furniture that exemplified the spirit of the age. The outside servants were led by head gardener Claude Tilbury, whose empire extended to hothouses that produced peaches and muscatel grapes. The lawns were kept short with a horse-drawn mower, the horse wearing special leather boots so his hooves would not spoil the surface.

To a small boy with a lively imagination and a taste for snails and solitude, the estate was paradise. Laddie tried to catch fish in the old pond in the walled garden. He and Lassie persuaded their mother and Tilbury to hang a swing from the drooping branch of an oak, stole raspberries from the kitchen garden and picked mint and kingcups on the banks of the streams. They followed the gardeners to the potting shed and built forts from winnowing fans, cane-bottom sieves and wooden rat-traps. A few months after moving to Lamer, the seven-year-old Laddie wrote to his mother, who was visiting her family in Bedford.

Dearest Mother,

The hounds came here this morning, and found [a fox] in Lamer Wood, and Lassie came with me and we followed them through Lamer Wood, over those fields to the outskirts of Hall's Wood by the Baxendales and I think they went the Kimpton way. We met Tilbury, Weakly with his gun and Clark on the mare I think it was by Hall's Wood – Lassie & I came home by Gustard Wood Common and got home in good time for Dinner.

Mrs Bright and I am going down to Wheathampstead today. Mrs Bright wants to get some PO [postal orders] at the Post Office. The others are not going out today again but are going to have their heads washed.

As an afterthought, and perhaps with encouragement, at the top of the first sheet he wrote, 'Mrs Bright is a very good girl.'

When the pond by the stables froze, Laddie and Lassie learned to skate by pushing chairs on the ice, and when the skating was over Tilbury and his henchmen cut blocks from the pond to store in the ice house. Later in the winter nurse made blackberry syrup for their coughs, and if the children didn't get better Dr Smallwood came and listened to their chests with his horn. In the summer they played croquet on the lawn, but Laddie was too short-sighted to win. He couldn't see as well as any of the girls, but the General thought he might grow out of it, not liking the idea of an imperfect son.

Honora and Charles Drake Garrard had presided over Victorian Wheathampstead like minor monarchs. Honora, who looked like the aged Queen Victoria, had been known as 'Lady' to the tenants and villagers. Towards the end she had been pushed about in a wicker wheelchair by a footman, and little girls were obliged to curtsey if they saw her. Most of the estate cottages still had a framed picture of her on the wall. The Cherry-Garrards quickly assumed their predecessors' dignified mantle. The General had no trouble adapting to his seigneurial role. Each day fresh table linen was required in the Lamer dining room, and to make sure that no mistake was made, after dinner he would dip his fingers into a fingerbowl and draw them across the cloth. By this time he was a stocky, imposing figure: the handlebar moustache had whitened and the crinkly hair slightly receded, emphasising his strong forehead. In Hertfordshire he served as a magistrate, just as he had in Berkshire. As a justice of the peace, he sat on the Bench, though when the local police constable hustled a poacher to the house he was required to administer a more ad hoc kind of justice: a possible confrontation with the General was a potent deterrent to a man with poaching on his mind. But he was a well-loved social figurehead. 'We knew him best,' the local vicar said many years later, 'as the kind country gentleman, always ready to help forward and support good works in our parish and elsewhere.'

Evelyn inherited the unofficial title of Lady and its responsibilities: quite a shift for a doctor's daughter. When she went shopping in St Albans, five miles away, shopkeepers ran out with trays of buttons and ribbons as her carriage approached so she need never descend. She visited the poorest cottagers, as she had done at Denford, often accompanied by a daughter or two, and if a tenant's child was ill Evelyn would appear at the door with a milk pudding.

It was always said that the architect Robert Adam had been employed at Lamer, at least in the design of the dining room and library; Laddie certainly grew up to believe it. (Sir Benet may have used him when he remodelled the house in the 1760s.) The reception rooms had marble fireplaces, carved chimney-pieces and superbly detailed cornices. They were extravagantly furnished with typical late-Victorian intensity: the drawing room heaved with rosewood and tortoiseshell cabinets, inlaid satinwood tabletops, lacquer writing desks and forests of Dresden and Derby china. A pair of great flute-legged console tables under dim Vauxhall looking-glasses were spread with ivory penknives, silver trowels and china baskets encrusted with flowers. Ancestral portraits were hung all over the house, though they congregated especially in the entrance hall, where dark, full-length Garrards were now obliged to jostle for wall space with Cherrys transported from Denford. Evelyn and the General grew accustomed to taking breakfast under seventeenth-century mayors in extravagant ruffs.

Behind the house, the General kept his eight horses in the eighteenth-century, cupolaed stable block. Nothing was too good for the Lamer horses. Henry Hobbs, the Denford coachman, had moved up to Hertfordshire to look after them, and he lived in a specially converted part of the stables with his young family. When out with the Master, Hobbs and the grooms wore a livery of cockaded top hat, beige breeches and prune coat complete with silver buttons embossed with the Cherry lion and Garrard leopard. Hobbs taught all the children to ride. The girls had to go side-saddle, and the General made them practise until they could sit ramrod straight, but when he was away they piled into the governess's cart to be towed by the Lamer donkey.

Sometimes Laddie went into the village with Hobbs to get a horse shod. They took the brougham (the carriage was reserved for more formal occasions) down Lamer Lane and over the Mill Bridge where the Lea formed a pool by the Bull Inn and yellow wagtails darted in and out of the reeds. Laddie loved the forge with its hoofy smell, the sizzle of the hot shoes in water and the flying sparks of struck metal.

On Sundays the horses were not taken out unless it was raining, and the family walked down to St Helen's in the village for Morning Service. Before leaving the house the children lined up in the hall to be inspected by the General. He was a martinet, and he brought his army training into his home; but he was a very lovable martinet, and his military severity was mitigated by his wife's indulgence.

St Helen's was an old flint-and-limestone church, slender-spired and daffodilled in spring. The General led his family to the Lamer chapel in the north transept, a place where the dead outnumbered the living. During Canon Davys' interminable sermons Laddie contemplated the lidded urns and swagged sarcophagi detailing the achievements and multitudinous progeny of his ancestors. He sat alongside a recumbent Sir John, the first baronet, his marble-cool wife Lady Elizabeth and, in the panel below, effigies of their fourteen children. The dead ones carried skulls into which, when his father's head was turned, Laddie poked his finger to see what lay behind.

The new lords of Lamer held skating parties in winter, and, in the summer, crayfishing parties on the banks of the Lea near Castle Farm. The General was a sociable fellow but a stickler for punctuality, and when the parties were over, he went round saying goodbye with his watch in his hand. Laddie and the girls socialised at the other big houses, the best party being the Children's Ball given by the Salisburys at Hatfield House, where there was a real band and a proper supper and wax candles – one year there was even a conjuror who baked a cake in a top hat and brought it out steaming. The Salisburys were top of the Hertfordshire gentry tree – when the Cherry-Garrards moved to Lamer, Gladstone had just narrowly ousted Lord Salisbury as prime minister. (The Tory titan was not yet finished with Downing Street, but he was to be the last prime minister to govern from the Lords.)*

---

* Evelyn got out her best gown for dinner at the Salisburys'. Hobbs' daughter remembered that her mistress chose less splendid attire when dining with Lord and Lady Cavan at

For those who marry late, ingrained domestic habits are harder to break. But familial intimacy is often sweeter, too. After decades of military life it was agreeable to hear a childish tune tinkle from the nursery, and to find a mewling baby on one's wife's knee in the drawing room. Besides, it was easy to slip down to the Naval and Military Club in London, or to receive Bedford pals at home. They came with their grooms, and a pile of freshly laundered horse blankets was stored in the harness room for visiting servants required to stay overnight.

In their old age, the Cherry-Garrard offspring recalled a blissful childhood and a happy parental marriage. The wear-and-tear of proximity never spoiled the magic for the General and his wife. It was known among the servants that they shared a bed – an unusual practice among the gentry – and it made them seem more human. After they arrived, Lamer quickly acquired a reputation as a good place to work, though the young parlourmaids complained that the General did not allow them to go out at night, and slacking and impropriety swiftly met with their reward. On one occasion, a footman failed to answer a late-night ring on the General's bell. A search was made, and the hapless man was discovered in a housemaid's bed. The footman was summoned to the General's presence, dismissed on the spot and ordered onto the first train out of Wheathampstead in the morning. The housemaid's mother was summoned the next day and she tearfully took her daughter home.

The General had always been a keen shooter and he continued to raise partridges and pheasants, as he had at Denford. He took his son out with him, and Laddie walked in the line, watching the beaters march ahead and marking the number of birds bagged in his father's morocco shooting notebook. Latin was another shared experience. Late in the afternoon, when the room was patchily lit by gas jets, the General gave Laddie lessons in the bow-fronted library. It didn't occur to the old man that the girls might have wanted to learn Latin, too.

Eighteen ninety-four was a rainy summer, and in August Laddie's Bedford grandmother died. His mother was often absent over those long, damp weeks. But there was to be a ruder shock before the trees in the park lost their leaves. Laddie was going away to school.

That September the eight-year-old Laddie started at the Grange prep school in Folkestone, Kent. He had a new trunk, and a wooden playbox

---

Wheathampstead House, though the servants couldn't decide whether it was because there were dogs in the house, or because the Cavans were merely Irish nobility.

with his name painted on the lid, and the cook made him up a large tin of mixed biscuits.

The Grange had been founded by the Reverend Arthur Hussey in the early years of the 1870s. The General had been so miserable at Harrow that he was attracted by the school's newness: it was not mired in the brutality of the old prep schools. In addition, Folkestone's position on the south coast gratified the Victorian obsession with the benefits of fresh air. At the time Laddie was despatched Folkestone was a deeply fashionable town: rich families decamped there for the summer, installing their servants in the big houses on the new wide avenues and indulging in the new craze for sitting on the beach in canvas chairs. The Grange was known around Lamer, and other Hertfordshire boys were sent away with Laddie. They were a nervous lot when they were decanted from the train at Radnor Park station, their spam-coloured legs sticking out from grey flannel shorts and their striped caps jammed over their eyes.

For Laddie the anxieties of the playground were exacerbated by his short sight, and his discomfiture at not being able to see fuelled his innate shyness and nervous disposition. But the Grange wasn't too bad: Hussey, still the headmaster, was popular with the boys. They called him Old Buzz. After classes they collected worms from the dark laurel boscage at the end of the playing field, and when it was warm high-collared masters marched them purposefully down to the harbour to bathe in the bitter English Channel. In July 1896 Laddie wrote home:

Dear Mother,
    Could you send me a new toothbrush as the one I have now has a lot of the brisels coming out. I have just been sitting out in the pavilion.
    It is only two weeks from the holidays.
    I am looking forward to the time when we wake up in the morning and find that we are going home.
    I am your very loving son
    Apsley.

No doubt his mother found time to send the toothbrush.

For most of Laddie's childhood Evelyn was either pregnant, or nursing, or both. Margaret, to be known as Peggy, made her appearance on 21 September 1896, when her brother was ten. He was now outnumbered four to one, and left alone in the school holidays to nurse his finches by the kitchen range, build crow's-nests in the trees and ride his pony. In the summer he corralled as many of the male staff as he could for games of cricket. Tom Hobbs, the coachman's son, was a mainstay of the team, and his niece recounts an episode that entered the lore of her own family:

> The young master did not much like being bowled or caught out, and once in a fit of temper threw a ball which hit the coachman's daughter on the head. For his bad-tempered action he was rebuked by Mrs Hobbs who had witnessed the outburst, the more so because he denied the act and tried to frame the footman. 'Fie, Fie, Master Apsley!' Mother said. 'That is not the way for a gentleman to behave.'

That year, after term ended in December Laddie went on holiday to Devonshire with his father while his mother was with her family in Bedford. They took the train, and stayed at the Torbay Hotel on the seafront at Torquay. 'Dear Mother,' Laddie wrote two days after their arrival,

> Father and I went to church this morning and after church we went to try and get ourselves warm but it came on to rain so we had to retreat to the hotel. You can't imagine how nice it is here especially when it does not rain and how I am enjoying myself. There was a collier in yesterday at least it has been in for a good time I should think as it was here when we came unloading the coal, it went out this morning early, we have got a very nice room facing the sea and not too big and not too small just ripping. Father and I went for a walk yesterday afternoon down by a place called Daddy's Hole, it was very nice and so pretty. I am going to try if we get some decent weather to get some shells for my collection. I hope the baby is all right and kicking I shall expect to have some very pretty music from her when I come back to Lamer. It was an awfully nice journey down here, and having our dinner in the train . . . mind you tell the baby when I come to Lamer to celebrate my arrival with a tune. With much love to all I am your very loving son Apsley.

In June 1897 Queen Victoria's Diamond Jubilee was celebrated from Zanzibar to Simla. The British Empire covered a quarter of the earth's land surface, Lord Salisbury was back at the helm of the nation, and there were still plenty of reasons for landowners to celebrate. The forebodings of Kipling, the adult Laddie's favourite author ('Lo, all our pomp of yesterday/Is one with Nineveh, and Tyre!'), were hardly representative of the national mood. In Wheathampstead the Jubilee was marked by a feast in Parson's Field next to the rectory lawn. The servants were given the day off. Dressed in their best clothes, they gathered for freckled cylinders of tongue, beer and rolled jam puddings. In the regrettable absence of the monarch herself, Evelyn glided between the tables doling out gifts while the village band played and the children raced donkeys. But Laddie was imprisoned at Folkestone. At the end of May he had written to his parents:

> Lots of boys are going up to the Jubilee, they are going up one day before and coming back one day after. I do not no what Mr Hussey is going to do about it but I think very likely we shall have 2 or 3 days holidays. My wrist is nearly all right we are having very changeable weather here. But it is not cold. I hope you are quite all right. The map we had on past Sunday was Spain and Portugal we have got to finish it today.
>
> I am your very loving son
> Apsley.

In the end they had boiled mutton and tapioca pudding and walked to the end of the road to watch the Jubilee bonfires.

In the summer of 1899, Laddie left the Grange for the last time. There was nothing to regret as he leant out of the train window and watched the columns of steam dissolve above Radnor Park station. He rather suspected that there might be worse to come at his next school, and he was right; but now he had the summer to enjoy at Lamer where, as ever, little had changed. The River Lea was still teeming with trout and crayfish, and his cricket pads were still in the back hall. He knew very little about the enormous world beyond the trouty river and the mighty chestnuts. It was to be a savage dawning.

That September Apsley submitted to his first weeks at Winchester College, a procedure likened by one old boy to the initiation rites of the Australian Aboriginal. Founded in 1382, Winchester was one of the top three public schools in Britain. The year Apsley was admitted, it came first in the league table of Higher Certificate passes, beating Rugby and Eton into joint second place. It was famed for producing an intellectual élite, and at Oxford and Cambridge, Wykehamists* were noted for their ambition, single-mindedness and self-reliance. The General chose the school in the touching belief that it was not like Harrow, which he had hated so intensely.

---

* Pupils were known as Wykehamists after the school's founder, William of Wykeham.

The trunk and wooden playbox were handed over to the station-master and despatched to school in the guard's van. Shortly afterwards a white-faced Apsley was enrolled as a commoner at Culver House, nicknamed 'Kenny's' after the housemaster, Theodore Kensington. During the first two weeks of that term – 'Short Half', in Winchester parlance – new pupils were indoctrinated into school culture under the tutelage of an older boy called a 'Father', and, after this fortnight was up, fagging began.

Kenny's was a red-brick, flat-fronted Victorian building in a quiet street to the west of the ancient part of the school. Inside, forty boys (eight were admitted each year) slept in a bare-floored, practically unheated dormitory. Every morning at 6.15 they were obliged to jump into a metal tub full of cold water, one after the other. There was so little privacy that the lavatories did not have doors. The boys dressed like miniature men, in stiff collars, ties and buttoned-up jackets, and at seven in the morning, after a spartan breakfast, they sat down to Morning Lines and Henry's Latin Primer in its mulberry cloth binding, each boy working in a cubicle in the ground-floor hall. They were all hungry all the time, and constipation was compulsory, as John Betjeman wrote later of his own public school.

The rigid respect for tradition at Winchester extended to a private tribal language which each boy had to learn. The canings doled out by prefects were called *tundings*, the cubicles were *toys* and boys were not allowed to use the word 'think' until they had been at the school for two years. Arnold Toynbee, later a famed historian and sage, was a prize-winning scholar close behind Apsley. (As a scholarship boy he lived in the fourteenth-century College buildings, not in one of the boarding houses.) 'For five years at Winchester,' Toynbee was to recall, 'I . . . tasted what life had been like for Primitive Man. One found oneself suddenly plunged into a world of arbitrary prohibitions and commandments (chiefly prohibitions).' A boy was not allowed to wear brown boots until his third year, Christian names were outlawed, and you had to refer to your parents as 'Mater' and 'Pater'. It was a gigantic exercise in control, which perhaps worked for confident boys. But it didn't do much for those of a more subtle plumage, especially if they had short sight.

The curriculum was embedded in the classical tradition, though it had been reformed, to a limited degree, in the decade before Apsley arrived. Mathematics, science and modern languages had been introduced, though the extent to which these subjects were taken seriously varied: French and German were taught by the maths masters. The thirteen-year-old Apsley embarked on a staple course of Latin, maths, English, history, divinity and some science. 'Except in the Army Class,' wrote Toynbee, 'education in

Winchester was nine-tenths classical. The reverse side of the excellence of the teaching of Latin and Greek was that other subjects were starved.' In the mental world of Winchester, Toynbee went on, 'we were hardly aware that science and technology were on the march; that they had joined hands with each other; and that mathematics had stooped to lend efficacious services to them both'. Apsley's attitude to science on his Antarctic expedition six years after he left school reveals the absence of any real education outside the humanities. He displayed the frenzied enthusiasm of the convert, almost giving his life for a little knowledge of the life cycle of the Emperor penguin.

Games were more than important; they were a cult. The most prestigious sports were cricket and a peculiar form of either six- or fifteen-a-side football. While Apsley was at Winchester one Richard Stafford Cripps starred in the Houses VI football team. He was to come within inches of 10 Downing Street.* The boys also went swimming under the lime trees at Gunner's Hole, a hundred-yard-long stretch of the River Itchen dredged of mud, took two long runs each week, and endured regular sessions in the gym. A boy called George Mallory was a star in this last department. He was a year behind Apsley and, as a mathematical scholar, a member of the Parnassian élite of Collegemen. But not all Apsley's peers came off the top shelf. The future Socialist MP and lawyer D. N. Pritt was the son of a Harlesden metal merchant. ('Under the system then still prevailing,' Pritt remembered, 'some 95 per cent of my work consisted of translating Latin and Greek into English, and English into those languages, in prose and in verse.')

The Boer War broke out during Apsley's first term at Winchester. Down at the bottom of Africa the Dutch settlers of the two Boer republics and their British neighbours in Cape Colony and Natal were still locked in bitter dispute, twenty years after the General buried his men on the plains of the Transvaal. In the second week of October 1899 the pent-up bitterness and violence exploded into full-scale war. The Boers were challenging British hegemony, and millions of imperial hearts quickened. The mood among the British was confident: few had any doubts about their right to dominate southern Africa or indeed anywhere else. Cecil Rhodes, colonial statesman, financier and until recently Prime Minister of Cape Colony, still expressed the hope that the British might win the United States back for the Empire.

---

* At the Treasury, Cripps led a ministerial team made up of himself and two other Wykehamists, Hugh Gaitskell and Douglas Jay.

The school was gripped with a febrile elation that put a stop to the rather wearisome talk of the new century. Patriotic fervour swept through the cloisters, masters pored over the morning newspapers and the school magazine – the *Wykehamist* – carried a proud list of alumni on their way to the front. Apsley had been weaned on stories exalting the defence of the Empire, and his experience at Winchester endorsed his father's attitudes. The ethos of the public schools at the end of the nineteenth century was imbued with the ideals of imperial glory, a ruling class and chivalry. The boys were indoctrinated with noble notions of honour, patriotism and leadership, so when a war came along they were gasping for it: war was the authenticating forge of nationhood. For the whole of that academic year, the 'School News' section in the *Wykehamist* teemed with war data – including a report of an Old Wykehamist dinner held in Pretoria during a pause in the fighting – and captains on leave hurried back to their alma mater to address boys longing to march off to wars of their own. The honour of the school and the glory of war were tightly entwined, and tangled in with it was an idealisation of death stoked by the Greek tragedians. Even as the Mentioned-in-Despatches lists melted into obituaries and some boys vanished from school to reappear wearing black armbands, there was still a sense that the pupils filing into the chapel lamented their ill luck at being born too late.

As for the reality of the war – the concentration camps where Boers were starved, the living skeletons of 'natives' crawling across the veldt by the hundred, the disease that killed thousands of proud young officers, the swooning military incompetence – of these things, the boys heard nothing.

On 22 January 1901 Queen Victoria died at Osborne, the royal residence on the Isle of Wight. She was eighty-one, and had been on the throne for sixty-three years. Two days later the entire school was summoned to the flint-faced Chamber Court. There the boys were marshalled into order and marched, in the rain, to Winchester Guildhall, where they listened to the formal announcement of the accession of Edward VII being read from the steps.

Wars and royal deaths notwithstanding, the school year unfurled in a succession of unchanging internal rituals interspersed with the meetings of a bewildering variety of clubs, the most prestigious of which was the Debating Society. Apsley was not one of the young bloods who stood up and declaimed in their best Ciceronian English about the moral necessity of war or the benefits of free trade, nor did he hold office in the Golf Club, the Shakespeare Society or the Orchestral Society. His school record was unblemished by achievement either in the classroom or on the sports field.

He showed no particular gift for turning Burke's speeches into Greek, and there were no early glimmerings of the limpid prose that characterised his mature writing. He won no prizes and did not bat for the 1st XI. Throughout his Winchester career he was a boy in the background, peeping shyly round a flint pillar or awkwardly relacing his football boots on a spongy touchline. It was impossible to foresee, in this introverted boy, the team player who would blossom in the Antarctic a decade later.

His sense of isolation was shared by many of his peers, though his excessive short-sightedness singled him out for special misery. For years the General refused to believe that his son could not see. Influenced by the army's refusal to allow soldiers to wear glasses, he considered imperfect vision a slur on the family name. But as Apsley's schoolwork grew increasingly demanding, the problem loomed too large even for the General to ignore, and when he was about fifteen the boy was at last kitted out with a pair of pebble-lensed glasses. (In 1902 the army relented, too.)

Shortly before he returned from Winchester at the end of his second year, Apsley acquired yet another sister, bringing the total to five. Edith was born at home on 7 July 1901, in her father's sixty-ninth year. The old soldier had just been made High Sheriff of Hertfordshire. It was a prestigious appointment, and the ceremony in Hertford lasted several days, necessitating a mass expedition from Lamer and a group booking at the Dimsdale Arms. At home the General had joined his ancestors on the dining-room wall: a dark and glossy three-quarter-length portrait had been commissioned, sat for and hung. The year after he was appointed Sheriff the venerable Lord Salisbury made his final exit from Downing Street, replaced by his languid nephew Arthur Balfour (the first prime minister to go to Buckingham Palace in a motor car). But how faintly the vibrations of the outside world reached Lamer during those years. The faded silk on the back of the upright piano; the taste of ginger beer and the smell of boiling strawberry jam; the sanctuary of the stable-yard: these were the immutable landmarks of the children's youth. The downy-faced Apsley still collected shells and moths and butterflies, but he was now allowed to attend Lamer Balls in the school holidays. (The General marched among the guests at midnight sharp, grasping his fob watch and saying goodbye.) He had been confirmed – a universal rite of passage in the public schools – after labouring over his catechism books. Compulsory chapel-keeping had beaten out any interest in organised religion, as it usually does. He was never attracted back to the Church. Like many, the adult Apsley had an instinctual yearning for the mystical but an intellectual inability to swallow the tenets of Christianity.

Other developmental milestones were more enjoyable than confirmation. During one school holiday, out shooting with Father, Apsley was handed a gun. He no longer had to trot behind the men, holding his father's shooting notebook. He had never been close to the younger girls, and now, as the school years marched on, their ice-floe of common experience shrank alarmingly. In the late summer of 1903 his mother took him down to London to buy new school clothes, and, for the last time, after shopping they ate custard ices in glass dishes under the trees outside Gunter's in Berkeley Square.

That autumn, Apsley became a House Prefect (in the final year it was difficult not to achieve that rank) and was at last qualified to boss the juniors around. One candidate was Charles Scott-Moncrieff, who had just arrived at Kenny's. He went on to be a magisterial translator of Proust, but at school he distinguished himself with a literary work of his own – a story of teenage fellatio which appeared in a school magazine (not the *Wykehamist*, sadly) and promptly brought the publication to a close.

Although in later life Apsley was a model of conventional Wykehamist self-sufficiency, it was a result of his natural shyness, not of absorption in the school's culture. He did not feel that he was a member of an especially prestigious club; he did not attend reunions, and kept in touch with few boys. It was not Winchester's fault: Apsley was not suited to large, overpowering crowds; he came into his own in smaller groups, and was never at ease with swells or bloods.

He left Winchester at a climactic moment in its modern history. The highlight of the school calendar was the Eton cricket match in June. Boys, parents and masters all attended, the maters trussed up in long frocks and elaborate hats, grasping parasols and languishing in deck chairs. Having lost to Eton three years in a row, in 1904 Winchester triumphed by eight wickets. Three weeks later, a team of Wykehamists also won the Public Schools' Shooting Championship, and the entire school went to the station to greet George Mallory and the other victorious marksmen. Apsley watched these events from the outside, pleased that he would soon be leaving Winchester and its cloistered rituals for the last time. But a fresh set of fears lay at the other end of the summer holidays. He had been offered a place to read Classics at Christ Church, his father's old Oxford college.

Oxford was throbbing with Edwardian ebullience, and Christ Church heaved with Byronic youths. Known as 'the House' (from the Latin *Aedes Christi*), it was reputedly the most aristocratic of the colleges; one of Apsley's contemporaries, describing the wooden noticeboards at the foot of each staircase which announced the occupants of the rooms above, noted, 'In other colleges the surnames alone were painted, but presumably the House was so full of noblemen that commoners had to have the distinguishing mark of Mr.'

Apsley was billeted in Old Library 6, and he kept the room for three years. To reach it he walked through the wide, tranquil space of Tom Quad, with its fountained lily pond and leaping Mercury, down into Cloisters and off into a passageway with a wood-panelled ceiling carved with bunches of grapes. Old Library was off this passageway, and 6 was a large room on the first floor. It had two oak doors and, in the opposite wall, a pair of arched sash windows that looked across a small courtyard onto the Venetian Gothic walls of the new Meadow Buildings. When Apsley sat quietly in his shabby leather armchair, he could hear the faint rattle of carts, wagons and dumpy horse-drawn omnibuses floating over from St Aldate's.

Apsley was a handsome eighteen-year-old, his dark brown hair straight, glossy and parted left of centre. His features were neat and well proportioned and his eyes chocolate-brown and velvety, like his mother's. But he was overly conscious of his wire-framed pebble glasses, and at college was prone to skulking between the columns of the library bays. He would hurry back to his room in the late afternoon light, past the butterscotch gargoyles of Cloisters, and listen to the crackly tunes of a distant gramophone while he prepared for the uncomfortable ritual of cutlets and watery cabbage in Hall. He did not make friends easily, and he struggled to master college etiquette. Freshmen were not to speak to senior men living on the same staircase; they were to wait until the seniors visited them and left their cards. Similarly, freshmen were not to take the armchairs in front of the fire in the junior common room as these were reserved for seniors. As for teaching, Oxford was still in the grip of conservative forces, many of the dons living in a Jurassic age of human consciousness. A few years before Apsley arrived at Oxford a tutor at Brasenose, a splendid college on the other side of the High Street, sent a letter of condolence to the parents of one of his undergraduates who had died. 'It may be of some consolation to you,' he wrote, 'to know that the young man would in any case have had to go down at the end of the present term owing to his failure to pass Responsions.'

Academic attitudes were similarly fossilised. The Provost of Oriel College, Dr C. L. Shadwell, elected in 1905, was proud to announce, 'Show me a researcher and I'll show you a fool.' A man who did plenty of research and was no fool was H. T. Tizard, an exact contemporary of Apsley's at Oxford (Tizard was at Magdalen) and later an eminent scientist and adviser to Churchill. The two men knew each other, Tizard resurfacing thirty years later to support Apsley's application to join the Athenaeum. He noted that far from extending the boundaries of knowledge, most Oxford dons of their vintage were 'content to live like gentlemen, passing to the younger generation the knowledge that had been amassed by others'.

Compton Mackenzie's novel *Sinister Street* is partially set in the Christ Church of the period. 'Nothing anywhere seemed as yet to hint that the general flippancy of Oxford which was merely an extension of the public school spirit was in danger of dying out', comments Mackenzie. 'Oxford was still the apotheosis of the amateur. It was still surprising when the head of a house or a don or an undergraduate achieved anything in a manner that did not savour of happy chance.' Apsley was adrift in another strangely closed community, a country boy who did not belong among the braying aristocrats roaming arm-in-arm through Tom Quad. Like Michael Fane, the protagonist of *Sinister Street*, it seemed to him that he alone was not in the club, and that he stood, a solitary figure, in the wings of a glittering show. He sat at his desk in the long evenings, a pool of light from his lamp flooding the pages of Thucydides, and gazed unhappily over at the blazing light from Meadows.

Then, after a few weeks, Apsley made a great discovery. Poor eyesight wasn't a handicap when it came to rowing. At almost five feet ten he was among the taller students, and though he was slightly built, he was fit. He immediately took part in trials for torpids, the spring-term intercollegiate races in eight-man boats. Soon he was rowing bow in the college 3rd VIII. He may have been quiet and shy, neither aristocratic nor wonderfully clever, but he could row, and that meant he belonged. He thrived in the enforced companionship of a small team, and since he had few outlets for his enthusiasms, rowing took on a great importance in his life. By the autumn of 1905 he was in the 1st IV. As a man in a college boat, he was one of the lucky ones who posed for crew photographs in the Palladian grandeur of Peckwater, standing nervously, jacket buttoned and hands in pockets, by the stone doorway emblazoned with rowing victories. The crews trained in the early morning, running from Meadow gate down the wide avenue to the shrouded river, where they carried their boat from the boathouse in the clammy mist. Torpids dominated the spring term, and summers revolved around the pistol shots of the Eights' Week races and parental visits to the boathouses for salmon mayonnaise, trembling jellies and a glass of hock.

The tyranny of games, so vice-like at Winchester, was broken at Oxford, and in an atmosphere of greater choice, Apsley, always anxious, found it easier to participate. Social rituals notwithstanding, Oxford was a release from the robotically prescribed routine of school. Stephen McKenna, a future journalist and Liberal politician and a near contemporary of Apsley's at the House, commented that 'many who had been despised and rejected at school began suddenly to shine as unexpected social lights'. Apsley was never a social light, but at university he could at least glow.

One who shone very brightly was George Mair, a modern history scholar who had a room near Old Library 6. Mair was an influential figure in college. He went on to become a modestly successful literary journalist, and when *The Worst Journey in the World* made Apsley famous fourteen years after he left Oxford, Mair remembered him as 'a dark, lean, rather silent man who was short-sighted and always wore spectacles. He used to row in the college boat, and used sometimes to afflict his friends by his anxiety as to whether he was pulling as well as he should.' Mair went on to deliver a convincing verdict on his friend's personality: 'Otherwise he was remarkable only for a certain taste in natural history, an extreme shyness, and a nervousness which was not what we commonly call nervousness, but rather a sensitive imagination which made him see further round things than other people, and, like a tightly stretched wire, made him react more quickly than other and duller men.' In later years Apsley was not just liable to react more quickly, but also to respond more profoundly than other men, sometimes with appalling consequences. A tightly stretched wire indeed.

Women were not admitted as full members of the university, and they scarcely featured in the lives of most male undergraduates. Twenty years later the art historian and Old Wykehamist Kenneth Clark wrote that 'it was practically impossible to meet a girl at Oxford', and he turned out to be quite good at meeting girls. A shy boy from Hertfordshire had no chance, even one with five sisters. One of Apsley's peers called it 'a life of familiarity without intimacy'. Of course, there were sentimental attach-ments in college; but if Apsley enjoyed any, their story has slipped away. Little is known of his emotional life during this period. Leonard Woolf, born in 1880, offers a clue to general attitudes towards sex at that time. 'How dense the barbaric darkness was,' wrote Woolf,

> in which the Victorian middle-class boy and youth was left to drift sexually is shown by the fact that no relation or teacher, indeed no adult, ever mentioned the subject of sex to me. No information or advice on this devastating fever in one's blood and brain was ever given to me.

Love and lust, like the functions of the bowels and bladder, were subjects which could not be discussed or even mentioned.

Stuart Mais (pronounced 'Mays') was among Apsley's friends at Christ Church. In later years, after being sacked as Professor of English from the new Cadet College at Cranwell, S. P. B. Mais became a well-known Fleet Street journalist.* The pair stayed in touch, and Mais, like Cherry a great nature lover, enjoyed going to stay at Lamer. More extrovert than his friend, Mais adored Oxford. 'In my time at any rate,' he wrote, 'life at "the House" was very much a country house existence. Our every want was instantly catered for. We had but to shout for our scout, and immediately the courteous, almost P. G. Wodehouse-like valet-butler would appear to attend to our wishes and see them carried out.' Apsley did not join the Union or indulge in the stew of political societies at Oxford. Union hacks dogmatising in their robust Johnsonian manner were anathema to him, and so were dazzling characters such as the aesthete Philip Sassoon and the toffs vomiting out of their windows after a session with their dining clubs. The High Tory conservatism of his father and his father's father ran through him like woodgrain.

As for work: Apsley floundered in oceans of Ovid and seas of Sallust. Increasingly, he felt that he wasn't cut out to be a classicist, and after grinding through his first-year exams he flung aside his Homer and switched to Modern History, a subject deemed suitable for students who were not quite up to Latin and Greek.

When he went home in the holidays, he found that little had changed except the elder girls' skirts, which were shorter. In the early mornings he jumped his horse, Harebell, over the estate's high hedges, and afterwards he sat in the kitchen under the row of copper pots eating bread and honey. But further afield, things really were changing. At the end of 1905 Balfour resigned as prime minister, and the following year he watched the general election from the sidelines, knowing his style of paternalism was doomed: the Liberals triumphed in an anti-Tory landslide unparalleled until 1945. A decade of Tory hegemony was over, and the General shuddered, along with the rest of the country's landowners. Furthermore, another enemy had entered the field. The Labour Representation Committee, the party's

---

* Mais was also a prolific book writer. One of his novels, *Caged Birds*, was memorably reviewed in the *New Statesman* by Rebecca West with the six words, 'How long, O Lord, how long.'

forerunner, was formed in 1900; by 1905, Labour candidates had trebled their share of the vote.

Another event in the closing weeks of 1905 was discussed avidly in the junior common rooms by young men with a taste for adventure. It did not have the seismic effect of a prime-ministerial resignation, but it was widely reported in the British press none the less. The Norwegian explorer Roald Amundsen had pioneered a route through the North-West Passage. Ever since Elizabeth I stood at her window to wave farewell to Martin Frobisher as he sailed from Greenwich in 1576, mariners and adventurers had sought to find a way from the Atlantic through to the Pacific. Confounded by ice and the jigsaw of an unmapped archipelago, none had succeeded. In Frobisher's day the goal had ultimately been commercial: the sea-route offered a short cut to the wealth of Cathay away from the baleful influence of Spain and Portugal. By the nineteenth century the dogged expeditioners were inspired by the reward of national and personal prestige. The Admiralty despatched a series of British naval ships to the high latitudes, culminating in Sir John Franklin's grisly 1845 endeavour. American expeditions joined the race, their stories enthralling the public waiting comfortably at home. Although a Briton, Commander Robert McClure, led the first transit of the elusive Passage, he did it in stages, in two ships and on a sledge. The dauntless Amundsen was the first man to sail through the North-West Passage in a single ship.

Apsley had read widely on the subject of exploration, and had recently devoured a copy of Robert Falcon Scott's *The Voyage of the 'Discovery'*, the story of the British National Antarctic Expedition of 1901–04. He immediately recognised the significance of Amundsen's feat in the Arctic. But he had no idea that even the North-West Passage would not mark the Norwegian's greatest achievement. That was yet to come.

In June 1906, on the fiftieth anniversary of military operations in India, the General's name appeared on the Birthday Honours List as a Companion of the Bath. He had been ill since the spring with an undiagnosed condition that made his legs swollen and painful. Apsley dashed back from Oxford whenever he could and sat for hours massaging his father's calves. When the old man was no longer able to run the estate his son acted *in loco parentis*. At the age of twenty he helped organise a voluminous inventory and valuation for insurance purposes. The resulting document ran to more than two hundred pages, including twenty-nine pages listing the family silver. He began to seek the advice of Arthur Farrer, a friend and former neighbour of the General's and a lawyer in his family firm in Lincoln's Inn

Fields in London.* The relationship between Apsley and Farrer, one which was to last many decades, now shifted gently into professional gear.

That October, though it was term time, Apsley was back at home, attending to the General. He wrote to Farrer:

> Father said he would very much like you to bring down the paper you spoke about. I hope you will pardon me for not telling him that it was not necessary for anyone to come, since I know that he very much likes to see you, so much so that I do not think you will mind the trouble though it must mean a lot to you. The Doctor says that it is impossible to say that he is any better, but he is not any worse, and, as was expected, the pain is leaving the right leg, which will enable him to be turned off his back, which is most important . . . Will you let me know yr day and train?

After Farrer's visit, Apsley wrote again. 'Sir Lander [the specialist] has just left. He says that he thinks Father is past the present crisis, but that he does not think he will recover quickly. Also he told me that though he does not say that Father will be actually crippled, he will never, he thinks, get about in the same way again . . . I only hope Father will not know this, if it is true . . .'

Some years previously the General had made a will, bequeathing appropriate portions to the girls, a life interest in Denford to Evelyn and the rest to his son. As was standard practice, the Lamer estate was entailed, which meant that it could not be sold or bequeathed to anyone except the heir by descent. Apsley in effect was to be the custodial owner until it passed to the next generation, as the General had been before him. But the old soldier had felt the winds of change. Seeing that things didn't look good for landowners, he decided to free his son's hand, and when Apsley turned twenty-one, on 2 January 1907, the General formally broke the entail. Fewer than forty years later, every inch of family land would be gone.

Back at Oxford, Apsley learned to fence during his third year, and in the autumn and summer, when there was no rowing practice, he took an early morning dip in the Cherwell. He progressed to the 2nd VIII, and, in the spring, to the transcendent glories of the 1st. Watching him on the river one morning, the boat club secretary noted in the log book that Cherry-Garrard 'showed promise', and in the autumn term of his fourth year he was duly given a trial for the University Boat Club. It was a tremendous

---

* Farrer & Co., still at the same address, are solicitors to the Queen.

honour, though he was not eventually selected, 'being very short in the water and not giving his crew time'. In the summer he had just missed a place in the college 1st VIII. Christ Church went on to go Head of the River for the first time in forty-nine years, inciting scenes of extravagant debauchery. A few weeks later Apsley was 'spare man' at the Henley Royal Regatta, obliged to watch from the bank in his straw boater. He determined to do better next year.

He spent the second half of his third year darting between Hertfordshire and Oxford. In May 1907 the family's old coachman, Hobbs, who had served the General and his horses since the Denford days, had a heart attack. The young master wrote to him from Oxford:

I was very sorry to hear a few days ago that you are not to work . . . I very much hope that this will find you feeling pretty fit, it's always pretty feeble work strolling about and not being allowed to do anything.

I am having a great time, I am not allowed to go into training yet, and so there is no chance of any very serious rowing for me yet, but I am going to row in some sculling races and also in a Four against a London Four on Whit Monday. I bathe every morning at seven, do very little work, play cricket and fence – so you see I am having a merry time . . . I am glad to hear Harebell is very fit and fresh; I only wish I had her here for a ride. I hope this good sun will do you and Father lots of good.

Hobbs was obliged to retire. When Apsley heard, he wrote again. 'I am very very sorry. You have been with us so many years, as long as, and longer than, I can remember – that we shall all miss you very much.'

On 15 June Apsley brought a cricket eleven over from Oxford to play a local team on Nomansland Common. It was a high point of a summer otherwise dominated by the General's painful illness. A doctor was now in almost permanent attendance. That summer, to celebrate the forthcoming Jubilee of the Relief of Lucknow, Lord Roberts led the survivors in a ceremony at the King's Levee, but the General was too ill to attend. He was invited to a Mutiny veterans' banquet, hosted by the *Daily Telegraph*, to take place in December, and, in a touching display of hope, the family spoke of their wish that he would be well enough to attend. In some dark place in their hearts, they must have known that he would not. In the autumn, after a tense summer at home, Apsley began his last year at Oxford. He moved into 19 Pembroke Street, sharing his modest lodgings with a postgraduate mathematical scholar. It was a narrow, higgledy-piggledy street two or three minutes' walk from the main entrance of the college, and 19 was one of the medieval houses on the left-hand side going up. It was a bad time. Telegrams arrived at the porter's lodge summoning Apsley home and he would dash off a note to his tutor and run to the station in the fog to catch the next train to London, arriving at Wheathampstead as the lampman propped his short ladder against the wall of the station house. Reporters called at Lamer for news and bulletins were issued in *The Times* as well as local papers. 'The seeds of his illness,' one report stated authoritatively in a pleasing example of journalistic imagination triumphing over evidence, 'were sown during the Indian Mutiny, probably at the Relief of Lucknow, where the General had a trying time.'

Apsley Cherry-Garrard senior died on 8 November 1907, shortly after two o'clock in the afternoon. He was seventy-five. The family were all there. The next day his coffin was brought into the drawing room. One of the wreaths was from Hobbs, and the message ran, 'In ever loving memory of a kind master, from his old coachman.' In her note thanking him, Evelyn, convulsed with grief and loss, wrote that she was feeling 'as if it cannot all be real, but that we must be in some awful dream, from which we shall wake presently'.

The funeral was to take place on Friday 15 November. The day before, Apsley wrote to Hobbs, 'I had thought of asking you to walk with the men in the procession tomorrow, but I thought of your heart and decided that perhaps it was better not. However as it is your wish to come we shall be most glad. Please tell Mr Owen [the local builder] or whoever is arranging the front part of the procession that I wish you to walk in front of the bier. I am sure Father would have liked you to do this.' As a postscript he added, 'You will have to regulate your pace according to the slow marches of the soldiers behind you.'

The General was buried on a grey November day in an eddy of fast-falling leaves. The men who worked on the estate met at the house and walked down to the village in front of the bearer party sent by his regiment. The pall covering the coffin was a Union Jack, and on it lay the old soldier's plumed helmet and sword; his medals were carried in front of the coffin. When the procession reached the station, the tenants joined the front of the group. The High Street was lined with people, shops were closed and blinds drawn. The bells of St Helen's rang half muffled, and hundreds attended the service. On Apsley's wreath, the message read simply, 'From Laddie'.

By this time, dead Garrards had moved out of the church and into the churchyard. The General was buried under a granite cross in the shadow of the slender broach spire. After the coffin was lowered, the girls stood on the lip of the grave in the glaucous twilight, and each dropped in a posy of lilies of the valley. Edith was six years old.

The obituary in the *St Albans Times* said, 'As a proof of his dislike for self-prominence it may be stated that the people of Wheathampstead were practically unaware of his brilliant military career, and some of his intimate friends knew little of the distinguished service rendered to his country in the Indian Mutiny and the several wars which followed.' He passed this endearing modesty down to his only son, along with a large fortune.

Loss flooded through the old house like water through a hole in a ship's hull. The remaining Cherry-Garrards had to get away, so they spent some weeks in that first awful winter without him in Brighton, the retirement home of Evelyn's father, Henry Sharpin, who had remarried after his first wife died. But on Good Friday 1908 they experienced another tragedy when Dr Sharpin died of a heart attack. They buried him in Bedford.

Apsley spent the winter and spring shuttling between Lamer, Brighton and Oxford. It was a desperate period for him, with Finals looming horribly and a cold, empty space where the central presence of his life had been. He struggled to balance the demands of the estate with the requirements of his degree course: he was frequently obliged to abandon his books to attend to some pressing matter on one of the properties. Besides Lamer and Denford, he was responsible for Little Wittenham, a large Cherry estate in north Berkshire.* In February he had to dash over there to inspect the school, which was in need of repair. Rowing was a bright spot. In Eights' Week he finally rowed in the 1st VIII, and Christ Church again triumphed. Following that, his crew won the Grand Challenge Cup at Henley Royal Regatta, beating off Eton by a length-and-a-half in a dramatic final. It was the first time the House had won the Grand.

In June, dressed in academic gown and mortarboard, he sloped along the High Street to Schools, the late-Victorian building that has struck terror into so many trembling students. He had spent much of his final year sorting out the General's affairs and running the estates, and he had buried his father and grandfather in the space of five months. The tension between competing demands and responsibilities, combined with a highly-strung disposition, was a heavy burden for a young man. No wonder he got a third-class degree.

He was back at Lamer when the news came through. It was not a

* Now, as a result of boundary changes, in Oxfordshire.

surprise, and anyway thirds were more common then than they are now. In the year Apsley graduated, a third of students got one; in Modern History it was the biggest overall category, with nineteen men achieving a fourth. Given the cult of the amateur that still persisted, in some quarters thirds were a source of pride.

3

Untrodden Fields

Apsley came down from Oxford in the summer of 1908 at a loose end, perplexed by the bewildering speed at which the world around him was changing. On the road, the battle between the horse and the internal combustion engine was edging towards its inexorable conclusion. Motorised taxis, motorised buses, Ford's announcement of the Model T, a car most middle-class people could afford, a royal commission to look into traffic congestion: for five years the pages of *The Times* had been crowded with stories about the motor car, and even in Wheathampstead representatives of the species had been sighted. Above ground, since Orville Wright had made the first powered flight at Kitty Hawk, North Carolina, in December 1903, non-flying flying machines had been pranged into apple trees on a weekly basis. More significantly, records were being made in the air with similar regularity. Below ground, too, distances shrank as electric underground trains rumbled out of London's Baker Street.

The newspapers were also burgeoning with ugly stories of social unrest. In October the young Liberal politician Winston Churchill made a speech in which he said that the perilous problem of unemployment demanded special remedies; those remedies would lead people into 'new and untrodden fields in British politics'. This kind of talk made Apsley uneasy. As the country marched towards progress and change, he felt curiously out of step. In his heart he was still a Victorian; in many ways he was to die a Victorian. But, like many men of his background, as he matured he longed to shake off the suffocating effects of his early years. 'It was not a question of unhappiness,' explained Lytton Strachey, 'so much as restriction and oppression – the subtle unperceived weight of the circumambient air.'

Apsley had the vague idea that he might study law, and he told his mother that this was his long-term plan – though he was not eager to begin immediately. He didn't need to work at all: the General's estate had been valued at £102,000 gross (£5 million today), and Lamer alone at £44,052 (over £2 million). Rents flowed in regularly and an extensive portfolio of stocks and shares yielded dividends and bonuses. But Apsley's spirit was restless, and he was looking for something real – something solid – to occupy his time. He recoiled from the sedate life of the country squire. Those who did not know him expected him to follow in his father's distinguished footsteps and take up soldiering. He admired his father hugely, but he was not of the warrior caste. Never a natural leader, Apsley was too neurotic for the army, and too afraid of making mistakes. What should he do? He accepted his responsibilities as head of the household, and felt his duty keenly; but he could not yet submit. Furthermore, without its dominating paterfamilias Lamer no longer seemed like home. The girls had created their own cosy domestic world on which external events had little bearing. They helped their mother in charity work, went off to stay with relations and organised heavy schedules of dancing classes, tea parties, plays and concerts. (The suffragettes might have been making progress elsewhere in Britain, but nobody chained herself to the Lamer railings.) Apsley was an outsider, even in his own house.

Travel offered the perfect short-term escape. Apsley had grown up on the General's stories of bivouacking on the veldt, and as a schoolboy he had thrilled to tales of tall-masted ships creaking in the pincers of an ice floe and doughty Britons battling malaria as they hacked their way to vast inland seas. He had plenty of money. The problem was that he had nowhere to go.

In this frame of mind, early in the autumn of 1908 Apsley had taken the train up to Scotland to stay at his cousin Reginald Smith's bungalow in Cortachy, near Kirriemuir. Smith was the son of one of the General's sisters. He was thirty years older than Apsley, and when he first swung his young cousin over his shoulders on the Denford lawns he was already a brilliant junior barrister.

A tall, patrician Old Etonian with dark skin and an elongated face, Reggie had a first-class degree in Classics. Despite having become a King's Counsel he had abandoned the law in order to head the London publishing firm of Smith, Elder & Co., whose list included Trollope, Browning and Thackeray. His wife Isabel's maiden name, confusingly, was also Smith: she was the daughter of the Smith, Elder publisher George Smith, who had discovered Charlotte Brontë. The childless Smiths lived in an elegant townhouse in Mayfair's Green Street, and since his father's death Apsley, always close to both of them, had turned to Reggie and Isabel for advice and companionship. A paternal figure so much nearer Apsley's age than the General had been, Reggie was a measured, sensitive man who below the surface was highly-strung and prone to anxiety, like his younger cousin.

Reggie was also the editor of the *Cornhill* magazine, in which capacity he had recently provoked a volley of angry comments from Virginia Woolf* ('that fool of a man') for rejecting a piece she had written. This egregious oversight notwithstanding, Reggie was intelligent, thoughtful and highly principled, and his long face usually wore a serious expression as he chewed on his pipe and peered down through his glasses. He was known for his courtesy and meticulous attention to detail, and a private income enabled him to pursue quality rather than profit in his professional life. Austere and spare in face and figure, he seemed formidable on first impression, but he had a big heart. His authors were devoted to him (at least six dedicated their books to him), and so were many with whom he worked to help run a hospital in a poor area of east London.

The Smiths had transformed their Scottish bungalow, called 'Burnside', from a shepherd's cottage into a homely shooting lodge. French doors in the dining room opened onto a rose-covered veranda and a garden which sloped down to a row of birch trees bordering the road through Glen Prosen. It was a cosy little lodge which smelt of griddled bannocks and sweet peas. That summer the Smiths had lent it to their close friends Edward and Oriana Wilson. And so Apsley arrived, bereaved, rudderless and vulnerable. The General had been dead for less than a year. His son walked smartly up the steep path to the lodge and met the man who would tower over the rest of his life like a colossus.

Edward Wilson, known as 'Bill', had been to the Antarctic on Scott's first expedition, which left England in 1901. He met Reginald Smith four years later when he accompanied Scott to the Smith, Elder offices to discuss the book of the expedition, which the firm duly published. Smith and Wilson were both meditative, judicious men with a highly developed moral sensibility, and they became great friends. The Wilsons were frequent visitors to Kirriemuir, and before Bill left on his second Antarctic expedition, Reggie gave him an engraved watch. 'From now onward till we return . . .' Wilson wrote in a thank-you note, 'not a single day will pass but I shall be reminded by the simple inscription on the back of the watch of the friend whose friendship has made all but the very highest principles

* Then still Virginia Stephen.

in life impossible. We feel that to possess the friendship of yourself and Mrs Smith is to possess something which will outlast watches, and will still be going when the last of them has stopped.'

Born in 1872, Wilson was a doctor's son from Cheltenham. The family lived in a ten-bedroom Regency house in the genteel streets of the town itself, and Wilson's mother Mary also leased a farm out towards the village of Leckhampton. A towering figure in the world of chicken breeding (she was the distinguished author of the definitive *ABC of Poultry*), Mary Wilson took the smallholding to enable her to experiment with cattle. It was there that her second son had spent his happiest days. As a teenager he was often to be found crouching over the bulrushes in the pond, examining young frogs and collecting tadpoles, or roaming over the gentle Cotswold hills observing nightjars silhouetted against the great spur of rock to the north. He liked to spend the night out in the woods, returning for breakfast with two plover's eggs in his pocket, and he knew the name of every bird that sang. A friend who went birding with him noted how observant he was. 'I have seen him,' recalled John Fraser, 'suddenly stop and then swoop down like a merlin hawk and produce a large grass snake. I had not seen it: Wilson had seen it . . . and had beaten the snake for quickness . . . He was tall and thin, rather like a thoroughbred racehorse.'

Following his father into medicine, Wilson studied at Cambridge, where he rowed in the college boat. But while pursuing further medical studies in London he contracted tuberculosis, and was obliged to take a year off in Switzerland. Against the odds, he recovered, but the disease left him with scarred lungs. He remained deeply involved with the natural world, and after qualifying as a doctor he continued to work as a zoologist and naturalist. Wilson was mostly interested in small things. When he was asked why he had made no contribution to the study of the stars, he replied that he would love to try, if only he could hold and examine a cluster of them in his hand. In the field of natural history he was a keen and gifted illustrator, a fact that was to stimulate Apsley to take up sketching and painting.

Wilson was a tall, lean figure with clear blue eyes, reddish-brown hair and a swift, raking stride. A committed Christian prone to asceticism, he strove to rise above the comforts of the flesh and draw closer to the God who lived in his heart. Once, staying in a hotel while away from home with his research, he realised that he was beginning to prefer bathing in hot water to cold, a bad sign, 'and something must be done to stop it'. He sought to sublimate the self, and aspired to a Christ-like ideal. As a young medical student he worked among the poor and resolved 'to let nothing stand in the way of doing everyone a good turn'. But he was not outwardly pious, in that he kept his religion to himself, and he was a genial companion. In public he was funny and playful, and when he was amused the corners of his mouth twisted into a quizzical smile. In short, he was a man of action and a mystic: a potent combination. He was also highly-strung like Reggie Smith, and suffered from a kind of social neurosis. As a young man he took sedatives before taxing social encounters, and it required far more courage for him to face an audience than to cross a crevasse. Apsley found Wilson's belief in a divine purpose deeply attractive, as it imposed a pattern on an otherwise inchoate, confusing universe. Besides recognising Wilson as a mentor, he saw an inner calm in the older man that he badly wanted.

Shortly before he left on the *Discovery*, Wilson married Oriana Souper, the daughter of a clergyman who was also a headmaster. She was the matron of a preparatory school. Like Wilson, Oriana was a committed Christian. Her relationship with her husband was tightly bound up with their religious faith. 'Without a love for God,' he wrote to her from the Antarctic, 'I can't imagine either loving you or being loved by you.'

Wilson had first become attracted to the Antarctic in 1900. He was spotted sketching at London Zoo by its Secretary, a friend of his father's and one of the organisers of Scott's first polar endeavour, the British National Antarctic Expedition which was to set sail the following year. Despite a poor health report, Wilson was selected as second medical officer, vertebrate zoologist and artist, and he turned out to be a vital presence, whether on board ship, out sledging or cooped up in the hut. He was quite capable of cavorting naked in the wardroom when horseplay broke out after dinner; yet he always had time to listen to a shipmate's troubles. On the *Discovery* expedition Wilson marched to within 500 miles of the Pole with Scott and Shackleton; he also carried out groundbreaking work on the embryology of the Emperor penguin.

Both Scott and his fellow explorer Ernest Shackleton were powerfully drawn to Wilson. Shackleton wrote to him in February 1907 ('My dear Billy') literally begging him to be second-in-command on his own *Nimrod* expedition: 'it will be a thousand times better with you'. Wilson was not only an outstanding sledger and inspirational scientist. He was also adaptable and good at improvising: key qualities in any camp. Most importantly, he was an unquenchable fountain of emotional support and wise counsel. But to Shackleton's bitter disappointment, Wilson wouldn't go with him. He had been appointed field researcher, physiologist and anatomist to the Department of Agriculture's Grouse Disease Inquiry, investigating a bizarre ailment that was decimating birds on British moors. It was a major project, and one that Wilson was committed to seeing through. But he was determined to return to the Antarctic when it was finished.

The polar regions were in fashion in the early years of the twentieth century. They represented the last white spaces on the map, mysterious, romantic and untamed, and the power of the unknown worked hard on the human spirit. Victorian explorers, geographers and chancers had filled in the map of Africa, naming its lakes, claiming its lands and gasping for their lives in its broiling climate. The icy purity at the world's ends encapsulated a more potent kind of romance. 'Of all the continents,' wrote a celebrated American explorer, 'Antarctica is the fairest, white and unspoiled, spacious and austere, fashioned in the clean, antiseptic quarries of an Ice Age.'

The High Arctic, remote and perilous though it was, had been at least partially charted by generations of explorers. The Antarctic still lay behind a hoary veil: before Captain James Cook's second voyage in 1772 many had believed that there was a fertile Shangri-La in the far south. Cook, the first man to cross the Antarctic Circle, laid the myth to rest when he announced that there could be no people down there: it was too cold. The continent itself was sighted through the sepulchral fog in 1820, and although it is not clear who spotted it first, it was probably the Estonian Thaddeus Bellingshausen, despatched south by Tsar Alexander I. Bellingshausen was a fine explorer, but it was the Englishman James Clark Ross who discovered great swathes of the ice shelf surrounding Antarctica during a Royal Navy voyage between 1839 and 1843. From the bridge of the ice-strengthened *Erebus*, Ross, reputedly the most handsome man in the navy, looked over at the glittering peaks of Victoria Land, and at a mighty smoking volcano that he named after his ship.

Sealers and whalers eddied round the bleak sub-Antarctic islands, but the golden age – the period that came to be known as the Heroic Age of Antarctic exploration – did not begin until the Sixth International Geographical Congress, which took place in London in 1895. At its closing session, Congress passed a resolution urging scientific societies throughout the world to start planning Antarctic expeditions, on the grounds that 'the exploration of the Antarctic regions is the greatest piece of geographical exploration still to be undertaken'. Congress had a point. Antarctica, the highest, driest, coldest and windiest continent, a landmass one-and-a-half-times the size of the United States, was still almost unknown: barely twenty-five expeditions had even glimpsed it.

Between 1897 and 1899, a multi-national, Belgian-led expedition discovered and mapped sections of the Antarctic coastline, and its ship, the *Belgica*, inadvertently became the first to winter in the pack ice of the Southern Ocean. The 26-year-old Roald Amundsen was on board, an accomplished sailor and skier keen to acquire valuable experience of the capricious and often murderous Antarctic conditions. Even the austere Norseman yielded to the romance of the south. 'Beauty is still sleeping,' he wrote of the Antarctic heartlands, 'but the kiss is coming, the kiss that shall wake her!'*

That same year Carsten Borchegrevink, a Norwegian by birth, led a British venture, raising the Union Jack over Antarctic land for the first time. Borchegrevink and his men went on to winter on the continent itself. Germans and Swedes led pioneering expeditions at the turn of the twentieth century, and in 1901 the young Royal Navy commander Robert Falcon Scott sailed south in the *Discovery*. By trekking inland, Scott and his companions undertook the first significant exploration of the Antarctic landmass. They were true pioneers, and their findings convinced the scientific establishment that a continent, as opposed to an archipelago, existed south of the Antarctic Circle.

French, Scottish, Norwegian and Argentine vessels, some of them whalers, continued to explore Antarctic waters, but it was Ernest Shackleton who was to come thrillingly close to the Pole. Having been invalided home with scurvy on Scott's *Discovery* expedition, in 1907 he sailed south on the *Nimrod*, in command, at last, of his own show. 'The stark polar lands,' wrote Shackleton, 'grip the hearts of the men who have lived on them in a manner that can be hardly understood by the people who have never got outside the pale of civilisation.' He discovered more than 300 miles of the main Antarctic mountain range, found coal deposits at Mount Buckley and claimed the Polar Plateau for Edward VII. In January 1909, the year after Apsley met Wilson at Burnside, Shackleton and three companions marched to within 112 miles of the South Pole. He was knighted later in the year.

Shackleton's near miss attracted intense publicity and raised the stakes considerably: the Pole, surely, was there for the taking. News swirled around geographical and naval circles that other nations were preparing to

---

* The image of a slumbering continent was popular among the first men to land in the Antarctic. The American Frederick Cook, the doctor on the *Belgica* expedition, wrote on his return that with the right backing, 'The combined armies of peace could . . . march into the white silence, the unbroken, icy slumber of centuries about the South Pole . . .'

launch expeditions: Japan, some said, or Germany. Emotions were already running high when the news came through that three months after Shackleton's dash towards the South Pole two Americans had reached the North Pole on separate expeditions. One was Frederick Cook, the doctor on the *Belgica*. His claim was soon questioned, and Commander Robert Peary of the US Navy was honoured as the first man to reach ninety degrees north.* The Antarctic was a fine setting for national chest-puffing. (It still is.)† British empire-builders never flinched from the conviction that the white spaces of the polar regions should be coloured pink just as vast tracts of the rest of the world had been in the nineteenth century. When it was reported that an American had reached the North Pole first, it became increasingly urgent for an Englishman to bag its southern counterpart. The South Pole was now perceived as the last great geographical prize, and Antarctica as the last remaining continent to be conquered by the triumphant armies of imperialism – a mighty *terra incognita* waiting to be ushered into the known world, like the dark continent before it.

In September 1907 Scott went up to Burnside to stay with the Wilsons. The Smiths were also there, and all five enjoyed the dying days of summer on the moors and in the rolling, coarse-grass fields around the lodge where they took picnics. Scott, Wilson and Reggie Smith went out shooting in the afternoons, and Scott once deliberately let a roe-deer leap away because it was so pretty.

Scott was four years older than Wilson and eighteen years older than Apsley. Born into an ordinary middle-class family in Devon, he had enlisted in the navy as a cadet when he was thirteen. His early career had been unexceptional, and it seemed unlikely that he would make a name for himself. When he was twenty-nine his circumstances unexpectedly changed for the worse: his father died and left the family penniless. The following year Scott's only brother also died. He had always been hard-pressed for cash, but now, already scraping by on the meagre pay of a lieutenant, Scott was solely responsible for his widowed mother and unmarried sisters.

Searching for a way to boost his career, in 1899, two years after his father

---

* Peary's claim has subsequently also been challenged, and he probably didn't get to the Pole. But at the time it was thought that he had.

† 'This is how it looked,' wrote Doris Lessing, who grew up in South Africa and was fascinated by Scott's expeditions, 'to quite a lot of people not European: there was little Europe, strutting and bossing up there in its little corner, like a pack of schoolboys fighting over a cake.'

died, Scott appealed to Sir Clements Markham to support his application to lead the forthcoming British expedition to the Antarctic. The aged and crusty Markham was president of the Royal Geographical Society, and as a young midshipman he had spent a winter in the Arctic on one of the searches for Sir John Franklin. Markham was a man of energy, passion and prejudice, a throwback to the glory days of British exploration. Scott had caught his eye many years earlier when, as an eighteen-year-old midshipman, he had won a cutters' race off the island of St Kitts. Markham was to be the powering force behind both the expeditions Scott led to the Antarctic.

A handsome man of medium height, with unusual dark blue eyes that sometimes looked almost purple, Scott had broad shoulders and a small waist, and at thirty his dark hair was already beginning to thin. His naval experience had not provided him with any of the specific skills that polar exploration demanded, and as a lieutenant he had specialised in torpedo work, hardly a useful asset when out sledging. But he was an ambitious, restless man who saw that the blank spaces of the Antarctic offered a tempting challenge to the commander who dared take his ship through the pack ice. A successful expedition would almost certainly lead to promotion, prestige and a secure financial footing: important considerations to a man with onerous responsibilities.

As for Markham, although his cherished expedition was a private venture he badly wanted a naval man in command. In addition, he believed that youth was more important in a leader than experience. Scott was still in his early thirties, and his enthusiasm impressed Markham. Shortly after being promoted to the rank of commander, Scott was appointed to lead the British National Antarctic Expedition.

The whole venture was organised under the auspices of the Royal Geographical Society, which championed exploration, and the Royal Society, which was dedicated to science. The differing demands of these twin goals almost inevitably led to conflict. During the chaotic years of planning and preparation, the Societies and the Admiralty clashed over the respective authority of the chief of scientific staff and the captain of the ship. Scott considered resignation when it seemed the scientists were winning; but in the end he was given sole command of both ship and expedition.

The *Discovery* finally set sail in 1901. Despite disappointments, and the drama of a costly relief expedition when the ship was frozen in, the whole venture was rightly judged a success. Scott and his men travelled far inland for the first time, examined the coast of Victoria Land and the Ross Ice

Shelf and discovered King Edward VII Land. Besides the exploration, expedition scientists contributed to an understanding of the magnetic fields of the southern hemisphere, vital information for Britain's maritime trade, and discovered plant fossils that threw new light on the continent's geological origins. The jubilant Scott was fêted on his return, and promoted to captain. He even sat at the King's table at Balmoral.

Among his friends and colleagues it was no secret that Scott planned to lead another expedition. He wanted to complete what he had started, and march to the South Pole. But he was so dependent on his naval pay that he could not afford to be precipitate. When he visited the Smiths' shooting lodge in September 1907, he was immersed in his plans, though he had made no public announcement. Before proceeding further, he wanted Wilson to sign up. The combination of physical prowess and quiet moral authority he had seen in Wilson throughout the *Discovery* years was irresistible to a man like Scott.

By the time Apsley arrived ten months later, it was decided. 'When I first knew Wilson,' he noted, 'it was certain that he and Scott were going south again if possible: they wanted to finish the job. I do not know whether Scott would have gone again without Wilson.'

In Edwardian Britain explorers embodied the imperialist ideal. By 1908 the very name of Scott evoked the whiff of romance, heroism and adventure, a heady mix that Apsley identified with his father. In the bracing Scottish breezes the 22-year-old walked with Wilson on his morning field trips through the glen, and following long afternoons shooting they sat on the balcony after dinner, watching the lights of Kirriemuir twinkle in the distance and listening to whitethroats singing in the saw-pit. Wilson's Antarctic plans struck a note of longing. Apsley resolved to follow their progress.

He battled on with family business throughout the autumn, returning briefly to Oxford in October to collect his degree. The Denford estate was now let. Everything had had to be valued for probate purposes, and hundreds of pages of legal documents trundled between Lincoln's Inn Fields and Lamer. One of the Denford lists included a garden swing, bushels of seed potatoes (two), and a chestnut cat (one), though according a value to the cat was a task that defeated even the scrupulous lawyers. Half-yearly accounts came in from Denford, Little Wittenham and an estate in Swansea on which Apsley had inherited the role of mortgagee, and farms and cottages on all of them demanded attention, as did the sprawling acres of Lamer itself.

As soon as the General died, Evelyn had started organising Lamer with a view to her own departure. As a widow with a son she was expected to move into a dower house so that her husband's heir could take his place as lord of the manor and bring up the next generation. ('I shall be only too pleased to see a daughter-in-law at Lamer,' she wrote to Apsley in 1910.) She had been well provided for: the General had bequeathed her the right either to reside at Denford or to live off the rent it brought. The trustees were to manage it all. As always, Evelyn bowed to her duty, though as Apsley showed no sign of marrying she did not move out of Lamer for nine years.

Poor Evelyn. The General was gone, Apsley badly wanted to go abroad and the older girls were loosening the apron strings. She was concerned about her youngest daughter, Edith, a physically weak child often confined to a wicker spinal chair. Edith is a shadowy figure in the family story, briefly appearing with her nurse and the spinal chair, usually looking on at events organised by her older sisters or parked under a chestnut tree. But she must have shaken off her disabilities: in the 1920s a photograph of her appeared in a local magazine standing on the summit of the Matterhorn.

Apsley found his chance to travel in an unlikely place: a church mission. The Oxford House in Bethnal Green in London's East End was one of the first missions of the settlement movement. Settlements were urban communities in which the educated classes set about the social reform of the poor. In 1884 the Oxford House had been founded on that principle by men from Keble College, partly in reaction to the élitism of the Anglican Church in late-Victorian Oxford. It provided a centre for religious, social and educational work through the promotion and management of clubs for men and boys. Missions were an integral part of public school and Oxbridge life, and active participation, as well as donations, were perceived as part of the seigneurial duty of the ruling classes. Apsley became familiar with settlement work at Winchester, and as an undergraduate he had helped out at a summer camp for East End boys. For him, as for many, it was more a question of social responsibility than religious commitment. Through his mission work, he made friends with the Head of the Oxford House, Harry Woollcombe.

Seventeen years Apsley's senior, Woollcombe came from an old Devon family with land and deep Tory roots. After graduating from Keble, he had followed his father's calling and taken holy orders. Still single, he was a short, jolly man, deeply religious, teetotal and, like Apsley, a keen nature enthusiast and pheasant shooter. Towards the end of 1908 he had accepted an appointment as travelling secretary of the Church of England Men's Society, an organisation with over 100,000 members committed to the promotion of muscular Christianity. In this capacity, Woollcombe was to carry the message on a three-year tour of Australia, New Zealand and South Africa.

Here was the obvious solution to Apsley's dilemma. He could sail to Australia with his friend, travel with him for a period and then split off on his own. Woollcombe was delighted with the plan. Evelyn was less pleased. She hated the idea of being left in charge of Lamer, let alone the other estates. But she didn't make things difficult, comforting herself with the knowledge that Apsley would be back within a year. Fortunately, she did not know what lay in the unfathomable future.

It seemed a good time to leave. In March 1909 panicky rumours surged over the country concerning the alarming growth in Germany's naval power, and two months later, as Apsley's ship was being loaded, parliament was obliged to step in to deny 'evidence' that Germany was plotting war. Imperial power was being shored up all over the globe, and at home Liberals and Conservatives were at each other's throats over free trade and Home Rule for Ireland with more than the usual measure of venom.

On 16 May Woollcombe and his young friend set sail from Plymouth on the Orient Steam Navigation Company's 6,400-ton steamer *Ormuz*, one of the best-known liners of her day ('the greyhound of the Southern Seas', according to *The Times*). They called at Gibraltar, Marseilles, Naples and Port Said before proceeding down the Suez Canal, where the crew of a passing ship hailed the *Ormuz* to ask which horse had won the Derby. After crossing the Arabian Sea to the western coast of India they steamed round to Ceylon, where Woollcombe hurtled ashore to address members of the Colombo branch of the Men's Society. On the longest leg of the journey, a haul over the Equator and down to Australia, the *Ormuz* battled the squally south-west monsoon while everyone on the upper deck was sick.

The Orient Line, of which the Steam Navigation Company was an offshoot, had recently lost the Australian mail contract, though its southbound ships, all beginning with 'O', still carried cargo as well as 400 passengers, of whom just over a quarter travelled first class like Apsley and Woollcombe. Their upper-deck cabins featured bathrooms with marble baths, and they dined in a saloon panelled with inlaid rosewood and mahogany and upholstered in velvet, its revolving chairs anchored to the floor to prevent diners from shooting across the carpet and colliding with the soup tureens. The first-class passengers dressed for dinner, the men in black or white tie, spats and watch chains and the women in elegant evening gowns. When the ship was in port coaling, there was plenty of time to stroll down the gangplank and indulge in some gentle tourism. In Naples Woollcombe and Apsley had a guided tour of nearby Pompeii, and at Port Said they were taken to the new mosque, where they were obliged to put on large slippers which looked like wicker baskets. At sea they lounged in cane chairs on the wide promenade deck, rising occasionally for a game of bucket quoits or deck billiards or even cricket, at which the passengers were regularly thrashed by the officers.

Apsley took to shipboard life immediately, even the impromptu dances on deck after sunset and the fancy-dress balls. While Woollcombe held evensong in his cabin, Apsley lounged in the smoking room, visited the on-board barber for a shave and noted the birds wheeling in the ship's wake, as well as the pretty girls leaning on the rails. His experience on the *Ormuz* left him with a love of cruising that was to last his whole life. Loosed from his moorings, the abundance of free time allowed him to relax, a task he found difficult on land, and being physically marooned enabled him to cast off his anxieties, too. He relished the contained world of an ocean-going ship, just as he was to relish an Antarctic hut.

They reached Fremantle, the port twelve miles south of Perth in Western Australia, on 17 June, just over a month after leaving England. The passengers crowded the decks as the ship hooted up to the mouth of the Swan River and into Princess Royal Harbour accompanied by a flotilla of tiny craft. The two men went straight up to Perth, and Apsley tagged along as Woollcombe toured around addressing meetings. The Church of England Men's Society was already well established in Australia, and at one venue 2,500 men turned up. From Western Australia the tour moved south to Adelaide, continued round to Tasmania ('the Bishop is a great Men's man') and travelled up to sub-tropical Queensland. At the end of September they surfaced in Brisbane, where Apsley heard the official news that Scott was planning a second expedition (it had been announced in *The Times* on 13 September).

From the start, Apsley was sure that this was for him. In his short acquaintance with Wilson he had glimpsed something he badly wanted: a clear sense of purpose and the chance of adventure. The newspapers reported that Wilson had been appointed chief of scientific staff, and Apsley immediately wrote to him to apply for service. He sent the letter via Reggie and informed both men that if necessary he could shorten his trip and sail straight home for an interview. It was not an empty gesture. He was determined to let nothing stand in the way of his application.

Leaving Woollcombe in Brisbane to continue his tour, Apsley struck out alone. He took a series of cargo ships up the coast of Queensland, through the Arafura Sea and on to the island of Celebes (now Sulawesi), sandwiched on the Equator between Borneo and the Spice Islands (now the Moluccas) in the Dutch East Indies. On the way up to China and Japan he passed through the Singapore Straits Settlements, then British. His arrival was anticipated by a raft of references unleashed on the expatriate community by Arthur Farrer, his lawyer, whose fulsome letters focused on Apsley's rowing achievements – it's difficult to see how these were going to come in handy in Singapore – and talked him up as 'a very cultivated, capable, nice fellow and a particular friend of mine. His father was a very good class and the son is like him.' After steaming up through the South and East China Seas, Apsley's ship stopped at the new dock in Nagasaki. Four years after emerging victorious from their war with Russia, the Japanese were well disposed towards the English, and Apsley particularly enjoyed travelling among them. The highlight of his adventures was a partial ascent of Mount Fuji.

By the end of the year he was in Calcutta, the capital, at that time, of British India. The expatriate community was large enough even to sustain Old Wykehamist dinners, though the leisurely pace of colonial life had been quickened that year by nationalist unrest, and the government was busy banning Gandhi's article on Indian Home Rule. Apsley left by rail for Lucknow, where his mail pursued him. Reggie wrote to say that he had discussed Apsley's application with Wilson, and reassured his cousin that he was not risking the chance of a place by remaining abroad. Expeditionary finances were perilous, and to further Apsley's cause Reggie had told Wilson that if he were accepted, he would not expect to be paid a salary. Smith went loyally on to thrash out the pros and cons of an Antarctic adventure, one of the cons being a delay on Apsley's planned call to the Bar. No doubt in some place in his heart Apsley put this on the 'pro' list.

He saw some of the Himalayas, including Kangchenjunga, the third highest mountain in the world, and at the beginning of 1910 he was back in Calcutta in time for his twenty-fourth birthday. He hurried to the main post office and discovered among his mail a reply from Wilson on British National Antarctic Expedition notepaper. It was dated 8 December 1909. 'My dear Cherry-Garrard,' wrote Wilson:

Your letter duly reached me and I have discussed your proposal with Captain Scott as with Reginald Smith ... The facts are these. Scott thinks that it is just possible that when we have filled up the actual scientific staff with the necessary experts in each branch, there may still be a vacancy for an adaptable helper, such as I am sure you would be; ready to lend a hand where it was wanted. Only, I must frankly say that as it is a matter of real importance in these shore parties to reduce numbers to a minimum, the reverse may be possible and there may be no room for any but the absolutely necessary staff.

If however you will allow the matter to stand over until you return, and if, after coming once more into closer touch with your home ties, you are still anxious to go, I can promise that your application will not have been forgotten, and will not have suffered by the waiting. Only at present it is quite impossible to make you any promise – I wish it were otherwise – and you must be prepared for disappointment. I am delighted to hear that you are enjoying your travels.

From the start, Wilson was unequivocal in his support. During their Scottish sojourn he had been impressed by Apsley's intelligence, enthusiasm and sensitivity, and by the time he received the younger man's formal application the foundations of their friendship were in place. Besides his natural affection, Wilson was influenced by his deep loyalty to Apsley's cousin. 'I am biased in favour of anyone who is a friend of Reginald Smith's,' he wrote, 'and you are more than that.'

When he received Wilson's letter, Apsley immediately wrote to Reggie, who replied on 3 February.

Dr Wilson is up to his ears with work and yet makes time to pay me constant visits and so does Captain Scott. They are getting on very well with their preparations and everything points to the *Terra Nova* [the expedition ship] starting in June . . . it looks as if should they not get to the Pole in the next two years they will stay on and make a third effort. 'We are going to get there this time', they say.

I need not say that your keen ambition to go is very much in my thoughts. And it will be a question which you only can decide whether you can ask your Mother to make the sacrifice which your going will mean to her. Apart from this there seem to me many reasons and inducements for you taking part in the venture if they can have you . . . Take good care of yourself and 'haste ye back' as you know we say in Scotland.

The rest of Apsley's mail revealed widespread anxiety over the January 1910 general election, an event precipitated by the refusal of the House of

Lords to pass Lloyd George's land-taxing budget the previous December. Apsley watched anxiously, via out-of-date newspapers in steamy expatriate drawing rooms, as the authority of the Lords was pitted against Liberal reforms, the latter including a graduated income tax culminating in a supertax on all incomes over £5,000. Power was shifting away from the landed estates and into London, a process which irritated Apsley intensely from start to finish. Taxation hurt, and like most middle- and large-scale landowners he protested indignantly at government plans to fund the desperately needed social reform programme with a little of his money; but the way the country was abandoning the status quo distressed him more profoundly.

The traveller returned at the beginning of April, six weeks earlier than his mother had expected. He had sailed across the Pacific to San Francisco, where he watched seals playing on the rocks outside the harbour and wondered if he would shortly be seeing a great deal more of them. But he abandoned plans to travel in California, anxious that further absence might jeopardise his Antarctic prospects. At home he basked in maternal attention and lavished his sisters with Japanese robes. He had been abroad for twelve months, and had thoroughly enjoyed himself; all he could think about now was when he could get away again. It was not just that travel offered an escape from squirearchical responsibilities and interminable correspondence with tenants and lawyers and land agents, though that was attractive enough. There was a deeper appeal, a visceral, illusory sense that one's true self lay somewhere out there, waiting to be uncovered.

On 7 April a telegram arrived at Lamer from Kensington. 'Welcome home delighted see you Devonshire Club tomorrow 5 o'clock.' It was from Wilson. Apsley rushed down to town, but after the meeting expressed grave doubts about his chances: he learned that 8,000 men had applied for a place on the expedition. Such was the lure of the poles. Ten days later Reggie reported a startling idea that had originated with Wilson. 'I have seen Wilson more than once about you,' he wrote, 'and I learn that the Antarctic land lies this way. Scott has not yet gathered as much money as he needs for the Expedition, and he finds that he can get volunteers – unqualified – who will subscribe in order to go.' Like many explorers before him and since, cash was Scott's main problem. Although the navy were lending him men and the government had made him a grant of £20,000, the expedition was not an official national undertaking. Scott was cobbling funds, equipment and personnel together from a wide range of sources: from anywhere he could.

'Putting it quite baldly,' Reggie continued, 'I learn that if you subscribe £1,000, there would be a good chance of your being accepted. If this is confirmed, as I expect, you will have a good prospect . . . The question then is whether you will think it right to volunteer in such terms? And will your going in this way, if you like to take the risk of subscribing a large sum . . . be in any way to your detriment or discomfort?

'This is really a matter for you and for you only. One man, I hear, a soldier from India, is going in this way. [This was Captain Oates.] And there may be more. I am sure that Wilson will do all that a good friend can do for you, but . . . you know already that your short sight will militate against you, perhaps increasing the chance of accident to you.'

On 19 April Apsley took the train to London again, this time to see Farrer. The usual matters were queuing up for attention: cottages at Denford, sanitation at Little Wittenham, monies due from the General's trust, decisions on stocks and shares. When the business was over they turned with some dismay to the uproar in the House of Commons, where the Liberals were preparing legislation that would effectively abolish the power of the Lords.

Two days later Apsley heard from Wilson that he had not been accepted on Scott's expedition.

'I am more sorry than I can say to have been the means of conveying to you your disappointment,' wrote Wilson. 'But there are two things that give me even more pain. One is that it should have been necessary for me to offend your sense of the fitness of things by suggesting that you might pay money for a place in the expedition, and the other is that the whole thing has been a very great disappointment to Reginald Smith, and I would have done anything in the world to have avoided that had it been possible.' In fact, Apsley had no scruples about his financial donation. It was perfectly standard for a member of an expedition to contribute funds then; and it would be now. But for Wilson the inner life was infinitely more important and more real than the outer, and he recognised the shadow of potential moral compromise in the scheme that he had proposed.

Apsley decided to make a noble gesture. He would give the thousand pounds anyway.

On 25 April, Wilson wrote again. It seemed that it was not over after all. 'Captain Scott wants to see you again and have a talk over things with you before giving you a final answer. Can you manage to be at the office, 36 Victoria Street, on Wednesday forenoon, say at 11 o'clock?' Eight thousand men might have applied but Apsley had Wilson's support: in Scott's eyes it was a powerful advantage. 'I have received your cheque,' Wilson continued, 'and I am withholding it, as Captain Scott wishes you to see him first. He says he must satisfy himself by a talk with you that there is no misunderstanding on the subject before coming to a determination, otherwise he feels you might both be in something of a false position. I believe he is right, and the time has come when you and he must understand one another. I can tell you one thing however, and that is that he very *much* appreciates the motive which induced you to send your subscription independently of your chance of being taken. That is an action which appeals to him, not because of the money for which he cares very little, except impersonally, insofar as it helps the Expedition to be a success, but because he knows what to expect of a man who felt it was the right thing to do.

'I know Scott intimately, as you know. I have known him now for ten years, and I believe in him so firmly that I am often sorry when he lays himself open to misunderstanding. I am sure that you will come to know him and believe in him as I do, and none the less because he is sometimes difficult. However you will soon see for yourself.

'Come prepared to be examined medically in the event of your being accepted, as we have arranged to overhaul everyone at the office that day . . .

'You have my heartiest good wishes.'

He was accepted on Wednesday 27 April. There was a spare place on the scientific staff after all, and Scott had taken a liking to Reggie's bright, keen young cousin. He almost failed his medical, because he could only see people on the other side of the road 'as vague blobs walking', but Wilson went and had a talk with Scott about it and they said he could go if he was prepared to take the additional risk. 'At that time,' Apsley wrote later, 'I would have taken anything.'

4

Winning All Hearts

The *Terra Nova* was a three-masted wooden whaler with auxiliary steam, and she reeked of blubber. She had already been to the Antarctic once: when the *Discovery* was stuck in the ice on Scott's first expedition both the *Terra Nova* and the *Morning* had been sent down as relief ships. The 747-ton *Terra Nova* sailed under the white ensign, a privilege accorded only, outside the Navy, to ships of the Royal Yacht Squadron. But by 1910 she was a battered old tub, hardly the ideal vessel for an enterprise on the scale of Scott's. 'The *Discovery* was a palace compared to the *Terra Nova*,' Wilson reckoned.

Apsley had been accepted on the expedition just five weeks before the ship was due to sail: a very short time to prepare for a trip that would last eighteen months at least. In addition to his personal arrangements, Scott asked him to learn to type, as he was taking two typewriters south and nobody knew how to use them. Farrer gamely took on the tricky job of obtaining life insurance, insurers not liking the sound of the Antarctic any more then than they do now. Apsley spent hectic days in London, lunching quickly at Harrods or at Reggie's house in Green Street and squeezing in one last night at the theatre with the Smiths, his head too full of lists to concentrate on Galsworthy's new play. At Lamer he sorted through a rubble of new purchases spread over the study floor between teetering piles of books, and the girls scuttled in with offers of knitted headwear. Lassie set about making a sledging flag, rushing down to the Kensington School of Art to learn a special new stitch that appeared the same at the back and the front. Having been waited on all his life, Apsley panicked at the thought of having to take his turn at the Primus, so he sloped into the kitchen and asked the appalled cook for lessons. Meanwhile the *Terra Nova* was being fitted out and provisioned at London's West India Docks, dwarfed by cargo vessels and gleaming liners.

The death of Edward VII at the beginning of May meant that a country already tense with industrial unrest and political acrimony became tenser. As one of the chief features of England's social disquiet was class hatred, the chance of escape was especially attractive to a young gentleman with land, money and a nervous cast of mind.

On 1 June the *Terra Nova* raised steam at the West India Docks, painted, polished and fluttering with flags. The wharf was bristling with the cocked hats of dignitaries, including that of Sir Clements Markham, the expedition's chief supporter. Markham's wife and Lady Bridgeman, the wife of the First Sea Lord, hoisted the white ensign, and the *Terra Nova* slipped down the Thames to the low elephant grief of ships' horns.

Apsley joined the ship at Cardiff, and Elsie and Mildred went to see him off. The girls stayed on board until the Barry Docks, and there they finally picked their way down the ship's ladder and climbed into the last tug back to Cardiff. Then the crew steamed away down the Bristol Channel, gleefully tossing overboard hundreds of tracts and periodicals left by earnest visitors, the flimsy sheets lifting briefly aloft before floating down to dissolve in the pewter water. Scott was not on board; he had stayed behind to drum up funds and make final arrangements, leaving his second-in-command, Lieutenant 'Teddy' Evans, in charge of a mixed company of thirty-nine navy men and civilians. Teddy was a jovial, ambitious young officer who relished the responsibility of leadership and wore it lightly. He had sailed to the Antarctic before, as second officer on the *Morning* expedition to free the *Discovery* from the ice. On that trip he had made up his mind that he would see more of the polar regions.

Before signing up on the *Terra Nova*, Evans had planned to mount an expedition of his own. Like Scott, he saw that the uncharted spaces at the bottom of the world offered a fine opportunity for a naval officer to make his name. But the country could not afford two expeditions. In the summer of 1909, with the discreet intervention of Sir Clements, the prospective leaders had reached an agreement. Evans would yield to Scott and hand over the monies he had already raised in exchange for the position of second-in-command on Scott's expedition.

While Scott was traipsing round the country drumming up cash, Evans had overseen the cleaning and refitting of the greasy old ship, and he had thrown himself into the task with gusto. 'I shall never forget the day I first visited the *Terra Nova* in the West India Docks,' he wrote years later. 'She looked so small and out of place . . . but I loved her from the day I saw her, because she was my first command.' Under his supervision, gangs of labourers removed the blubber tanks, cleansed and whitewashed the hold and scrubbed and disinfected the bilges. They built storerooms and laboratories, erected an ice house on the upper deck and fitted out bunks around the saloon. Then the ship had to be provisioned, and on a severely limited budget. 'The verb "to wangle",' Evans wrote, 'had not yet appeared in the English language, so we just "obtained".'

The sense of rivalry between Evans and Scott never disappeared. They were profoundly different characters: Evans a boisterous extrovert with the common touch, Scott a reserved introvert with a diffident manner. Their relationship was uneasy, and it was not clear how it would evolve.

The *Terra Nova*'s crew consisted mostly of naval officers and ratings, but they had been joined by six of the expedition's twelve scientific staff; the rest were to meet the ship in New Zealand. All twelve were automatically classified as officers. They included two men untrained in any scientific field and called 'adaptable helpers' by Scott. Apsley was one. His title was zoological assistant, and his duties essentially involved assisting Wilson with his specimens. The other 'adaptable helper' was Captain Lawrence 'Titus' Oates, a soldier in the Inniskilling Dragoons, a cavalry regiment. Oates' few words were caustic. Of the multitudinous well-wishers who had crowded the decks before the ship left Cardiff, he remarked that only the telephone operator was a gentleman.

The *Terra Nova* was no Orient liner. She rolled fifty degrees each way, and Apsley was seasick for the first few days, manfully typing out notices and general orders for Evans while looking very green. But after less than a week at sea he was able to record in his diary, 'Every prospect of a really good time. Setting sail on Sunday afternoon I got quite done; I feel very soft after a year's travelling, which makes one fit, but anything but hard.'

His bunk was in the nursery, so called because it housed the youngest members of the expedition. Next to the engine room and boilers, and, annoyingly, providing a short cut to both, the nursery was larger than the other cabins, with six bunks as well as the ship's library and a pianola equipped with bulky rolls of music. The floor was permanently layered with a deep jumble of boots and overcoats, and in the gloom it was almost impossible for a man to find his own kit.

Apsley was determined to meet the stiff challenges of a crowded ship run according to unfamiliar naval rules. He kept three clocks and two wristwatches above his bunk to make absolutely sure that he did not miss his shift on deck. To the amusement of the other nursery residents he often spoke out loud in his sleep and went sleepwalking twice, rescued both times by Tryggve Gran, a Norwegian skiing expert and the youngest man on the expedition. Apsley took the inevitable teasing gracefully; one of his shipmates noted that he had 'an ever-ready laugh'. It was a useful asset.

They anchored at Funchal in Madeira on 23 June. The town was hot, swarming with lizards and ants, and the cobbled streets smelt of flowers, drains and onions. Apsley and two other men went up the mountain, first in a funicular then on foot, lunched at a hotel ('excellent food – I had a bath, better still'), ate pounds of loquats (yellow, plum-like fruits), then went to another hotel for dinner. 'This is always to be remembered as an A1 day,' he wrote in his diary. In a letter from Funchal, Wilson told Reggie, 'I really never have seen anyone with such a constant expression of "this is what I have been looking for" on his face.'

Less than three months later, on 6 September, another crew of polar explorers anchored off Madeira. They were a leaner, sleeker group: only nineteen men all told. Their leader was Roald Amundsen. He had been yearning for another great adventure since sailing through the North-West Passage in 1905, the year his country gained independence from Sweden. A reserved, ascetic bachelor with pale, icy blue eyes and a certain inscrutability, after his successful 1908 expedition Amundsen had set his sights on the North Pole. On a lecture tour to England in 1907 he had asked the great Arctic explorer Fridtjof Nansen, at the time serving in London as Norway's first ambassador to Britain, if he could sail in the doughty *Fram*, a ship Nansen knew well (she was state property, but Nansen had absolute moral authority in the field of exploration in Norway). Nansen had been dreaming of taking the *Fram* to the Antarctic and of conquering the South Pole, but he reluctantly yielded to the younger man. 'And so with a bleeding heart,' he told Amundsen years later, 'I gave up the plan I had prepared for so long, and which would have crowned my life, in favour of your voyage, because I saw it as the right thing to do, and the way which would bring most to Norway.'

In November 1908 Amundsen unveiled his plans for the North Pole, and the King and Queen of Norway opened the subscription list. Amundsen claimed that his main object was a scientific study of the polar sea, but this was disingenuous: he rarely paid any attention to science. His plans were known in England, and when Scott visited Norway to test equipment he tried to meet him in order to discuss scientific collaboration between the respective north and south expeditions. But Amundsen avoided Scott.

★ ★ ★

The *Terra Nova* leaked so much that when she was under sail the crew had to man the hand pumps amidships every four hours; by the time they left Madeira Apsley had already written in his diary, 'The pump is going to be a bit of a nightmare.' And it was. When the engines were going he took his turn as stoker ('I think I shall dream of great monumental stones of coal which cannot be moved'), and in the early weeks he also worked for the navigator, Lieutenant Harry Pennell.

The 28-year-old Pennell was a relentless hard worker who was always willing to lend a hand trimming coal if he wasn't occupied on the bridge or up in the crow's nest. Besides keeping a meticulous ship's log, which included a detailed record of all animals sighted, he spent hours working on magnetic observations as a hobby. He never seemed to go to bed: when he felt an urgent need to sleep he simply lay down under his chart table. He was cheerful ('as happy as the day is long', according to Apsley), steady and sober – though not too sober, as he danced hornpipes at inopportune moments. 'He was father and mother to every man on board his ship,' Apsley wrote. 'He knew all their troubles, smoothed over many a difficulty, helped them not to get drunk.' Wilson rated him 'by far the most capable man on the whole expedition'. On the journey down to South Africa Apsley helped Pennell take observations (and was praised for his neat handwriting and accuracy), and they often drank cocoa together in the quiet stillness of the early watch as dawn spilled over the ocean. Cherry came to admire Pennell hugely, and so did many others. 'He is only eighteen months older than I am,' wrote Birdie Bowers, 'and when I think of all he has in his brain I begin to wonder if I know anything at all.'

Unlike the *Discovery*, which had caused so much trouble when she froze in, the *Terra Nova* was not going to remain in the Antarctic during the winter. Her job was to land a party of men on an island close to the Antarctic continent and return to New Zealand. The shore party would then overwinter in their hut. As navigator, Pennell was not required to stay: he would captain the ship back to New Zealand, and take her back down to Scott in the spring. Many of the men who were staying were sorry that they would not have Pennell as a companion through the long darkness of the polar night.

Every day was hotter than the last after Madeira, and by the end of June the deck scalded the men's bare feet. In the tropics they slept outside, and when it rained they ran around naked to get clean. Apsley and Wilson bedded down on top of the ice house between the great squares of sail rising fore and aft. They all placed bets on what day they would reach South Africa, set up a whale watch and leant over the rail to inspect glassy

Portuguese men-of-war twisting in the clear blue water. Most of all they liked discussing the Antarctic. A sledging committee was formed with Apsley nominally the secretary, and the men who had been south before lectured the others on the vagaries of that unknown continent.

Apsley had learned to steer and was now confidently furling sail aloft with the seamen, the first among the civilians on board to do so. 'Enjoying myself greatly,' he ended his 17 July diary entry, two days after they had celebrated crossing the Equator with elaborate high jinks. In the doldrums they reverted to steam power. 'I have been more fit yesterday and today than I have been since I joined,' he wrote. No wonder, after four-hour shifts in the furnace of a stokehold, and in the tropics to boot.

They were chronically short of water, as the tanks were too small. One result, according to Charles 'Silas' Wright, was 'the lack of something decent to drink. One does pall of champagne, beer and ginger ale in the course of time.' Twenty-three-year-old Wright, a Canadian, was already a much-loved member of the company. After graduating from college in Toronto he had won a scholarship enabling him to take up a place to study physics at Cambridge. There he began work on natural penetration radiation and became friends with Thomas Griffith Taylor, a British-born geologist who had grown up in Australia. Taylor had gone through Sydney University with Douglas Mawson, the Australian explorer (also British-born) who had sledged to the South Magnetic Pole on Shackleton's *Nimrod* expedition. Encouraged by his Cambridge tutors as well as by Mawson, Taylor applied for the post of physiographer and geologist on the *Terra Nova*. When he was accepted, Wright decided to have a shot at the still-vacant position of physicist. He liked the idea of continuing his measurements of penetrating radiation on the journey down to the Antarctic, but his primary motivation was curiosity about that immense continent and its little-known topography. In fact, he was desperate to go south with Scott. The problem was that his application was rejected.

Undaunted, Taylor announced that the two of them should go down to London, face Scott and Wilson and persuade them to change their minds. They set off on foot, with twelve hard-boiled eggs and a few bars of chocolate to sustain them, and walked the fifty miles in a day.

It worked. Like most of the *Terra Nova* scientists, Wright was engaged on the flat rate of four pounds a week for the first year. (It was uncertain if the expedition would remain for a second year, and if it did, salaries would have to be renegotiated.) He was quickly nicknamed 'Silas', on the grounds that it was the most 'Yankee' name the others could think of. Cherry described him as 'robust, willing and uncompromising', and along with his friend 'Griff' Taylor, Silas injected a healthy dose of irreverence into expeditionary life. Like Cherry, he was short-sighted, but he made up for the difficulties this caused him out on the trail with his athleticism and unflagging energy. After the first season Scott described him as 'good-hearted, strong, keen, striving to saturate his mind with the ice problems of this wonderful region'. Silas was a committed physicist and physiographer, though it was probably in the field of glaciology that he made his greatest contribution to the expedition's scientific programme.

Sing-songs were a regular occurrence in the wardroom (not surprising, after all that champagne), 'though there was hardly anybody in it who could sing'. Instead of grace, at the start of most meals they sang a music-hall song about the 'Sisters Hardbake with the goo-goo eyes', and schoolboy rough-and-tumble inevitably followed. One night, Wilson recorded in his diary, 'Campbell, Cherry-Garrard and I held the nursery, which has two doors, against the rest of the wardroom. The struggle lasted an hour or two and half of us were nearly naked towards the finish, having had our clothes torn off our backs.' Nicknames proliferated. Girls' names were popular, with Pennell metamorphosing into 'Penelope' and Edward Nelson, a biologist, into 'Marie'. As the oldest man on board Wilson was dubbed 'Uncle Bill', and Scott was known respectfully as 'the Owner', the standard naval term for the captain of a warship. Apsley was inevitably 'Cherry' (sometimes pronounced 'Chewwy'), and the name stuck until the end of his life.* The lower ranks were naturally suspicious of hyphens and called him 'Mr Gerard'.

On 26 July the *Terra Nova* reached South Trinidad (now the Brazilian Ilha da Trindade), a coral-ringed, uninhabited volcanic island 680 miles east of Brazil. Several parties went ashore: Cherry set off to find specimens with Wilson and Pennell. Pursued by locusts and red-legged flies, they climbed up the crumbling lava and basalt almost to the top of the island and picnicked on captain's biscuits among the yellow land crabs while the sun burnt all the blue from the sky. When a swell rose, the men who had stayed on board hoisted a warning flag and fired a rocket to call the scattered parties back. Cherry and his two companions scrambled down, denting their guns, but the sea was already too rough for the ship's boats to land, and the men were obliged to swim one by one through the surf among cruising sharks. Cherry noted Wilson's psychological leadership during the

---

* Finding myself among thirty British men on an Antarctic base eighty-five years later I was gratified to see that nicknames were still going strong. A man with the surname Garrard (no relation) had, pleasingly, been named 'Cherry'.

crisis: 'When we first got down to the shore and things were looking nasty, Wilson sat down on the top of a rock and ate a biscuit in the coolest possible manner. It was an example to avoid all panicking, for he did not want the biscuit.'

'One of the days of a man's life and an exciting ending,' Cherry wrote in his diary that evening. The reality of the trip – even the gruesome hours shovelling coal – was endorsing the vision he had glimpsed during his long walks across the Scottish moors with Wilson. After an uncertain journey through school and university, he had at last found congenial companion-ship, a genuine outlet for his talents and true adventure authenticated by a clearly defined purpose. The relief was inexpressible.

He spent the next day skinning the birds they had shot on South Trinidad, staying up all night to get the job done. Together with Wilson he worked in a small lab on the upper deck which he had painted and fitted with specimen shelves. Cherry loved learning from his sympathetic mentor in this cubby-hole, and he was turning out to be a practically adroit zoological assistant. Under Wilson's tutelage, he had also taken up sketching. But his primary debt to the older man was emotional. When it was all over, Teddy Evans noted in his account of the expedition, 'Wilson took Cherry-Garrard under his wing and brought him up as it were in the shadow of his own unselfish character.'

They rounded the Cape of Good Hope and on 16 August anchored in the sheltered bay at Simonstown, just south of Cape Town. It had taken them two months to reach South Africa; they now had eighteen days on land, and mail waiting.

Cherry, Oates, Henry Bowers and Edward Atkinson, a quiet navy doctor and parasitologist, stayed out at Coghill's Hotel in Wynberg, up in the hills about five miles south of Cape Town. 'We are [a] peaceloving party,' wrote Bowers, 'and want quiet and little gaiety.' The foursome got on well ('we usually hunt in a quartet'), and Bowers and Cherry had already laid the foundations of a friendship that was to be one of the closest of the expedition. 'Cherry-Garrard is a great pal of mine,' Bowers wrote to his sister May, describing him as 'our young millionaire . . . a thorough gentleman and very keen'.

The 27-year-old Bowers was a short, solid Scot with red hair, limbs as tough as teak and a hooked nose which had conferred the nickname 'Birdie'. He had inherited a passion for seafaring from his father, a hardy old seadog who had died when his adoring son was four. The widowed Emily Bowers, left to fend for herself in modest but not indigent circumstances, had devoted herself to her son and his two elder sisters. Birdie accepted his position as head of the family, and like Scott he gladly supported his widowed mother. But like Scott he went to sea as a teenager despite the pulls of kinship. When he was fourteen he enrolled as a cadet on the training ship HMS *Worcester*, and in 1899 qualified for the Merchant Service. For six years he worked his way through the ranks, gaining valuable experience under steam and sail. In 1905 he was gazetted as a sub-lieutenant to the Royal Indian Marine, a service which ranked second in prestige only to the Royal Navy.

The lower ranks adored Bowers. He was a good-tempered, hard-working officer and a cheery optimist who exuded warm good sense: as one of his sisters said, 'There wasn't a twist in him.' He was devoid of intellectual pretension or aspiration. He simply marched resolutely through life getting things done, eschewing undue attention and avoiding show. Indeed, Bowers was almost unnaturally modest, a trait that was in part a consequence of his goblin-like appearance. In his attitudes he was an imperialist, a Conservative and a patriot. 'I love my country,' he once wrote, 'and trust that I shall not be found wanting when the day comes to act.' Above all, he was a deeply religious man whose life was grounded in his faith. Standing alone on deck in the long night watches, contemplating a becalmed and starry ocean, he often sensed the mystical presence of Christ, and he wrote movingly about this subject in his long letters home to his mother and sisters.

In the Indian Marines Bowers sharpened his navigational skills on the Irrawaddy in Burma, polished up his Hindustani and qualified as a lieutenant before proceeding to the Persian Gulf to serve on a battle-cruiser. His constitution and strength were legendary, and he was hungry for adventure. The challenges of the Antarctic called him with sirens' voices. 'Ever since I went within three degrees of the Antarctic Circle, I looked due South,' he wrote in 1907. 'I have thought – as I thought then – that's my mark . . . Reading Captain Scott's books (2 vols) on the *Discovery* Expedition made me as keen as mustard.' When he read news of Shackleton's thrilling journey towards the Pole on the *Nimrod* expedition, he wrote home, 'If only they will leave the South Pole itself alone for a bit they may give me a chance. Don't laugh!'

Nobody laughed. As a young cadet Bowers had been introduced to Sir Clements Markham, and he made such an impression that in 1909 the old man recommended him to Scott for the *Terra Nova*. The suggestion was enthusiastically endorsed by Bowers' old commandant on the *Worcester*, and, to Birdie's unending delight, he was accepted without an interview and without submitting a formal application.

It was a difficult time for Emily Bowers, who was distraught to see her son vanish again, and to such an impossibly remote destination. Their parting scenes at Waterloo station in London as Birdie caught the train to Portsmouth to meet the *Terra Nova* were inhibited by the presence of a truckload of coffins on the platform alongside them.

'Well, we're landed with him now and must make the best of it,' Scott allegedly said to Wilson when they finally met their new recruit. Scott was taken aback by the quasi-comical appearance of this muscle-bound, five-foot-four-inch sailor with red hair, a pink face and a large nose. But Scott never regretted his decision. Bowers was appointed primarily as a junior officer in charge of expedition stores, possibly the most arduous and thankless position on board. Scott was consistently impressed by his mastery of detail, astonishing hard work and stamina, and the crew quickly got a measure of the man when, on one of his first days on duty, Birdie fell nineteen feet into the ship's hold, stood up, retrieved his peaked cap and carried on as if nothing had happened.

Scott and his wife Kathleen had sailed directly to the Cape in a merchant ship. Soon after their arrival they went out to Wynberg, turning up at Coghill's to find Cherry and the others in bed. Two other wives joined their husbands in Simonstown. These were Hilda Evans, wife of Scott's second-in-command, and Wilson's wife Oriana. Some of the men were irritated by their presence ('the wives are much in evidence'). But it was Kathleen Scott who was most in evidence. She was suspected of having too much influence over her husband.

The least conventional thing about Scott was his choice of wife: Kathleen Bruce was a sculptress given to bohemian behaviour and exotic friends. After a strict upbringing in a Jacobean rectory she had gone off to Paris to study art – a daring course of action in 1901. There she became close to Rodin, who taught and encouraged her; and to the avant-garde dancer Isadora Duncan, whose illegitimate child she later helped deliver. Kathleen loved to dance herself, but not on a stage: preferably barefoot in the garden, as she was happier outdoors. She had met Scott in 1907 at a lunch party given by Mabel Beardsley, sister of the illustrator Aubrey (there were scandalous rumours that the two had enjoyed an incestuous relationship). Scott had been famous since his return from the Antarctic on his first expedition, and he was a draw at any social function. 'I glowed rather foolishly and suddenly,' Kathleen remembered, 'when I clearly saw him ask his neighbour who I was.' She was not beautiful, but she was striking, even handsome, with long, thick and slightly frizzy chestnut hair, and throughout her life she was pursued by amorous men. In 1908

Kathleen married her handsome captain ('Darling,' she had promised him, 'I will be good when we're married'), and the following year their son Peter was born, Kathleen having spent much of her pregnancy sleeping on a beach wrapped in a blanket. She loved babies almost as much as she loved men.

Kathleen held forceful opinions, none expressed more regularly or with more conviction than her view that women were far less interesting than men. If she was bored, as she often was in the company of more conventional women, she found it difficult not to reveal her feelings. Scott often had her with him, and everyone could see that he discussed expeditionary matters with her in detail, and that she had much to say on every subject.

A herd of young British officers bound for the Antarctic, many in uniform, must have had a devastating effect on the young women of the small Cape colony. At one dance Birdie was introduced to the Misses Williams, two young sisters who turned out to be 'little rippers and ladies too'. So much for wanting a quiet time. A few days later the Misses Williams came aboard, Birdie reported to his sister May, 'with staid and proper Cherry-Garrard who had accidentally appeared from nowhere when they wanted to come down'. Cherry went on to 'make hay' with the Misses Williams. He might have been shy in large groups or at cocktail parties, but he was not diffident with women, or if he was, he overcame his diffidence when an opportunity presented itself. He issued Birdie with peremptory orders to organise a day out with the girls.

At 8.30 on Wednesday morning Birdie and Cherry got hold of a car and driver and called at the Williams' residence in Cape Town. After being introduced to the girls' parents ('the Pater, a lawyer . . . a very sound chap indeed') they motored off with Kitty and Betty to Hoow-Hoek, about fifty-five miles to the south-west. Birdie let Cherry pick his girl. 'As I was not in the least particular I let Cherry – who was somewhat near the line one knows so well – have his choice while I kept out of the way with Miss Betty – an absolutely ripping little girl.' What Betty made of it was not recorded.

After lunch and a stroll they started back in high spirits, but ten miles later, in the middle of rolling moorland, the car broke down. They were obliged to walk five miles to the nearest village. 'Cherry took a shorter cut by another way to get us time to wire and the girls and yours truly plugged on for what seemed like crossing Africa before we sighted the village. They stuck it out most pluckily against a stiff breeze . . .' The hapless driver was eventually set up for the night in his car and Cherry and Birdie joined the girls at the village hotel, having meanwhile reassured the Pater by wire. They had a sing-song in the parlour. 'The proprietress,' continued Birdie, 'who looked upon us all with suspicion, looked in from time to time. At 10 p.m. she assured us that the motor could not come and said she had got a room for the ladies and indicated that Cherry and I had better quit.' As she spoke, they heard a toot. 'We had a jolly drive back though it was a wild night and arrived at 2 a.m. when we found the Pater waiting up . . .'

Birdie had fallen for Miss Betty. 'Perhaps it is well I am off and I should not answer for myself after a little longer acquaintance . . . I don't think so though. Both Cherry and I are able to see things as they should be though he – not being a sailor and having gone deeper – will like it less than I.' However deep Cherry had gone, he was determined to conceal it from his mother. Later, before parcelling up his journal for despatch to Lamer where Evelyn was instructed to read it instead of a letter, he wrote up his South African entries without a single reference to his *coup de coeur*. 'I did a lot of shopping,' he concluded.

Meanwhile, who should turn up in Cape Town but Harry Woollcombe, last sighted in Brisbane. He was still preaching furiously for the Church of England Men's Society, and had arrived in South Africa after an exhausting tour through New Zealand. He took Cherry off to meet the Archbishop and other eminent Cape Town personages, all less appealing than Miss Kitty. It was a busy time. Besides sightseeing (Cherry went up Table Mountain by Skeleton Gorge) there was a banquet to attend and mail to send.

They set sail again on 2 September, and Scott took over the command as far as Melbourne, sending Wilson on to Australia by steamship to recruit another geologist and continue fund-raising. Everyone was disappointed that Wilson was temporarily leaving the ship. 'It will be terrible without "our Bill",' wrote Birdie, 'as he was always the balancing point in the mess.' Wilson, meanwhile, was keen to reassure Reggie that the faith they had invested in their protégé was being rewarded. 'It is delightful to find,' he wrote, 'that he [Cherry] is such a real favourite with everyone. . . . You need have no fears for his eyesight. I have so often watched him and have been struck by the absence of all handicap when he might have been bothered by glasses . . .'

Shortly after the *Terra Nova* left Simonstown she steamed into the famous gales of the roaring forties. All the crew could do was put the engines at dead slow and sail as close to the wind as possible. The little ship rose on the crest of one mountain of water after another, plunging into the foamy valleys in between and rolling sharply, flinging anyone on deck against the rail. Men on the first and middle watches went aloft in the dark in seventy-mile-an-hour winds and driving hail, unable to see the canvas that was flapping crazily four feet away. Despite having broken a small bone in his wrist the night they left South Africa, Cherry learned to reef sails and to work flattened against the yard-arm, and he weathered the storms like an old hand. A member of the expedition later wrote that he was 'one of the landsmen who took kindly to a sailor's life', and Wilson reported gleefully to Reggie that Cherry was 'as strong as a horse'.

For this leg of the journey Cherry was the sole zoologist. He applied himself to the task with vigour, noting on 14 September that he had been lucky with the bird line and caught three Cape pigeons, two great grey shearwaters and one black-breasted petrel. Below deck the seamen were preparing camping gear, sewing up food bags and repairing lampwick bindings, while in the wardroom sledging plans were again discussed avidly. Cherry discovered that he had already been selected for the important journey with dogs, ponies and sledges to cache stores on the ice in preparation for the dash to the Pole. He was thrilled.

The men who did not know Scott now had the opportunity to see him in action. He was more aloof, as a captain, than his second-in-command Evans: according to Silas Wright, Scott 'takes no part in skylarking – but always looks on with a grin', whereas Evans, known as 'the Skipper', 'has a taste for rowdyism'. Short, muscular Evans had a range of wardroom tricks up his sleeve. He was able to pick a man up by his teeth (by getting hold of his belt, for example), and was famed for his ability to rip a pack of cards in half. 'Evans is leader in all these things,' an observer wrote of the larks. The difference in personality and leadership style between Scott and his second-in-command was felt keenly throughout the expedition – and after it.

Scott was forty-two years old. He was not a fatherly leader. He was a reserved man, and, like Cherry, he was not at ease at cocktail parties. But Scott was more volatile, and he was subject to black moods that lasted for days. Temperamentally he was more complicated than his peers, especially in his self-doubt, which tortured him. He believed that he was by nature indolent, and that his most vital task was to triumph over his baser self. But he had worked tirelessly to raise funds for the expedition, trailing round the country addressing damp, half-empty halls in provincial towns, sometimes, through no fault of his own, bringing in as little as twenty pounds in a night. Throughout the months of preparation Scott put his shoulder to the punishing wheel of fund-raising without complaint, and he could be very persuasive. Nobody enjoys that kind of work, but Scott enjoyed it less than most. He used to say that the worst part of an expedition was over when the preparation was finished.

The scientists, mostly civilians, were unfamiliar with naval systems and traditions, and they instinctively identified with Wilson. Furthermore, Wilson was always willing to answer their questions and listen to their complaints. Good-natured Bill was one of the few men on the expedition who didn't grow critical of Scott's temper, and it was he, not the leader, who inspired superlatives from almost everyone. 'To all his comrades,' Raymond Priestley remembered, '[he was] the nearest thing to a perfect man they ever knew or can hope to know.'

At Port Melbourne the ship was met by a launch bearing Wilson, his wife Oriana, Kathleen, Hilda Evans and the mailbag. It was dark and lashing with rain, and the sea was rolling heavily, but the women had insisted on persevering, bullying Wilson, who was steering, into submission. 'I hope,' he wrote in his diary afterwards, 'it will never fall to my lot to have more than one wife at a time to look after, at any rate in a motor launch, in a running sea at night time.'

Cherry had been invited to stay with the Reverend W. H. Fitchett, a friend of his cousin Reggie Smith. A keen traveller and author, whose uplifting books included the bestselling *Deeds that Won the Empire*, Fitchett had met Cherry through Reggie on a recent visit to England. He was principal of the Methodist Ladies' College out at Hawthorn, where he and his family also lived. 'Cherry-Garrard had a look of the stoke-hole about him,' recalled Fitchett affectionately. 'He was the picture of health, with his face bronzed. He wore a soft shirt, his nails were broken and dirty, his hands horny, but he was the same charming, sweet-natured gentleman as ever, and we greatly enjoyed having him with us.'

The college was a multi-pinnacled, pseudo-Gothic affair of the kind popular with Australian settlers at the end of the nineteenth century. The girls were in residence, and when a dashing young Englishman appeared *en route* to the Antarctic they rushed for their cameras and autograph books and vied to be his tennis partner. It was difficult to imagine a more attractive welcome.

Fitchett had heard a good deal about Wilson from Reggie, and Uncle Bill and his wife were duly invited out to the college. After they had gone Fitchett eagerly wrote to Reggie:

Mrs Wilson told me that she heard Captain Scott discussing the members of the staff with Wilson, and he summed up Apsley Cherry-Garrard saying, 'He is tip-top always.' They will select the party for the actual dash for the Pole on the test of their fitness when the moment comes for the adventure, and Dr Wilson told me that he thought Apsley Cherry-Garrard would be one of the chosen party. He is justifying his claim to a place in it by his cheerfulness, his pluck, and his activity.

The expedition left Melbourne on 16 October after some changes of personnel. Once again, Scott wasn't with them: he was to rejoin them in New Zealand. Before they finally departed, the ship was inspected by an Australian admiral who paused at the sight of Nigger, the expedition cat, reclining magisterially in the hammock the seamen had made him, complete with bedding and pillow.*

In Melbourne Scott had picked up a cable announcing news which was to alter the course of polar history and shape his own destiny. It read simply, '*Beg leave to inform you* Fram *proceeding Antarctic. Amundsen.*'

On 1 September 1909, embroiled in preparations for his North Pole bid, Amundsen had opened a newspaper and read that someone else had got there first (two people, actually). The air went out of his project as if from a balloon. The tall, inscrutable Norseman with ice-blue eyes considered his position, and kept his own counsel. His lively imagination was fuelled by his powerful ambition: like most explorers, he saw little point in coming second. He had been travelling and training on ice since he was a boy, and he was one of the most experienced ice-men alive. Above all, Amundsen was a man who wanted to make a splash.

He made up his mind to switch poles. Like all expedition leaders, he would certainly return to colossal debt, and it would be far easier to raise funds after the event if he planted the Norwegian flag at the South Pole, rather than following others to its northern counterpart (there was to be no footling around with science after all). With characteristic flair, and with the *Fram* due to sail in a matter of months, Amundsen did not reveal his new plans to the public, to his backers, or to his crew. He kept silent, and made the startling announcement on the deck of the *Fram* off Madeira. (The cable to Scott was despatched by Amundsen's brother Leon, who left the ship at Madeira.) Each man on board was given the opportunity to quit

---

* Nigger was black, with white whiskers on the port side. He was very popular and much photographed, especially after he had mastered a couple of tricks such as jumping through a hoop formed by a man's arms. When he got a fright and leapt overboard the following year, the ship hove to, a boat was lowered, and the cat saved. In 1912, when the *Terra Nova* was returning from her second journey to the Antarctic, he went up into the rigging one day with the men, as was his custom, and disappeared during a squall.

the expedition, and offered a free passage home. None took it. They were going to the South Pole.

When Scott allowed the news to spread, Cherry and the other men were not greatly disturbed. They had no idea of its devastating implications. But what the telegram meant, Cherry wrote with hindsight, was, 'I shall be at the South Pole before you.'

Cherry shovelled coal relentlessly. It was a horrible job, and the men doing it were stung mercilessly by 'stokehold flies': drops of hot oil from the engines above that dripped on the backs of their necks as they stooped to shovel. At this stage of the journey they were burning 'patent fuel', which made their eyes and skin sting horribly as it was full of pitch and resin. 'We are all a bit stale,' he wrote on 24 October, 'and I think New Zealand will do us good.' But even stale, uncomfortable and spotted with burning oil, he was happier than he had ever been.

In a small, cramped ship which made ceaseless demands, the most capable men were bound to emerge. In Australia Cherry wrote that, 'Among the executive officers Scott was putting more and more trust in Campbell.' Victor Campbell was first officer aboard the *Terra Nova* and a shy, steely Old Etonian in flight from a troubled marriage. A quiet and distinguished man with a high forehead and a strong chin, Campbell had transferred to the Royal Navy from the Merchant Service, though he had retired in 1902 at the age of twenty-seven. He lived part of each year in Norway, where he had become an accomplished skier; it was his love of skiing, in part, that had led him to join the expedition (he was the only man who could ski, except Gran, the young Norwegian). As first officer he had been responsible for routine and discipline on the voyage south, and as a result he had been nicknamed 'the Wicked Mate'. 'I was very frightened of Campbell,' Cherry claimed; but the first officer was no martinet. 'Campbell as the "President of the Purity Brigade" wears a halo,' Wilson recorded in his diary, 'but it has been broken so often that it hardly holds together and has a permanent cant.'

Cherry continued to impress Scott. 'Cherry-Garrard has won all hearts,' he wrote to Reggie. 'He shows himself ready for any sort of hard work and is always to the front when the toughest jobs are on hand. He is the most unselfish, kind-hearted fellow . . .' It was not a small achievement. Before they left home there had been sniggers at Cherry's startling lack of any kind of qualification for the expedition; men had joked that he had been selected for his handy knowledge of Latin and Greek. (Titus Oates, the other 'adaptable helper', at least had experience with horses.) 'You will be equally glad to know that he is exceedingly happy,' Scott continued. 'I haven't asked if he is, but when I see his cheerful brown face charged with enthusiasm and wreathed in smiles I cannot doubt it – but indeed it is a good life for any young man who has the right stuff in him.'

On 28 October the *Terra Nova* steamed into Lyttelton in New Zealand. Cherry was again able to stay with a friendly family known to his own people, this time the Burtons, the English occupants of St Michael's Vicarage in St Albans, just outside Christchurch. There was work to be done at the docks, but also time for fishing and dancing.

Cherry found a large pile of mail waiting for him in New Zealand. To compensate for her son's second lengthy absence Evelyn deluged him with letters, telegrams, parcels and newspapers. At home she and the girls pored over reports of the expedition in the *Sphere*, looked up the *Terra Nova*'s position in the family atlas and compared her progress with the accounts in their well-thumbed copies of Scott's *Voyage of the 'Discovery'* and Shackleton's *Heart of the Antarctic*. Pages of her letters concerned a crisis which had developed at Lamer three months after Cherry left. (Several people had mysteriously fallen ill; the cause was eventually located in malfunctioning drains.) She relied heavily on Farrer and Reggie, who frequently wrote to each other three times a day over some aspect of Cherry's affairs ('minding his cakes at home', Reggie called it). Bank pass-books whizzed between them as they handled tottering piles of stocks and investments, as well as accounts for Denford, Lamer and the other estates. How relieved Cherry must have been to leave it all behind.

On 20 November Evelyn began a letter to her son to which she added each week for nine months, when it went south to catch the relief ship. It was 1910, yet in the very first entry she recorded, 'We are all working up "Voluntary Aid Detachments" in case of war. Your offer of Lamer for a Hospital in case of Invasion has been accepted.' (He stuck to it, too: four years later Lamer became a convalescent hospital.) She saw herself as a caretaker in her son's absence ('I feel you have left me in a place of great trust') and was painfully anxious for him to approve of her decisions. 'I am so very glad to find you think we did right about the drains,' she told him after he had written from Lyttelton. She was praying hard, and 'in the night when I wake up you are my first thought always'. (As she was bursting with pride about his exploits, Cherry was afraid that she might publish his journal when he mailed it home, so he wrote to her firmly from New Zealand banning such a project.) On Christmas Day, she said, they drank to his health round the dining-room table, 'and hoped it would not be long before you brought a wife to Lamer'. They had twenty-nine years to wait.

★   ★   ★

In Lyttelton the unloaded ship went into dry dock for a complete overhaul and was caulked to stop the leak that had kept the hand pumps occupied for the entire voyage. Taking the early train from Christchurch, Cherry worked as a stevedore as she was restowed. Her cargo now included New Zealand cheese, butter, bacon, ham and tongues, all of it colour-coded. Kathleen Scott was once more in evidence, positioning herself on the dock like a skirted sentry and checking all packages as they went on. Two prefabricated huts had been transported from London in pieces for the wintering party, and the skeletons of these were erected on a piece of wasteland near the dock. Finally the dogs and ponies waiting on Quail Island crowded on board; the well-travelled dog-handler, Cecil Meares, had brought them from Siberia. Meares knew a lot about dogs, but not a great deal about ponies.

Ponies had been used to pull sledges on at least one Arctic expedition. Shackleton had been the first to take them south, on the *Nimrod*. Despite the fact that the beasts had not performed well in the Antarctic, Scott had chosen to take ponies as well as dogs on the *Terra Nova*. It was an odd decision: Shackleton had described the way the ponies sank into soft surfaces, whereas lighter dogs could travel rapidly over the same snow. Furthermore, the ponies Scott had brought were inadequate. Oates was in charge of them, but, crucially, he had not accompanied Meares to Siberia to select them. As soon as he saw them in New Zealand he knew that they were a bunch of old crocks. '*Nobby*,' read his diary catalogue after he had inspected the ponies for the first time. 'Aged. Goes with stiff hocks. Spavin near hind. Best pony we have.'

Kathleen and Oriana Wilson both wrote to Evelyn from New Zealand, their letters bursting with compliments about Cherry. But goodwill among the wives had its limits, and Kathleen and Hilda Evans squabbled so intemperately in New Zealand that Oates recounted, 'There was more blood and hair flying about the hotel than you would see in a Chicago slaughterhouse in a month.' Kathleen was disgusted with the other wives, whom she perceived as dim, simpering little women clinging pathetically to their men. 'If ever Con [Scott] has another expedition,' she scribbled in her diary in New Zealand, 'then the wives must be chosen more carefully than the men.' When the mild-mannered Birdie learned of the rows among the wives he concluded,

I don't know who to blame, but somehow I don't like Mrs Scott . . . Nobody likes her on the expedition and the painful silence when she arrives is the only jarring note of the whole thing. There is no secret that she runs us all just now and what she says is done – through the Owner. Now nobody likes a schemer and she is one undoubtedly . . . We all feel that the sooner we are away the better.

At noon on 26 November the Bishop of Christchurch took a service among the steering equipment on deck. The officers crowded onto the poop with the local dignitaries and the sun glinted off their gold-laced uniforms for the last time in months or years. At the end of the service Petty Officer Evans was discovered to be drunk; so drunk that he ended up in the water. There were two Evanses on the *Terra Nova*. One was Teddy, Scott's second-in-command. The other belonged below decks. Edgar 'Taff' Evans was a huge Welshman with large appetites. He had served under Scott in warmer waters on HMS *Majestic* and then in the Antarctic on the *Discovery* expedition. They had even dangled down a crevasse together. Taff had got spectacularly drunk once before on the expedition, when he had had to be carried back to the ship after a farewell dinner in Cardiff. A wily, popular tentmate who drew on a bottomless fund of navy yarns, he knew he was in favour with Scott, and was determined to make a name for himself in the south this time. Scott considered him 'wonderfully capable', and had put him in charge of sledging equipment.

After he had been fished out of the Lyttelton docks Taff was ordered home on the grounds that he had disgraced the expedition. But he wheedled his way round Scott and rejoined the ship at her final stop in Port Chalmers, much to the fury of Teddy Evans, who wanted him banished. The disagreement over Taff contributed to the tension that had been simmering for months between Scott and Teddy, and at Port Chalmers a row finally erupted. Scott made a decision which Evans interpreted as a slur on his honesty, and it 'was the last straw in the heavy load that broke the camel's back': Teddy told colleagues privately that he intended to resign unless a clear understanding was reached between him and Scott. The trouble was exacerbated, according to Birdie, by the excessive jealousy of the wives, each goading her husband to gain ground over the other. Several officers decided they would resign in sympathy if Teddy quit, and they asked Cherry if he would join them. But he refused. He would have been happy to see Evans go. 'From the first,' he wrote, 'I had never liked Evans.' Behind Teddy's relentless high spirits Cherry saw a shallow man with none of Scott's complexity or Wilson's thoughtful altruism.* For a brief, tense

---

* Cherry came to believe that Evans had obtained his position as Scott's second-in-command through deception. Although Evans surrendered the funds he had raised for his own expedition in exchange for his place on Scott's, the sum turned out to be far less than

period at the last port before the merciless Southern Ocean, the expedition was in jeopardy. Finally, with Bill acting as peacemaker, Scott and Evans reached an agreement. 'May it never be known,' Birdie wrote to his mother, 'how very nearly the *Terra Nova* came to not sailing at the last few hours.'

Six scientists and a photographer joined the ship in New Zealand, bringing the total, including new seamen, to sixty-five. Among the recruits a chirpy Australian geologist soon made his mark in the wardroom. The 27-year-old Frank Debenham was the strapping son of a New South Wales parson. A recent graduate of Sydney University, he had applied for service with the encouragement of his tutor, Professor (later Sir) Edgeworth David, the geologist who had played an important part on Shackleton's 1907 *Nimrod* expedition to the Antarctic. 'Deb', as he was known, had been selected by Wilson when he went ahead to Australia (the sparkle in his eye clinched it, according to Wilson), and the appointment was sanctioned by Scott during an interview in a Sydney hotel room. One of three geologists on the expedition, Deb was to contribute a great deal both to geological and cartographic work. He was practical and versatile, emerging as a competent illustrator and photographer, and like Cherry he could hold his own at the pianola. Scott described him as sturdy, and Cherry said this was exactly the right word: he was a robust figure with an open, cheeky face. Deb was modest and warm-hearted, but in the privacy of his diary and his letters home he was not afraid to be critical; his attitude to Scott, in particular, became deeply ambiguous. He and Cherry grew close during the first year of the expedition and remained close for five decades. 'In a quiet way,' Deb wrote of Cherry in his diary, 'he is a rattling good chap, and true as steel.'

Herbert Ponting, the expedition photographer, also joined the expedition in New Zealand, having sailed by P. & O. steamer from London. Ponting was a talented photographer with years of experience and keen commercial ambition that was not complemented by business acumen. He had a cropped, dark moustache, and his face was hard, like a face stamped on a coin. Yet another who was nervy by disposition, when he couldn't set his shots up perfectly he quickly became very agitated. Ponting had reached an agreement with Scott to film both stills and a moving picture, which he called a kinematograph, and he took himself so seriously that he insisted on

---

he had suggested. Cherry privately accused Evans of '[trying] to raise a mutiny' at Port Chalmers, presumably over the reinstatement of Taff Evans. 'It seems incredible,' Cherry wrote furiously years after the event, 'that Scott should have written (at Port Chalmers) "all is well".'

being called 'camera artist'. The men soon became irritated at being asked to pose all the time (it was called 'to pont'), especially as they almost froze in the process, and they found it difficult to avoid making fun of Ponting. Before leaving home he had been told that pepper was a great thing to keep your feet warm, and he had brought a case of cayenne to put in his boots.

After the Bishop's service, at three o'clock the *Terra Nova* steamed out of the sunny Lyttelton docks. Special trains had brought crowds of well-wishers who pressed together in the balmy November afternoon, waving little flags and shouting 'Good luck!' as the *Terra Nova* shrank into the blue. Cherry was not on board; he took the train to Port Chalmers, where he picked up well-wishing telegrams, sent a wire to his mother and went to one last dance, oddly dressed as he had left his decent gear behind in Lyttelton. The expedition set off from New Zealand in bright sunshine on 29 November. The people of Dunedin, the town just south of Port Chalmers, had been given a half-day's holiday, and thousands more turned out on the wharf to say goodbye. A pair of decked-out tugs escorted the ship to the Heads and small craft continued into the open sea until, one by one, they dropped away, their hoots fading into the chaos of civilisation stretching northwards behind them.

The overloaded *Terra Nova* lay low in the water. Sixteen-foot-long crates shrouded in tarpaulins and containing three motor sledges with caterpillar treads took up most of the deck, along with stacks of timber for the huts. Two of the motor sledge cases and a baulk of timber formed a corral for some of the thirty-three dogs, who spent the first days trying to gnaw through their chains. The last 30 tons of coal of the 460-odd tons on board were stowed in bags next to drums of petrol and paraffin, which were in turn cased in wood. More dogs were chained on top of the fuel supplies, and five tons of dog biscuits were jammed below. Immediately in front of the motor sledges, a hundred carcasses of frozen mutton and several carcasses of beef were stored in the ice house, ten dogs chained to a brass rail above them. Next door, the sad eyes of four ponies poked out from their stalls. The other fifteen ponies were stabled in the forecastle above the seamen's quarters, where their urine seeped through the leaky deck onto the unfortunate human cargo below. Besides Nigger, the on-board zoo included a blue Persian kitten, several pet rabbits (one soon flattened by a pony), a couple of squirrels and a guinea pig who lived in a cigar box that was subsequently dropped overboard by mistake.

The men celebrated their rupture from the world by having their hair cut on deck with horse clippers, a procedure that left most of them looking like criminals. But the mood of playful indulgence was soon brought to an abrupt conclusion.

The Southern Ocean can be pitiless. 'Dante tells us,' Cherry wrote in *The Worst Journey*, 'that those who have committed carnal sin are tossed about ceaselessly by the most furious winds in the second circle of Hell. The corresponding hell on earth is found in the southern oceans . . .' Only two days out of New Zealand, a furious gale rolled out of the lurid purple skies to the south and almost swallowed the *Terra Nova*. With freezing fingers Cherry lashed and relashed cargo as tons of water crashed on board in 35-foot waves and screaming gusts clawed at the bags of coal and crates of petrol. The main pumps became choked by a mixture of oil and coal dust that formed evil little cakes, and as the deck was submerged, the men couldn't get to the hand pumps to clear it. When Cherry put his head into the wardroom he saw grave faces, and above the roar of the storm he heard shouted talk about provisioning the lifeboats. The men decided to cut the engine and drill a hole in the engine-room bulkheads to reach the hand pump-well; it seemed to be the only chance left. The *Terra Nova* rolled and dipped, lifeless without sail or steam, while exhausted men waist-deep in oil and watery coal dust fought to save her. They were put on bailing shifts, two hours on and two hours off all day and all night, passing buckets from the boiler room to the upper deck, standing on tiny metal ladders and covered in bilge oil. The men at the bottom of the chain worked naked, and still boiled, and those at the top froze. 'As I looked into the depths,' remembered geologist Ray Priestley, who was standing near the top of the line, 'I could see the stark-naked figures of my comrades in the chain, heaving heavy buckets from one to the other and grunting as they came.' Cherry was seasick, but bailed all through the storm, vomiting where he stood.

They lost ten tons of precious coal and scores of cases of petrol. Two ponies died (many more were nearly hanged by their halters), and so did a dog, though another hound, Osman, was washed overboard by one wave and brought back again by the next. Cherry did not sleep for forty-eight hours. 'For sheer downright misery,' he decided, 'give me a hurricane, not too warm, the yard of a sailing ship, a wet sail and a bout of seasickness.'

The cabins were now even more crowded, engorged with four-foot-long canvas sausage bags of Antarctic clothing that had been issued to each man. Most of the company had brought their own supplementary gear, and all kinds of peculiar outfits, especially hats, appeared on the poop deck as the mercury fell. Griff Taylor, one of the geologists, noted, 'One scientist reverted to a fashionable Tudor garb, to wit, a long, speckled knitted tunic reaching the knees, and a pair of very long thick blue stockings.' Griff was a gaunt, untamed figure, though Cherry wrote that 'a halo of good fellowship' atoned for his wild appearance. He was outspoken, witty and likeable, and he talked so much that the dog-handler Cecil Meares nicknamed him 'Ram-Jatsass'. The others eventually discovered that this meant 'verbally flowing eternally' in a Tibetan dialect.

Cherry had dreaded going aloft in those latitudes, but when he did, he found that it wasn't so bad. As the temperature dropped to 34 degrees, new birds circled the ship. Wilson snared an Antarctic petrel, and Cherry learned to identify whales from a spotter's guide pinned to the wardroom wall. Early in the morning of 9 December a cry came from the crow's nest, 'Large iceberg ahead, sir.' When the steward appeared in the nursery, adding the news to his greeting, for once they all sprang out of bed. On deck, squinting in the buttery light, they saw a tabular berg, eighty feet in height and a mile long, its fissured cliffs pocked with foamy caverns at the deep green waterline and shimmering in the dry polar air.

At this stage they were getting about two hours of darkness a night. 'We are shaking down capitally with all our new hands,' Cherry wrote. 'When we are so close together it does not take long . . . I thought that after leaving New Zealand it would be rather hard to reconcile oneself to such an isolated existence. But I would not go back now for anything.' He was earning a reputation as a solid team player, and was such a smiler that his nickname often turned into 'Cheery' or, affectionately, 'Cheery Black-guard'.

Soon after they encountered their first berg, they entered the pack ice. This was much further north than Scott had anticipated. 'One of the best mornings I have ever spent,' rejoiced Cherry. 'Bump! We have just charged our first ice!' On 10 December the ship crossed the Antarctic Circle, and there was great excitement on deck when streaky brown crabeater seals were spotted lounging on the floes. Men leant over the shuddering forecastle rail to watch the iron-plated prow battering the pack ice in an unearthly cacophony of swishing and grinding. As if in retaliation, the pack thickened around them into frozen waves thirty feet high. The pack ice of the Ross Sea in the sunshine is an incomparable sight, the burnished coppers and rosy pinks of the austral skies reflecting off glittering and translucent bergy whites. That night, the sun did not set. 'It was more than a wonderful day,' wrote Cherry.

While the ship was stuck in the ice they lowered a plank over the side and practised skiing. They also had to exercise the dogs and water ship. The overworked condenser was struggling to produce enough drinking water, and as salt drains out of the top layer of old sea ice they were able to replenish their supply by hacking off large chunks with a pick and passing them aboard in a relay. It was so mild that they were able to go bareheaded, and so still that at the regular Sunday service held on deck their hymns broke the silence. Initially someone played the pianola at church. This was not a success, as the machine operated with rolls of music and resolutely refused to produce hymns, spontaneously bursting into 'Knees Up, Mother Brown' after Scott had intoned the collect.

The men were captivated by the sight of their first penguins, quickly identifed as Adélies. Someone threw a potato over the side, causing a sensation among the birds, who were so enthralled with the tuber that they camped around it. 'I have never thought of anything as good as this life,' Cherry wrote in his diary. 'The novelty, interest, colour, animal life and good fellowship go to make up an almost ideal picnic.'

There were low moments. Cherry cut his hand on a flensing knife and found it dreary not being able to work, obliged instead 'to moon around with a gun' or read Nansen's *Farthest North* on his damp bunk. The leak supposedly mended in Lyttelton had not been mended at all, and bailing was a Casaubon-like enterprise. If there was any chance of movement Pennell or Teddy Evans stood in the crow's nest, guiding the ship through lanes of blue water by shouting to the steersman through a megaphone. Progress was painfully slow, which was agony for Scott, who was desperate to begin his sledging programme: he needed to make one major journey laying in depôts of food and fuel before the first Antarctic winter. It was bad luck to have met the pack ice this far north. Scott watched his coal supplies being burnt down and his ponies and dogs losing condition and voiced his dread that if they were held up for much longer they might have to winter in the pack ice. 'What an exasperating game this is –' he confided to his diary, 'one cannot tell what is going to happen in the next half or even quarter of an hour. At one moment everything looks flourishing, the next one begins to doubt if it is possible to get through.'

Blue whales 100 feet long fluked round the ship, their jets of pale grey fog squirting 15 feet into the air. A leopard seal reminded Cherry of the sea monster in Kipling, and one of the scientists found eighteen penguins in the creature's stomach. At last, on 19 December, Cherry's hand had healed well enough for him to get back to skinning his zoological specimens. That day he saw his first Weddell, the enormous mottled seal that lives further south than any other, its sharp teeth enabling it to keep holes open in the ice. Two days later, Midsummer Day (the temperature was twenty degrees below freezing), he went out onto the ice and fell through twice, whereupon he was 'ignominiously called back by Scott' in front of everyone. 'Felt a bit chippy . . .' he confided in his diary that evening, 'but put it down to overeating and no exercise.' Scott's admonition had brought on the chippiness, not too much food. The wire was stretched as tightly as ever.

The weather had been cloudy for most of the slog through the pack, much to Ponting's annoyance. But Christmas Eve was windless and sunny, the bergs shimmering in a limpid light and the pack crunching gently. Dinner deteriorated into a 'general scrap' in the wardroom. 'Titus dragged all Bill's clothes off,' Cherry noted, 'and Bill burst naked into the wardroom dragging Titus along on his back.'

For Cherry, the next day was 'the most Christmassy Christmas I have ever had'. He opened a parcel of calendars and cards from home, doling the calendars out as presents and saving the cards for the following Christmas. Evelyn had sent so many packages down to New Zealand, in fact, that he was able to present his colleagues with a range of supplies. Griff recorded that although he had known Cherry for some time, 'A most acceptable pair of Jaeger socks brought about our real introduction!' (He also noted privately that his benefactor was 'very pleasant but with the Oxford shyness with newcomers'.) Cherry was generous by temperament. In later years, when he had become awkward and something of a curmudgeon, he remained a loyal and munificent friend. 'Cherry is very generous,' Birdie wrote to his mother on the journey to New Zealand, 'and one has to fight with him all the time to keep him from paying for everything.'

After church the lower ranks had mutton for Christmas dinner; they didn't think penguin was good enough for the occasion. The officers and scientists had their celebration in the evening. The wardroom was decked with sledging flags, of which Cherry's, depicting the family arms, was given place of honour on the wall. The table was laid with a new blue cloth, and after bowls of salted almonds the stewards served up turtle soup, stewed penguin breasts in redcurrant jelly (not unlike jugged hare, according to Ponting), roast beef and Yorkshire pudding, asparagus, flaming plum pudding, mince pies, preserved fruits and a jumbo box of Fry's chocolates, the lot sluiced down with champagne, port and liqueurs. After the meal Ponting played his banjo and, going twice round the table, everybody had to contribute a song, though Gran made a speech instead. 'I do think in my mind of Captain Scott this time next year,' he said in his staccato Norwegian accent, 'sitting quite close to the South Pole, a little frost-bitten on the nose perhaps but very warm inside. We do always say in our country that bad luck in the first of an expedition do mean good luck in the end and so I do not mind our sticking in the pack for this so long time.'

Shortly after Christmas they were able to sunbathe on deck, crammed into the slivers of open space lying face against tail like sardines. At midnight on 29 December the *Terra Nova* left the pack ice and entered open water. They had spent almost three weeks at the whim of the pack, far more than anticipated. Unknown to them, less than a week later the *Fram* entered the pack ice. She took just four days to clear it.

On the last day of 1910 the rigging was crusted with icicles and the air filled with driving snow. Cherry was seasick again and went to bed, but someone crept into the nursery and whispered in his ear, 'Have you seen the land?' Cherry went up wrapped in blankets. 'And there they were: the most glorious peaks appearing, as it were like satin, above the clouds, the only white in a dark horizon.' The peaks were Mount Sabine and the Admiralty Range, over a hundred miles away but indubitably on the Antarctic continent.

The next day was clear and sharp, 'the very air permeated with vitality'. Below decks, a seaman's rabbit had given birth to seventeen little bunnies. 'Our previous troubles,' Birdie wrote to May, 'seem to have fizzled out with the glad New Year.' On 2 January 1911, Cherry's twenty-fifth birthday, they spotted Mount Erebus in the distance. 'I have seen Fuji,' Cherry wrote in *The Worst Journey*,

> the most dainty and graceful of mountains; and also Kangchenjunga: only Michael Angelo among men could have conceived such grandeur. But give me Erebus for my friend. Whoever made Erebus knew all the charm of horizontal lines, and the lines of Erebus are for the most part nearer the horizontal than the vertical. And so he is the most restful mountain in the world, and I was glad when I knew that our hut would lie at his feet. And always there floated from his crater the lazy banner of his cloud of steam.

Scott planned to establish his base on Ross Island, a volcanic landmass just off the Antarctic coast. The *Discovery* men knew the island well, as they had sledged over most of it. It lay in the Ross Sea, and was separated from the mainland on one side by a wide channel called McMurdo Sound. Specifically, Scott intended to set up camp near the Cape Crozier headland where *Discovery* men had found an Emperor penguin rookery – the first anyone had ever seen.

As they approached Crozier's basalt cliffs, Cherry and five other men rowed over in a whaler. But he was so nervous that he could not row properly. 'I made an awful ass of myself,' he confessed to his diary, 'not being able to manage my oar at all, and I spent my time catching crabs, until even Scott said under his breath, "Oh! Steady on!" ' But they couldn't find a place to land – the swell was too heavy. Then, on the short row back to the ship, a crag snapped off the cliffs and hundreds of tons of volcanic rock crashed into the sea a few yards from the boat, enveloping them in dust and ice.

Wilson was frustrated at their failure to land, as he was longing to investigate the Emperor penguin colony and continue the work on the bird's breeding cycle that he had begun on the *Discovery*. As it was, he watched a stranded chick on the bay ice in a stage of development that nobody had ever seen before, the wings already feathered like an adult's, but much of the body still covered in down. Wilson was to learn more of the Crozier penguins; and so was Cherry.

They steamed on to McMurdo Sound in search of a landing, carrying out a detailed running survey of Ross Island. 'Many watched all night', recalled Cherry, 'as this new world unfolded itself, cape by cape and mountain by mountain.' Early in the morning, when it was sunny and calm, the sea scored blue and white, the pack loose and whales spouting all around, Wilson was invariably alone in the crow's nest, 'my private chapel'. It was a familiar landscape to this deeply thoughtful man. 'These days are with one for all time – they are never to be forgotten,' he wrote in his diary, 'and they are to be found nowhere else in all the world but at the poles. The peace of God which passeth all understanding reigns here in these days.'

The transcendent beauty of the Antarctic has always awakened a deep sense of wonder in the human spirit. The scale, the purity, the un-ownedness: these are characteristics that stimulate contemplation. Then, and now, it would be impossible, looking out at the incandescent band of purply blue light that lies between ice and sky on an Antarctic horizon, not to think about forces beyond the human plane. From the fecund coast to the sterile interior, the dignity of the landscape shines a light onto a corner of the human psyche that is rarely lit among the gas bills and rain-splattered streets of home. 'There, if anywhere,' wrote the chronically unsentimental Griff Taylor, 'is life worthwhile.' 'Antarctica,' said the nature-writer Barry Lopez, 'reflects the mystery that we call God.'

After much confabulation, Scott picked out a low headland of eruptive rock north of a point the *Discovery* people knew as the Skuary. Ice anchors were laid, and Scott, Wilson and Evans left the blubbery *Terra Nova* and walked a mile over the sea ice to the headland. Scott had decided: this place was their home. He named it Cape Evans.

5

Out of the World

For a week everyone worked nineteen hours a day setting up quarters for the twenty-five men who were to stay for the winter. The constant daylight disoriented them at first, and they were constrained by an epidemic of snow-blindness. But the clean and bracing Antarctic air felt fine. The dogs were in excellent form, dragging their leaders down the gangplank and running light loads between ship and shore while hurling themselves gleefully at marauding penguins. The ponies also began pulling loads (a two-year supply of fuel, food and other essentials had to come off the ship), and Cherry, soon dark with sunburn and dirt, was assigned to pony-leading. It was a devilish job, as the beasts were committed bolters, but he gained valuable experience in an important field, and Scott noted his talent for handling animals.

The site of the hut had been selected partly for the access it offered to the Ross Ice Shelf, then known as the Great Ice Barrier. This immense sheet of floating ice, about the size of France, was to provide Scott's route onto the continent itself.* Scott was going to have to cross the Barrier and march through a gap in the Transantarctic Mountains in order to reach the Polar Plateau and, ultimately, the Pole. Ross Island abutted the Barrier, and Scott had positioned his winter quarters on a black sand beach on the northern side of a spur of Mount Erebus. The Pole was over 860 miles away.

It had been an unusually warm summer, and as a result Cape Evans faced an expanse of open water. From their new home the men could see the mountains glittering on the other side of McMurdo Sound, while the walls

---

* Many floating ice shelves fill embayments (recesses) in the Antarctic coast, all fed by glaciers and ice streams flowing off the land like icing sliding off a wedding cake.

of passing icebergs reflected the saffron sun and crinkled sapphire water. The four Dellbridge Islands lay within three miles of the hut, all inundated volcanic craters, and along the coast in both directions rippling glaciers tumbled from the slopes of Erebus.

The highlight of the first week ashore was an episode involving Ponting and a pod of hungry killer whales who burst up from under a floe just as he had set his camera down upon it. Next, one of the motor sledges disappeared. The first two had been successfully unloaded, but the third crashed through thin ice and sank, a disaster felt keenly by Scott, who had invested a great deal of hope and effort in his motors. They were four-cylinder monsters with caterpillar tracks and air-cooled engines, specifically designed for use on snow and lacking both steering and brakes. Although touted as forerunners of the tank, they had an upholstered chair on each end and resembled not so much military ordinance as vehicles for transporting elderly members of the royal family among adulatory crowds. The two surviving sledges were able to ferry stores ashore, and Scott still cherished the hope they would do much more, and help him reach the Pole. The shrewder of his men already had their doubts.

With stores neatly arranged around the hut and guarded by pairs of upright skis, the Union Jack was hoisted. On the ship Cherry unhooked the royal family from the wardroom wall and sledged them to the hut. He was sorry that the King and Queen could not see themselves whizzing over the floe. Finally the pianola was also sledged over, and the first tune it played was 'Home, Sweet Home'.

Fifty feet long, twenty-five feet wide and nine feet to the eaves, the hut was heated by a huge round stove that dominated the interior like a lighthouse. Off the entrance porch a passage led to stables built onto the side, where Titus Oates and Anton, a Russian groom, tended the ponies. Once a jockey in Moscow, Anton was four feet ten and spoke very little English. Linguistic difficulties notwithstanding, he was already devoted to Titus.

In the main body of the hut a bulkhead of packing cases divided the officers' quarters at the far end from the galley and the seamen's berths nearer the porch. Cherry was billeted with Birdie, Titus, Dr Atkinson ('Atch') and the dog-handler, Cecil Meares, in the warren of bunks known as the Tenements. Along the wall furthest from the porch the scientists had their lab tables and Ponting his darkroom, where he also slept. 'It is wonderfully comfortable,' Cherry wrote, 'and the gramophone sounds ripping – Melba, Caruso, Scotti, Clara Butt . . .' Even the seal rissoles tasted good.

He was subject to difficult moods, even at this happy time. On 12 January he wrote, 'This evening a variety of things went wrong and I felt very chippy. I am going to turn in with a little Tennyson for company.' He cheered up two days later when Scott asked him if he would lead ponies on the depôt journey. It was a great honour.

The depôt journey was a key feature of Scott's strategy, and the first step towards the Pole. To prepare for the crucial polar trek the following spring, caches or depôts of fuel, manfood and animal fodder had to be laid as close to the Pole as possible before the winter set in. Only about twelve weeks of daylight remained in which to accomplish this task. Yet it had to be done, as the window of light and weather the following summer would allow only for the great march itself. Everything depended on the ponies. They were to pull the biggest loads, and Scott, who was to lead the depôt journey, selected his best men to handle them. Cherry's inclusion meant that he was to gain valuable sledging experience early in the expedition, making it almost certain that he would be included in the Southern Journey – and perhaps even go to the Pole itself.

Although he had brought supplies for two years, Scott was still hoping that he could get to the Pole and back the following summer, in which case everyone would leave with the ship without staying a second winter. From the start, this had looked ambitious. The ship was returning to New Zealand for the winter, and it was impossible to predict whether, and when, ice conditions would allow her back to Cape Evans. More significantly, Scott and the polar party would have to get back before the sea ice began to freeze. But Scott was keen to avoid the expense of a further year, as it would involve another costly trip down to the Antarctic for the *Terra Nova* as well as extra salaries for the men.

Scott had planned an ambitious scientific programme. A core of scientists were to remain at the hut, gathering data which they could then analyse in their makeshift labs. Others were to leave Cape Evans to collect material from more distant parts of the continent. The most significant splinter group, the Eastern Party, was to be led by the experienced skier Victor Campbell, first officer on the *Terra Nova*. The aim of this six-man team was to explore and geologise along a section of Antarctic coastline to the east. A smaller group of geologists, led by Griff Taylor, was to spend several weeks collecting specimens in the Western Mountains.

The ship went off, carrying the Eastern Party, which was to be dropped on King Edward VII Land – the part of the Antarctic that lay beyond the eastern edge of the Barrier – to explore and winter. In addition, Griff's four-man Western Geological Party was landed at Butter Point. After depositing the Eastern Party, Pennell was to captain the ship to New Zealand, where she would spend the southern winter before returning to the Antarctic at the end of 1911, again under Pennell's command. The *Terra Nova* was carrying the first batch of Ponting's photographs and the last mail the wintering men would be able to send for a year. Both Scott and Wilson again took the trouble to write to Cherry's people, telling them what a valuable member of the team he had turned out to be (Scott said he was one of the best pony leaders and that he was 'ready for everything'). Cherry himself churned out piles of letters, among them a missive to Kitty Williams in Cape Town. In his business correspondence he revealed to Farrer that 'a second year [in the Antarctic] has been seriously debated for the first time'. He had decided that if most men were staying on, and if he were given a definite job, then he too would stay. He knew it would be a shock to his mother,* and he apologised to Farrer for putting a further burden on him and Smith, as it meant that they would be saddled with his extensive affairs until 1913. But he asked Farrer to send another year's power of attorney when the ship returned. 'I am enjoying every moment of the day and night,' he told him.

Cherry wasn't sorry to see the ship go. 'I expect you are just done with the election,' he wrote to Farrer. 'I wish I knew the result here, but we are so out of the world that further than that we are fairly content to know nothing.'

On 24 January thirteen men, eight ponies and twenty-six dogs set off on the depôt-laying journey, a round trip of about three hundred miles. It was a vital six-week mission, for Scott's chances of reaching the Pole depended on it; yet after their unloading and hut-building efforts the men were exhausted before they even started on their first sledging journey. 'If we sat down on a packing case,' Cherry wrote, 'we went to sleep.' But the job had to be done, and the dead, dark polar winter loomed ominously close. 'We finally left camp,' noted Cherry, 'in a state of hurry bordering upon panic.'

The first week slipped by in a miasma of snow-blindness, long days on the trail and prayers on Sunday. And yet, and yet – the crust of surface ice that snapped underfoot, the meaty fragrance from the bubbling pot, the flutter of the canvas tent flaps, the thin band of apricot and petrol blue that hung over the Transantarctic Mountains and the pallid sun that shed a

---

* 'It is a terrible blow to me that you are seriously thinking about staying out there another year,' she wrote on 14 May after getting the news.

watery light over thousands of miles of ice: Cherry never forgot those first days of sledging. They hauled up from the sea ice onto the soft surface of the Barrier, which the ponies did not like, and confronted their first deep crevasses, often many feet wide. Picking their way over the corrugated snow bridges that hid the most treacherous holes, they began laying depôts immediately.

Cherry revelled in the newness of this adventure. 'Every seal-hole was of interest,' he wrote, 'and every type of windswept snow a novelty.' But there was little time to admire the landscape. 'As we came up to Camp Five,' he recorded, 'we floundered into a pocket of soft snow in which one pony after another plunged deeper and deeper until they were buried up to their bellies and could move no more ... My own pony somehow got through with his sledge to the other side, and every moment I expected the ground to fall below us and a chasm to swallow us up.'

At Corner Camp, so called because there the trail turned due south, a three-day blizzard obliged them to lie up. Cherry admitted that the rest was welcome. 'Cherry-Garrard is remarkable,' Scott wrote, 'because of his eyes. He can only see through glasses and has to wrestle with all sorts of inconvenience in consequence. Yet one could never guess it – for he manages somehow to do more than his fair share of the work.' The autumn temperatures on the Barrier were much lower than Scott had expected, and the ponies, each pulling 900 pounds, suffered terribly. Oates had not changed his mind about the poor quality of his charges, and anyway the Antarctic is a grim place for ponies – even decent ones. Scott fretted constantly about the beasts, and according to Cherry felt their sufferings more than the animals themselves. As the ponies found the going easier when the surface hardened up, Scott decided to march at night when temperatures were lower; so days were turned on their heads (an easy thing to do in 24-hour daylight). But on 13 February the three weakest ponies and their leaders turned back, and shortly afterwards two of the animals died on the trail. Teddy Evans remembered the last days of the pony Blossom. 'It was surprising what spirit the little brute had,' he wrote. 'If we started to march away Blossom staggered along after us, looking like a spectre against the white background of snow. We kept on giving him up and making to kill him, but he actually struggled on for over thirty miles before falling down and dying in his tracks.'

Cherry continued south, moving into a tent with Scott, Wilson and the dog-handler Meares. 'He [Cherry] is excellent,' Scott noted, 'and is quickly learning all the tips for looking after himself and his gear.' Because of the blizzard they were not as far south as they had hoped. Scott had wanted to lay the last depôt on the 80th parallel, but instead they stopped at 79 degrees 29 minutes south, depositing a ton of provisions and assorted equipment about 150 miles from the hut at a place they christened One Ton Depôt, a toponym that came to haunt Cherry. Had the depôt-laying party been able to struggle on for another march or two and lay a depôt further south, or had the Corner Camp blizzard not come in to delay them, Scott and his two companions, staggering back from the Pole the next summer, would probably have reached the depôt and lived. But expeditions are made of chance and circumstance, with risks and hazards at every turn. From the start, Scott was gambling that the things he could not control would go his way. But there were an awful lot of them.

On the way back from One Ton Cherry began his turn as cook, deeply worried that his companions would either starve or be poisoned. He made a huge 'hoosh' or thick soup from pemmican (a cakey slab of dried, pounded meat and melted beef fat), water, arrowroot, curry power and biscuit, and reported 'everybody as happy as ninepins'. The next day Scott said, 'Cherry, you are going far to earn our eternal gratitude – I have never had such a dry hoosh as far as I can remember.' But Scott got indigestion.

They covered a whacking thirty-eight miles one day, then ten dogs fell down a crevasse. Scott and the others just managed to anchor the sledge in time, to stop it following the dogs down. After dangling on their leather trace for more than an hour, eight dogs were hauled out, then Scott was lowered into the crack to rescue the last two. (Cherry offered to go, saying that he often went down the well at home.) It was a miraculous escape for men and dogs, and the latter celebrated with a tremendous fight with the other team. When it was over, snug in the tent, Cherry wrote in his diary, 'There is a pleasant air of friendship about, rather more than usual. I feel that a man who never says much in the way of prayers would say one tonight.' 'My companions today were excellent,' Scott reported, 'Wilson and Cherry-Garrard if anything the most intelligently and readily helpful.' But years later Cherry was to note in the margin of his journal, 'Up to this day Scott had been talking to Meares of how the dogs would go to the Pole. After this, I never heard him say that.'

At Hut Point, named after a shelter built by *Discovery* men eight years previously, they found news so dramatic that it left them reeling. The *Terra Nova* had returned to Ross Island after heavy pack ice had prevented her from dropping Campbell and his men on King Edward VII Land. But she had left messages in the Hut Point shelter. They included the startling information that Amundsen had been sighted unloading stores in the Bay of Whales, just off the eastern edge of the Barrier. He had decided to position his base on the floating Barrier itself: a bold, innovative and potentially risky move.

Nobody had suspected that the Norwegians would be starting from the same side of the continent as Scott, or that they would be so well positioned: their base was over sixty miles nearer the Pole than Cape Evans. Furthermore – and this was devastating news – Amundsen had over a hundred dogs. 'I never thought he could have got so many dogs safely to the ice,' Scott wrote in his diary. Dogs could cope with early spring temperatures and surfaces, which ponies could not. 'But above all and beyond,' Scott acknowledged ruefully, 'he [Amundsen] can start his journey early in the season – an impossible condition with ponies.'

Visits had been exchanged between the ships.* As the *Terra Nova* steamed away from the Bay of Whales, geologist Ray Priestley, one of Campbell's party, noted, 'The world will watch with interest a race for the Pole next year, a race which may go either way . . .' Meanwhile the Norwegians had all started sneezing. They had caught colds from their unexpected visitors.

The hut erupted like a volcano at the news of Amundsen's proximity. 'For an hour or so we were furiously angry,' Cherry wrote, 'and were possessed with the insane sense that we must go to the Bay of Whales and have it out with Amundsen . . . we had just paid the first instalment of the heartbreaking labour of making a path to the Pole; and we felt, however unreasonably, that we had earned the first right of way.' When they woke on 24 February Scott leapt out of his bag and said, 'By Jove what a chance we have missed – we might have taken Amundsen and sent him back on the ship.' Cherry later elaborated on this: 'Scott said we could go and fight Amundsen. There was no law south of sixty.' This was an absurd reaction, typical of the competitive urge of the Admiralty and British empire-builders in general, all of whom thought they had a prior claim to any far-off land on which they had set their sights. Amundsen had every right to be where he was.

Wilson calmed Scott down, arguing that there might well be no law south of sixty, but at some point they would have to go north of sixty. 'We had hours of it . . .' Cherry continued. 'Bill said to me, "We had a bad time with Scott on the *Discovery*: but never anything like this."' In his rational moments, Scott acknowledged that the important thing was to carry on as if

---

* Both sides were apprehensive about this meeting. When the Norwegian watchman spotted the *Terra Nova* he prepared himself for all eventualities by loading his gun with six bullets and looking up 'How are you this morning?' in the ship's English phrase book.

. nothing had happened, and 'to go forward and do our best for the honour of the country without fear or panic'.

As for Campbell, having failed to find a place to disembark on King Edward VII Land, etiquette had prevented him from establishing a base close to the Norwegians, so the ship had continued 500 miles along the Barrier edge and then northwards to land the party in South Victoria Land. This was the part of the continent to the north of the western, Ross Island edge of the Barrier. The Eastern Party was renamed the Northern Party. On 18 February 1911 they were duly landed on the beach at Cape Adare, in great haste as the ship was running short of coal for the journey back to New Zealand. They were to be out for two long winters.

Sledging parties were still battling it out on the Barrier, finishing the depôt work. Another pony died. Cherry's unease with Teddy Evans was beginning to solidify into overt, if private, criticism. Atch (Dr Atkinson) had been out on the trail with Evans. 'He said it was a terrible thing to say of anyone,' Cherry confided to his diary, 'but Evans was not pulling.' Later, Deb told Cherry that he had had the same experience out sledging with Evans; Silas too was disenchanted ('Teddy a quitter'). Furthermore, Evans had been criticising Scott behind his back: Birdie had gone to Cherry one night 'almost in tears' to talk about his treacherous carping. Scott himself was having doubts about Evans. He described him privately as 'a queer study – his boyish enthusiasm carries all along till one sees clearly the childish limitations of its foundation and appreciates that it is not a rock to be built upon . . . There are problems ahead here for I cannot consider him fitted for a supreme position . . . It was curious to note how his value (in this respect) suddenly diminished as he stepped on shore . . .'

Evans found it difficult to stick to the rules. As a boy he had been expelled from school and detained by the police for pilfering. But he had talent. While a naval cadet, despite regular misdemeanours he had impressed his superiors and won an excellent reputation. He was to have a glorious war, and in peacetime he would rise to the top of the navy. While he quickly hardened into an archetypal enemy in Cherry's imagination, and to a lesser extent in the imaginations of others, he was not without supporters on the expedition. Campbell was a firm friend in later years; the taciturn Oates respected him; and even Birdie, so hurt by his tales out of school, was sympathetic to the man ('He is the best of skippers and friends'). Men less wedded to ideals and codes of honour than Cherry would say Evans' criticisms of Scott in the Antarctic were no worse than might be heard on the bridge of any warship. Evans' weaknesses were his mercurial temperament and his feline way of ingratiating himself. 'He is a man of moods,' concluded Birdie. 'A good friend – but like most Welshmen, a bad enemy.'

Cherry had been out with a sledging party ferrying stores from Hut Point to Corner Camp. On the way back, leading four ponies off the Barrier, he camped on the sea ice with Birdie and an Irish seaman called Tom Crean. A strong and immensely able petty officer with broad shoulders and a deep chest, Crean was one of the best polar travellers in the whole history of exploration. He had left his family farm in County Kerry and signed on with the Royal Navy ten days before his sixteenth birthday. Eight years later, serving on a navy ship in New Zealand, he had been recruited to fill a vacancy on Scott's *Discovery*. He acquitted himself with such distinction in the Antarctic that when Scott went back to sea after the expedition he asked to take Crean with him. In 1909, as soon as his plans for a second polar venture were made public, Scott again applied to the Admiralty for Crean's services. Crean had an insatiable appetite for adventure as well as an iron constitution, and at the age of thirty-two he had no hesitation about following Scott into the unknown for a second time.

The small caravan of men and ponies had had a taxing journey through black mist, but despite that, and the usual rigours of an icy camp, the mood was calm, the men were content, and the only upset in an otherwise peaceful evening occurred when Birdie, who was cook, mistook curry powder for cocoa. Even then Crean swigged the drink back before realising anything was wrong.

In the night, thinking that he could hear his pony attacking the oats, Birdie went out in his socks. The sea ice under the camp had broken up, and they were stranded on a small floe between long black tongues of boiling ocean. 'The tops of the hills were visible,' Birdie wrote home later, 'but all below was thin mist and as far as the eye could see there was nothing solid; it was all broken up, and heaving up and down with the swell.' Cherry's pony, Guts, had already gone ('a dark streak of water alone showed the place where the ice had opened under him'). Birdie poked his head into the tent and announced that they were floating out to sea.

Striking camp in record time, they began leaping from floe to floe, avoiding the prowling killer whales and coaxing the ponies over the furious water when the channels between the islands of ice narrowed. 'Very little was said,' Bowers wrote. 'Crean like most bluejackets behaved as if he had done this sort of thing often before.' Using the twelve-foot sledges as bridges to cross the widest channels of water, after six hours they reached the heavier floes near the fast ice of the Barrier. Bowers sent Crean off with a message to Scott, who was camped not far away. Cherry and Birdie waited with the ponies on a floe in the middle of it all, 'utterly done. I remember thinking what a beautiful place the world was.' Broken sea ice promises a tasty crop of seal for killer whales. They shot up vertically to stare over the lip of the floe, their huge black and white heads and piggy eyes only a few yards from the tent flaps. Cherry had heartburn and cramp. 'I suppose there is no doubt,' he recorded in his diary as he squatted on a sledge on the bobbing floe, 'we are in the devil of a hole.'

'It was not a pleasant day that Cherry and I spent all alone there,' wrote Bowers, 'knowing as we did that it only wanted a zephyr from the south to send us irretrievably out to sea.' As the day wore on, skua gulls, eager for carrion, settled on a nearby floe. Scott, Oates and Crean eventually appeared on the edge of the Barrier. Throwing down a rope, Scott shouted at Bowers to climb to safety using the sledges as ladders.

'What about the ponies and sledges?' Bowers shouted back.

'I don't care a damn about the ponies and sledges, it's you I want,' yelled Scott. 'Between us and the Barrier,' Cherry wrote, 'was a lane of some fifty yards wide, a seething cauldron. Bergs were calving off as we watched: and capsizing: and hitting other bergs, splitting into two and falling apart. The killers filled the whole place. Looking downwards into a hole between our berg and the next, a hole not bigger than a small room, we saw at least six whales.'

As Scott pulled the men up, he said, 'This is the end of the Pole.' He had invested so much hope in the ponies, and with four more gone before the journey to the Pole had even begun he saw little hope of success. The dogs alone could not pull four or five months' worth of food and fuel: Scott did not have enough of them. He was tense with anxiety and dismay. They pitched camp, and Birdie, realising how much was at stake, persuaded Scott that they should try to rescue the three drifting ponies who were waiting trustingly for their nosebags on a clunking floe. 'The others meanwhile, a little overwrought,' Scott wrote; 'Scott was the man who was overwrought,' Cherry remembered. When they got to the drifting ponies, Punch leapt for it, but fell in, and after a struggle lay motionless in the frothy water. The men looked down at the still, white corpse in sorrow and despair. Then Punch snorted. A horrified Scott covered his face with his hands. 'Oh! Cherry, Cherry,' he cried, 'why didn't you tell me he wasn't dead?' But they couldn't get Punch out, so Oates brained him with a pick.

In the end they saved one pony. Of the eight that had started the depôt journey, two were still alive. On 2 March Scott wrote in his diary, 'The events of the past 48 hours bid fair to wreck the expedition, and the only one comfort is the miraculous avoidance of loss of life.'

Back at Hut Point, Cherry and eleven others had to wait for the sea ice to freeze: it was their only route back to the main hut fifteen miles away at Cape Evans. It took a month longer than they had expected, leaving them stranded in the old *Discovery* shelter as autumn slid into winter. It was not a friendly hut. There was no outlet for the blubber stove, so the interior was permanently murky and filled with acrid smoke, and as neither walls nor roof were insulated it was rarely warm. They had exhausted their sledging supplies and were dependent on seals for food, fuel and light, though they had plenty of biscuit (delicious fried in blubber) and a small store of luxuries such as chocolate, lentils and raisins. Improvisation is the key to happiness in any camp, but attempts to manufacture an acetylene gas plant from a case of carbide they dug out resulted in several minor explosions before the project was abandoned. The men were black, and smelt of blubber. When Griff Taylor's Geological Party got in after six weeks exploring the dry valleys in the Western Mountains they failed to recognise their sooty companions. These four new arrivals brought the population of the hut to sixteen.

They went climbing, or crouched in the lee of rocks on top of Observation Hill, sketching the glowing amber landscapes of late autumn. 'We spent . . . our evenings in long discussions which seldom settled anything,' Cherry wrote. Sitting on packing cases, they smoked in the dim glow of candles and the blubber lamp before spreading their reindeer-pelt sleeping bags on the floor. Water dripped on them all night, though after six weeks' hard sledging they were able to sleep for twelve hours at a stretch without any difficulty. 'Perhaps this is not everybody's notion of a good time,' Cherry wrote, 'but it was good enough for us.'

Still dreaming of sea ice and killer whales, a week later, on 16 March, he went out with the last sledging party of the season to boost the depôt at Corner Camp. It was an eight-day trip. The temperature floundered in the minus thirties and forties and the wind shrieked furiously down from the Plateau. Silas wrote:

Supper by candlelight in frozen sweaty gear with hoarfrost down one's neck and over everything. The metal cooker and Primus blistering at every touch. Then a struggle to unroll the frozen bags, change into frozen finnesko [reindeer-skin footwear, with fur on the outside] and wet warm socks . . . With luck you have melted the bag after two hours shivering and then you have all the feelings of a wet bath sponge till joy comes in the morning.

Even then, it took them an hour to put their boots back on.

At Hut Point, anxieties pressed upon Scott. 'Bit by bit I am losing all faith in the dogs,' he noted in his diary. As the days shortened the men lapsed into what Cherry described as 'a very lazy and rather irritating existence waiting for the sea to freeze, which it does about every 24 hours, and then comes the wind and out it goes'. A dubious mass of brownish glue turned up under some snow and was found to be ten-year-old Bovril – a major discovery. They thawed out some old copies of the *Girl's Own Paper*, and a battered edition of Stanley Weyman's *My Lady Rotha*, which they all read, the suspense of the plot permanent since the end was missing. After the last box of lavatory paper had been counted out – twenty-nine sheets were issued to each man – back numbers of the *Contemporary Review* ('contemporary to ten years ago') fulfilled a useful function.

At last, on 11 April nine men, including Scott, left for the hazardous crossing to Cape Evans, leaving Cherry and the others to bring back the dogs and ponies when the sea ice thickened.

The seven grease-covered men left at Hut Point had run out of most things, but they were a happy party. On Easter Sunday Titus Oates made a special tinned haddock breakfast, a biscuit and cheese hoosh for lunch, and a pemmican fry for dinner, using a precious tin of Nestlé's milk for the cocoa and tea. (Titus was full of 'Robinson Crusoe genius', according to Teddy Evans.) It was minus 25 outside. 'Those Hut Point days,' remembered Cherry, 'would prove some of the happiest of my life. Just enough to eat and keep us warm, no more – no frills or trimmings: there is many a worse and more elaborate life . . . the luxuries of civilisation satisfy only those wants which they themselves create.'

When Cherry finally arrived back at Cape Evans he hadn't washed or shaved for twelve weeks and three days. His beard was white and grey. The men from Hut Point were so filthy that their anxious companions at Cape Evans at first thought they were the Norwegians. But what a welcome they had in the warm, dry hut. Light, noise, cutlery, clean faces – they sat next to the huge round stove and worked their way through a feast which included rice pudding, figs and custard and a bucket of cocoa. The primitive hut had been transformed. Telephones connected it with two science shelters and a sophisticated acetylene lighting system had been installed. 'Today has been the greatest fun,' Cherry wrote two days after he got in, 'fitting up my bunk, fitting up shelves, unpacking my Kiplings, and now getting into *The Light that Failed* for the fifth or sixth time.' Cherry identified with many of Kipling's motley cast of heroes, none more closely than Dick Heldar from *The Light that Failed*. He latched on to Heldar's urge to travel to find his vocation (his 'go-fever'), his poor sight and his puzzled consideration of the eternal conflict between art and action. The novel as a whole endorsed the conservative, anti-feminist world-view that Cherry had absorbed throughout his youth, as well as his father's attitudes to Indians, and to foreigners in general. 'The sun rose for the last time after service this morning . . .' Cherry continued in his diary. 'It was a beautiful sight behind the glacier – the ice cliffs quite green, and all round bathed in a rosy glow fading into pure orange ochre.'

A pony and a dog had died while the men were out laying depôts, and round in the stables, Anton, his English unimproved, was hunched over a blubber stove making bran mash. The surviving ponies were horribly thin – 'regular hat racks', according to Deb.

In the brief silver twilight, the Antarctic quivered on the cusp between day and night. Measured in mass and energy, the growth and decay of Antarctic sea ice are the greatest seasonal events on earth. Around the hut, the ice cracked like a whip as the surface cooled and contracted, and a pallid mist stole over the freezing Sound and glazed the bergs, clamped in now for the winter. Finally the opalescent light faded into the chilled blackness of the polar night.

They might not have had light, but with so much sea frozen the men had more solid territory to explore. On clear days, guided by the ghostly outline of Erebus, they roamed the glaciers and islands among which they were marooned and skied under the great dark walls of the ice cliffs. Most had pet projects to occupy the spare winter hours: Cherry was designing and building a stone taxidermy lab. But, again, a note of unease crept into his diary. 'I feel very unsettled coming back to this easy life,' he wrote. He began sleeptalking more frequently. 'Every morning now,' he wrote on 25 April, 'there is a recital of the curious things I have said in my sleep. Last night I gave a speech on the gramophone.'

The sixteen officers and scientists and nine seamen settled into their winter routine. They were called at 8.15. The cook served up fried seal's liver and porridge for breakfast, but as everyone liked porridge there was never enough to go round. If it was fine, in the morning Cherry, Titus and Birdie took the ponies out in the moonlight, its soft beams silvering the crenellated bergs. Sometimes they helped the scientists with their work, or assisted the cook in fetching supplies (on one occasion two men were almost killed by a 500-pound case of hams flying through the air in an eighty-mile-an-hour wind). They returned with ice in their beards to clear the long table of its cargo of books, charts and glass tubes and lay it up for lunch. The meal consisted of bread, butter, jam or cheese (on alternate days), and, twice a week, sardines or lambs' tongues. Tea and cocoa were followed by pipes, and then, unless a blizzard was raging, they went out again, returning for hut work and a spot of pianola before dinner. The evening repast always began with tinned soup, which was followed by seal or penguin (seal's liver curry was popular) and mutton on Sundays, served with tinned vegetables. They drank diluted lime juice – often with a suspicious penguin flavour derived from the ice slopes from which they quarried their water – for its anti-scorbutic properties. Alcohol was served only on birthdays and other special occasions. (A careful record was kept to ensure that each man had only one birthday a year.)

Scott had arranged a winter lecture programme, scheduling three talks a week (everyone except him thought this was too many). Some lectures were gripping, but when Deb spoke on volcanoes several people fell alseep, and after Silas Wright, the physicist, had held forth on 'The Constitution of Matter', he recorded in his diary, 'Wonder if any of them knew what I was talking about.' Ponting had brought his slide collections with him, and his illustrated talks were popular, though Cherry noted sniffily that his lecture on Burma 'showed merely a tourist's knowledge of the country'.

The acetylene was turned off at about half-past ten in the evening, whereupon the hut was dark except for the glow of the galley stove and the silhouette of the nightwatchman preparing his supper by oil lamp. If it was calm outside only snores, the ticks of the instruments or the whine of a dog broke up the silence. But it is rarely calm in an Antarctic winter. More often, the roars and howls of a blizzard shook the hut and hurled pebbles against the wooden walls.

The scientists pressed on during the dark months. Hydrogen-filled balloons attached to fine silk thread floated off, carrying temperature and pressure recorders. Atch, the quiet navy doctor, was doubling up as a parasitologist, and his corner of the hut bristled with culture-ovens, test-tubes and microscopes, the man himself quietly crooning among them. Alongside him Simpson's Corner, the kingdom of meteorologist George Simpson, was crammed with every kind of weather-measuring device from barometers, thermometers and thermographs to an anemometer connected to input tubes on the roof (it was rechristened the Blizzometer). The biologists caught fish in a trap lowered into an ice hole; having been sketched and dissected, the fish were eaten, though without much enthusiasm.

Scott took an interest in every experiment. He had an oddly religious attitude to the work. 'Science –' he wrote in his diary on 9 May, 'the rock foundation of all effort!' He remembered how, a decade earlier, the conflict between science and exploration had almost ended his first expedition before it had begun, and he was determined that neither should be neglected in 1911. From the beginning Scott regularly proclaimed that the aims of the expedition were twofold: to continue the scientific and geographical work begun on his previous expedition, and to plant the Union Jack in the ice at the South Pole. But the twin goals formed an uneasy alliance. When it was all over, Cherry concluded that it had been an error to pursue both.

Scott asked Cherry to edit the expedition newspaper. The tradition of the polar newspaper had been established on Arctic expeditions. It was enthusiastically taken up by the *Discovery* men, and Shackleton had become the first editor of the *South Polar Times*. Desperate to do a good job, Cherry began by nailing a flour box to a wall alongside a notice inviting anonymous contributions for the first edition. While he waited, he read Dickens's *Barnaby Rudge*, wrote a report on the building of snow huts for Scott, and put the roof on his stone taxidermy lab.

The lecture at which nobody slept was Scott's, for he unfolded his plans for the polar journey. Cape Evans to ninety south and back was over 1,700 miles. Scott intended to get to the Polar Plateau by sledging up the 100-mile-long Beardmore Glacier which flowed through a gap in the Transantarctic Mountains and drained into the Ross Ice Shelf. The Beardmore had been discovered by Shackleton during the *Nimrod* expedition, and Scott was relying heavily on his reports. Scott's experience on the depôt journey, when the temperatures on the Barrier had been so low, had convinced him that he should wait until November before starting out for the Pole. It meant that the polar party would not be back until late March, and Scott officially called for volunteers to stay a second year.

Scott's transport arrangements had been the subject of endless debate and speculation in the hut, and now he revealed that he was taking the ponies only to the foot of the Beardmore. As for the dogs: he was sure they would not make it even that far. It was to be manhauling alone for the long, last leg to the Pole – just like the epic British expeditions to the Arctic in which teams of men in leather harnesses had stooped in the slicing wind to drag wooden sledges with names such as *Hotspur* and *Resolute*. Many of Scott's men had absorbed the quaint British romanticisation of manhauling. 'It will be a fine thing,' wrote Birdie, 'to do that plateau with man-haulage in these days of the supposed decadence of the British race.' The idea that decadence might be foiled by good old teeth-gritting and pulling would be farcical, had it not turned out to be tragic.

Dogs had achieved remarkable success in the Arctic, both for indigenous peoples and explorers. Yet Sir Clements Markham was fatally prejudiced against them, preferring the old system, which he seemed to think was more British. Behind his illogical ideas there lay the conviction that mighty Britons had little to learn from foreigners. American explorers were often more willing to adapt: Robert Peary was one of many who had learned vitally useful dog-driving skills from the peoples of Greenland. Scott had absorbed some of Markham's opinions on the questionable value of dogs. In addition, both Shackleton and Scott had been influenced by what they perceived to be the poor performance of dogs on the *Discovery* venture. In fact, dogs had achieved some success on that expedition. Such failures as there were had come about as a result of faulty diet and handling.

Scott had confessed in his diary that he was losing faith in the dogs he had brought down on the *Terra Nova*, but the fact was that he had never had much. The geologist Ray Priestley summed it up like this: 'Scott took the British naval tradition with him to the south, and his own streak of sentiment caused him, combined with some ineptitude in dog management, to return from his first journey still further certain that dogs were of little use.' Cecil Meares, the man in charge of the dogs, thought Scott regularly took poor decisions regarding the animals. It was a crucial failing on Scott's part, horribly apparent from a reading of Amundsen's account of his own expedition to the South Pole, in which the dogs emerge with more distinct personalities than the men. 'If we had a watchword,' Amundsen wrote, 'it was dogs first and dogs all the time.' 'The fact of the matter is,' Deb concluded years later, 'that neither Scott nor Shackleton, the two great exponents of manhauling, understood the management of sledge dogs.'

Scott was a likeable man. Though Cherry came to be critical of some aspects of his leadership, he respected him, and his deep affection for him never really wavered. 'He was eager to accept suggestions if they were workable,' he was to write of Scott in *The Worst Journey*, 'and always keen to sift even the most unlikely theories if by any means they could be shaped to a desired end . . . Essentially an attractive personality, with strong likes and dislikes, he excelled in making his followers his friends by a few words of sympathy or praise: I have never known anybody, man or woman, who could be so attractive when he chose.' When he wrote that Scott was 'a subtle character, full of lights and shades', Cherry could have been describing himself. 'But few who knew him realized how shy and reserved the man was, and it was partly for this reason that he so often laid himself open to misunderstanding.

'Add to this that he was sensitive, femininely sensitive, to a degree which might be considered a fault, and it will be clear that leadership to such a man may be almost a martyrdom.' In the original typescript Cherry wrote, 'nightmare' in place of 'martyrdom'. To lead none the less: Cherry recognised what a triumph it was. 'Temperamentally,' he continued, '[he] was a weak man, and might very easily have been an autocrat. As it was he had moods and depressions which might last for weeks . . . He cried more easily than any man I have ever known.

'What pulled Scott through was character, sheer good grain, which ran over and under and through his weaker self and clamped it together. It would be stupid to say he had all the virtues: he had, for instance, little sense of humour, and he was a bad judge of men.' This was a harsh criticism. Cherry was thinking primarily of Evans, and Scott *had* recognised that Teddy was difficult. He had recorded misgivings about other men in his diary too. Gran was 'a lazy, posing fellow . . . who never does his share of work', and it had been 'a terrible mistake to bring him'; 'Meares hates exercise'; Simpson displayed 'cocksureness'; and poor old Nelson, one of the biologists, was both idle and 'a young man whose habit of life is that of the pot-house politician'.

The first year of the expedition was not the one long idyll that later accounts suggested. Few expeditions ever are. The records were sanitised as a matter of course: Scott's critical remarks were excised from the published version of the diary. Many men never made their views public. Meares told Oates' mother Caroline privately, 'there used to be great trouble and unhappiness. Captain Scott would swear all day at [Teddy] Evans and the others.' Meares said it was shocking, 'and the worst was it was not possible to get away from the rows'. Discontent was focused on Scott. Atch told Caroline Oates, 'Captain Scott would be very rude and not behave well and then be very friendly and try to make it up.' Deb confided to his mother that Scott was 'not in the least popular'. Cherry went on to draw a less hagiographic portrait of Scott in his own account (and he was duly vilified for it in some quarters), but he remained silent on the rows in New Zealand, the undignified bickering and the accusations against Evans. In the context of the pressures and tensions of isolation and danger, and measured against the record of other expeditions, the unpleasantness was not excessive. Some men made no mention of trouble, even in the privacy of their diaries. Simpson, the meteorologist, noted how well everyone got on, all the time. 'He is certainly a great man,' he wrote of Scott, 'and one feels that if his polar venture does not succeed it will be through no want of thought or ability on the part of the leader.' And on the whole, Scott was pleased with his team. Throughout his diary he is lavish in his praise.

At the beginning of May they played the first of many nine-a-side football matches on the ice. Twenty minutes each half was enough in those temperatures. Atch was the best player, and Gran had represented Norway, whereas Anton had never seen a football before and was not sure what side he was on until shortly before the match ended. A few days later an ice hockey match was abandoned when the puck, which they had made from shellac and paraffin wax, shattered as soon as it was struck.

On 12 June Cherry went to Cape Royds for a night with Birdie. A few miles along the coast from Cape Evans, Royds was the site of Shackleton's *Nimrod* hut. On a previous visit, Ponting had unearthed a pile of illustrated newspapers displaying his own work. Leafing through them back at Cape Evans, Cherry's eye was caught by a photograph of the shapely Marie Lohr. He asked Ponting if he could have that page of the newspaper. The delighted Ponting thought his colleague wanted his photograph of the Jungfrau, which was on the other side of Miss Lohr, and generously offered to mount it. 'I got badly ragged in "Virtue Villa" when it was found by Titus that I did not want Ponting's photo,' Cherry recorded in his diary. But Miss Lohr went up on the wall next to his bunk.

Before the dash for the Pole, there was to be another great journey – the most ambitious of all the journeys. The first sledging expedition ever undertaken on the Barrier in the polar darkness, its object was to collect Emperor penguin embryos from the rookery sixty-seven miles away at Cape Crozier. Nobody had ever seen an early Emperor embryo; before Scott's first expedition, the bird had been almost entirely unknown. On that earlier venture Wilson had made two summer visits to Crozier, manhauling across the ice shelf from Hut Point, and once he had camped in the pressure ridges for a month. He had discovered that the Emperor incubates its egg on sea ice in winter – an extraordinary phenomenon of the natural world – and had begun to piece together its life cycle. In his published report he said it was a great disappointment to him that although they had brought back abandoned eggs and young chicks, they had been unable to obtain early embryos. It was obvious that the recovery of embryos would have to involve a winter journey, and he put forward the idea of building a stone igloo near the rookery where he would be able to cut out the embryos before the eggs froze. He knew it would be a tough trip: he had had a horrible time among the Emperors in summer. 'Cape Crozier,' he wrote with foreboding, 'is a focus for wind and storm, where every breath is converted, by the configuration of Mounts Erebus and Terror, into a regular drifting blizzard full of snow.'

He and Scott had none the less been planning this winter trip for more than a year. They knew it was risky, but it offered a tempting zoological prize. 'The possibility that we have in the Emperor penguin,' Wilson had written in his report, 'the nearest approach to a primitive form not only of a penguin, but of a bird, makes the future working out of its embryology a matter of the greatest possible importance.'

Wilson thought the study of the Emperor embryo would shed light on the history of its ancestors. He had been deeply influenced by the work of the German biologist and philosopher Ernst Haeckel, an enthusiastic early Darwinist. In 1866 Haeckel had published his 'biogenetic' law, more often stated as 'ontogeny recapitulates phylogeny'. Haeckel proposed that the embryonic stages (ontogeny) of each animal sequentially repeat the evolutionary history (phylogeny) of its type. According to Haeckel, the gill slits of the early human embryo repeat our ancient past as fish. As the Emperor penguin was at that time thought to be the most primitive bird, the logical conclusion was that a study of its embryology would reveal the origin of birds and their relationship to other vertebrates. What a tool ontogeny-recapitulating-phylogeny would have been to evolutionists if it had worked! The hypothesis was discredited around the time the *Terra Nova* sailed, but it persisted in popular culture. As for the idea that Emperors, and penguins in general, were the most primitive birds, ornithologists and palaeontologists now tend to agree that flightless birds evolved from birds with flight, rather than the other way round.

Wilson had asked Cherry and Birdie to go with him on the winter journey (he told his wife they were the two he liked most, besides the fact that they were the best sledgers). The three of them had already spent weeks preparing equipment. Each was taking different rations with a view to determining the most effective combination of fats and carbohydrates. Cherry's stone hut building had been useful practice – they were going to build an igloo at Crozier as Wilson had suggested seven years previously. But Cherry was quite unprepared, mentally and physically, for the horrors that lay ahead. On 19 June he wrote in his diary that he had got 'a bad needle about the Cape Crozier journey: I think it may be awful work'. That day the temperature crashed to minus 33 again, and when Silas went out in his pyjamas first thing to take a reading, as was his custom, his nose was frostbitten in under two minutes. (The cooling effect of the wind meant that the temperature on his skin would have been even colder – a phenomenon that had not yet been named the wind-chill factor.) On 21 June, the day before the expedition's midwinter celebration, Cherry wrote, 'a good bust out will I think do a lot to buck up people all round. There is no doubt that most men are, naturally, feeling this long night a bit, and some I think a good deal, especially the last two or three days. I feel very chippy some days myself, but very seldom.'

Midwinter Day, an important psychological turning-point in the Antarctic, did turn out to be a 'good bust out'. Cherry presented the *South Polar Times* to Scott with everyone gathered round him at the head of the table. It ran to more than fifty pages, and included prints by Ponting and watercolours by Wilson as well as a strong selection of poetry and prose, and lots of jokes. Bernard Day, the motor engineer, had made a binding from grey sealskin and plywood, and carved a monogram on the cover. Scott proceeded to read most of it out loud, interrupted by uproarious laughter and indignant barracking. Much of the material was in praise of sledging:

> O Blubber Lamp! O Blubber Lamp!
> I wish that I could tell,
> The glamour of thy smoky-gleam,
> The savour of thy smell.

'The funniest part now,' Cherry wrote, light-headed with relief, 'is to see everybody going round and spotting who wrote the different things. They are quite wrong, and quite certain they are right.' At dinner he sat next to Scott, who got a bit drunk, and 'it was very funny to see him blossom out'. A Rabelaisian meal was followed by the entry of a flaming Christmas tree and speeches all round; but when it came to Cherry's turn he said that he thought everything to be said had been said. He wasn't the speech-making kind. And he had a winter journey on his mind.

6

Even with God

ilson reckoned that Emperors laid their eggs towards the end of June. In order to collect embryos at the optimum stage of incubation, three men set out on the twenty-seventh of that month 'on the weirdest bird's-nesting expedition that has ever been or will be'. Ponting got out his magnesium flash powder and photographed them in harness on the glassy ice in front of the hut. They were hauling over 750 pounds – six weeks' food and fuel, pickling equipment and camping gear – on two nine-foot sledges, one sledge toggled on behind the other. They were not taking dogs, preferring to pull their own sledges the sixty-seven miles each way. At the last minute they even decided to leave their skis behind. Cherry was frightened; he admitted it later.

'This winter travel,' Scott wrote in the hut that night, 'is a new and bold venture, but the right men have gone to attempt it.' In fact, he had his doubts about the wisdom of such a dangerous journey, and had allowed Wilson to talk him into it. Scott was susceptible to the temptations of scientific discovery, and the Darwinian prize dangling in front of him was irresistible: Darwin had been keenly debated, even by non-scientists, for as long as Scott could remember. During the long sledging journey towards the Pole on the *Discovery* expedition Scott, Shackleton and Wilson had taken it in turns to read aloud from *On the Origin of Species* while swaddled in their three-man sleeping bag. But even Wilson acknowledged that at Crozier they were in for 'a regular snorter'.

On the second day, hauling the sledges up onto the Barrier, Cherry got all his fingers frostbitten, leaving blisters an inch long. 'I was a fool,' he wrote, 'to take my hands out of my mitts to haul on the ropes.' That evening the temperature fell to minus 47. When they started marching, the Barrier surfaces were as soft and powdery as arrowroot. Fifteen seconds after stepping outside the tent, their clothes froze into iron armour, and they couldn't move from the waist up until the garments thawed again at the next meal. Even their heads were frozen in position, and they quickly learned that they had to start pulling with their necks bent low. Their sweat froze and accumulated in the layers of their clothes. Cherry's glasses iced up and had to be abandoned ('must be sure not to let any inability arising from this get on my nerves,' he resolved). Everything was harder in the dark. Cooking was so difficult that they took turns day by day instead of following their usual weekly roster. The butter (all they had was biscuit, butter and pemmican) shattered like glass when they put a knife to it. On 30 June Cherry wrote in his diary, 'It does not look as if we [can] pull this off.' They had a record low of minus 66, and in his sleeping bag Cherry shivered until his back seemed to break: 'They talk of chattering teeth: but when your body chatters you may call yourself cold.'* The hours spent in the sleeping bags were torture, as the sweat melted from their clothes and into the bags, where it froze into steely sheets. At one stage they got frostbitten even while they lay inside. In the morning it took four or five hours to strike camp and get into harness, two men forcing each frozen strait-jacket into shape to get the other man in it. When they entered a bay protected from the high wind, the surface of the snow was not swept and hardened as it was elsewhere. Instead it was 'a mass of the hardest and smallest snow crystals to pull through which in cold temperatures was just like pulling through sand'. Soon it became so bad that they couldn't pull

---

* The reader may wonder if minus 60 feels any colder than minus 40. My own experience has taught me that it does. Before I went to the Antarctic I glibly assumed that once I had got used to low temperatures it wouldn't matter terribly if they were in the minus twenties or thirties or forties. I soon learned otherwise. At minus 15 I was able to spend a few minutes repositioning the wire of a radio antenna without gloves. At minus 30 this was a perilous venture: I could manage less than half a minute gloveless before my fingers turned into wooden chipolatas. At minus 45 I could not take any outer gloves off, let alone the polypropylene liners. My lungs hurt when I inhaled such bitter air, my balaclava froze hard to my mouth and I had to massage my nose to prevent the moisture in my nostrils freezing. (Once I threw a mug of boiling tea in the air at around minus 46 and the liquid froze before it hit the ice.) A few degrees made a huge difference to my ability to function, and, as a result, after a few months in the Antarctic I was able to judge the temperature fairly accurately just by standing still.

All this, of course, is without wind. A 25-mile-an-hour wind turns a modest ambient temperature of minus 20 into a brutal minus 74 that would freeze exposed flesh in seconds. I once experienced minus 115 with wind-chill at a camp I had at Cape Evans. That day my companion and I had to stay outside for some time anchoring our hut to ensure that it did not go careering off across McMurdo Sound. I can't recommend it.

both sledges and had to begin the hell of relay, taking one sledge at a time and going back for the other. This meant that they were travelling three miles for every mile of progress. They could not read the compass in the dark, and regularly struck three or four boxes of matches before one would light. 'Generally we steered by Jupiter,' Cherry wrote later, 'and I never see him now without recalling his friendship in those days.'

The second of July was 'a terrible day. I felt absolutely done up at lunch.' Cherry's blisters were worse, and they froze, and his big toes were frostbitten; at the end of each day's march he could feel that his heart was beating very slowly. Sometimes, he wrote, 'it was difficult not to howl'. Instead he invented a formula which he repeated like a mantra: 'You've got it in the neck, stick it, stick it.' On 5 July soft new snow made the surface almost impossible, and they managed only a funereal one-and-a-half miles, recording a noon temperature of minus 76. 'The day lives in my memory as that on which I found out that records are not worth making,' he wrote. Bill kept apologising, and saying he had never dreamt it would be so bad.

Besides the trials of winter sledging, Bill had to bear the responsibility of leadership. The wellbeing of his two companions was always on his mind: he asked them how they were at regular intervals, and undertook whatever small task he could to alleviate their miseries. As a doctor, he felt he should be the most vigilant when it came to frostbite. He wrote in his diary:

> I had to keep a very watchful eye on three pairs of feet and continually when one asked if they were cold, it was only to be told that they had been cold, but the owner didn't think they were frozen as they were most comfortable. I had to judge then whether they were really warmer or actually frozen, and sometimes it was exceedingly difficult to tell what was happening even with one's own feet.

Besides his concern for the safety of Cherry and Birdie, Wilson was determined not to let Scott down. 'Bill had a tremendous respect for Scott,' Cherry wrote. Even when things were at their most desperate on the winter journey, Bill was anxious not to forget equipment which Scott might need for the forthcoming season. 'Scott will never forgive me if I leave gear behind,' he said. Cherry noted that while thorough attention to equipment was an important aspect of sledging, 'it is a principle which can be carried to excess'.

On the depôt journey, Cherry wrote to his mother later, 'the temperature was down to minus 43, and we thought ourselves fine fellows: now . . . we know that we were quite warm'. They began to think of the minus fifties as a rare luxury. Day-dreaming was one of the pleasures of summer sledging: Cherry liked to think about the hot chocolate sauce that was served at Claridge's, or a pretty girl ('or girls'). But there were no wistful imaginings while marching on a winter journey. His mind shut down to everything but the torments of the moment.

It took him forty-five minutes to chip his way into his sleeping bag each night, as during the day it froze flat like a slab of tombstone granite. The bag was too big for him, which was a serious problem: it meant that once he was in he couldn't get the air inside warm. He had a bout of heartburn. But on 7 July he had a better night and was able to write, 'There is something after all rather good in doing something never done before.' The aurora was always ahead of them as they travelled east, the sky draped with swaying curtains of electric green, orange and pink as soft topaz searchlights criss-crossed the dark sky. On one occasion the three of them lay on their backs in the snow to look at these mysterious southern lights. But without his glasses Cherry was too near-sighted to see anything but a luminous blur.

On 9 July the temperature rose to a tropical minus 36 and they were able to pull both sledges at the same time. They were now marching constantly among crevasses, disastrously handicapped by their frozen rigidity. 'If we had been dressed in lead,' Cherry thought, 'we should have been able to move our arms and necks and heads more easily than we could now.' They were in the lee of Mount Terror, Erebus's extinct twin, and in the tumultuous pressure ridges folded tightly at its feet a three-day blizzard pinned them down, sodden and steamy. They were very worried about their oil supply. They were burning more than planned.

On 14 July they found themselves under a mountain of black pressure ridges. All three men fell and swung on the lip of apparently bottomless crevasses. 'My nerves,' acknowledged Cherry, 'were about on edge at the end of the day.' And who can wonder.

It took nineteen days to get to Cape Crozier. 'I for one,' Cherry recorded, 'had come to that point of suffering at which I did not really care if only I could die without much pain. They talk of the heroism of the dying – they little know – it would be so easy to die, a dose of morphia, a friendly crevasse, and blissful sleep. The trouble is to go on . . .'

It was too difficult to talk much. One discussion about what constituted a cold snap lasted a week, with two or three comments added each day. 'Do things slowly,' wrote Cherry, 'always slowly. That was the burden of Wilson's leadership.' He described Bill as 'Always patient, self-possessed, unruffled, he was the only man on earth who could have led this journey.'

'I think we are all right,' Bill would say, 'as long as our appetites are good.' Yet Cherry admitted later that there was nothing he had wanted to do more than turn back. 'I was quite sure that to dream of Cape Crozier was the wildest lunacy.'

On 15 July they arrived at the knoll on the slopes of Mount Terror where 800-foot cliffs to seaward formed Cape Crozier. This windy place was to be their base for the egg-collecting. They had arrived, at least, and it perked them up. 'It is wonderful how our cares have vanished,' Cherry wrote. They pitched camp and climbed higher to build the stone igloo in which they planned to pickle their little Emperors. About seven feet in diameter, the igloo was roofed with canvas and banked with rocks and snow; they said they must be living in a transitional period between the glacial and the palaeolithic ages. In the moonlight they could see a great field of pressure ridges like giant furrows running right up to the Barrier edge, and beyond it the frozen Ross Sea, sheathed in ivory frost smoke. It is a hostile enough spot, even in summer.*

Once they reached the Cape, Cherry stopped writing his journal: if he breathed near a sheet of paper it was instantly covered with a film of ice through which the pencil wouldn't bite.

It took three days to finish the igloo; then they had to find their way to the penguin rookery. Wilson, who had made the trip in daylight, led the way close under the cliffs, often on his hands and knees. Without landmarks they lost their way in the morass of ridges, chaotic ice blocks and mazy crevasses bridged with snowdrift. Despite hugging the cliffs they blundered into deep holes. Cherry couldn't see the cracks even when the other two pointed them out, and he fell down constantly. He loathed crevasses in daylight, but now he realised that the weeks he had spent negotiating them in summer 'were a Sunday School treat compared to our days of blind-man's buff . . . among the crevasses of Cape Crozier'.

Then they heard the metallic cries of the Emperors.

Late in the afternoon they reached an impasse and were forced, reluctantly, to turn round and return to the knoll. The next day, climbing in the short period of dim midday twilight, they roped together and found a better route, cutting steps in the ice with their axes and using their sledge as a

---

* I was there in February. Flying low over the icefields round Mount Terror, the Texan helicopter pilot pointed down at the gnarled pressure ridges. 'See those?' he said over the headset. 'You could drive a truck through them.' As for the igloo, a ring of stones about ten inches high had survived. When we landed next to it, the heavy VXE-6 helicopter swung in the wind like a rocking chair.

bridge over soft crevasse lids. Two miles down they reached the cliffs leading to the rookery and glimpsed a hundred birds huddled on the sea ice, trumpeting and shuffling – and with eggs on their toes.

'After indescribable effort and hardship,' Cherry wrote, 'we were witnessing a marvel of the natural world, and we were the first and only men who had ever done so; we had within our grasp material which might prove of the utmost importance to science; we were turning theories into facts with every observation we made – and we had but a moment to give.'

Alone of all creatures, Emperors incubate and hatch their young in the polar winter. In May the female lays a single egg which she passes almost immediately to her mate on the ice before heading out to sea to feed. The male incubates the egg in a brood pouch above his toes for over two months, in darkness, without food or drink, in temperatures of minus forty and fifty and sixty. To conserve body heat he huddles together with the other males from his rookery, each bird taking a turn on the windward edge. The tightly packed group does not move more than a few feet during this two-month incubation period. The fattened female returns a day or two before the chick hatches in mid July. But Wilson didn't know any of that.

The men were not elated: they were too anxious about the imminence of total darkness and the ominous wind from the south. They were still not at sea level. Initially foiled by walls of ice, Wilson eventually found a hole like a fox's burrow. They wriggled through and found themselves on the rim of a dwarf ice cliff. One of them had to stay up there, to haul the others back. Cherry was the obvious candidate: his short sight made him the least able. As he waited, ice axe fixed in a crevasse, Bill and Birdie got to the rookery, collected five eggs and killed three birds to flense for the blubber stove. Then they were hoisted back up the cliff.

As they struggled back to the igloo, the thin light drained beyond the horizon. On the steep slopes, Cherry couldn't even see the footholds they had cut with their axes on the way down. He had to kick indiscriminately to get a toe-hold. Bill said, 'Cherry, you *must* learn how to use an ice axe.' Birdie was proving the most physically robust, Cherry the least. He fell and fell in his blindness, breaking both the precious eggs he was carrying; the grease did his gloves good, he noticed later. It was beginning to blow hard, and they almost missed the igloo. Sleepless, icy and dog-tired in the dark and the wind and the drift, 'we were already beginning to think of death as a friend'.

They moved into the igloo for the first time as a blizzard set in, and pitched their tent outside the entrance. During dinner, a blob of boiling blubber flew into Wilson's eye, injuring it so badly that he thought he was going to lose it, though he didn't tell the others that.

They had only one tin of oil left. Then, some time in the early hours of 22 July, the tent blew away.

It had taken them almost three weeks to get to Crozier. Could they possibly get back without a tent?

The igloo, sucking in drift like a vacuum, was close to collapse, and everything inside was under six inches of snow. The men shouted at each other over the roar of the blizzard. In his book Cherry talks about his lack of hope and impious attitude; in his diary, written up back at the hut, he recorded, 'I said my prayers and waited.' The day after the tent went, the canvas roof and door of the igloo were whipped away in strips, the blocks that had secured them crashing all around. The men retreated into the sleeping bags as if to their graves. For forty-eight hours they lay in the open igloo in darkness, without food or drink, mummified in snow. Birdie and Bill sang hymns, and when he caught snatches of a tune, Cherry joined in. The remaining ribbons of canvas cracked like a continual firing squad (at the hut sixty-seven miles away the anemometer was recording windspeeds of over seventy-five miles an hour). Bill prayed hard. The second day was his birthday, and Birdie thumped him at intervals to see if he was still alive.

Has any man or woman ever come closer to the limits of endurance? I doubt it. Cherry freely admitted that he had no hope of survival. 'I might have speculated on my chances of going to Heaven,' he recalled, 'but candidly I did not care.' Confronting death, he thought about his life, and regretted the parts he had wasted. 'The road to Hell might be paved with good intentions: the road to Heaven is paved with lost opportunities. I wanted those years over again. What fun I would have had with them: what glorious fun! . . . and I wanted peaches and syrup – badly.' He resolved to get some morphine from the medical case if things got unbearable. 'Yes, comfortable warm reader,' he wrote. 'Men do not fear death, they fear the pain of dying.'

After two days and two nights without a meal they struggled to prepare tea and pemmican, rising from their snow coffins to sit up in their bags and pull the floor cloth over their heads to protect the thin Primus pyre. By then, the blubber stove had given up. The tea was choked with reindeer hair from the bags as well as penguin feathers, dirt and debris, but how delicious it was. The blubber left in the pot meant it had a burnt taste, and for the rest of his life singed food gave Cherry a Proustian rush.

In a lull in the blizzard they went out, and Birdie found the tent on a lower slope. It was like an Old Testament miracle. The tent had gone up poles and all like a shut umbrella, and was perfectly usable. 'Our lives had been taken away and given back to us,' Cherry wrote. 'We were so thankful, we said nothing.'

Bill wasn't prepared to risk further delay in those murderous temperatures with so little oil. There was no question now of pickling the booty before they got back to the hut – if they ever did. So they turned for home, Cherry feeling 'as if I should crack'. They were all weak. Yet Birdie had not even used the down bag each had brought as a reserve lining for the reindeer-pelt sleeping bags. He had offered his to Cherry on the way out to Crozier, and Cherry had refused. Now, getting closer to collapse every day, he accepted. 'I felt a brute to take it,' Cherry wrote, 'but I was feeling useless unless I got some sleep.'

Birdie's stamina and his ability to withstand the cold had already become legendary on the expedition. His tough, strong limbs never tired, and he found a way round every difficulty. Before setting out on the winter journey he had constructed a special hat with extensions to protect his long nose from frostbite. He looked out for the hardest jobs – he had been the one to lug the biggest stones to the igloo – and he took responsibility for the meteorological instruments. Throughout the Crozier trip he kept an excellent weather log ('a masterpiece', according to the official meteorologist), despite the fact that touching metal with naked fingers for even a fraction of a second led to frostbite. 'He was up and out of his bag continually,' Cherry wrote in his description of the blizzard on the knoll, 'stopping up holes, pressing against bits of roof to try and prevent the flapping and so forth. He was magnificent.'

Before leaving Cape Evans Birdie had secretly stowed two tins of sweets on one of the sledges as a surprise for the others, one to celebrate their arrival at the knoll, and the other for Bill's birthday. When things were at their gravest, he was able to infect the others with his positive outlook. After the tent blew away and they were lying like mummies he lent out of his bag and yelled, 'We're all right', and they shouted back that they agreed. 'Despite the fact that we knew we only said so because we were all wrong,' wrote Cherry, 'this statement was helpful.'

Birdie always wanted to go on. After they had recovered the tent, he wrote in his diary, 'I think he [Wilson] thought he had landed us in a bad corner and was determined to go straight home, though I was for one other tap at the rookery.' But he had voluntarily placed himself under Bill's orders for the trip, and did not demur when Bill decided on retreat.

The temperature hovered at the colder end of the minus forties and they stepped into thinly crusted crevasses. Birdie tied himself to the tent at night as human ballast to stop it from taking off again. They struggled onto the windless bight of the Barrier with its ghostly fogs and mists, guided when they were lucky by vague silhouetted shapes which might be yards or miles away. Most of Cherry's teeth split from the cold. He slept on his feet, and woke when he bumped into Birdie. 'The day's march was bliss compared to the night's rest,' he wrote, 'and both were awful.' You've got it in the neck, stick it, stick it.

Towards the end of July they had some light. Six days marching ahead if they were lucky; five days, four—

'Antarctic exploration is seldom as bad as you imagine, seldom as bad as it sounds,' Cherry wrote later. 'But this journey had beggared our language: no words could express its horror.' It was the other two who made it bearable. Sledging, Cherry said, was by far the greatest test of character. The winter journey was sledging at its hardest, yet 'I saw self-sacrifice standing every test'. Over and over again he was to talk about his companions' selflessness; it was a quality he prized above almost every other. 'In civilization,' he wrote in *The Worst Journey*, 'men are taken at their own valuation because there are so many ways of concealment, and there is so little time, perhaps even so little understanding. Not so down South. These two men ... were gold, pure, shining, unalloyed. Words cannot express how good their companionship was.' Even a winter journey had not shaken Wilson's still centre. His strongest language had been, 'I think we reached bedrock last night.' Wilson saw God's purpose in his suffering, and was able, as a result, to bear all hardship with grace and dignity. As always, he sought to sublimate the self. After they had got back to the hut, he wrote a report of the journey for Scott. The episode when the boiling oil flew into his eye was summarily dismissed with the words, 'I was incapacitated for the time being.' To Cherry, Bill was a light in the darkness.

As for Birdie, Cherry described him as one of the two or three greatest friends of his life. Birdie simply refused to admit difficulties; according to Cherry he had 'few doubts and no fears'. How attractive that was to a young man wreathed in anxiety. 'He made life look simple,' Cherry wrote. 'Perhaps it really is.'

They arrived at the Cape Evans hut in the evening of 1 August, thirty-five days after setting out. As they approached, Bill said, 'Spread out well and they will be able to see that there are three men.' But nobody saw them until they were at the door. They struggled out of their harnesses before it opened, and a voice said, 'By Jove! Here is the Crozier Party.'

Then there was pandemonium.

They were seized by pyjama-clad figures trying to prise off their armour, until finally the clothes had to be cut off their bodies (someone suggested a can-opener). The next morning Cherry's sodden pile weighed twenty-four pounds. He looked about thirty years older than he had when he had set off, his cadaverous face scarred and corrugated, nose dark, eyes dull and hands white and wrinkled with damp. Griff wrote in his diary, 'Cherry staggered in looking like nothing human. He had on a big noseguard covering all but his eyes, and huge icicles and frost stuck out like duck's bills from his lips.' Ponting said he had seen the same look on some half-starved Russian prisoners' faces at Mukden. The three men sat at the table behind slabs of bread and tin jugs of cocoa, choking with unaccountable laughter at George Robey on the gramophone. Scott said, 'You know, this is the hardest journey ever made.' Then they slipped into warm bags. 'I managed to keep awake long enough,' Cherry remembered, 'to think that paradise must feel something like this.'

'We slept ten thousand thousand years,' he wrote. Then they got up for a haircut, bath and shave. Their extremities swelled and came out in rashes, some of Cherry's toenails were falling off and his fingers were useless. 'We are looked upon as beings who have come back from another world,' he noted. Two hours after each meal he wanted to eat another one; and in between he raided his mother's supply of Turkish delight. Astonishingly, he had lost only one pound in weight (the other two had lost three-and-a-half pounds each). In his diary, Scott wrote:

> The result of this effort is the appeal it makes to our imagination as one of the most gallant stories in polar history. That men should wander forth in the depth of a polar night to face the most dismal cold and the fiercest gales in darkness is something new; that they should have persisted in this effort in spite of every adversity for five full weeks is heroic. It makes a tale for our generation which I hope may not be lost in the telling.

Had Scott been right at the outset? Had 'the right men' attempted the winter journey? 'I don't know,' Cherry wrote years later. He had no doubts about Birdie and Bill; but himself – he always had doubts about himself. 'Probably Lashly [leading stoker William Lashly] would have made the best third, but Bill had a prejudice against seamen for a journey like this.' Wilson told Scott that although Cherry had suffered the most, 'his spirit never wavered for a moment', and in his official report to Scott he wrote that it would be impossible to say too much of Cherry as a sledging companion. So perhaps Scott had been right.

How much did they really achieve? Wilson had intended to camp at Crozier and examine the birds for some time; in the event he only made it down to the rookery once. When he examined the three eggs that he had collected, the embryos turned out to be older than he expected. He was disappointed. 'Wilson,' Gran recorded, 'considers the journey to have been fruitless as regards study of the penguin.' Bill's report concluded, 'We had attempted too difficult an undertaking without light in the winter.' More seriously, the reserves of three key sledgers had been depleted before the trek to the Pole had even begun. To Amundsen, such a journey would have been unthinkable.

Nobody ever learned much from the three eggs, which were too far developed to test Haeckel's theory, or from the experiments with rations and sledging gear. But Cherry brought something back from Cape Crozier that was infinitely more precious than a penguin's egg. He had to find redemption in the journey, or it would all have been a colossal waste of time; later, after his two companions died, that thought became unbearable. His reward for the worst journey was an affirmation of the value of dignity and the abnegation of the self. There were no promises attached to the trek – the effort brought its own rewards. What mattered was 'the response of the spirit', and it is the same whatever your personal Crozier. 'I'll swear there was still a grace about us when we staggered in,' Cherry wrote. 'And we kept our tempers – even with God.'

The hut had been so quiet while they were away that according to Gran's diary a change of underwear constituted 'a very eventful day'. They were rubbing along all right, given the psychological demands of a polar winter. On 18 July Deb wrote, 'Tempers are beginning to get just a little shaky in one or two cases but produce nothing worse than sarcasm and we still keep up the *Terra Nova*'s reputation as a happy ship.'* It wasn't bad going. The next winter they would look back on it as a picnic.

Everyone was talking about the great trek to the Pole, and the long table was piled with rations queuing up to be weighed and bagged in readiness

---

* He stuck to his judgement, with one caveat: Scott. 'The marvellous part of it is,' Deb wrote, 'that the Owner is the single exception to a general sense of comradeship and jollity amongst all of us.'

for the journey. Sixteen men were to set out in stages: four with the motors, ten with ponies and two with dogs. Various parties would be sent back as the march progressed, leaving four men to make a final slog to ninety south. Cherry knew he was going, but not how far. He was prickling with apprehension. The Crozier trip had taxed his strength, and he took longer to recover than the other two. The toll was mental as well as physical. 'As I get more and more fit,' he wrote on 10 August, 'I find I get times when I get a bit "down" . . . Once I got very down about the Southern Journey – feeling that the whole journey was an impossibility.' Yet he was immersed in preparations. At Scott's request he was typing out data from Shackleton's book, panic rising in his throat as his fingers hit the keys:

> Ever since we came back from Cape Crozier I seem to, in an undefined way, be given a kind of reputation for sledging which I am sure I do not deserve. I would much rather this did not happen: the possibility of breaking down on the Glacier, or Plateau if I get there, is bad enough when you know that nothing much is expected of you: to start with a reputation, however small, to live up to, would be worse.

The next day the clouds dissolved from the smoking peak of Erebus and 'that really horrible feeling of depression has gone with the blizzard'. When the sun peeped above the sea north of the hut on 21 August, it lifted everyone's spirits with it. Shouting and singing out on the rubbly sea ice around the polished bergs, Ponting wrote, 'We felt like boys again, and acted, too, like boys.' In the hut, Atch gave a lecture on scurvy. Scott had seen scurvy on his first polar expedition. 'It seems very far away from us this time,' he wrote in his diary. But it wasn't.

Cherry was mostly concerned with the ponies and the *South Polar Times*. He grew tired of the newspaper, but when the second issue came out, it was judged better than the first ('Poor Cherry perspired over the editorial,' wrote Scott). As for the ponies, Scott let him choose his own animal for the polar journey. In the end Cherry picked Michael, spending hours exercising him or quizzing Oates about horse management in the stables. One day, as they sat on opposite sides of the smelly blubber stove making a bran mash for a sick pony, Titus suddenly looked over at Cherry through the blue smoke and said, 'It's you or me for the Pole.' He had guessed – correctly, as it turned out – the way Scott's mind was working.

Cherry admired Oates, 'the cheerful and lovable old pessimist', and they had much in common. The only independently wealthy gentlemen on the expedition, both were quasi-feudal lords of the manor and both had been despatched to public school as a matter of course. Titus had not cared for school; he was not the first young man to emerge from Eton signally lacking in mathematical and grammatical ability. ('I intended Oates to superintend the forage arrangements,' Scott recorded, 'but arrays of figures however simply expressed are too much for him.') As a captain in the 6th Inniskilling Dragoons he had served with distinction in South Africa, where he had been badly wounded in the thigh fighting the Boers, and after recovering he had completed tours of duty in Ireland, Egypt and India. He was tall and dignified, with a military bearing, and besides being taciturn he was slow of speech when he did eventually come out with something. At Cape Evans he spent most of his time in the frigid stables. The only picture above his bunk was a portrait of Napoleon, and the only book he read was Napier's *History of the War in the Peninsula*. Yet he emerges as a likeable character (perhaps because he says so little); one of the most likeable. He and Cherry were the leading upper-deck Conservatives, locked in perpetual warfare against the Liberal faction. Both had absorbed the jingoistic prejudices of Englishmen of their class, and both were deeply suspicious of all foreigners. Despite that, Titus took the most sanguine view of Amundsen's change of plan. 'I personally,' he wrote, 'don't see it is underhand to keep your mouth shut.' Temperamentally, Cherry and Titus were profoundly different. Titus was the archetypal man of action, his vision directed ceaselessly outwards. Cherry was a man of attenuated sensibility, whereas Titus was rough and ready.

Wilson was concerned, as the southern journey approached, that Scott was venting his frustration at the 'great string of rotten unsound ponies' on Oates, who was entirely blameless as he had not picked them: it was he who had kept them alive, smuggling extra forage on board at Christchurch at his own expense and toiling in the frosted stables day and night. 'He is spoken to,' Wilson wrote, 'rather as though he was to blame whenever anything goes wrong with them, and of course he doesn't like it.'

Indeed he did not. 'I dislike Scott intensely,' Oates wrote to his mother, 'and would chuck the thing if it was not that we are a British expedition and must beat these Norwegians.'

As for Cherry, still the old worries persisted. After his night watch on 23 September he felt 'more than extra mouldy'. He was making his way through the row of Kiplings he had brought, and wondering whether he wanted to stay another year. Much depended on the news from Lamer when the ship arrived in January – if indeed she did come in January. He wrote his mother a 29-page summary of events so far, telling her that he weighed a stone more than he had when he left home and including a detailed bulletin of his day-to-day activities, with scale maps of his sledging journeys. He told her not to take much notice of Shackleton's hair-raising account of his perilous summit journey – published to general acclaim in 1909 and still selling well – as it was written '*to appeal to the public*', and that really there was very little danger. This latter was entirely untrue, but how many of us have not glossed the truth to purchase maternal calm?

Daylight rushed over the continent like a spring tide, and all over the frozen sea swollen female Weddells gnawed open holes and flopped onto the ice to pup. When the little seals appeared they gained five pounds a day; to the men it was like watching dough rise. Sledging parties set off to dig out the depôts laid the preceding autumn, and in the middle of September Scott went on a trip to the west for a fortnight. Nobody was sure why he had gone; they surmised that he wanted some sledging practice. Soon after he returned Cherry perceived that the Owner had become 'worried and unhappy'. He had reason to worry. Several men were incapacitated by injuries, two of the ponies were in poor condition, a dog died, and days before departure the aluminium axle casing on one of the motors split. Scott would have been much gloomier had he known that on 20 October Amundsen was to start for the Pole with fifty-two dogs.

Since learning the explosive news that Amundsen was based not over a thousand miles away on the other side of the continent but just along the Barrier, sixty miles closer to the Pole, Scott's men had often speculated about the Norwegians' intentions. Their proximity had inevitably fuelled the sense of competition that lurked in all minds. The general feeling was that Amundsen had chosen a risky spot for his base, and might have already been thwarted by the instability of the Barrier ice. But everyone knew, whether they admitted it or not, that if Amundsen had come through the winter, his skill at handling his dogs meant that he would be travelling towards the Pole faster than Scott.

A third edition of the *South Polar Times* appeared on 15 October, this time including a 'Ladies' Letter' featuring polar fashion advice by 'Jessamine' (Deb). But Cherry was in a pickle. Back in June Scott had prepared notes for the officers and scientists taking part in the journey to the Pole. Each man, Scott decreed, should have a rudimentary knowledge of navigation so that in an emergency he could steer a sledge home. He should also be able to take observations with a theodolite, work out the altitude of the meridian and much else. The non-scientists threw themselves into the task of acquiring these skills, none more assiduously than Cherry. But now he went to Scott with a pale face: he was ashamed to tell him, he said, that he couldn't be counted on as a navigator. At first, Scott didn't know what he was talking about. Then it emerged that Cherry had determined to master the most abstruse navigational problems, and after hours tussling with log tables and compasses despaired of ever being able to do it. Scott confided in a letter to Reggie that there wasn't one chance in a hundred that Cherry would have to navigate, and that if that one chance came off he would need only the simplest skills; but Scott was pleased to have chosen a man who took his work so seriously. Cherry's powers of concentration and application seemed to work on just two settings: on and off. There was no 'moderate'. And as for that one chance in a hundred . . .

The motor party was the first to start on the long-awaited southern journey, lurching off in chilly sunshine on 24 October. The two surviving machines were hitched to sledges of food and fodder which they were to leave on the Barrier. Four men accompanied them: steward F. J. Hooper and Teddy Evans steered the crawling juggernauts, while engineer Bernard Day and leading stoker William Lashly kept the engines running. Or rather, they didn't. The combination of primitive air-cooled motors, inadequate caterpillar tracks and slippery surfaces conspired against the little team, and by the end of the first week, both machines had broken down. The men had to haul the loads themselves. 'I can't say I am sorry because I am not,' Lashly noted when the second motor broke; coaxing the beasts to life each morning had been agony. On 9 November the four men reached one degree south of One Ton Depôt and waited for the others.

The pony party, comprising ten men and ten animals, left on 1 November. They were divided into three groups, Cherry and his pony Michael marching with Scott and Wilson and their beasts. But the teams were soon miles apart, as the ponies were so erratic. 'It reminded me,' wrote Scott, 'of a regatta or a somewhat disorganised fleet with ships of very unequal speed.' On the way to One Ton, this straggling caravan passed the abandoned motors. It was a blow to Scott. Even though he had suspected the motors would let him down, and had planned accordingly, he had badly wanted to prove that they could be useful in the Antarctic. 'At the back of his mind,' Cherry wrote, 'I feel sure, was the wish to abolish the cruelty which the use of ponies and dogs necessarily entails.'

They marched at night, so the ponies could rest in the warmer day. It was hard work; but not for a man who had been to Cape Crozier in midwinter. 'My personal impression of this early summer sledging on the Barrier,' Cherry wrote, 'was one of constant wonder at its comfort. One had forgotten that a tent could be warm and a sleeping-bag dry.' He slept deeply and well after those long days on the march, lulled into his dreams by the sound of the ponies tethered outside, munching their supper in the sun. But the weather turned ('it was about as poisonous as one could wish') and Scott became anxious and gloomy. It took 15 days for the pony party to reach One Ton, 150 miles from Hut Point. Once there, 'a prolonged Council of War' was held, with Scott summoning various men into his tent; these conferences, Cherry felt, were always 'serio-comic'. The main issue concerned the ponies: how much food and rest they needed, and how much marching they had left in them. Scott decided to get them just to the foot of the Beardmore Glacier, though some would be killed on the way. His diary is a sustained expression of anguish about the beasts.

They were aiming for fifteen miles a day, laying depôts for the returning parties every seventy-five miles. The temperature was hovering at around minus 18. The faster dog teams, led by Meares and his assistant, Dimitri Gerof, had caught them up before One Ton, and from then on the demoralised leaders of the clapped-out ponies faced a daily struggle to keep up. According to Scott's instructions, Meares was to take the dogs part of the way across the Barrier and then return to the hut no later than 19 December. In January they would then be able to make a second journey to One Ton to depôt rations for the men marching back.

Now, a few days out of One Ton, dogs, ponies and men met the four-man motorless motor party, who had passed the time reading *The Pickwick Papers* out loud.

Cherry had been out for three weeks when the first pony was shot, and after that two men turned back, carrying to Simpson,* in temporary charge at the hut, fresh orders for dogs and men at the end of the season. This left fourteen in the southern party. Then the weather turned once more, with sharp southerly winds and thick snowfall, and in the chalky light of the Barrier another pony was killed. Everyone felt depressed in the bad weather. Cherry, reading the ostensibly consoling verses of *In Memoriam* in the tent from his green leatherbound Tennyson ('Ring, happy bells, across the snow'), tried to focus on nobler things, but in reality his life revolved around Michael, his pony. 'I go all the way on man-hauling,' he wrote on 29 November, 'pony driving is a rotten, pottering job.' That day, after almost 350 miles of monotony, the fog rolled back like a scroll and they saw

---

* Simpson the meteorologist was now universally known as 'Sunny Jim' on account of his dashing quiff, which made him look like a popular cartoon figure who appeared on cereal packets.

the mountains towering over the Barrier ahead, turbaned in straw-coloured cloud and gleaming in sunlight. Overall, Scott reckoned it was 'touch and go'.

On the first day of December they laid their last depôt on the Barrier. It was their twenty-seventh camp. They had been out for a month, and had marched more than 370 miles – but they were not yet half-way to the Pole. Cherry had been sharing a tent with Scott, which he enjoyed. Some men found the Owner obsessively neat and tidy in his domestic arrangements, with every item allocated its special place in the tent. But Cherry liked that. He found order reassuring.

They shot two more ponies before a thick blizzard obliterated the sight of the next tent. The men were constantly digging the ponies out and rebuilding the wind-breaker walls which they raised around them at each camp. Only the dogs were comfortable, entombed beneath the drifting snow. Scott was bewildered by the lethal rapidity with which the weather could change. But it cleared, and the mountains coalesced out of the mist again. 'Gallant little Michael', his shanks weathered and his black eyes dulled, was shot on 4 December. The next day, Cherry ate him.

The men had been crossing ridges of ice twelve or even twenty feet high, but at least they could see the mountains ahead getting bigger, and to the left the outflow of the Beardmore Glacier was now visible, stretching away like a series of huge waves. According to Scott's original plan, Meares, his assistant Dimitri and the twenty-three dogs were to have turned back earlier, but the animals were travelling so well that the Owner changed his mind. The dogs continued southwards. Then, a major blizzard pinned them all down for four days at a camp they called the Slough of Despond (an image relentlessly invoked to conjure the horror of the trenches three years later). The temperature shot above freezing, which meant they were soggy. A rivulet of brown tobacco juice trickled from Titus's bag. Scott had not expected significant summer blizzards, and was tormented by the delay. 'Oh!' he wrote, 'but this is too crushing.' The most serious repercussion, according to Scott, was that they started eating summit rations – food earmarked for the Beardmore and beyond. Even the indomitable Birdie was fed up.

Pressed against the green walls of the tent, clothes clinging wetly and a line of sopping socks and balaclavas dripping above their heads, they listened to the patter of falling snow and the flapping of the canvas. There was nothing to do but finish their books. Cherry swapped *The Little Minister* with Silas for Dante's *Inferno*. He had lent his Tennyson to Bill, who was busy rhapsodising over *In Memoriam*, 'a perfect piece of faith and hope'.

Scott suggested that if the blizzard continued they would have to turn the tents upside down and use them as boats. But on 9 December they dug the sledges out from under four feet of drift and groped forward. The last ponies were killed, so exhausted at the end that the men could goad them only five or six yards forward before they collapsed and sank into the snow. The beasts had got them to the edge of the Barrier and up to the gap between the mainland and Mount Hope, a peak sticking up through the ice sheet. Reddish granite crags thrust upwards on its right side, and on the left the pale sun gilded its sugary tips between delicate bands of cirrus clouds. Standing in the shadow of the mountain, Scott thanked Titus for getting the ponies so far.

They were late, on account of the unseasonal blizzard. Soft snow made terrible going for the sledges, though the dogs were still running well. Scott must have begun to regret his transport decisions. On 11 December three 4-man teams pulling 500 pounds a sledge started up the dreaded 100-mile Beardmore. They had appalling powdery snow instead of the hard ice Shackleton had described (they were constantly comparing their performance with his).

As the others started up the glacier, Meares, Dimitri and the dog teams finally turned back, 345 miles further on than Scott had originally intended. Though he had been impressed with the dogs' performance on the Barrier, he did not think they could cope with the Beardmore. This left twelve in the southern party.

Many men were snow-blind and the Pole was still more than 280 miles away. No crust had formed over the soft surface snow, and their back-breaking pulls covered only a mile or two a day, exhausting them physically and mentally. The sledges regularly sank in over a foot deep, and the men had to take off their skis to right them when they toppled over. Some days the crevasses were everywhere, and it was difficult to find a safe surface on which to make camp. They got so hot pulling that they marched in singlets, their lips cracked and bleeding and their faces blistered and scabby. Yet they all claimed to be enjoying themselves. In the middle of crucifying marches, near-misses and frostbitten extremities, Cherry began his diary entry for 17 December, 'This morning was just like an exciting day on the scenic railway at Earl's Court.'

Scott's anxiety over the ponies had been transferred to the weather and the surfaces, and he noted that Cherry and Petty Officer Pat Keohane were

the weakest in their team, 'though both put their utmost into the traces'.★
He was less satisfied that Teddy Evans was doing his best. 'I had expected
failure from the animals,' he wrote, 'but not from the men – I must blame
Lieut. Evans much – he shows a terrible lack of judgement.' Scott didn't
seem to remember that Evans and Lashly had been pulling for longer than
the others, as they had taken over the loads of the defunct motors before
the rest of the men had even left Cape Evans.

As the Beardmore opened onto the Polar Plateau, they came across
stretches of hard blue ice slashed with deep grooves by the ferocious
katabatic winds that swept down the glacier. On 18 December the men
beat their own record: fourteen miles ('and a better march than Shackleton
ever managed on the Beardmore'). They had risen to 5,800 feet. That day,
Bill revealed to Cherry that Scott had told him who was likely to be
continuing south to the Pole. One of the most difficult choices lay between
Titus and Cherry, 'but things being close, it was *seniores priores*'. It looked as
if Titus, the older man, was on his way to the Pole.

On 20 December, after a whopping march, Cherry was putting on his
reindeer-fur boots a little way behind the tent when Scott padded up to
him.

'I'm afraid I have rather a blow for you,' Scott said softly.

Cherry knew what was coming.

'I think it is especially hard on you,' Scott murmured.

'I hope I have not disappointed you, sir,' Cherry replied. Scott caught
hold of his arm. 'No, no, no. At the bottom of the glacier I was hardly
expecting to go on myself.'

Scott had two doctors with him on the Plateau, and now he sent one of
them, Atkinson (Atch), back to Cape Evans with Cherry. Silas and
Keohane were also returning. Atch, the senior navy man, was in command.
The seven Scott had selected to sledge on with him were Wilson, Bowers,
Oates, Teddy Evans and, from the ranks, Taff Evans, Tom Crean and
leading stoker William Lashly. A quietly articulate teetotaller from
Hampshire, 44-year-old Lashly had served on the *Discovery*, like Taff and
Crean. He had returned from that expedition garlanded with praise (among
other notable achievements he had saved Scott's life by pulling him out of a
crevasse), and Markham once called him 'the best man in the engine
room'. In 1910 Lashly had volunteered to return to the Antarctic with
Scott. He was a tireless worker, and popular on both decks.

★ Cherry was annoyed when he read this in Scott's published diary. 'Wilson,' he noted,
'wrote that I was completely fit.'

The eight who were continuing south wrote letters for the others to take back to the ship. 'Please write to Mrs Cherry-Garrard,' Wilson asked his wife, 'and say how splendidly her son has worked on this sledge journey. He . . . has made himself beloved by everyone – a regular brick to work and a splendid tent mate.' Scott had already written a similar letter to Reggie. 'He is the most unselfish good-natured fellow in the world, with plenty of intelligence and bottomless pluck. He is extremely popular . . . I hope you will let his people know what golden opinions he has deserved and won.'

The twenty-first of December was the last day of Cherry's march towards the south. In seven weeks he had travelled 575 miles, pulled his sledge beyond 85 degrees south, and risen above 7,000 feet.

There was a 'mournful air' in camp as they prepared to spend their last night together. Bill went into the tent while Cherry was cooking and told him that Scott could see he had been 'pulling his guts out for him all the way'. The hoosh smelled rich and meaty, blotting out the tang of fuel in the air. But it was a wretched parting.

Cherry gave away all the gear he could spare and turned for the long march down the Beardmore and back across the Barrier. 'Scott has only to average seven [geographical] miles a day to get to the Pole – it's practically a cert for him,' he noted in his diary. Scott gave Atch further instructions regarding the dogs. He was to make sure someone brought them out to One Ton in February to meet the polar party on its way back. 'With the depôt [of dog food] which has been laid [at One Ton],' he said, 'come as far as you can.' Scott's orders for the end of the season were becoming fatally confused.

On the return march Cherry's small party immediately met badly crevassed ice. 'Had a hell of a time,' wrote Keohane. 'We were going down holes as fast as we got out of them [and] every ten paces Dr Atkinson went down one big one head first and got brought up by his harness.' The four men all suffered from sickness and a touch of dysentery, and their hands got very 'puddingy'. Camping under a leaden sky on Christmas Eve, Cherry thought about the lighted streets and shop windows of London and all the feasts at home. But after their pemmican dinner they had 'a good whack of cocoa with half a pound of McKellar's plum pudding cooked in it in a bag'. ('Had a bad bellyake,' wrote Keohane the next day.) Cherry left cosy little notes on the depôts for Bill and Birdie. 'I will take on your pyjama trousers from the pony depôt,' he informed Bill on the twenty-eighth. 'You should see my wonderful sketches! We had a very happy Xmas & the pudding was fine. Heaps of love and good luck to you all.'

Except on Christmas Day, they were hungry all the time. ('I watched my companions' faces with their eyes and necks falling in . . . One day I got a piece of looking-glass and found I looked just the same.') But he was cheerful. 'My birthday,' he recorded on 2 January 1912, 'and given some more grub I don't want a better.' He was twenty-six. They had an extra biscuit for lunch in his honour. A few days later he dreamt he was buying chocolate and buns on the platform of Hatfield railway station, and one night he sat up in his bag and called out, 'Within a yard of the Great Hoosh!'

They were following Meares' tracks, depôt to depôt, cairn to cairn. It was hard, but all right, and they averaged sixteen miles a day up to One Ton in the bad Barrier light. They were obsessed by the depôt at One Ton: had the men at the hut sledged out to leave food for the returning parties? Had Meares taken more than his fair share on his way home? 'As I lay in my bag here,' wrote Keohane, 'I think of all the food ever I left behind that I could not eat I wish I had it now.' On 15 January they reached One Ton. It had been laid – the great hoosh at last.

Eleven days later they sledged up to Hut Point, bursting with expectation as they thought the ship had probably arrived with the mail. Instead they found a note from Meares saying that the ship was not in. But at least she had been sighted: she was waiting for more ice to melt.

In three months Cherry had travelled over 1,100 miles.

When the *Terra Nova* was at last able to lay anchor in the bay, Cherry got a pillow-case full of mail. At home top billing went to Lassie's marriage to George Herbert Shorting, a widower with two children who was vicar of Kimpton, a village near Lamer. The wedding was related in exhaustive detail in a fifty-page epic. 'I miss you horribly and want you at every turn,' Evelyn wrote in her catalogue of events, which included a lengthy description of police crowd control at the church. She even threatened to sail out to meet him. And he did feel pangs, as he sat on his scratchy bunk and read about the heatwave and the girls and the things he knew so very well. 'I thought as I drove up from the train yesterday I had never seen Lamer looking so beautiful,' his mother told him. 'Gorgeous tints of green, with all the flowering trees out and masses of white chestnut blossom. The garden radiates with rhododendrons, lilies, laburnums . . .'

He ploughed through his business correspondence, which included a supertax return, lease renewals, papers relating to the trust fund set up in accordance with the General's will, the purchase of stocks, reports from land agents at both Lamer and Denford, and much, much more. As for the wider world (which meant England), Oxford had won the Boat Race, and apart from that the main topics were the loss of the House of Lords' power of veto and the widespread labour unrest which so characterised 1911. Cherry found it all 'absolutely bewildering. England seems to have gone back to the days of the Reform Bill or the Chartist agitation.' (Thirty-nine years later he described these first reports from home as 'the rumblings of the storms to come'.) Letters from Harry Woollcombe revealed that he had carried the word with such exemplary zeal that he had collapsed with heart strain on the way to India and had returned home to Devon. From there he wrote about the proliferation of strikes and the alarming social disorder they towed in their wake. 'Personally,' fulminated the reverend, 'I hope it will galvanise our class into realising that we simply must pull ourselves together and consider the "social evil" and not talk rot about the "discomforts of the poor".'

The *Terra Nova* had brought provisions for the third year: new sledges, fourteen dogs and seven mules which, at Titus's suggestion, Scott had requested from India to replace the ponies. When unloading began, Cherry wore himself out sledging twenty miles a day between ship and shore. He received cases and cases of gear from Evelyn and Reggie, among it thirty scarves, sixty books and an eighteen-gallon cask of sherry. The ship steamed off to pick up a party out geologising in the west, and to relieve Campbell and his men. On her way down to Cape Evans in January she had collected Campbell's party and moved them to a new site further along the coast. The plan was that she should return six weeks later and bring the men home to Cape Evans.

Cherry tried to reply to his multitudinous correspondents before the *Terra Nova* called in briefly on her way back to New Zealand. His letters to Lamer were detailed and loving, in his characteristic, understated way, inspired in part by his father's long, tender correspondence from bloodier battlefields. On the business front, he drew up a testamentary document bequeathing £4,000 (£185,000 in 2001) to Scott in the event of his death before their return to England. Cape Crozier and the sea ice incident had brought death to life.

As late summer clouds began to rake the mountain tops across the Sound, the hut-dwellers waited for the last returning party to sledge in with news. Everyone speculated on which three Scott had chosen to accompany him to the Pole. Each man at Cape Evans was convinced that he could pick a winning team. Silas thought that both he and Cherry had been in better shape than Teddy at the top of the Beardmore. 'Scott a fool,' Silas wrote in camp on the night the announcement was made. 'Too wild to write more tonight.' (Convinced that Teddy was a shirker and a hypocrite, Silas had wanted to push him down a crevasse. Cherry confided to his journal that it was a pity he hadn't.) Oates was limping from his South African wound, and on the glacier he privately revealed to Atch that he wasn't fit to continue. Cherry considered it was a mistake to take a limping man; Scott, he thought, should have asked his doctors' advice.*

The men in the hut also talked incessantly about who was going back to New Zealand with the ship. Meares definitely was, so on 13 February it was Atch, not he, who left for Hut Point to prepare to sledge to One Ton as Scott had instructed. He took Dimitri and the dogs with him.

Six days later, Atch was making the final adjustment to the leather sledge straps on the slippery platform of rock outside the *Discovery* hut. When he straightened up, he saw a man stumbling out of the icefields to the south.

Atch hurried out, and as he approached the tottering, wind-scoured and frost-scarred wreck he recognised Tom Crean. Crean was the stalwart Irish seaman who had leapt across the floes to get help when Cherry, Birdie and the ponies had been caught on the sea ice. Ensconced in the hut, he revealed that Teddy Evans was lying in a tent thirty-five miles out on the Barrier, perilously ill after collapsing with scurvy. Crean had left Lashly nursing Evans, and walked in alone to get help.

This, then, was the last returning party – but where was the fourth man?

Atch and Dimitri strained with expectation. Crean took a swig of cocoa. Then he spoke. *There was no fourth man.* Scott had decided it was five for the Pole.

Atch was obliged to abandon his plans for One Ton in order to take the dogs out to rescue Evans. Delayed by a blizzard, he waited at Hut Point, and Crean poured out the rest of the story. After Cherry and the first returning party had turned round at the top of the Beardmore on 22 December, the eight remaining men had sledged on across the Plateau among crevasses 'as big as Regent Street' until 4 January, when Scott announced that Wilson, Bowers, Titus and Taff Evans were going with him to the Pole. The last returning party, Teddy Evans, Crean and Lashly, turned for home at an altitude of about 9,000 feet barely 163 miles from the Pole, leaving Scott and his men almost certain of success ('I think the British flag will be the only one to fly there,' Bowers wrote). Evans had more verbal orders from Scott about the dogs: they were to come further

---

* Wilson thought Scott took Titus because he wanted the army represented at the Pole.

south to meet him on his way back, and hurry him back to Cape Evans before the ship left. These orders were forgotten in the ensuing drama.

Hauling in a reduced team of three was a terrible struggle ('too great a sacrifice'). After struggling for hundreds of miles Teddy Evans developed scurvy (Lashly noted, 'he is turning black and blue and several other colours as well'), and was towed on the sledge until heavy snow prevented further pulling. Then Crean, who had already racked up 1,500 miles, marched 35 more over 18 hours in a miniature polar epic all of his own. The blizzard broke half an hour after he came in.

Back on the Barrier Lashly was left to take care of a man falling slowly towards death. He and Evans had no food except a few paraffin-soaked biscuits.

As soon as the blizzard broke, Atch and Dimitri set off to rescue the two men. When they reached the tent, the lead dog, a dark grey and white husky called Krisravitsa, went right inside and licked the patient's cheek. 'I kissed his old hairy Siberian face with the kiss that was meant for Lashly,' Evans recorded. After restorative onions and cake, and a medical examination, Evans was towed back to Hut Point.* Lashly had been out for four months. When he got in he wrote in his diary that now they were keen to get their mail. 'How funny,' he wrote, 'we should always be looking for something else, now we are safe.'

Atch decided that Evans was too sick to be left without a doctor, and, as he was the only doctor, it meant someone else had to take the dogs to One Ton with Dimitri. He despatched two men to Cape Evans with a note suggesting Silas or Cherry for the job. Silas could not be spared from the scientific work. 'I'm right in it,' Cherry wrote in his diary. He had neither navigated nor driven dogs before, winter was closing in, and he had to reach a depôt 150 miles out on the featureless Barrier. This was the chance in a hundred that Scott had doubted would ever come.

The dogs strained in the traces. Then they stampeded away with a howl, the sledge runners swishing and freezing air rushing at the drivers' faces. Cherry found navigation devilishly hard: since his goggles were fogging, he

---

* Evans asked Atch if he was going to have to go home on the ship, and the doctor said that he was. Evans was pleased, as before turning round at the top of the Beardmore Scott had ordered him home anyway. (In a letter to Joseph Kinsey, his agent in New Zealand, Scott wrote that Evans had to be sent home 'as it would not do to leave him in charge here in case I am late returning'.) Evans could now legitimately claim to have been invalided home rather than sent back in disgrace by Scott. Yet Scott had also furnished Evans with a letter of recommendation which duly led to his promotion to the rank of commander. In later years Cherry got in a stew over the role of Evans at this point in the expedition.

had to rely on Dimitri to spot the cairns. The light was diminishing daily, and on 28 February they were obliged to use a candle in the tent for the first time. Fears crowded into Cherry's journal. They got to One Ton, but they had a cold coming of it. The weather was so bad for four of the next six days that it was either impossible to push on further south, or pointless as they would have almost certainly missed another party in the milky drift. Furthermore, they were running out of dog food, none having been depôted at One Ton, and so could only move south by killing dogs. Yet Cherry's verbal instructions from Atch included the order that he was on no account to risk the dogs: Scott had stipulated that they were to be saved for sledging the following season. It did not cross Cherry's mind to disobey those orders; and, anyway, according to Scott's schedule there was still plenty of time for the polar party to get in. 'I had no reason,' he wrote in *The Worst Journey*, 'to suppose that the polar party could be in want of food.'

Both Atch and Cherry thought the dog party was going out to meet Scott at One Ton and help him get back quickly so that he could send mail out with the ship – including, hopefully, news of his triumph, as he was desperate to reach the public before the Norwegians. But by this time Scott thought their job – or someone's job – was to save the lives of the polar party by bringing food and fuel south of One Ton. The deadly misunderstanding was a result of confused and conflicting orders.

At an early juncture, Scott had left instructions for extra dog food and man food to be taken to One Ton. This was for the party which was to hurry him back to the ship on his return journey. But the decision to take the dogs 345 miles further than planned on the way to the Pole had had a domino effect. It meant that Cecil Meares, who was in charge of the dogs, returned to the hut too late to undertake further reprovisioning trips, as he was going home with the ship before the second winter. Although others did the reprovisioning, and man food was laid at One Ton, in the confusion and comings and goings of parties and the ship, dog food had been forgotten.

In the meantime, on Scott's return journey much of the oil left in the depôts had evaporated, leaving him short. This fuel shortage, the unexpectedly poor weather and the polar party's sickness meant that the men and dogs at One Ton now had a very different role from the one Cherry had imagined: to save Scott's men by taking food and fuel out to them. But Cherry could not know this. He could not travel further south with the dogs as he had no food for them; but he did not know it had become a matter of life or death.

While Cherry was waiting there at One Ton, Scott was lying in his sleeping bag writing in the queer greenish light of a polar tent, 'We hope against hope that the dogs have been to Mt Hooper [a depôt south of One Ton]; then we might pull through.' But they had not, and he did not.[*]

Soon after arriving at One Ton, Dimitri began to suffer badly from the cold. First he had a bad head, then a bad right arm and side which developed into partial paralysis. Cherry did what he could for him, and they waited, in brutal Barrier temperatures, a tiny dot in hundreds of miles of swirling snow. If it cleared for an instant, they convinced themselves they could see the polar party coming in, gulled by the delusive light.

On 10 March, with just enough dog food for the return journey, Cherry laid a small depôt and started for home, leaving a pencilled note in a film canister for Scott. 'Dear Sir', it said, 'We leave this morning with the dogs for Hut Point. We have made no depôts on the way in being off course all the way, and so I have not been able to leave you a note before. Yours sincerely, Apsley Cherry-Garrard.'[†] Eleven days later, Scott, Bill and Birdie were dying just twelve and a half miles to the south.

On the eight-day return journey Cherry contended with open crevasses, ravenous, raving dogs, and a sick man. Dimitri's right side was now completely useless, and for the last days he was immobilised. It was Cherry who filled the aluminium cooker with gritty snow, grappled with stiff, flapping canvas and lashed leaden sleeping bags to the sledges. He was worried about everything on this trek: finding a route, the weather, the condition of the sea ice near Hut Point, Dimitri. 'Lately I have felt that it has almost been too much,' he wrote ominously.

They reached the *Discovery* shelter at Hut Point on 16 March. Atch and Keohane were there; in his official report Atch wrote, 'Cherry-Garrard under the circumstances and according to his instructions was in my judgement quite right in everything he did. I am absolutely certain no other officer of the Expedition could have done better.' He noted that when they got in, 'Both men were in exceedingly poor condition, Cherry-Garrard's state causing me serious alarm.' The ship had left.

Thirty-six years later, Cherry was thrashing it all out for the umpteenth

---

[*] Near the end, Scott seems to have realised the muddle he had unleashed. When he got to his Mount Hooper depôt and found that the dogs had not been brought that far south, he concluded, 'It's a miserable jumble.' The comment was deleted from the published diary.
[†] Three and a half years later, Dick Richards and other members of Shackleton's Ross Sea Party found Cherry's note. The supplies Cherry depôted at One Ton were of incalculable help to them, in a desperate situation themselves: 'At last we have struck gold in the Antarctic,' Ernest Joyce wrote that night. So Cherry's journey was not in vain.

time with his friend and mentor George Bernard Shaw, then ninety-two. 'If the depôt [of dog food] had been laid,' Shaw asked him (thanks to Cherry, polar travel had been dropped into the boundless reservoir of Shavian expertise), 'would you have gone on?' 'Of course,' Cherry said.

If there had been food for them at One Ton, Cherry would have taken the dogs on after the weather cleared. He might have found the polar party and three or four of them might have lived.

7

It is the Tent

In the murky sanctuary of Hut Point Cherry collapsed, overwhelmed by exhaustion and tension. He was experiencing a breakdown, its physical symptoms including fainting fits and depression so crushing that some days he could barely get up. Dimitri, by contrast, staged a miraculous recovery. 'It is sad,' Cherry wrote, 'that he has really been shamming ill . . . He just hasn't got the guts.'*

As the Western Mountains shrank into the polar night, Cherry started hearing bells, and 'hardly cared what happened'. Atch diagnosed heart strain. Whatever was wrong with him, Cherry was definitely too ill to be considered for a final sledge journey to look for the polar party. A note of foreboding entered his journal as he waited for news, although he kept telling himself that he had no reason to be especially anxious about his friends: according to Scott's schedule they were not expected for some days. The men's marches during the first fortnight on the Plateau had been excellent, and they had caught up with Shackleton's dates before the last five struck out alone. Scott himself was confident. 'What castles one builds now hopefully that the Pole is ours,' he wrote the day after the last supporting party left him.

Then, as the leaves fell from the calendar, the men at Hut Point began to wonder, and worry took hold. Not one but two groups were out: when the *Terra Nova* had returned briefly on her way back to New Zealand she brought the news that bad ice conditions had prevented her from picking up Campbell and the five other members of the geologising Northern

---

* In later years Cherry asked a doctor specialising in psychiatric illness about Dimitri, and the man diagnosed hysterical hemiplegia.

Party. Already absent for a year, they were now stranded 230 miles up the coast. Like Scott and his men, they only had small tents to protect them against the horrors of the Antarctic winter. But Campbell had supplies, and the six of them could probably survive until the spring in an ice cave or igloo. The polar party, on the other hand, would certainly perish in the sunless winter if they did not make it back to Cape Evans soon. 'Atch and I look at one another – and he looks and I feel quite haggard with anxiety,' Cherry wrote. As each day passed, the spectre of disaster solidified. One night, asleep in their bunks, they were woken by knocks at the window. Atch shouted, 'Hullo! Cherry, they're in!' Keohane yelled, 'Who's cook?' and they all rushed out, hearts pounding. But it was a dog, slapping the window with his tail.

With painful frequency someone spotted figures sledging in, they all raced outside, and each time, 'hope sprang up anew'. Atch and another man sledged more than thirty miles out on the Barrier in the hope that they might meet the polar party. But conditions were atrocious, and in the bad light Atch finally acknowledged that the search was hopeless. On 30 March he recorded that he was 'morally certain that the party had perished'.

They were again trapped at Hut Point by open water. The *Discovery* shelter there was fifteen miles along the coast from Cape Evans, and the only route back was across the sea ice – if it ever froze. Although he had good days, Cherry was weak, and suffered from chronic headaches and a swollen throat. He too was now certain that his friends were dead. On 2 April he wrote, 'I think I have been down into hell.' A week later he was left alone for four days, so feeble that he was obliged to crawl about on his hands and knees. Like many of his later illnesses, this one had no name: it was more a random collection of symptoms than a specific condition. He took morphine, and lay on the floor in his crusty sleeping bag in the bitter hut, periodically dragging himself over to the stove to feed it blubber as the walls swam away and the floor heaved and sank like a wave. The dogs took advantage of his infirmity, and he said he could easily have killed the lot of them.

The sun left them on 23 April, the sea finally froze, and a week later Cherry sledged back to Cape Evans in the perpetual twilight that marks the hiatus between summer and winter in the unforgiving Antarctic. He had had six weeks' rest since coming in from the dog journey to One Ton with Dimitri, but when he arrived at Cape Evans he was 'more or less an invalid'.

Nine men had gone with the ship, including Ponting, Griff and the sick Teddy Evans, and two had landed, leaving thirteen at Cape Evans for the winter, many of them exhausted. The six-strong 'officers' contingent comprised Cherry, Atch, Silas, Deb, biologist Edward 'Marie' Nelson and the 23-year-old Norwegian skiing expert Gran. Anticipating a bulging mail bag, Gran had been horrified to receive only one item, and that was a bill. But he rallied, and made himself useful with the animals during the winter, successfully deploying a football pump to give a mule an enema. By default, Atch was in charge, unless Campbell were to turn up. They had plenty of everything they needed, and recognised the importance of routine and activity to stave off despair. A handful of hyacinth bulbs that had come down with the ship bloomed blue in a basin of wet sawdust.

Four years older than Cherry but not quite as handsome, Atch was strong and nimble (as a medical student he had been the hospital light heavyweight boxing champion). He spent his early years in Trinidad in the company of his parents and five sisters, and was educated in England, joining the navy as a surgeon two years after qualifying. He worked primarily as a researcher, and had published a paper on gonorrhoeal rheumatism, possibly not the most useful area of expertise in the polar regions. As there was little medical work to do on the expedition, Atch had also been engaged as a parasitologist, and he was often to be found enthusiastically delving in the entrails of penguins. In later years, when he was working on his polar worms in a lab at the London School of Tropical Medicine, he named a new species *garrardi*.

A quiet, diligent man with impeccable manners, Atch turned out to be a popular and gifted leader, and throughout the emotional carnage of the second winter he was also a magnificent confidant for the sick Cherry. He kept a grip on morale by maintaining naval discipline (the officers and scientists continued to mess separately from the seamen) and issuing each man with orders. Cherry was appointed official recorder of events, and told to continue with his taxidermy, and with the *South Polar Times*, and, in between, to rest.

When they got home, someone had to write up the expedition records. Atch and Cherry both felt passionately that if Teddy Evans, as second-in-command, were to take on the task they would end up with 'a garbled, disloyal account'. Their worries drew them together. But Atch had a sense of perspective, whereas the idea of Evans 'taking over' became an obsession with Cherry. He brooded on it in the hut and expressed his views in a letter to Reggie, whose firm was to publish the official expedition book. His main criticism was that Evans had spoken disloyally of Scott behind his back: a serious violation of Cherry's code of honour. 'Evans has been the one blot,' he told Reggie, 'on what I believe is the best expedition which has ever sailed.' At the same time, Cherry began writing Scott's story, and the seed of *The Worst Journey* was planted.

Blizzards imprisoned them for weeks. The seamen were much taken up with the mules which had been sent down from India to replace the ponies, and in their free time they entertained themselves with games. 'This winter is passing a lot better than I thought it would under the circumstances,' wrote Keohane. 'It is no doubt owing to our skelleywag board everybody is very keen on winning.' Without complaint they followed a regime that might have seemed brutal at home. 'We usually wear our underclothing about a month,' recorded Petty Officer Thomas Williamson cheerfully. 'Now that we have run out of soap,' he added, 'we shall be obliged to wear them much longer periods.' On the other side of the partition Cherry discharged his duties and read, subsisting on a conventional diet of Dickens, Charlotte Brontë, Arnold Bennett, Rider Haggard and Anthony Hope. For light relief he pored over reports of the coronation of George V in the illustrated papers sent down by his old Winchester housemaster, Theodore 'Kenny' Kensington. He improved his painting, and when he got bored of penguin wings and parasitic rock cones he drew ink studies of cancan dancers, gorgeous Lautrecian creatures never previously sighted south of the Antarctic Circle. One day he astonished everyone with a break of 102 at billiards, which they played on a miniature folding table, one of the rackety wooden balls no longer being recognisably round. With a depleted roster he was no longer able to escape lecturing, speaking in May on rowing and in July on Florence under the Medici. (Oscar Wilde once lectured on a similar subject to the red-shirted miners of Leadville, Colorado, though the miners were more enthusiastic than Scott's grizzled seamen.)

On Midwinter's Day the bunting, flags and Christmas tree were manfully wheeled out again, and the menu extended to *noisettes d'agneau Darwinian* and *charlotte russe glacé à la Beardmore*. Soon the light began seeping back into the edges of the dark sky, and for a whole fortnight Cherry had only one headache. He watched the seals glissade through the black water, outlined in the phosphorescence, and one day he saw an eruption of Erebus in which flames seemed to shoot thousands of feet into the air, fall and rise, fall and rise; then disappear. But blizzards brought his depression back. ('It is of some scientific interest to be a living blizzometer, but I wouldn't recommend it even to my enemies, if there are any about.') He had already lost seven pounds and now he shed a further half a stone in the course of a month 'that has been one continual fight against a kind of nervous strain and sick headaches'. He concealed his depression from everyone except Atch, more or less. 'Cherry was his usual cheerful self,' Silas remembered, 'but rather subdued by the loss of his two greatest friends.' In fact, he was reeling from the most profound emotional shock of his life. More often than the others knew, he retreated to the private colonies of the imagination. In his dreams the polar party appeared at the door of the hut; and then he woke again to the same, sickening horror. He had stabbing pains in his heart: stumbling in the bleak psychic landscape of bereavement and trapped on a frigid cape, he internalised his trauma so completely that it manifested itself in physical symptoms.

Cherry said afterwards that this second winter was 'a ghastly experience'. It was a bitter and desolate sequel to the happiness and fulfilment of the early part of the expedition. 'The scenery has lost much of its beauty to us,' Deb wrote, 'the auroras are cheap and the cold rather colder.' It was hardly surprising: every day they slept alongside empty bunks.

On 27 August the sun returned to Cape Evans, at last. The hut was still snowed in, but the familiar jagged battlements of the Western Mountains thickened in the gloom, and the lower slopes of Erebus, their friend, gleamed in the pale, frosty light of early spring.

Cherry too had emerged from gloom, and soon he was 'top dog' for the first time in many months. He finished the lugubrious job of packing Bill's and Birdie's possessions, a task assigned to him by Atch, and after listing the contents of each box in one of his slim hardback notebooks he nailed down the lids for the return journey. The female seals were popping up again, bursting like overripe melons, and the first visiting parties of Emperors came calling. Cherry went over to Cape Royds, and to Hut Point, but he was determined not to go sledging for the fun of it: 'God knows I have done enough hard sledging to want no "objectless" trips.'

Something inside him had broken. He no longer had Bill's lofty ideals and Birdie's unremitting selflessness to guide him. At the beginning of October he was furious when Atch asked him to take on some sledging errands. 'It is all I can do not to speak out sometimes,' he wrote; but he spoke to his journal instead. 'There is not a dangerous or hard job which has ever been done down here that I have not done – depôt journey, ponies on the sea ice, winter journey, southern journey, unloading ship, dog journey to south – work till an inevitable breakdown which has given me such hell this winter as I hope never to suffer again.' Once he had begun, he couldn't stop. 'And when we got back from three months' sledging last year we sledged on unloading the ship, up early and late to bed – while the men on the ship who could hardly waddle for fat took alternate days on and off. Never again – never!'

His shapeless feelings of loss and grief now found an outlet in bitterness. While he was not given time to concentrate on his taxidermy, 'others sit round the table reading novels . . . And God alone knows where it will all end. Likely or not in a crevasse . . . There's only four or five months more and they can all go to hell.' Bill's cherished 'forgetfulness of self' was a long way off. In the shifting layers of Cherry's unconscious he displaced his hostility towards Scott (at some level responsible for the deaths of Birdie and Bill) onto his companions in the hut, and, more permanently, onto the absent Evans.

Day after day the men had chewed over the problem of where to concentrate their resources when the light returned. They could either sledge south, in the hope of finding out what had happened to the dead polar party, or west and north to try to relieve Campbell and his Northern Party, who could very well be alive. It was difficult to put the dead above the living, but unlikely that the ice would be good enough to reach Campbell, and there was also an outside chance that he had been relieved by the *Terra Nova* on her way north. If he had not, and they did go, by the time they got to him Campbell would be out of danger one way or the other: either he would have set off for Cape Evans, or he would soon be relieved by the ship on her way back south. The Cape Evans men had a clear duty, on the other hand, to tell the public what had happened to Scott. Most of them thought the five-strong polar party had gone down a crevasse, though one or two suspected they had died of scurvy.* While they reckoned there was little chance of finding bodies, Scott always left notes on his depôts, and a search might yield at least some information. When Atch called for a vote, everyone wanted to go south except Lashly, who abstained.

Cherry was sent out depôt-laying in preparation, fuming that he would not be back at the Cape Evans hut before the search journey began. But out on the trail, it wasn't so bad. The white-gold clouds of spring drifted hazily around the lower slopes of Erebus, the rim of the crater glowed against the cobalt sky, and the smell of fuel when the Primus flame whooshed rekindled the romance of a southern camp.

At the end of October twelve men set off for the Barrier with dogs and mules. They marched on for a fortnight in moderate conditions, the

---

* They probably had died of scurvy, though Cherry was always adamant that this was not the case.

temperatures bouncing between minus 7 and minus 29. The mules were not a success. While they enjoyed tea leaves and tobacco, they did not care for their own rations, and a great deal of human energy was expended in coaxing them to eat.

In the morning of 12 November, twelve-and-a-half miles south of One Ton, Cherry was driving a dog team when he saw Silas and the mules turn off course and swerve to the right in a sparkling cloud of ice particles that sprayed wide in a soaring arc. Silas had seen what he thought was a cairn, and something black next to it. 'A vague kind of wonder,' Cherry remembered, 'gradually gave way to real alarm.' Silas, realising what he had found, signalled to the others; he felt it would be sacrilegious to make a noise. They all went up to this mound of snow, and stopped, mules weary, dogs frisky, men afraid. Silas came across to Cherry.

He said, 'It is the tent.'

Someone brushed away a small column of snow on the top of the mound, revealing the green flap of a tent ventilator. Two of them found the entrance, and went in through the funnel and then past the inner bamboos. But the snow banked up outside made it too dark to see anything, so they started shovelling it away from the cambric walls. Slowly the ghostly outlines formed. There were three of them.

Scott was in the middle, the flaps of his bag thrown back, one hand stretched over Bill to his right. Bill's hands were folded over his chest. Birdie lay with his feet to the door. Their skin was yellow and glassy, like old alabaster, and they were mottled with frostbite. Everything was tidy.

'That scene can never leave my memory,' Cherry wrote.

As Atch searched in Scott's bag for his diary, the others heard a crack, like a shot being fired. Years later, Gran could still hear that sound. 'It was something breaking,' he said. 'It was Scott's arm.' They found everything: diaries, letters, film, thirty-five pounds of geological specimens dragged hundreds of miles from the Beardmore, and Cherry's copy of Tennyson in its green leather binding. They learned from the diaries that Amundsen had got to the Pole first, news that seemed at that moment to be of no importance whatever. They learned too that Scott had run out of oil, less than thirteen miles from the plenty of One Ton.

They dug down to find Scott's sledge, and put up their own tent. Atch sat inside and went through Scott's diary, according to the instructions on the cover, then gathered everyone together to read them the bones of the story.

After the last returning party had gone back, the five men had continued doggedly across the Plateau with only four pairs of skis between them. The inclusion of an extra man at the last moment had other serious implications: more fuel was required for cooking, and rations had been prepared in quantities of four. But they knew the Pole – the grail – was close. Then, on 16 January, Birdie spotted a tiny scrap of black flapping in the wind. It was a Norwegian flag. 'All the day-dreams must go,' Scott wrote. The next evening they reached the Pole itself, their hands freezing through double woollen and fur mitts. 'It was a very bitter day,' Wilson noted in his diary. They camped, planted a flag ('our poor slighted Union Jack'), and took observations. Amundsen had left a tent, some equipment and a cordial note for Scott. They were only a month behind him.

Five Norwegians had reached the Pole on 14 December 1911. They had pioneered a new route, avoiding the Beardmore, and had not been encumbered with ponies. Apart from one false start that almost ended in disaster (Amundsen had set out too early, and low temperatures drove him back to his hut), there had been no major setbacks. 'We are going like greyhounds,' the Norwegian leader wrote on the Barrier. The men had practically grown up on skis – one was a former national champion – and they drove some of their dogs all the way to the Pole. Furthermore, they were not stopping to survey or load their sledges with rocks.* By the time he returned to his hut, despite appalling fog and desperately challenging terrain, Amundsen had covered over 1,600 miles in 99 days.

Scott and his companions, meanwhile, had turned for home – 860 miles away. A sail rigged to the sledge speeded them along, but temperatures were low, surfaces poor and their spirits broken. Taff Evans had a nasty cut on his hand which refused to heal; he was especially run down, and gradually became 'rather dull and incapable'. He and Oates were badly frostbitten. Everyone was hungry, and, given the altitude, more than usually thirsty. After a cold seven weeks on the Plateau, they struggled down the Beardmore and onto the Barrier, battling crevasses, snow-blindness, falls, cold and more cold. Evans, whom Scott had originally thought the strongest man of the party, was on an irreversible downward trajectory, and on 16 February he collapsed. He struggled up, but the next day he broke down completely, and by the time they got him into the tent he was comatose. He never regained consciousness. They had watched him die, slowly, for many days.

They slogged on, colder and weaker. Scott's diary for these weeks is a

---

* During the course of the expedition the Norwegians explored new territory and made significant discoveries. But though they did make meteorological and geological observations, they did not pursue an ambitious scientific programme like Scott's.

lament of misfortune, like a chorus in a Greek tragedy. Each day unfurled in a slow, mental scream of anguish about their chances of finding the next depôt. When they did reach the depôts they found them short of oil (the result of evaporation and leakage). The weather turned bad – much colder than Scott could reasonably have expected on the Barrier at that time of year – and Titus's feet were black with frostbite. 'We are in a *very* queer street,' Scott noted with robust English understatement. On Amundsen's return journey a month earlier his food depôts had been so plentiful, he noted in his diary, that he and party were 'living among the fleshpots of Egypt'.

On about 17 March Oates said at lunch that he could not go on; he wanted them to leave him there in his bag. But they would not, and he went on, one more agonising march with a huge swollen foot frostbitten over and over again. He had given his diary to Wilson, asking him to pass it on to his mother, who was, he said, the only woman he had ever loved. That night he turned in hoping never to wake, but that passive exit was denied him. In the morning a thick blizzard was blowing. Oates said, 'I am just going outside and may be some time.' They did go and look for him, but they did not find him.

'Should this be found,' Scott wrote, 'I want these facts recorded. Oates' last thoughts were of his Mother, but immediately before he took pride in thinking that his regiment would be pleased with the bold way in which he met his death.'

They staggered on, 'and though we constantly talk of fetching through, I don't think any one of us believes it in his heart'. At their sixtieth camp since the Pole, less than thirteen miles from the bounty of One Ton, they had nine days of blizzard, and that was the end. They had pitched the tent for the last time five days after Cherry and Dimitri arrived back at Hut Point with the dogs. Scott had no fuel left, and hardly any food. His feet were so bad he could scarcely walk ('amputation is the least I can hope for now'), and Birdie and Bill were planning to go on to the next depôt alone; but the blizzard put a stop to that. Scott made the last entry in his diary on 29 March. 'For God's sake,' he wrote, 'look after our people.'

They left farewell letters, thawing their fingers to write by the wispy flame of an improvised spirit lamp. 'Death has no terrors for me,' Wilson wrote to his parents, and he begged his wife not to be unhappy, since 'all is for the best . . . my love is as living for you as ever'. Birdie tore a flimsy leaf from a notebook and wrote to his mother for the last time. He signed off, 'Your ever loving Son to the end in this life and the next when we will meet and where God shall wipe away all tears from our eyes.'

'He was one of the two or three greatest friends of my life,' Cherry wrote later of Birdie, who had died aged twenty-eight. As for Bill, he had been more than a friend. He had offered a hand to a fearful young man who came to love him sincerely. 'How cold are your feet, Cherry?' Bill had asked when they faced death together at Crozier. 'Very cold,' Cherry replied. 'That's all right,' Bill said, 'so are mine.'

Besides his letters, Scott left a 'Message to the Public'. It began with the assertion that the causes of the disaster were not due to faulty organisation but to misfortune, citing specifically the loss of pony transport on the depôt journey the previous season, which meant they had started late; the poor weather; and the soft snow in the lower reaches of the Beardmore. Despite all that, he said they would have got through had it not been for Oates' prolonged sickness, the shortage of fuel in the depôts, and the last blizzard. 'We are weak,' he concluded, 'writing is difficult, but for my own sake I do not regret this journey, which has shown that Englishmen can endure hardships, help one another, and meet death with as great a fortitude as in the past. We took risks, we knew we took them . . . Had we lived, I should have had a tale to tell of the hardihood, endurance, and courage of my companions which would have stirred the heart of every Englishman.'

They had not been expecting this. They had thought the bodies were dangling down some crevasse on the far-off Beardmore. They stood there, stamping their feet softly, lost in shock, until Atch found the Prayer Book. Then they gathered on the gleaming ice shelf with their balaclavas in their hands, and Atch read the lesson from the Burial Service into the deep Barrier silence. They did not move their friends, but Cherry searched for Bill's watch to give to his widow. He found the cheery little notes that he had left on the depôts folded in his pyjama pockets. Outside, sheets of emerald clouds rippled across the southern sky. In Cherry's bursting heart, something died.

They removed the tent poles and collapsed the cambric over the three bodies. Then they built a twelve-foot cairn over the tomb, and made a cross out of skis for the top. On either side they placed the two sledges, upright. In a metal cylinder on a bamboo they put a note commemorating the three dead men in the snow and the two out there on the ice. It cited inclement weather and lack of fuel as the cause of death. 'The Lord giveth,' the note ended, 'and the Lord taketh away.'

'I do not know how long we were there,' Cherry wrote, 'but when all was finished . . . it was midnight of some day.' Gran said that he envied them. 'They died having done something great. How hard must not death be having done nothing.' Cherry was already haunted. 'I for one,' he wrote, 'shall be very glad to leave this place.'

'The question of what we might have done for them with the dog teams is terribly on my mind,' Cherry wrote in his diary, 'but we obeyed instructions . . . and I know that we did our best.' In an attempt to clear his mind he sat down on a sledge and wrote out the sequence of events that had led to his dog journey to One Ton with Dimitri. He badly wanted to make it clear that he had had no food with which to take the dogs on. He now knew that if he had pressed on through the blizzard, he could have left oil and food on cairns which Scott and the others might have seen. If he had made good progress, and killed some dogs to feed the others, he might even have met the polar party and shepherded them home. Cherry sat among the immense, bloodless icefields as men began unlashing sledges, and recriminations without end began to rain down.

Subsequent climate data reveals that the temperatures Scott experienced on the homeward trek across the Barrier were lower than average; over some periods as much as twenty degrees lower. The unseasonably cold conditions were a significant factor in the disaster. Cherry crucified himself over the repercussions of his decisions during the crisis at One Ton, but the facts indicate that the polar party would almost certainly have died even if he had sledged on. The facts, however, did not determine Cherry's personal tragedy.

He was sorry that the question of oil shortage had arisen, as it implied selfishness, or at best carelessness, on the part of the returning teams. (They did not then know how the shortage had arisen.) 'We were always careful,' Cherry wrote fretfully that night in his diary, 'to take a little less than we were entitled to.'

The following day they marched south to look for Titus's body, the gritty wind in their faces and the light poor. They found just his sleeping bag, empty except for his socks. Near the spot where he had walked out they built another cairn, and another cross, with a note written on a page torn from Cherry's sketchbook. Signed by Cherry and Atch, it began, 'Hereabouts died a very gallant gentleman.'

They reached Hut Point a week later, and Cherry went up to the entrance. After a minute or two he rushed back to the others, 'his face transformed'. On a note pinned to the door he read that Campbell and his men had arrived at Cape Evans. Finally, they had good news. 'It is the happiest day for nearly a year – almost the only happy one,' Cherry rejoiced. They soon got over to Cape Evans themselves and sat up to hear the story.

What Campbell and his five men endured beggars belief, even in the steely annals of Antarctic hardship. They had been out from February 1911 until November 1913. Their first season at Cape Adare was successful: geologist Ray Priestley collected important specimens and they charted new territory, though they were hemmed in by unclimbable glaciers, and so could not penetrate the hinterland. (During this time they published their own newspaper, the *Adélie Annual*, which included a cookery column.) In January 1912 they were picked up by the *Terra Nova* on her way from New Zealand and deposited further down the coast, but when exceptionally bad ice conditions prevented her from relieving them, they made their home in an ice cave on Inexpressible Island (it was they who named it). The cave was nine feet by twelve, and five-feet-six high, which meant they could never stand upright. They spent much of their second winter lying in their bags talking about food. They had to ration themselves to one match a day to light the stove, and their practically all-meat diet meant that the acid content of their urine was exceptionally high, with the result that they wet themselves all the time and everyone had haemorrhoids. When Campbell had a touch of dysentery he got his penis frostbitten. 'The road to hell might be paved with good intentions,' one of the party wrote, 'but it seemed probable that hell itself would be paved something after the style of Inexpressible Island.' But they saved twenty-five raisins apiece to celebrate birthdays, and held divine service on Sundays. Finally, not having washed or changed their clothes for eight months, they sledged the 230 miles back to Cape Evans, still friends.

That they survived at all was due in no small part to the outstanding leadership of Campbell, who, as the senior navy man, now took over command at Cape Evans. Everyone tried to be cheerful, but all they wanted to do was go home. 'Hope I have set foot on Barrier for last time,' Silas noted in his diary. Cherry had to type up Scott's 'Message to the Public' ready for telegraphic despatch round the globe when the ship reached New Zealand, and it brought on 'a terrible fit of the blues'. They even saw their dead companions, as they went into Ponting's darkroom and developed the films that had lain on the snow next to Scott's body for eight months. Five men posed woodenly at the Pole, hairy faces solid with ice. Birdie was holding the string to open the camera shutter.

As an antidote, Cherry went off to Cape Royds for three weeks to pickle Adélie penguin embryos. The weather was good; he had the companionship of Atch, who had gone with him to work on parasites; and as for the food – tins of boiled chicken, kidneys, ginger, Garibaldi biscuits: 'Truly Shackleton's expedition must have fed like turkey cocks from all the delicacies here.' Best of all, they had fresh buttered skua gull eggs for breakfast. Besides taking copious notes on the behaviour of Adélies for an article he planned to write, Cherry sketched, skinned and indulged his taste for solid Victorian novels by knocking off *Adam Bede*. One afternoon he worked out his own sledging record, and found that he had clocked up a whacking thirty-three weeks and four days on the Barrier, and that he had been absent from Cape Evans for forty-eight weeks and four days. His sledging total was 3,059 miles, higher than any other man's. He was proud. More than that, he was pleased to get the embryos done, as he knew it was what Bill would have wanted.

They went back to Cape Evans for Christmas, the return journey 'more like a steeplechase in deep snow than anything else'. It was not a happy holiday. They did manage a good meal, though all the wine was gone and they were obliged to drink liqueurs. There was little to do now except wait for the ship. They had packed up, ready to leave at short notice, and the words 'When I get home . . .' rang round the hut like a refrain. It was agreed that anyone who wanted could take a dog back to England with him, and Cherry settled on Kris, the hairy dark grey and white Siberian who had slavered over the sick Evans. Cherry ascribed to Kris the character of a Bolshevik – though he was immensely fond of him none the less.

January dragged on. The ship was frequently sighted, and always turned out to be an iceberg. On the seventeenth they decided to prepare for another winter. It was a grim prospect. They were almost out of coal, so were going to start cooking with seal oil. Food was to be rationed. Campbell issued orders to begin slaughtering seals.

After breakfast the next day Cherry went off to hunt while some of the others started carving a meat store in the ice. He killed and cut up two blubbery Weddells, and at about midday walked back to the hut across the hummocky headland. Everyone was out working, the air was still, and the chop-chop of ice axes sang out over the cape. Suddenly the bows of the *Terra Nova* glided out from behind the snout of the Barne Glacier.

The yells were wild.

On the ship, almost every man was on deck, straining into binoculars or telescopes. Many of the old crew were there, including the industrious navigator Harry Pennell, who had enjoyed an uneventful winter in New Zealand after the taxing journey up from Antarctica at the end of the previous season. But this time Pennell was not in command: he had yielded to Teddy Evans, who had recovered from scurvy and been promoted, becoming the youngest commander in the navy. The doughty old *Terra Nova* had been specially scrubbed, yards had been squared, ropes coiled and the ensign hoisted. The wardroom table was decked with flags and ribbons, champagne had been fetched up from the hold, and ranks of cigars, cigarettes and chocolates stood ready for duty. As the ship approached the ice foot at Cape Evans, her engines were cut. The shore party gave three cheers, and the ship's company replied. 'Are you all well?' Teddy Evans shouted through a megaphone from the bridge. There was a pause. Then Campbell shouted back:

'The Polar Party died on their return from the Pole: we have their records.'

The men on shore worked all night loading, then shot the last mules and shut up the hut, leaving it well provisioned for whoever might come next. When they sailed round to Cape Royds to pick up the zoological specimens left at Shackleton's hut, Cherry watched Cape Evans recede without regret: he never wanted to see it again. 'The pleasant memories,' he wrote in his diary, 'are all swallowed up in the bad ones.' He had been in the Antarctic for almost exactly two years.

He was given his old bunk on the ship. Besides beer, apples and the latest waltz on the gramophone, his chief joy was the mail. He had become an uncle, Lassie and her vicar having produced a little girl whom they named Susan. His multitudinous parcels and packing cases included a home-baked Dundee cake and a six-year supply of oilskins. Besides private news, he luxuriated in newspapers and magazines. 'The last year,' he wrote, 'has fulfilled the promises of the year before in English home politics: there are big changes coming, and we who believe they are for the bad, will be unable to do much about them.'

They had decided to erect a cross on Observation Hill, near Hut Point, to commemorate the five dead men. The ship's carpenter made a fine one from Australian jarrah wood, and quotations from the Bible were put forward as possible inscriptions. Cherry suggested the last line of Tennyson's 'Ulysses' instead: 'To strive, to seek, to find and not to yield.' He was pleased when his idea was taken up. The erection of this impressive cross was their last task, and while he was on the hill Cherry put a piece of lava in his pocket to send to Bill's widow. The cross stood nine feet out of the rock, and many feet into the ground. Lying on his bunk that night, Cherry wrote, 'I do not believe it will ever move.'*

* It did. I was there eighty-four years later when a small party of Americans repaired it after it had fallen in a blizzard. They re-erected it in a simple ceremony. Cherry would have been pleased.

They coasted alongside the Western Mountains up to Granite Harbour. Denis Lillie trawled for specimens, crouching on the poop surrounded by forests of jars, sponges and spiny starfish. Two years Cherry's senior, with sand-yellow hair and marble-blue eyes, Lillie was a genial character who had sailed down to the Antarctic with the *Terra Nova* and returned to winter in New Zealand, where he had worked on whales and fossils. Before the expedition he had studied Natural Sciences at Birmingham and Cambridge, and although he was not a distinguished student, he was an enthusiastic biologist who went on to publish a number of papers. A gifted artist, on the journey down to the Antarctic he had produced a series of excellent silhouette-style caricatures which were eventually reproduced in the *South Polar Times*. Lillie was popular on the ship, though he was probably the most unconventional man Scott had: he was deeply intellectual and was more interested in matters of the spirit than in schoolboy pranks. He had a number of eccentric, even cranky ideas which he happily aired as the *Terra Nova* pushed her way north, despite the fact that most of his theories were greeted at best with stupefaction by the others. He believed in reincarnation, for example, and thought he had been a Persian or a Roman in a previous existence. Reincarnated or not, Cherry liked him.

They picked up Campbell's geological specimens from Inexpressible Island, left a depôt for future explorers and turned for home through heavy pack ice, counting first the weeks, then the days, then the hours. Everyone was seasick. The bergs were so large, and so close, that once, leaving the wardroom, Cherry nearly struck his head on one. As the *Terra Nova* sailed north, he read reports of the expedition in the preceding year's newspapers. Evans' role, grossly distorted, featured prominently in all of them. It was too much. 'I should like to see things put in their right proportion,' Cherry wrote in his diary, 'and that man branded the traitor and liar he is.' He trawled through the weekly *Times* noting the inaccuracies, mostly concerning Evans' arduous sledging. 'I wonder if all the print in *The Times* is equally unreliable,' he mused, not the first person to ask such a question, or the last. 'It's fairly sickening and it makes one lose one's faith in everything – a man chosen out of 8,000 volunteers and now "the youngest commander in the Navy".' He was deeply disillusioned. 'One started with such high hopes, expecting men to get their desserts – and one's hopes have come to worse than nothing . . . There may be honour among thieves – there is none among adventurers.'

Evans had been appalled to learn of Scott's actions on the return journey from the Pole. In particular, he thought Scott a fool to have dragged the rock specimens on the sledge when the entire party was so weak. In a letter to one of the expedition's supporters four days before the *Terra Nova* reached New Zealand he pointed out that he himself had displayed more prudence. 'It seems to me extraordinary,' Evans wrote, 'that in the face of such obstacles they stuck to all their records and specimens. We dumped ours . . . I must say I considered the safety of my party before the value of the records and extra stores . . . Apparently Scott did not. His sledge contained 150 lbs of trash. He ought to have left it . . .' His gift for self-promotion did not desert him. 'Their *biggest* day's march on the Barrier was 9 miles,' he crowed, 'against our *average* 16.' This was vintage Evans. 'Why should I be modest?' he once asked a vice-admiral.

While Cherry boiled, Evans was busy in the wardroom establishing a six-man committee for winding up the expedition. Atch, who was on it, reported to Cherry in low tones that Evans wanted to doctor Scott's 'Message to the Public' before it was cabled to the world at large. Specifically, he wanted to omit the references to the oil shortages. Atch was determined to stop him.

Cherry and Atch were already close, and now they were thrown together in their desire to prevent Evans from taking over. Cherry recognised that his angry outbursts about Atch in his diary in October had been unfair, as his friend had been doing his best in a difficult situation. 'I consider him to be straight as a die,' he now wrote. Once again, Atch grew alarmed at Cherry's overwrought state. He told him he needed a complete change and plenty to occupy him when he got back. 'I see he is afraid that things generally are worrying me too much,' Cherry recorded.

In the early hours of 10 February the *Terra Nova* crept into Oamaru on the east coast of New Zealand like a phantom ship. 'With what mixed feelings,' Cherry remembered later, 'we smelt the old familiar woods and grassy slopes, and saw the shadowy outlines of human homes.' Atch and Pennell landed incognito to send the official telegram (including Scott's comment on the oil shortage: Atch had won), and the ship cruised around for a day to allow the news to get to the relatives first, and to fulfil the expedition's exclusive contract with the Central News Agency. Cherry had a bath, shaved off his beard and got out a new blue landing suit. How strange it felt to be sheathed in its stiff cleanness.

They steamed through Lyttelton Heads at dawn on 12 February, the white ensign at half-mast. The harbour master chugged out to meet them, bringing Atch and Pennell, who had gone on from Oamaru. 'Come down here a minute,' Atch shouted to Cherry over the growl of the engine. The tug belched out its exhaust fumes. 'It's made a tremendous impression,' he said conspiratorially when Cherry got to him. 'I had no idea it would make so much.'

The Empire was in mourning. Scott's 'Message to the Public' and the story of Oates' end had gone to the heart of the civilised world. In London the King and Queen spoke out publicly in sympathy, as did the Prime Minister and representatives of both Houses of Parliament. Messages poured in from beyond the Empire: President Taft sent a telegram to King George from New York, and the Italian Chamber of Deputies voted to convey their sympathies to the House of Commons. The myth-making began before the survivors even got their land legs. Scott and his dead companions gratified the need of the hour for heroes who could demonstrate that Britain was still great (*The Times* announced confidently that their actions proved Britons were still 'capable of maintaining the Empire that our fathers builded'). Only seven months before the news of Scott broke, the press had had an orgy over the *Titanic* disaster. Here was another monster story – the second in a year – facilitating feet, not inches, of column space hymning the uplifting virtues of gallantry in the teeth of catastrophe. And now, by an unwitting sleight of hand, it seemed that the polar party had won after all. Defeat on this earthly plain would surely be supplanted by British victory in the world to come: *The Times* concluded that the real value of the expedition was 'moral and spiritual'. The Admiralty decided that their men – Scott and Taff Evans – had been killed in action. In his luminous death Oates embodied the code of the era (or what was perhaps already the past era), that of chivalry and sacrifice.

Cherry again stayed with the Burtons, who were standing on the wharf to meet him in the pale morning sunshine. For years he remembered the first night in a soft bed and the first dinner off a white tablecloth with gleaming silver spoons and forks. He relished the bright colours and the balmy air, had a number of baths, and found that he could not sleep. The day after he arrived, Oriana Wilson asked him to visit her at the home of Joseph Kinsey, the expedition agent, where she was staying. She had sailed down from England early and enjoyed happy travels in New Zealand while waiting for Bill. She heard the news while on the train to Christchurch from a newspaper vendor parading along the platform shouting, 'Scott's dead! Scott's dead!' Cherry hurried over, and Ory read him part of Bill's last letter and told him all the nice things Bill had said about him. She wanted him to handle Bill's things. 'She is as fine a woman as he was a man,' Cherry concluded.

Thousands came to Lyttelton and Christchurch to offer their condolences, messages poured in from all over the world and flags up and down the country fluttered sadly at half-mast. Cherry went to a memorial service at the cathedral. 'I believe I am only just beginning to realise what has happened,' he wrote. The day after the service he had one of his headaches, and got annoyed at the small talk over dinner at the Burtons': 'the old, old story of running down colonials, which I cannot keep silent about'. Meanwhile he was occupied by a myriad expedition affairs, as well as arrangements for his passage home. He met up with Atch, who was himself embroiled in meetings and arrangements. Atch told him that Evans was 'quite hysterical'.

The press had little information and much space to fill (a Toronto newspaper reported soberly the day the *Terra Nova* reached Lyttelton that sixty-six men had died), and as always, the critics were ready. Cherry read in several American papers that 'all that could be done was not done', and in *The Times* that the returning parties might have 'tapped' oil from the depôts, leaving Scott short. Worse, many editorials focused on the inaction of Cherry and Dimitri during their dog journey to One Ton. The *Sydney Morning Herald* cited a rumour 'that relations between the present heads of the expedition are more than a little strained, and the suggestion is made this may possibly be in connection with the work of the relief parties in March of last year'. It was not all the fault of the newsmen. The bulletins sent out to the press by the committee were truncated, and sometimes manipulated. Cherry was furious that Evans and others had referred to his already infamous dog journey to One Ton as a relief journey, a term he angrily rejected. And above all the noise Cherry heard the parroted cry *cui bono* – what was the point of these hazardous expeditions? 'All these questions and many others were discussed by comfortable old gentlemen sitting plumply before their club fire with a condensed official report and some pages of hearsay on their knees,' he wrote later in an unpublished draft of *The Worst Journey*. 'Given one April day on the Barrier they themselves would have curled up and died.'

His mother cabled her sympathy. 'Do not worry about press criticism,' he wired back. 'I know all we could do was done there was not shadow dissension among us all the year please post this Reggie Apsley.' She cabled in reply that 'congratulations' were pouring in to Lamer on his safe return. 'Longing to get you home', she added.

The public had no idea of the sequence of events that had resulted in Cherry being stuck at One Ton. Nobody was interested in that kind of tedious detail. 'All kinds of wild conjectures in the papers this morning,'

Cherry wrote in his diary on 15 February. The reports included Dimitri's assertion that he had wanted to take the dogs on alone from One Ton. If Cherry had allowed Dimitri to go on, pundits mused, he might have found the polar party alive. Cherry tried to keep calm. 'I don't know that it matters,' he wrote bravely. There were bright spots. He saw more of Mrs Wilson ('Oh! She is wonderful') and dined with Kinsey's daughter at her house on Papanui Road. 'Beautiful table, good dinner, pretty girls in London frocks: what does a miserable explorer want better than that?' Sunday was a good day, as there were no papers. He played tennis, and enjoyed an excursion to Ashley Gorge, smelling the pines with his host Henry Burton.

He had foreseen criticism: in the last weeks on the ice he had discussed the reaction they would face with Atch and the others. But he had never imagined it would be personal; it hadn't crossed his mind that people would say he could have – should have – gone on from One Ton. He sat in his room at the Burtons' and went back to his journal. Leafing through to the note he had written on the Barrier after finding the bodies, he added to it, 'It seems to be necessary to point out that when we started back from One Ton Depôt we had no reason to suppose that there was anything wrong with the polar party.' He had thought this was obvious; but it wasn't. On 21 February he wrote:

a horrid day. Everybody everywhere seemed to be saying the wrong thing. One asked whether 'there would have to be an enquiry': a shopman told me they had been supposing all kinds of things about my journey south etc ad nauseam. I wish official sources would tell the truth and finish the whole rotten business. Meanwhile I am in the dirt tub and except an official denial of rumours nothing has been done. What a rotten end it is to a good expedition.

'Official sources', however, persisted in not telling the whole story. On the day Evans left for England Cherry found papers on the floor of the *Terra Nova* wardroom which included information about Scott's original orders for the dogs. These papers would, he inferred, almost certainly have been tossed over the side had he not picked them up, and he ascribed what was probably carelessness to a cover-up concocted by Evans and Francis Drake, a navy paymaster and the expedition secretary.

Lilian Burton wrote to Evelyn that Cherry was strong and well and bright. 'He looks just a little older,' she said tactfully, 'and one can see the shadow on his face in repose which the awful strain of these last two years must leave for a while.' Atch again told him to rest, and to take a roundabout journey home, but Cherry had already organised his passage on a mail ship. He would not leave the country until the zoological specimens were either despatched to England or safely donated to museums in New Zealand. There was time for golf and more tennis, and even a little theatre, but it was interspersed with mail, telegrams, visits to Ory and organisation of the specimens. Atch went up to Wellington to meet Kathleen, now Lady Scott, when her ship arrived. She too wanted the matter of the oil shortage kept as quiet as possible, and again Atch put his foot down.

At least Kathleen was not prepared to hand control to Evans, especially after she had read the criticisms of him in her husband's diary. This was a relief to Cherry. 'It is a horrid business,' he wrote, 'for her and for everybody: but there it is, and it would be an everlasting shame if the story of this expedition were told by the one big failure on it.' A few days later Cherry received a note from Kathleen. 'I know', she told him, 'how splendidly you stuck through it all . . . I feel you've borne the strain with a heroism equal to anybody's, and bless you for it.' He was very glad, and wrote to Reggie that she was one of the few people whose opinion mattered to him.

On 6 March the *Terra Nova* sailed for England under Pennell's command with Cherry's dog, Kris, howling cravenly on deck in a most un-Bolshevik manner. Cherry was then free to spend more time with Kinsey. Scott had thought a lot of him, and now Cherry took a liking to him too, partly because Kinsey was suspicious of Evans. He gave Cherry a copy of Scott's last letter to him, written in the tent. 'You will pull the expedition together I'm sure,' it said. 'Teddy Evans is not to be trusted over much though he means well.'

Cherry spent his last week in New Zealand playing tennis, motoring about the countryside and sorting specimens at Christchurch Museum. He was touched by a letter he received from Deb, already back in Sydney, exclaiming that he was 'damned disgusted' about the misunderstandings in the newspapers, especially the one about Dimitri wanting to go on from One Ton. It made him boil, fulminated Deb, 'that the men who should have did not set the papers right on that point, even at the expense of showing Dimitri up . . . But I believe these things will only make us stick closer together, and anyhow damn the world!'

On 17 March Cherry left Lyttelton on the mail steamer *Osterley* with a note from Atch in his pocket wishing him *bon voyage* and thanking him for his loyalty. New Zealand had been a mixed experience. There was sweetness in the return to the world – the exotic colours, the ripe fruit, the new faces. On the other hand, reading about himself in the papers had been agony. But he kept his head. At one point he said it almost seemed as if the interlude in the Antarctic had never happened. It had already taken on the quality of a dream.

8

Kipling in Real Life

The *Osterley* steamed wearily into the Bay of Naples through a warm April shower, and on the glistening wharf Evelyn and her daughters Peggy and Edith strained for the first sight of Laddie. After a very happy reunion they sailed back to Plymouth together and were soon gratefully enveloped within the familiar quiet bustle of Lamer. The servants had prepared for the young master's return with mounting excitement, and only one was disappointed: Mrs Hyde, the aged wife of a long-serving gardener, had been standing at the window of the lodge all morning, waiting eagerly for the carriage bearing Cherry home at last. But when she went into the kitchen to put the kettle on, the carriage swept up the drive unseen.

It was as he remembered. He walked out on the shaved lawn in the cool night air and stood in the shadows of the chestnuts. Owls were hooting in the pear trees, nightjars chugging in the wood, and in the walled garden the willows flexed their limbs over the pond. Crayfish still jittered in the shallows of the Lea at the bottom of the slope, and laburnum and lilac still bloomed on the wall of the kitchen garden where raspberry canes were standing guard, neatly trussed with Tilbury's green twine. Indoors the silk was a little more faded on the back of the piano, but his gloomy relatives still glowered down from their old positions on the walls. These were the places of his childhood imaginings, and they embodied something deeply loved.

He dangled his gurgling baby niece Susan on his knee, and shook the hand of his new brother-in-law the vicar, whose two children from his previous marriage had found a second home at Lamer. As for the girls, Elsie had been to Jamaica and New York before coming out to meet him in

Italy, and Mildred was about to go to India: as a neighbour wrote to Evelyn, there must have been a travelling microbe lurking among the family genes.

There was a mountain of business, as usual, including fresh drafts of his sisters' settlements, Lassie's marriage necessitating complicated changes. On the estates tenants had vacated, electricity had been installed and cottages built, and in his study Cherry perused the prices of prudently purchased debenture stock. He had come back a richer man. Rents had been flowing in from Denford, Lamer, Little Wittenham and the Watling Street house in London, and at the end of 1913 he received a payment from the Swansea estate on which he had inherited the role of mortgagee to the tune of £27,500 (well over a million today). He instructed his brokers to reinvest.

Beyond the gentle slopes of Hertfordshire, expedition business pressed upon him. Days after his return he hurried down to the hectic Victoria Street offices, where letters were going out in their hundreds on black-edged expedition paper, soliciting funds (the expedition had virtually gone bankrupt while its members were in the Antarctic), thanking donors and keeping relatives informed. Teddy Evans, much in evidence, was recovering from fresh tragedy: his wife Hilda had died of peritonitis on the journey home from New Zealand. But he threw himself into expedition work, and addressed an audience of 9,000 at the Albert Hall. On Atch's advice, Cherry was on the platform alongside him, maintaining an appearance of taciturn dignity while churning hotly inside. More happily, Cherry was able to pick up Kris, who was a free hound after eight days in quarantine.

Cherry was drawn to the families of his dead friends. He became fond of Birdie's mother Emily ('Sometimes you seem a little bit of him left to me,' she told him), and his sister Mary, known as May, and he went down to Henley-on-Thames for tea with Scott's mother and one of his sisters. He often saw Kathleen. But of all the relatives, he was closest to Oriana Wilson. Like Kathleen and Scott's mother she had been up to Lamer in his absence, and now she and Cherry embarked on a friendship that was to last until her death in 1945. A tall and handsome, though not beautiful, woman, Ory was restless and independent, and she hated publicity, a characteristic that appealed deeply to Cherry. She had a strong smile with a hint of the iceberg, and was reserved and friendly at the same time. If she didn't like someone – Kathleen Scott, for instance – she behaved as if that person didn't exist. She felt protective of Cherry, as her husband had. But she was not as soft as Bill.

On 14 June the *Terra Nova* sailed into Cardiff under Pennell's command, three years after she had left. There were no banquets. Cherry was there to meet her, and so were Ory and Caroline Oates, Titus's formidable mother. Mrs Oates had already read her son's diary, as it had been brought back ahead of the ship, and she had been interviewing survivors in an attempt to establish what had really happened ('Oh, he was just champion,' one of the seamen kept saying when remembering Titus). A strong and intelligent woman quite capable of reading between the lines, she did not accept the notion of heroic explorers dying for the honour of their country: she suspected that Scott had been a bungler. Teddy Evans and Atch both told her that Titus had regretted going on the expedition – on one occasion he had to be talked out of returning with the ship before the southern journey had even begun. Her son, Caroline concluded, had been 'disgusted with the way in which the whole thing was done'.

A few weeks later King George received the *Terra Nova* men at Buckingham Palace to present them with Polar medals.* The officers lined up with gleaming buttons and burnished epaulettes while the scientists and Cherry skulked in the background in top hats and spats. The widows had been invited, and afterwards everyone thronged into a reception at Caxton Hall for sherry and stewed tea. The King told Ponting he hoped every British schoolboy would see his pictures, as they were sure to promote the spirit of adventure that had made the Empire. As it turned out many hundreds of thousands of schoolboys did; but it was too late for the Empire.

Atch and other friendly Antarcticans went up and down to Lamer, where their trains were met at the station by the rackety Lamer carriage. They slept outside in the green surge of summer, Cherry's tribe of sisters entertained them on the piano, and the mowing machine buzzed lazily down the slope to the river as they finished their picnics with wobbly puddings and bottled blackberries. It was not quite the fabled Edwardian country house set, but it was an agreeably cosy scaled-down version.

Ory was often there that first summer. Cherry had been helping her locate and sort Bill's possessions. She offered him his green leather copy of Tennyson back, but Cherry wanted her to keep it. Ory too was suspicious of the London committee, now in full spate marshalling material for publication, raising funds for the widows and moulding the public image of

---

* The officers and scientists were also awarded medals by the Royal Geographical Society; the senior navy men were promoted; and Crean and Lashly got the Albert Medal for saving Teddy Evans' life.

the dead heroes. It was chaired by the autocratic figure of Lord Curzon, president of the Royal Geographical Society since 1911, former viceroy of India and a man, Cherry noted, whom nobody in England would dare gainsay. The expedition belonged to the committee now. In June Cherry was told off by Francis Drake, its secretary, for communicating with a firm which had donated a typewriter to the *Terra Nova* back in 1910. 'It is very undesirable,' Drake wrote officiously, 'to have any interference in our business arrangements . . . You should have consulted either Captain Evans or myself.' Depressed by the direction post-expedition events were taking, Cherry was cheered only by indications from Kathleen that Teddy was not going to have it all his own way. ('Reginald Smith,' she confided to her diary in October, 'comes to show me a preposterous letter written by that disgraceful creature Evans.')

Reggie suggested that Cherry have the volumes of his journal typed up by a secretary at his firm's offices. Before handing them over, Cherry went through them carefully underlining critical passages which were to be edited out of the typed version. After the job was done, the original handwritten notebooks were locked in the Lamer strong room. At the same time, Leonard Huxley, a former schoolmaster and one of Reggie's readers at Smith, Elder, was editing Scott's diaries for publication and commissioning supplementary material. At Huxley's request, Cherry lent him a copy of his typed journals. Huxley told Smith they were 'gorgeous'.

Meanwhile, late in the summer of 1913, Cherry delivered the three Emperor penguin eggs from Crozier to the Natural History branch of the British Museum, that supreme piece of bombastic Victorian architecture in South Kensington. At first, a junior assistant was reluctant even to accept the bitterly won specimens. Cherry was passed to a senior member of staff and then forced to wait in a corridor while the man conversed at length with a more important visitor. Finally, someone grudgingly took the eggs in, and with immense difficulty Cherry extracted a receipt. To compound the insult, when Cherry visited the museum some time later accompanied by Grace, one of Scott's sisters, the first person they spoke to denied ever having seen the eggs ('How stupid that minor custodian was!' Grace remembered).

The frosty reaction of the museum staff was memorably parodied, nine years later, in *The Worst Journey*: Cherry represents himself as the Heroic Explorer in the exchange, his frustration rising to a murderous plot in the hushed museum corridors. The episode was a potent metaphor for Cherry's fractured ideals, and as the book took shape in his mind the painful disparity between the effort of retrieving the eggs and the response they met with at the museum came to exemplify one of his central themes. (Furthermore, when Dr C. W. Parsons published the official results of the embryo work many years later, he concluded that 'neither [the three Emperor embryos nor the series of Adélie embryos] has added greatly to our knowledge of penguin embryology'.)*

Called *Scott's Last Expedition* and appended with supplementary material, Scott's diaries appeared in two volumes in October 1913. They were received with widespread acclaim. The long review in *Punch*, unsigned but in fact written by A. A. Milne, noted, 'There is courage and strength and loyalty and love shining out of the second volume no less than out of the first.' Cherry believed Milne's thoughtful piece was 'quite the nicest thing that has been written on the expedition'. But he was uneasy with the glib heroism which Scott's prose fostered in the public imagination. Scott and the myth-makers had turned the story into a simple allegory of the Christian journey, a sort of *Pilgrim's Progress* on ice. Yet Cherry's two best friends were dead, and no amount of allegories could bring them back. Cherry was struggling not to blame Scott; he was not yet able to acknowledge his anger towards him, even to himself. Later, he came to feel deeply threatened by *Scott's Last Expedition*, convinced that it didn't tell the whole story, or even the true story. It was an unfair assessment, and a reflection of Cherry's lack of perspective. Scott's diaries were edited for publication, but not substantially. Most of the cuts dealt with critical remarks: it was natural for a leader to express doubts about individuals in the privacy of his diary, and equally natural for his remarks to be edited out when the diaries were published. Cherry's general unhappiness about the excisions had not yet formed in 1913, but he was disturbed by one point in *Scott's Last Expedition* from the day it appeared. The book failed to make it clear that Scott had taken the dogs on further than planned, and that as a result of jumbled orders there was no dog food laid at One Ton.

Cherry suspected the committee of a cover-up to make Scott look perfect. Nobody was prepared to say that the dog food depôt had never been laid: not Evans, not Kathleen, not Curzon. Atch tried to say it, but he was bludgeoned into quietude. Seeing that Atch had little weight against the steamrolling tactics of the committee, Cherry decided to go to Lincoln's Inn Fields for an official interview with Farrer, who was the expedition's solicitor as well as his own. But Farrer wasn't playing. 'They

---

* Professor Cossar Ewart of Edinburgh University had produced an interim report indicating that the embryos might shed some light on the relationship between scales and feathers. Cherry still believed that an Emperor embryo would reveal the missing link between birds and reptiles.

would not listen,' he insisted when Cherry said he wanted to go up before the committee himself to explain the role of his dog journey. 'They will say you are overstrained. You see, there must be no scandal.' It was not just a refusal: it was an implied threat. 'The committee,' Cherry noted in the margin of his Antarctic journal, 'meant to hush up everything. I was to be sacrificed.'

The other Antarcticans had taken up where they had left off before the expedition, the navy men returning to service, the scientists to their research. Atch, who as a naval research surgeon was in both camps, was working on his polar parasites at the London School of Tropical Medicine. The civilian scientists were writing up their material as well as arranging postgraduate or teaching positions to supplement their meagre incomes. There had been endless talk, during the long days spent waiting for the ship, of how they would manage to produce their reports on the paltry expedition fees. They were all full of plans.

Silas Wright went straight back to Cambridge and took up a position as lecturer in surveying and cartography in the Department of Geography. In 1914 he married one of Ray Priestley's sisters. Griff Taylor, who had come home after the first year down south, had been working for the Australian federal government, carrying out geological surveys. In 1913 he was granted permission to move to England to collaborate with the other Antarctic scientists. He joined Silas at Cambridge, and married another Priestley sister. Deb (Frank Debenham) also moved to England to finish his postgraduate studies at Cambridge, taking up a place at Caius, Wilson's old college. As for Ponting, he had produced his moving picture film and had a heavy lecture programme planned for 1914.

Leading stoker William Lashly was forty-five when he returned from the Antarctic. He was discharged from the navy with a pension; but, with characteristic determination, the day after he was formally released he enlisted in the Naval Reserve. For Lashly's colleague Tom Crean the call of the Antarctic remained irresistible. In the spring of 1914 he was again loaned by the navy to a ship heading for the polar regions. He was returning to the Antarctic with Shackleton, serving – not in the ranks but as second officer – on an ambitious expedition which was to be the first to march the whole way across the continent. According to Shackleton's plan, his ship, the *Endurance*, was to deposit a small party on the Weddell Sea coast, from where the men would march to the Pole, on across the Plateau and down the Beardmore to Cape Evans. On the last leg they would pick up depôts laid by another party left by the *Aurora* on the Ross Sea side.

Unlike his former shipmates, Cherry had no fixed plans, and no career to follow. When the grouse season opened he went up to the Smiths' Scottish cottage to cool down with a spot of shooting on the moors of Glen Prosen. It was where he had met Wilson, so the ghosts were there too. He strode along the broomy banks of the South Esk streams and dwelt on what to do next with his life, still keen to acquire a profession. His interminable correspondence with his solicitor had led him to abandon his plan to study law. He now turned instead to medicine, a career with the defined sense of purpose that he sought. He was surrounded by successful doctors on his mother's side of the family and, more significantly, he was still under Bill's influence ('I feel how happy Bill would be to know that you are doing this,' Ory wrote). But he had no real conception of the years of hard labour involved in qualifying as a doctor from a standing start as a 27-year-old with a mediocre history degree and a taste for travel.

None the less, as the first plane trees yellowed on the cambered streets of the capital he began hospital work as a junior trainee observer. Right from the start he found it difficult to apply himself to the job, as he was still spending much of his time sorting the expedition's zoological specimens at the Natural History Museum. He had also begun working up his notes on Antarctic birds for official publication, corresponding on the subject with Sidney Harmer, a zealous departmental head at the museum. It was the start of an unhappy and misguided attempt to reproduce an academic report as if he were a scientist. As for the relationship with Harmer, it was to end very badly indeed.

In addition, Cherry was busy giving illustrated lectures on the Antarctic to schools and working men's clubs around Wheathampstead. When Ponting found out that his slides were being used, he fired off a long and aggrieved letter insisting that he had exclusive rights in expedition images. Cherry hosed him down, pointing out that his lectures were small and free of charge, and Ponting was extinguished until the following February, when he learned that Cherry was speaking in Leeds. Once again he erupted into thunderous protest. The disagreement finally petered out when the pair united against a common enemy: Evans. In the summer of 1913 Teddy had embarked on an ambitious lecture tour of his own. He was still officially on cordial terms with Cherry, who chaired his lecture in St Albans that November, but Ponting was furious that Evans was using his expedition slides so fecklessly.

Meanwhile Kathleen wanted to know what was to be done about the *South Polar Times*. In the end Cherry handed the originals over to Reggie to prepare for reproduction, and the early numbers subsequently went on display at the British Museum. Cherry was annoyed to see that they were labelled 'Lent by Lady Scott', as he didn't consider them hers to lend. He was beginning to feel wary of Kathleen. 'Lady Scott's possessive instinct,' he noted, 'not only of Scott but of the whole expedition, is a very strong one.' He kept the final volume to himself.

Since Cherry had left Cape Evans and its bitter memories he had been coping with both bereavement and a growing sense of personal betrayal by Evans, the committee and the press. Now, as he settled back in to the rhythms of home, he also had to acknowledge the collapse of the moral certainties that had characterised the England of his youth.

Between the death of Edward VII and the war, a period which coincided almost exactly with the absence of Scott's second expedition, Britain had been traumatised by a series of shattering challenges to the existing order. The House of Lords had lost its power of veto (the crucial vote took place the day Lassie walked up the aisle), and the notion of the paternal responsibility of the noble few had vanished with it. The Liberals had been preparing legislation to abolish the power of the Lords just before the *Terra Nova* left England, and while he was in the Antarctic Cherry had read reports of its progress when the ship brought news. Back at home in the aftermath of the great parliamentary drama – probably the greatest of the century – he recognised that the ground had shifted under the feet of his class. In his childhood the cabinet had been peopled with mighty landowners such as the bearded giant Lord Salisbury down the road at Hatfield House. Now the absolute power of the Lords had been removed, the vast landed estates were crippled, and well-fed patricians like the General no longer spoke for the masses.

After August 1911 turbulence on other fronts had further shaken the tottering British establishment. The notion of Home Rule in Ireland had preoccupied the nation for years, and while Scott was struggling up the Beardmore it had become an obsession. There was even talk of civil war. In 1913 the Lords twice rejected the Home Rule Bill, and in the spring of 1914 a fresh Home Rule crisis engulfed the country. The idea of an Irish parliament was even more alien to thorough-going imperialists like Cherry than the objectives of the suffragette movement, another symbol of the rejection of the existing order. The women, as intrepid, brave and pioneering as any polar explorer, had come a long way since the *Terra Nova* sailed out of Cardiff. In the summer of 1912 they had started setting fire to post-boxes, and in the first months of 1914 they embarked on a more ambitious arson spree. There was still no evidence of conflagration in

Wheathampstead, but Cherry noted with bewilderment that the pretty girls walking through St James's Park near the expedition offices were no longer trussed up in Victorian fashions that thrust out their buttocks and breasts.

Finally, the wave of labour unrest that had unsettled Cherry when he learned of it in the Antarctic ('the rumblings of the storms to come') had indeed continued on its unstoppable trajectory. By the summer of 1914 a general strike was looming out of the foggy hinterland. In his absence, the security of Cherry's past had dissolved like so many fragments of ice. Throughout his childhood he had inhaled the vapour of paternalistic Toryism and the moral seriousness of Victorian virtue; it was part of him. He was not yet thirty, and he was a relic.

On the cultural front, too, iconoclastic new movements had sprung forth in almost every arena. Sergei Diaghilev's ballet had caused a sensation, and at the end of May 1914 London was shocked by the deeply modern music of Richard Strauss. Kathleen Scott's friend Isadora Duncan had been enjoying fabulous success for some time – she had even danced for King Edward – but many were still offended by her free-style methods and the tunic in which she insisted on deploying them. A Post-Impressionist exhibition at a London gallery had provoked an angry and almost hysterical reaction among critics and public alike. On the lower cultural slopes, moving pictures continued to capture the popular imagination. The men had come back from the ice to find that the number of cinemas in London had quadrupled.

Antarctica, like the past, was a place where the anxieties of the twentieth century did not intrude. The expedition cut like a canyon between Cherry's childhood and the rest of his life, and when he looked back beyond it to his youth he saw, dimly, the lost world of Rupert Brooke, the flaxen-haired poet who, rightly or wrongly, came to embody the romantic, self-sacrificing ideal of the young Englishman of Cherry's generation. After the war, Brooke's poetry appealed to many nostalgic for the certainty of the past, a sunlit era when the Grantchester clock stood permanently at ten to three. But for Cherry, it was not the war that had transformed that world of lyrical innocence. By the spring of 1914 it was already gone.

The allure of an Antarctic explorer was comparable to that of a major sports star in our own less heroic age, and when good looks, a whopping income and a country seat were thrown in it wasn't surprising that Cherry found himself surrounded by pretty girls. Over the winter of 1913 he had become attached to one admirer in particular, and if they weren't dancing to the ragtime that was all the rage at the Berkeley Hotel or breathing in cigar smoke at the Café Royal, Cherry was showing her off in the chaotic expedition offices or at Reggie and Isabel's house in Green Street. She remains anonymous, as no information about her has survived.

Yet he was still immersed in the expedition. For many years after his return from the ice Cherry quietly undertook small acts of kindness towards the *Terra Nova* crewmen; during the war he was even on the look-out for needy *Discovery* men. The chief beneficiary was Petty Officer George Abbott, a naval gymnastics instructor and wrestling champion who had been a member of Campbell's Northern Party. Despite severing the tendons of three fingers in a disagreement with a Weddell seal, Abbott had held up well during the horrors of Inexpressible Island, but on the voyage home he had a breakdown. Especially sensitive to cases of nervous collapse, a condition with which he closely identified, Cherry went down to visit Abbott in hospital in Southampton and paid for his treatment. When Abbott lost his pension because he had been transferred from a naval hospital to a civil one, Cherry campaigned on his behalf and secured his rights, a process which eventually culminated in general reforms in the treatment of invalided servicemen.

Cherry had plenty to do, but despite his new girlfriend and his half-baked medical plans, he didn't have enough to think about. Atch saw yet again that his tendency to dwell on the expedition and its aftermath was threatening his mental wellbeing. He had an idea. He had just been seconded to a medical research expedition to eastern China led by Dr Robert Leiper, a distinguished Scottish helminthologist at the London School of Tropical Medicine and a scientist so devoted to his subject that he once swallowed a fish tapeworm to observe the effect it had upon his stomach. The expedition had been funded both to investigate a parasitic flatworm which was finding its way inside British seamen in Chinese waters and causing Asiatic schistosomiasis, and to study the spread of bilharziasis. Why didn't Cherry come along to help out for a month or two in his familiar role as zoological assistant?

This was just the ticket. A chance to escape again, and on a medical expedition to boot. Cherry was soon off on another round of visits gathering equipment and supplies, his Harrods account bending under the strain. In the middle of the preparations a letter arrived at Lamer which was to have a decisive effect on the course of the next decade. It was from Colonel H. G. Lyons, secretary of the expedition's publications committee. After a poor start ('Dear Mr Garrad'), Lyons revealed that Evans, who as Scott's deputy was naturally first in line to write the official narrative of the expedition, was too busy to take on the job. Would Cherry do it? This too was Atch's suggestion. It was what both he and Cherry had wanted all along. Cherry immediately wrote to Lyons, gleefully accepting his offer. They agreed to meet on his return from China.

On 20 February 1914, ten months after he had arrived home from the Antarctic, Cherry boarded the P. & O. steamer SS *Malwa* with Leiper and Atch. Reggie was to accompany them as far as Marseilles. Kathleen and Ory saw them off as if they were returning to the Antarctic, and the event was recorded in *The Times*. 'Among all the heroes of the [*Terra Nova*] expedition,' trilled the report, 'survivors state that no-one acquitted himself more usefully than Mr Cherry-Garrard.'

As the air on deck grew warmer, Cherry wore the old arguments threadbare with Atch and once again relished the confined freedom of an oceangoing ship. But at Port Said he was intercepted by a wire from Farrer concerning the tenants of Watling Street, the old Garrard property in the City of London. The house had been occupied for many years by a large firm of cotton traders who wanted to buy the dilapidated property so that they could pull it down and build a new one. Farrer advised him to sell, interest being more favourable than rent. Cherry cabled back *Yes*.

After an uneventful passage through the Suez Canal and the Red Sea they crossed the Indian Ocean and changed ships in Colombo, arriving in a rainy Shanghai on 30 March. Proximity to both the coast and the Yangtze River made the city an ideal base for an expedition researching a condition afflicting people living and working close to water (in some regions sixty per cent of the population had the disease). Leiper and his men hired a houseboat, turned it into a floating laboratory and pottered up the canals of the Yangtze, the main trade route to the largest silk- and tea-producing regions of China. Their first task was to find an infected patient from whom they could collect the worm's eggs.

Since Cherry's last visit to Asia on his cargo ship tour, China had lost her emperor. The parliament established to replace dynastic succession was barely lurching from one week to the next, threatened by such baleful enemies as the army and even more volatile warlords. Before setting off on the houseboat, Cherry wrote to Farrer from Shanghai's Astor House Hotel.

The country is in a most disturbed state. White Wolf looks like setting up an independent kingdom in Szechuan, and he is a better soldier than the Imperial troops; trade is more or less at a standstill, one man shot himself 3 days ago owing to financial difficulties and I hear that there are many in the same state. At present this part of China seems all right as regards safety – but they are expecting another revolution later on and they say that it is going to be much worse than the last. The general opinion is that China is in practically the same state as 400 years ago and they may do just the same things.

Cherry was carrying round a small maroon Winsor & Newton notebook in which to jot suggestions for his official expedition narrative. From the outset he and Atch were concerned about potential editorial interference from committee bogeyman Lyons, already a Porlockian figure in Cherry's imagination. But Cherry was too methodical to hold off important list-making. Jiggling in a rickshaw along the muddy lanes that filleted the fertile lowlands abutting the canals, he compiled a rough inventory of drawings to be commissioned ('eye goggles, sledge, tapered runners of sledge . . .') and a formidable 'To Do' list which included requests to relatives for permission to use the polar party's notebooks; correspondence with suppliers asking for details of exactly what had been supplied; and multitudinous notes to himself ('Find out the cause of the fur falling out of the sleeping bags'). He started writing letters to this effect, and posted them when he returned to a chilly Shanghai, where he found time to carouse in the club-rooms with Atch (as a sizeable port and manufacturing centre Shanghai had a lively expatriate community). His good watch was stolen.

The search for an infected patient had proved fruitless, and to exacerbate their scientific problems, Atch and Leiper were quarrelling bitterly. Cherry did his best to support Atch. But he was only half in China. 'Get details of acetylene gas plant,' he noted in the maroon book one day, and on another, 'Plentiful supply of nails needed for boots.' The notebook became a kind of brainstorming receptacle, each thought neatly separated from the next by a ruled line. The volume which would come out of it, in Cherry's mind, was to be both official history and travel guide: it would include an elaborate descriptive list of every item used by every member of the British Antarctic Expedition, rather like an upmarket scout manual. His sorrow was still too deep for more pliable words.

After a glorious rail journey on his own up through Harbin to Siberia and across central Russia, Cherry arrived home on 10 May to find *The Times* sprouting with stories about the escalating crisis among the great powers, and the news that in the National Gallery a suffragette had slashed Velázquez's 'Rokeby Venus' with a meat cleaver. He had enjoyed his adventure immensely. Atch had been sorry to see him go: 'I have missed you a very great deal,' he wrote from Shanghai later in the month. Atch was not the only one missing Cherry. His letters contained greetings from a woman called Maidie. 'She asked me to say,' wrote Atch, 'she was always thinking about Chewwy-Gawward.'

Meanwhile, Cherry broke up with his English girlfriend. Nothing is known of the cause of the rupture, but judging from the consolatory words despatched from Shanghai by Atch, Cherry was badly shocked. 'Some day you will meet Miss Right,' Atch offered lamely. Cherry cheered himself up with plans for another trip to Shanghai. The search for human patients had been abandoned, and Atch and Leiper, still quarrelling, were now looking for infected dogs.*

At the beginning of June Cherry went down to London to meet Lyons at the Army and Navy Club. He asked directly what his authority would be as the writer of the official narrative, and was assured that he would have a free hand. On that happy understanding, Cherry issued Lyons with a list of requests to various people for information about their work on the expedition. It included enquiries about photographic gear to Ponting, who, when Lyons forwarded the questions, immediately replied that he was too busy to answer.

Hospital work was abandoned – for good, as it turned out – as Cherry threw himself into research for the book. He was soon drowning in material. He spent many days in London, and started going round to firms who had supplied the expedition with equipment and food. At the beginning of July he broke off to take the train over to Cheltenham. There he joined thousands of people watching Sir Clements Markham unveil a memorial to Wilson. Sculpted by Kathleen (who modelled Bill's bottom half on Cherry's corduroy trousers, which she had borrowed), it was an imposing larger-than-life bronze depicting Bill in his sledging harness.

Cherry saw a lot of Kathleen in 1914, despite his developing wariness. She refused to play the part of the distraught and housebound widow. Her first priority was her five-year-old son Peter, but from time to time she still disappeared on her exotic travels: at the beginning of the year she went to the Sahara alone. Her social life was fearsomely active. She had luncheon and dinner engagements almost every day, often squeezing in a tea party too, and Herbert Asquith, the Prime Minister, regularly turned up at her house for a confidential talk. Besides all that she remained devoted to her

---

* A groundbreaking paper on the spread of Asiatic schistosomiasis, co-authored by Leiper and Atch, was published in the *British Medical Journal* in 1915. With the help of pioneering work by Japanese scientists they had discovered that the parasite entered sailors' feet while they were swabbing decks. Atch later turned away from parasitology, but Leiper went on to become an international authority on very small worms.

sculpture, and was rarely short of commissions. She sculpted Kris, Cherry's Antarctic dog, despite the fact that he refused to lie down. (Kris was now living in grander style than any polar dog before or since. Cherry had had a special pen built behind the house, with a properly drained floor laid with white tiles, a wrought-iron gate and a board inside spelling out Kris's full name – 'Kris the Beautiful' – in Russian.)

Sculpture was one of the few subjects in which Kathleen and Cherry found genuine communion. Although Cherry was conventional by nature, he responded to artistic excellence rather than established models of what constituted art. Stumping briskly round the London galleries with an eye to acquisition, he embraced newness. He bought a Rodin bust at a time when Rodin represented the most *avant* of the avant-garde, and began to build a modestly impressive collection for Lamer which foxed the servants and flummoxed visiting clergy for decades.

Fresh interests did not displace his obsessions. He scrutinised the press for references to the expedition, and when he spotted errors he fired off letters demanding corrections. As these were usually minor, and often in minor publications, he cut a rather ridiculous figure, a youthful Sir Bufton Tufton marooned in a study deep in a leafy shire. Scanning *The Times* over breakfast one morning he noticed that the sculptor Albert Hodge, commissioned to carve a memorial to the dead men, had included on the back a trophy depicting snowshoes. Cherry leapt for pen and paper. 'We never used snowshoes,' he told Hodge firmly. 'Always ski.' More seriously, he was increasingly convinced that lean and hungry conspirators were at work hushing up aspects of the expedition that did not fit the heroic ideal: an omission in the typed version of his journal was ascribed to collusion between someone at the Smith, Elder offices and Lord Curzon. The evidence is inconclusive, the theory unconvincing; but both fuelled Cherry's anxieties for years.

Cherry had been so pleased, on the other hand, with what A. A. Milne had written about *Scott's Last Expedition* that when a facsimile of the *South Polar Times* was published, he sent him a copy. Milne duly obliged him in print. 'I cannot read or see too much of the men who are my heroes,' he wrote in *Punch*, confessing that when it came to Wilson's illustrations, 'I envy Mr Cherry-Garrard so prolific and brilliant a contributor.' The warm-hearted review focused on an article by Griff called 'The Bipes', purporting to be a paper given by Titus's escaped rabbit to the Royal Society of Rabbits on the subject of the wingless bipeds at Cape Evans. Cherry appeared in the piece as a Bipe classified as B. Kiplingi. 'This is an interesting type,' ran his taxonomic description. 'He is adorned with a cheery smile, accessory transparent membranes over the eyes and literary leanings . . . I found a series of beautiful little journals in his burrow labelled Kiplingi which deal with portions of his career . . .' Griff's observation was sound: Cherry was devoted to Kipling and his robust imperial ideas (on some subliminal level he also identified with the dark, depressive strain present in both the man and the work). In a fit of reverential munificence when sorting through his Antarctic packing cases, he decided to send his well-thumbed copy of *Kim* to its author. The novel had been read by almost everyone in the shore party. 'I can say quite truthfully,' Cherry wrote to his hero, 'that there were no books which we had which were so much used, gave so much food for conversation or more enjoyment.'

Nineteen fourteen was a gorgeous summer, and at home Cherry and Evelyn had cook's special plum cake for tea underneath the flowering chestnuts while Lassie's daughter Susan toddled after butterflies. Indoors the sash windows were left permanently open and sunblinds were unfurled to protect the motionless ancestors. Cambridge was only an hour away, and, as Deb, Silas, Griff and several other expedition men were ensconced there as postgraduates or junior fellows, Cherry often zipped over in his new, low-slung motor car, still a rare sight on the quiet Hertfordshire lanes. He was immensely fond of Deb in particular, and regularly dragged him away from his specimens in the Sedgwick Museum. Deb was still deeply involved in matters expeditionary, since he was writing up the geological results, and although he was to evolve into more of a geographer than a geologist he remained a central figure in the British polar community for many years. He was straight, a characteristic that ranked highly with Cherry, spoke his mind, and liked to have fun.

In the early summer days they picnicked in the elmy sunshine of the Backs with Silas and Griff or, if their girls were with them, punted indecorously along the Cam, sometimes joined for short visits by Harry Pennell, the cheerful, steady navigator on the *Terra Nova* who had worked so hard that he had slept under his chart table. Everyone, especially Cherry, admired Pennell tremendously.

The crisis precipitated by the assassination of the Archduke Franz Ferdinand and his wife in Sarajevo on 28 June did not rattle them: there had already been two Balkan wars in three years, and parliament remained preoccupied with Home Rule. Cherry was feeling satisfied with his own position regarding the estates and his extensive portfolio. 'My income seems to be increasing considerably,' he wrote to Farrer two days before the decisive Austrian ultimatum to Serbia at the end of July. Britain continued to remain neutral, while busily preparing her battleships. On 3

August long, grey columns of soldiers marched into Belgium, and at eleven o'clock the following evening, at the end of a hot, tense bank holiday weekend, Britain declared war on Germany.

Men like Cherry with an ingrained sense of duty threw themselves at the war ('Now, God be thanked', wrote Rupert Brooke, 'Who has matched us with His hour'). Within days he had offered to organise Lamer as a fifty-bed Red Cross hospital for wounded officers, a plan he had harboured for many years; but that, of course, was nothing like enough. He had to act. While he was engaged in discussions about the hospital, the famous surgeon Sir Frederick Treves, a luminary of the Red Cross, had the idea that dogs might be usefully deployed at the front to sniff out wounded men. As an experienced dog-handler, this was a perfect job for Cherry. A major in Harrow offered his pack of bloodhounds, and arrangements were hastily made while the country erupted in jingoistic frenzy and the black lines of the German advance crept down the maps.

Uniforms and passports were provided by the Red Cross, though Cherry and the major were to pay their own expenses and operate as an independent unit attached to the Belgian army. On 19 August – two weeks after war was declared – Cherry, the major and the yapping bloodhounds boarded a ferry to Ostend. But after three days and 'an awful wild goose chase' they were back, each with his tail firmly between his legs. It had become clear almost as soon as they arrived in Belgium that with communications cut by the Germans it was impossible to work dogs at the front. As Cherry ruefully acknowledged, 'We might have as well run a confectioner's shop as try and work dogs.' Red Cross people motored out to them from Brussels and Sir Arthur Keogh, who led the first Red Cross commission to Belgium, announced that Cherry and the major had better take the dogs home.

The idea that dogs might have a role to play in the unfolding slaughter was a poignant symbol of public innocence in the late summer of 1914. As for Cherry, he felt vaguely humiliated and, rather unfairly, resented the way he had been hurried into a hare-brained scheme. In any event, it was a bad start to the war.

In Wheathampstead the villagers were borne along by a tide of patriotic enthusiasm bordering on hysteria, but apart from the sweaty swarm to the recruiting office, there was little to do. Newspapers were scanned for instructive articles on war preparation, notices went up about blackout arrangements and the price of butter rose. *The Times* ran a helpful column advising readers to instruct their keepers not to feed corn to pheasants. The press bristled with the same patriotic language extolling duty and sacrifice that they had used about Scott not much more than a year before.

Cherry badly wanted a job. Each day, as he came down to breakfast, his father's stare became more reproachful. But a colonic disorder had been troubling him since the end of the Antarctic expedition, and his doctor refused to pass him fit for service. Enlisting, therefore, was out of the question. He considered a position helping to run a converted yacht as a hospital for the wounded, but it never came to anything. There was also talk of working as an orderly in the Royal Army Medical Corps, and Sir Frederick offered him a car to transport wounded men. That, too, fell through. In the middle of September he finally hit on the idea of despatch riding. This, surely, was a useful job, and one that he could do well. He worried that his eyesight might let him down, but bought a Douglas motorcycle anyway and set about learning how it worked.

He was quickly accepted as a private into the 14th Signalling Company of the Royal Engineers and sent down to Aldershot for training. The RE had so many casualties among its first batch of despatch riders that it determined to prepare the next lot more effectively, and Cherry was sent out on signalling and ordinary training. 'Here I am living as a Tommy,' he wrote to Farrer, 'and a good life too.' He was very pleased to have got the job. His eyes were still an issue, but his commanding officer said he would find him other work if his sight became a problem. Cherry enjoyed the barracks rough-and-tumble with 150 other men, smoking incessantly, fighting for a place in the porridge queue and laying bets for an extra sardine at tea. 'They are a splendid lot of men,' he wrote. 'It's just Kipling in real life!'

It is a comment – freighted with terrible irony – that exemplifies the sporting, high-jinxy concept of war prevalent in the British army at that time. Nobody had experienced an all-out European war: in living memory, there hadn't been one.

In the second week of October Cherry was informed that a wire had arrived from a commander in the Admiralty asking if he would accept an appointment with an armoured car squadron. He was baffled. He had not applied for the job; he had not applied for anything in the navy. He got leave and hurried up to Reggie's in Green Street, wondering if he wanted a commission at all. 'I am not sure,' he wrote to Farrer, 'that I don't prefer to see this through as an NCO [he was about to be promoted] in a good RE company with a lot of rough but very good diamonds, rather than becoming an Officer Boy.' It was an admirably egalitarian urge. But Cherry went on: 'The one thing which fairly makes me squirm is to have to salute the very young and raw material of the said boys!' Squirming was out of the question.

He accepted the commission. At first the Royal Engineers refused to transfer him, but they eventually relented, and on 15 October he left Aldershot for good. It was an abrupt departure. He gave his motorcycle to his captain as a parting gift, and headed back to London. Farrer, it turned out, had been his benefactor. By chance he had met Lady Boothby, whose husband was a commander in the Royal Naval Air Service. Together with Captain (later Admiral) Murray Sueter, Director of the Air Department, Boothby was in the process of raising a division of men to take a fleet of armoured motor cars out to the front. Like Scott, as a young officer Sueter had specialised in torpedo work, and the pair had served together in the Pacific. When Scott was preparing to go south for the second time, Sueter had advised him on the doomed caterpillar motor sledges that were to cause so much anxiety in the Antarctic. As a result, Sueter had followed the progress of the expedition closely. So when Boothby mentioned the name Cherry-Garrard, Sueter immediately recognised it, and few commanding officers would have turned down one of Scott's men. On 18 October Cherry was granted a temporary commission as a lieutenant in the Royal Naval Volunteer Reserve and appointed to the RNAS (Armoured Car Division).

He rushed around getting measured for his uniform. On 9 November he was promoted to the rank of temporary lieutenant-commander and posted to the command of No. 5 Squadron, Armoured Cars. Like most of the armoured car officers, he was not required to undergo the standard navy medical.

The Royal Naval Air Service had only recently been formalised. It was still regarded with grave suspicion by crusty naval officers who neither trusted nor believed in the utility of air power. Its most potent ally had been Churchill, then First Lord of the Admiralty, who had supported it through difficult beginnings and encouraged it to grow. Within this nascent naval air organisation, the even more anomalous armoured car division had evolved as a result of Wing Commander C. R. Samson's successes with motors in Belgium and northern France in the first weeks of the war. Operating out of Dunkirk, the swashbuckling Samson had led a small force carrying out reconnaissance missions by air and using cars to raid the German flanks by land. Observing the usefulness of cars for ground work, Samson had one of his vehicles fitted with a Maxim gun, thereby creating

Lamer.

Evelyn Cherry and her first-born,
Apsley George Benet, in 1886.

General Apsley Cherry-Garrard and his
wife Evelyn, with their children Mildred
(*standing*), Elsie (*centre*), Ida ('Lassie'; *second
from right*) and Apsley, posing at Lamer
in 1896 for the distinguished royal
photographer Frederick Thurston. Evelyn
is pregnant with Margaret ('Peggy').

Culver House at Winchester College in 1903 (*Apsley is circled*). The house was known as 'Kenny's' after its housemaster Theodore Kensington (*seated centre*).

Christ Church 2nd Torpid, 1906. Apsley is in the back row on the far right.

Apsley in the dell at Lamer, aged twenty-one.

Reggie Smith, Isabel Smith, Oriana Wilson and Robert Scott picnicking at Kirriemuir, 1907.

The *Terra Nova* weathers the Southern Ocean.

Assistant zoologist on board the *Terra Nova*: 'I have never seen anyone with such a constant expression of "this is what I have been looking for" on his face.'

The *Terra Nova* in the ice.

Home: the hut at Cape Evans.

The Tenements: Cherry (*bottom left*); Birdie Bowers (*standing*); Titus Oates (*centre*);
Cecil Meares (*top right*); Atch (*bottom right*).

Camping near the Transantarctic Mountains.

Atch in his lab at the back of the hut: 'I consider him to be straight as a die.'

A sledging party leaves Ross Island and heads for the Barrier.

'Even now, the Antarctic is to the rest of the earth as the Abode of the Gods was to the ancient Chaldees, a precipitous and mammoth land lying far beyond the seas.'

'This winter travel is a new and bold venture, but the right men have gone to attempt it.' Birdie Bowers, Bill Wilson and Cherry set out on the winter journey to Cape Crozier.

'But this journey had beggared our language: no words could express its horror.'

1.   THIS is the House that
Cherry built."
2.   THIS is the Ridge that
topped the Moraine
     That supported the House
that Cherry built.
3.   THESE are the Rocks and
Boulders "Erratic",
Composing the walls - with lavas "Basic" -
     That stood on the Ridge that topped the Moraine etc.
4.   THIS is the Sledge and Canvas strong
That formed a roof about ten feet long,
     To cover the Rocks and Boulders "Erratic",
Composing the Walls - with lavas "Basic" - etc.
5.   THESE are the Ice-blocks hard and stout
That were placed so carefully round about,

The South Polar Times:
'Poor Cherry perspired over the editorial,' wrote Scott.

Scott's birthday dinner,
Cape Evans, 6 June 1911.
Left to right: Atch, Cecil Meares,
Titus Oates (*standing*), Cherry,
Griff Taylor, Edward Nelson,
Teddy Evans, Scott, Bill Wilson,
George 'Sunny Jim' Simpson,
Tryggve Gran (*standing*), Birdie
Bowers, Silas Wright, Frank 'Deb'
Debenham, Bernard Day.

(*Left*) Silas Wright: 'robust, willing and uncompromising'. (*Above*) Biologist Denis Lillie, working on his sponges on the *Terra Nova*. (*Below*) 'It will be a fine thing to do that plateau with man-haulage in these days of the supposed decadence of the British race.' The polar party on the final slog to the South Pole. Birdie Bowers has the camera.

One Ton Depôt.

'If you march your Winter Journeys you will have your reward,
so long as all you want is a penguin's egg.'

Lieutenant-Commander Cherry-Garrard at Lamer.
During the First World War the house was converted into a convalescent home.

Picnicking near Lamer:
Charlotte Shaw, Pussy Russell Cooke, Cherry, Peter Scott, Kathleen Scott, GBS.

Cherry and Angela on their wedding day.

Cherry in the 1940s, birding on the South Downs.

Cruising (i): 1930s.

Cruising (ii): 1950s.

'It makes a tale for our generation which I hope may not be lost in the telling.'

the first armoured car of the conflict. Churchill, alert to the potential of motorised instruments of war, authorised immediate developmental investment, and by the middle of September officers and marines were being enlisted for a modest armoured car force.

The first armoured cars looked like regular sedan convertibles with toughened bonnets. Josiah Wedgwood, an RNVR lieutenant-commander who trained with Cherry, was one of the first officers to take a squadron of armoured cars across the Channel. He was patrolling in one of his vehicles the day the Germans took Lille. 'They called it an armoured car,' he said. 'I remember that the tyres were armoured, and so was the radiator, and the chauffeur sat in a sort of armoured extinguisher. But we were not armoured, and the armour elsewhere made us feel indecently exposed.' By the end of 1914 the cars had evolved into the classic Rolls-Royce. It all staggered forward in a chaotic kind of way, like most things in that war; perhaps in all wars.

Cherry raised his squadron himself (one of his recruits was Petty Officer George Abbott, who had recovered from his breakdown), and headquartered it at Lamer, now colonised by platoons of starched nurses setting up their wards. The men were billeted in outbuildings and the officers in the house, and the cars themselves were kept next to the stables. The estate thronged with activity. When they had leave the men made sharply for the Cricketer's Arms or the Bull, regaling the villagers with spurious information about the revolving turrets in their new Rolls-Royces. Cherry rushed between Lamer and an armoured car training ground near Goring-on-Thames. 'We shall be ready to go over in three weeks,' he wrote to Farrer in December, 'but whether they will send us yet with the roads as they are is another thing.' As the casualty lists in *The Times* grew longer, he felt that his absence was treacherous.

Life continued at Lamer, hospital and war notwithstanding. On 18 November Mildred married Peter Ashton, a Wykehamist from Lancashire. Evelyn liked her second son-in-law, despite his lack of funds. He had already volunteered, and the following year he served at Gallipoli ('this damn peninsula') with the Herefordshires. He went on to win a Military Cross and was mentioned in despatches four times.

By the end of the year, with both sides locked into a trench system trailing from the North Sea to Switzerland, none of the supposed 'breakthroughs' on the Western Front had come to anything. There had been no swift, decisive victories; just deadlock, and widows.

Armoured cars continued their good work in Belgium and northern France. They were deployed in the series of diversionary attacks launched by the Allies in March 1915 to break the stalemate: No. 2 Squadron, under Lieutenant-Commander the Duke of Westminster, participated in the unsuccessful attempt to drive the Germans back from the village of Neuve Chapelle. After this battle, Cherry's squadron mobilised at last.

They arrived in France in April, a cruel month on the front. The armoured car division, spread across all the theatres of war, had swollen to nearly 200 officers, 2,000 men and 1,000 motor vehicles. The cars themselves were evolving rapidly: they now had more crew protection and were camouflaged. Some towed trailers loaded with three-pounder guns, and others had Vickers-Maxim machine-guns poking out of their revolving turrets. They had started to look vaguely like tanks on wheels. Most squadrons were attached to army corps in the line, but No. 5 and one other remained in Dunkirk, based in the northern suburb of Mâlo-les-Bains.

Cherry spent most of his time over the border in Belgium, driving staff officers around alongside columns of men trudging through the mist in their waterproof capes while lone farmers struggled to keep crops alive outside the little towns dumb with shock and damp. The flats of ploughed land were punctuated by windmills and the wooded ridges by grey-roofed châteaux that looked down on fields of cornflowers. Back in Dunkirk Cherry dealt with a daily stream of runners and their tiresome bureaucratic enquiries, and shuttled back and forth to the repair shop in a cavernous shed at the Forges et Chantiers ship-building yard near the brothels. Local kids hung around on the muddy cobbles of the docks, ogling the cars and angling for a tin of bully beef. At night, shells flickered in the sky above the black rows of willows and poplars, and in the thicket behind the mess a nightingale sang on in the clammy darkness.

Fortnum & Mason hampers arrived from Evelyn packed with goose-liver pâté, tinned butter, chocolate and other essential complements to the mess fare. Cherry drilled his men very early, after their bacon and eggs, and if there was nothing to do later in the morning there were impromptu football matches, the uneven pitch marked off by hedgy rolls of barbed wire. The men thought it was cushy enough. As for Cherry, the all-male communal life had strong resonances. He revelled in the ragging, the glow of physical fitness and the common purpose. But after what he had been through, there was something hollow about the military. It was as if the Germans were a manufactured enemy, compared with the Antarctic.* He

---

* In a draft paragraph of *The Worst Journey* that never made it into print he discoursed on how much the Antarctic had to teach 'the stereotyped respectability of the City Man'. Being in the Antarctic was like climbing a mountain and getting 'an untrammelled view' of what

was sickened by the rhetoric of the English papers, which leant ever more heavily on the old public school traditions of loyalty, honour and chivalry. A stranger reading the *Wykehamist*, which many officers had sent out to France, would have thought the war was a knightly quest. But Cherry had discovered that life failed to fit the neat patterns of chivalric rhetoric, and he was never quite taken in by the team spirit of the Great War.

When Cherry's division arrived in Flanders the Germans were trying to prise the Allies out of Ypres and push forward to the Channel ports. No reports have survived on the specific activities of 5 Squadron. Cherry almost certainly didn't see any direct action, though his armoured cars continued their support work. Night after night throughout May news came in to the mess of British disasters at Aubers Ridge, Festubert and other godless places. Cherry could do little except look through the window and watch the light of star shells dilating against a sickle moon. John Buchan's long account of the Second Battle of Ypres in *The Times* (which praised the detachment of armoured cars that had assisted the cavalry) ended with the dying words of a Captain in the 9th Lancers. 'Tell them I die happy,' gasped the unlucky man. 'I loved my squadron.' Only according to Buchan he was not unlucky at all. 'Has the whole duty, love and service of a regimental officer,' he wondered, 'ever been more beautifully summed up?'

A section of armoured cars with Maxim guns was attached to two cavalry divisions near Ypres, constituting, according to Josiah Wedgwood, 'the first mechanised cavalry'. The cars were now moving men between the forward, support and reserve trenches at times when telephone communication was cut and widespread gas prevented unprotected travel. One strategist, General de Lisle, reported to the Admiralty that the work of the cars attached to the first cavalry division towards the end of May had revealed that 'in trench warfare and in any future advance these armoured cars would prove a most valuable addition to the cavalry division'. Despite their successes, once the battle lines had been established and the trenches dug, opportunities for vehicles that had to stick to roads were severely limited. By May several armoured car squadrons, Wedgwood's included, had already left for Gallipoli and Egypt, where conditions were more suitable for wheeled vehicles. No. 5 Squadron was duly sent back to Britain to await instruction. 'Thus at the very moment when the new armoured

---

before was obscured by clouds and complications. 'War is another such mountain, but it loses by being artificial, whereas the Antarctic is natural.'

car force was coming into effective existence at much expense and on a considerable scale,' Churchill concluded in a lengthy report written after the war, 'it was confronted with an obstacle and a military situation which rendered its employment practically impossible.'

For most of June 1915 Cherry and his squadron were again headquartered at Lamer, now fully operational as a Red Cross officers' convalescent hospital. Pieces of paper were glued to the old doors ('WARD B') and arrows stuck to the frames of the bemused ancestors, but Evelyn was in magnificent command, supported by grey-and-blue uniformed Voluntary Aid Detachment nurses including the eighteen-year-old Peggy. Mildred, Edith and Elsie were also living at home. Many patients were sufficiently convalesced for Evelyn to institute strict rules of conduct, and she summarily informed the hapless Peggy, for once in a position to have some fun, that Cherry-Garrard girls did not chase officers.

Almost all the other Antarcticans had joined up as soon as war was declared: even the 46-year-old Ponting applied for service as a field photographer. Atch, still examining Chinese parasites in September 1914, had been obliged to abandon Leiper and report for active duty. In 1915 he was despatched to Cape Helles on the Gallipoli peninsula with orders to investigate the fly-borne diseases that were affecting the troops. He later moved to the Western Front, served with siege-gun crews in Flanders and fought on the Somme, where he got a DSO. After a stint in northern Russia, in 1918 he suffered horrific injuries while serving on HMS *Glatton* in Dover harbour. The new ship caught fire and had to be torpedoed by a destroyer before her magazine went up. Briefly knocked unconscious by the explosion, Atch was blinded, burned and forced to pull shards of hot metal from his leg, yet by feeling his way between decks he rescued several other men before making his escape. He was awarded the Albert Medal, and partially recovered his sight.

Atch was not the only one to have a distinguished war. Campbell came out of retirement and returned to the navy as a commander. He was sent to the Dardanelles, where he won a DSO. Teddy Evans was also awarded a DSO for a bravura performance commanding the destroyer HMS *Broke* in 1917. Together with one other ship, the *Broke* engaged six German destroyers that were about to attack Dover. Three were sunk, and the others retreated. Evans, observing a number of Germans in the water begging to be saved, leant over the bridge and shouted, 'Remember the *Lusitania*?'

Silas had joined the Royal Engineers as a second lieutenant and gone over to France at about the same time as Cherry. There he worked on the development of wireless techniques for the French army, was twice mentioned in despatches and won the Military Cross. He was a major before the war ended, and after being transferred to the General Staff as a staff officer in Wireless Intelligence, he was awarded an OBE. Priestley rose to the rank of major in the Royal Engineers and was mentioned in despatches like his old shipmate Silas, as was Gran, who flew for the Royal Flying Corps and was credited with the destruction of seventeen German planes. Cecil Meares, an intelligence officer for many years, also joined the Royal Flying Corps. He ended the war as a lieutenant-colonel.

When war was declared Deb had just returned to Australia for a scientific conference. On hearing the news, he sailed straight back to England on the same ship and joined up as a lieutenant with the 7th Oxford and Bucks Light Infantry. He was a major by 1915, served in France and Greece, and was invalided home in 1916 (a few months after he left, most of his battalion was wiped out). Deb quickly recovered from his injuries, and remained on light home duties for the rest of the war.

As for Tom Crean, he had left for the Antarctic the week war began. Shackleton had offered the services of his expedition to the war effort, but on the day the *Endurance* was due to sail, the Admiralty cabled back with the single word, 'Proceed'. Crean's former shipmate Lashly, now in the Naval Reserve, had signed up on HMS *Inflexible*. His ship was badly damaged in the Dardanelles, but Lashly survived, remaining in service until after the war ended.

At the end of June 1915 Cherry was summoned down to divisional headquarters at Wormwood Scrubs in London. He was there to demonstrate a prototype vehicle to an Admiralty committee developing an armoured landship capable of negotiating mud, barbed wire and trenches. The committee was chaired by the recently demoted Churchill, now Chancellor of the Duchy of Lancaster and the most senior supporter of the nascent machine (if his new armoured cars couldn't go *round* the trenches, he argued, some method should be found enabling them to go *over* them). Caterpillar-tracked farm machines had been in use for some years (Scott's motor sledges were an adapted version of the early tractor) and H. G. Wells had confidently deployed quasi-tanks on the page, but tracks had never yet been effectively used for military purposes (Lord Kitchener, Secretary of State for War, dismissed the armoured tractor as 'a pretty mechanical toy'). Caterpillar tracks were obviously ideal for trench conditions, and early in 1915 a specially formed RNAS squadron had carried out a series of experiments which would lead to the construction of a vehicle code-named the tank (to preserve secrecy it was disguised as a water-tanker). The project was based at the Scrubs, and there, because of his Antarctic experience with tracked motors, Cherry was asked to show off one of the machines under consideration, a tiny Killen-Strait tractor built in Wisconsin on three sets of tracks like a tricycle and equipped by the navy with a special net-cutter. While Churchill, the new Minister of Munitions, David Lloyd George, and a row of Admiralty brass hats looked on, the Killen-Strait ceremoniously clambered over piles of railway sleepers and barricades of scrap metal before making a final assault on a maze of barbed wire with the net-cutter. It was a vaguely farcical occasion, but they were on to something. In February 1916 the army ordered a hundred tanks, and in the autumn His Majesty's Landships were deployed on the Western Front.

Cherry went back down to London at the beginning of July, basing himself at the Piccadilly Hotel while he tried to get orders for his squadron. The hotel was teeming with uniformed officers and the platforms of Victoria station were striped with rows of soldiers, asleep or sitting on their packs and smoking. Outside, men on leave walked the normal streets, absurdly conscious of the short distance that separated their two irreconcilable worlds.

Then, quite suddenly, he collapsed. It was his old colonic problem, first diagnosed as colitis mucous ('contracted in his expedition to Antarctic [sic]') and eventually as ulcerative colitis. In retrospect, he said he had known he was not well when the war started. 'Before I had recovered from the heavy overdraft made on my strength by the expedition,' he wrote in *The Worst Journey*, 'I found myself in Flanders looking after a fleet of armoured cars.'

Ulcerative colitis is a chronic inflammatory disease of the large intestine and rectum, its chief symptom being diarrhoea, often acute. Its cause is unknown, its cure uncertain even eighty-five years later; and it is highly unpredictable. It can extend through the entire large bowel and lead to thickening of the intestinal wall. Other symptoms include abdominal pain, weight loss, a high temperature and the emanation of startling gurgles from the stomach regions. Attacks can be triggered by many factors, including, significantly, anxiety, and the disease is often associated with nervous disorders.

At around the same time, Cherry's unit was disbanded. It was a tremendous disappointment. The men were despatched to barracks to await billets elsewhere (many were shipped off to the front almost immediately) and the officers dispersed to other branches of the RNAS. In August the board of the Admiralty and the War Office agreed to put an end to the whole anomalous position of cars in an air service within a navy. All the armoured car squadrons of the RNAS, and all the other ground services that had grown up like ivy around it, were immediately transferred to the army.

For Cherry it was all over anyway. Conveniently, he now lived in a convalescent home. He kept his old bedroom, and had his own nurse, who happened to be particularly beautiful. But as he looked down from his window and watched the sweet chestnuts bloom in the park and the pipistrelle bats loop around the stable block, it seemed a bitter end to the summer.

9

The War had Won

The last months of 1915 were grim. At Loos 16,000 British troops were killed in 19 days, and the advance of the line was still measured in yards per week. The public had not forgotten Scott in this harvest of death. He was sent out to the trenches as inspirational fuel: Ponting's kinematograph was being shown to the regiments in France, images of the white battlefield of the south inspiring the Tommies before they went over the top. A grateful Forces chaplain wrote Ponting a thank-you letter from the front. 'We all feel,' he wrote, 'we have inherited from Oates and his comrades a legacy and heritage of inestimable value in seeing through our present work.'

Oates' surviving comrades, however, were in need of some inspiration themselves. Atch was having a ghastly time on the Gallipoli peninsula, Deb's battalion had suffered heavy losses in France when the village in which it was billeted was unexpectedly shelled, and poor old Ponting had been rejected by the War Office on the grounds that he was too old to serve as a field photographer. Pennell was commander on HMS *Queen Mary*. On 17 December he wrote to Cherry, 'The war from a naval (big ship) point of view is about as dull as it could be. However, this fleet is the advance force of the Grand Fleet so if and when the Huns come out, we ought to be there.' The Huns were indeed to come out, and Pennell was there, and it was not dull.

Cherry hoped he might soon be well enough to return to duty. But where? He seriously considered going out to join Atch, although Turkey might not have been the ideal spot for a man with acute diarrhoea. After debating the matter by post, in September Atch duly asked the Admiralty to send his friend out to support him with a squadron of armoured cars. But

Cherry still had bad bouts of colitis, and then he got flu on top. In November he was granted three months' further sick leave on full pay.

By the beginning of 1916 he had lost more weight, and was still very weak. In addition, he was horribly jumpy. Evelyn fended off visitors. He read *The Times* when he was up to it, either in bed or in the firelit library where the bald branches of the chestnuts danced on the glass-fronted bookcases. Despite the heavily glossed version of events served up to the public, a glance through the news pages did not provide a cheery start to the day for a sick and gloomy man quite capable of reading between the lines. He kept in touch with the men who had served in his unit as best he could, but as the war lurched from week to week letters from the field consisted of little more than a farrago of rumours. Cherry sent cheques to the men he had commanded: it was the nearest he ever came to a paternal relationship. Their mail to him was censored, and as a result often laughably anodyne, given the circumstances in which it was written. A missive from Private E. Snelling that arrived at Lamer in June 1916 is typical of so many hundreds of thousands that went out from the lousy hell of the trenches. 'We have had some very nice weather lately,' Snelling told Cherry helpfully, 'been quite hot but these last few days have been stormy.' Still, many of the men had happy memories of Lamer Park. 'I very much miss the cheery mess we had in Squadron Five,' wrote another young seaman. 'I suppose it is always afterwards that we really appreciate anything fully and I realise that very much now. I hope one day we shall meet again but the world is so big and life so terribly busy that it is unlikely. But they were great days.'

When he felt well Cherry was able to get out and walk through the leaf litter in the woods, the air viscous with the smell of rotting foliage. He watched young women root-gathering in the adjoining fields and hurrying off to their shifts at the new helmet factory in the village. It was whispered in the factory that Lord Cavan, a prominent Wheathampstead figure, had had a hand in the removal of Cherry's inactive squadron from Lamer Park, as he suspected the men were time-wasters. It seems unlikely: Cavan had written warmly to Cherry at about that time. But it shows what an uncomfortable position Cherry was in. A woman in Ayot sent him a white feather, and he received an anonymous letter accusing him of cowardice. He turned to Reggie, as usual, for advice and support, but it was another bitter pill. His illness was as real as a shrapnel wound; if it was linked to or caused by something that was not physical, it was not less of an illness. That was a difficult thing to explain. And anyway, as his exact contemporary

Siegfried Sassoon wrote, 'The intimate mental history of any man who went to the War would make unheroic reading.'

The pram returned to the back hall early in 1916 when Mildred and Peter's son, another Peter, was born in an upstairs bedroom. The domestic routines of home did not comfort Cherry. He had never shared the concerns of his mother and sisters, and his vague sense of alienation now became more acute. At any rate, he preferred shooting to babies, and was well enough to bag a pheasant or two to celebrate his thirtieth birthday. But that February the Admiralty put him on half pay. As usual it was Atch who saw that he was in trouble. 'Look here old chap,' he wrote. 'I believe a change of scene and taking your mind off things completely would very likely benefit you.' He had unilaterally suggested to their Antarctic colleague Denis Lillie in Cambridge that he and Cherry plan a motor tour together. 'Please forgive any interference,' Atch asked Cherry after confessing what he had done, 'but I would like to see you well . . . If it will relieve you write and tell me to be damned.' As for Atch himself, he had ended the previous year in hospital with pleurisy. He was appalled at what had gone on in the Dardanelles. More than 265,000 Allied soldiers were killed, wounded or missing following a series of botched attacks on the Gallipoli peninsula. 'The public,' he told Cherry, 'have not the smallest inkling of what happened.'

In the spring, Cherry's health improved steadily. He put on weight, and was mentally strong enough to compose irate letters about his purchase of War Loan stock and his supertax, though he commented that 'the constant poisoning from the bacillus and the sickness has left me rather a jumpy wreck'. The doctors ordered no hard work for at least nine months. 'I don't think there is much wrong with me,' he wrote to Farrer, 'except that this has left me very ragged out and the places inside which have been wrong are still tender, and so they keep me in bed still.'

He was well enough to return to his official narrative. Contact was briefly re-established with Lyons, who had himself been battling to locate members of the expedition – those who were still alive, that is – and get hold of their notes. But the niggling concern over authority would not go away. 'I have written to Lyons,' Cherry told Farrer, 'that I see he tacitly agrees that I was given a free hand.' That was it for Lyons. Cherry did not contact him again for two-and-a-half years, by which time the book had crystallised, and was not an official narrative at all.

The convalescent hospital had closed, and in April 1916 Evelyn announced that she could no longer afford to live at Lamer and was moving out. This, as she admitted privately to Farrer, was not quite the truth. She had fulfilled her role as guardian of the hearth, and she wanted Cherry to feel free to take his father's place as paterfamilias. Evelyn's sense of duty was even more finely tuned than her son's. Within a month she had found a house to rent in Weston, on the outskirts of Southampton, and she threw herself into the task of interviewing servants. Cherry didn't do much to dissuade her, and started looking for a housekeeper for Lamer. In the summer, Evelyn went, taking her three unmarried daughters with her.

For the first time, Cherry was alone at Lamer. The house was quiet without the rustle of cretonne skirts and the peals of girlish chatter. He was not immune to the stillness; but it did not displease him. As the daffodils bloomed in the park he retreated to the summer house near the pond. It had a handle enabling the sitter to revolve it on its base and enjoy the sun at all angles. There, in the stillness behind the high yew hedge, he watched the oaks and beeches flower and observed the progress of a family of robins nesting in the willow. He noted the arrival of a hen sparrowhawk, and listed the species of tits hovering around the fruit trees. It was a stay against the chaos of the war, and he absorbed himself in the smallness of his garden while the world went mad.

He felt he was getting better, though he continued to spend part of every day in bed. Towards the end of May the doctor had said he didn't think there was much wrong with the actual wall of the intestines any more. A specialist confirmed that he had no ulceration left, but that there was still plenty of inflammation. 'I am very gradually to get on my legs a bit,' Cherry reported to Farrer, 'and in under a year I ought to be able to lead a fairly normal life, but the process will cause an increase of pain and sickness.'

Although his physical health was mending, his mental state remained uncertain. In the first months of the year he had finally assembled his Adélie penguin notes and submitted them to Dr Sidney Harmer at the Natural History Museum. The notes were little more than a transcript of Cherry's diary, and Harmer judged that they were not publishable as they stood. When he was politely informed of the fact, Cherry exploded, claiming, inaccurately, that he had submitted the work in the form of rough notes and simply wanted an expert opinion. In his oddly unreasonable response to the shell-shocked Harmer, he continued:

I shall be most interested to see how far those scientists, who have lived their comfortable lives in England, and who work out the material given to them by men who have been in the Antarctic, recognise the help given them by such men almost always after hardship, generally at some risk to their lives, sometimes at considerable risk to their future health.

At the end of his vituperative letter he came to the point, to the thing that had been rankling for three years, since he had walked into the museum with three eggs in a small box. He had noted a spirit more than once at the museum which implied 'that it is an honour conferred upon the collector that his results should be accepted'. He would cite, he said, 'one example only. I handed over the Cape Crozier embryos, which nearly cost three men their lives, and has cost one man his health, to your museum personally, and . . . your representative never even said "*thanks*".'

Antarctica claimed headlines, even in war. Shackleton had been away for nineteen months when in March 1916 news came through that the *Aurora*, *Endurance*'s sister ship, had broken free of her moorings, leaving ten men stranded without adequate supplies at Cape Evans. Their plight was attracting extensive press coverage. Cherry had never met Shackleton, but he had been prejudiced against him by events that had unfolded eight years previously. Before setting out on the *Nimrod* expedition in 1907, Shackleton had reached an honourable arrangement with Scott, promising not to land in the part of the Antarctic around McMurdo Sound that Scott considered his own. ('I don't want to be selfish at anyone's expense,' Scott had written to him, 'and least of all at that one of my own people, but still I think anyone who has had [anything] to do with exploration will regard this region primarily as mine.') But Shackleton had been forced into landing in that very area by the treacherous ice conditions that blocked his preferred route. He had not had a choice; there was nowhere else to go. To Wilson, however, a broken promise was an irredeemable sin. 'I wish to God,' he wrote to Shackleton on his return, 'you had done any mortal thing in the whole world rather than break the promise you had made.' He subsequently ended his friendship with his old sledging mate. It was Wilson's moral disapproval that influenced Cherry. When the *Endurance* was about to leave in 1914 he had loyally, if pointlessly, taken up Wilson's baton, writing indignantly to Kathleen to ask whether Shackleton had said anything about using the Cape Evans hut and stores. 'Do you think,' he huffed, 'he means to walk into our hut and use it without asking permission as *his* hut?' But now, with the men stranded, he wrote to *The Times*, reassuring the public that the Ross Sea party would not be short of food at Cape Evans, and listing the stores left there in characteristic detail (456 pounds of cocoa, 608 pounds of lard and margarine . . .).

Only three months after the news of the *Aurora* broke, the full story of Shackleton's expedition thrilled a jaded nation. On 19 January 1915 the ice had frozen around the *Endurance*. She zigzagged for a thousand miles in the pincers of a floe, and after a long fight was crushed like an almond in a nutcracker. There was to be no transcontinental marching after all: facing apparently insuperable odds, Shackleton had to rescue his men from the maw of death. The twenty-eight castaways tried to haul supplies over the floating ice to land, but it was an impossible undertaking. They set up camp for six months instead, drifting hundreds of miles as they waited. They shot the dogs, and the carpenter's cat. When the floes broke up they launched the three lifeboats they had salvaged from the *Endurance* and sailed to Elephant Island, an outpost of the South Shetlands. There was no hope of rescue, so six men set out in the best of the small boats and, navigating by dead reckoning, sailed 900 miles across the Southern Ocean. Close to land after seventeen days, freezing, wet and seriously dehydrated, they ran into a hurricane. 'Darkness settled on six men driving a boat slamming at the seas and steadily baling death overboard,' wrote the skipper, Frank Worsley. 'The pale snow-capped peak gleamed aloft, resting on black shades of cliffs and rocks, fringed by a roaring line of foaming breakers – white horses of the hurricane, whose pounding hooves we felt, in imagination, smashing our frail craft.' When Shackleton reached the whaling station at Stromness on South Georgia, he asked the bemused manager when the war had ended. It was May 1916.

One of the five Shackleton had chosen to accompany him on his epic open boat journey was the feisty Irish seaman Tom Crean, Cherry's old shipmate. Like most of the *Endurance* men, Crean enlisted for active duty as soon as he returned from South Georgia. ('Emerged from a war with Nature,' wrote Shackleton's photographer, Frank Hurley, 'we were destined to take our places in a war of nations. Life is one long call to conflict, anyway.') Cherry sent Crean a cheque to help him on his feet. 'We've had a hot time of it in the last 12 months,' the seaman wrote back with characteristic understatement. 'I must say the Boss [Shackleton] is a splendid gentleman and I done my duty towards him to the last.' Cherry expressed guarded admiration for what the Boss had achieved. He had felt from the outset that the expedition was a 'desperate venture', and reckoned it was lucky that the *Endurance* went down when she did, convinced that if Shackleton had started on his march he would have met a more terminal kind of disaster. By the time he had finished *The Worst Journey* he was prepared to be more positive about Shackleton's qualities. 'For a joint scientific and geographical piece of organisation,' Cherry wrote, 'give me

Scott; for a Winter Journey, Wilson; for a dash to the Pole and nothing else, Amundsen: and if I am in the devil of a hole and want to get out of it, give me Shackleton every time.'

With the land armies locked in stalemate in France, on 31 May 1916 the Grand Fleet steamed into the Battle of Jutland. Perusing *The Times* while lounging in the revolving summer house in his tweed knickerbockers two days later, Cherry read that Harry Pennell had gone down with the *Queen Mary*. As he let the paper fall, happy memories of the wardroom rose like milk to the boil. The loss of Pennell touched him more profoundly than the columns of the glorious dead he skimmed each morning; what a mundane task that had become. He expressed his grief in a passage he planned to include in his book, but never in fact published. Those feelings were too personal for the public domain. 'When you have a standard of work set by men like Wilson and Bowers,' he wrote,

> you cannot go much higher. But Wilson always said that he could not touch Pennell. I do not know why he never had a nervous breakdown, because he simply could not go to sleep ... But Wilson, Bowers and Pennell are all gone now – for Pennell was in the *Queen Mary* at Jutland, and we are left to talk of eight-hour days,* and even that would not be so bad if we worked them! In Pennell's heaven they will work thirty hours in the day ... He will perhaps keep the Celestial Log Book, and the record of the animals sighted ... And every now and then he would ask for leave to go and take some of his friends in Hell out for dinner. I hope he will ask me.

There had been talk of the 'Big Push' since the beginning of June, and it came just as the swifts marked the arrival of summer in Lamer Park. On Saturday 1 July, one of the most horrible days in the history of humanity, the Battle of the Somme began. In the shimmering sunshine the British army suffered higher casualties than on any other day in its existence: almost 20,000 men were killed by German machine-guns. The Somme offensive unfurled in a deadly cascade of misjudgement and mismanagement (though not according to *The Times*) and ended in complete Allied failure. Among British troops it became known as 'the Great Fuck-Up'. There was a terrible pathos about the self-delusion on the home front.

---

* Industrial unrest on the home front was all over the papers, notably among the munitions workers on Clydeside.

What had been gained on the Somme, except the calligraphy of dry bones? No wonder the likes of Sassoon began their long keen of disillusioned protest. Cherry was beginning to sympathise with the pacifists. He, too, perceived the war through the lens of irony, and could no longer subsume the slaughter into the myth of Arthurian chivalry he had been taught at school. After the Somme, Cherry shared the view of Edmund Blunden that 'neither race had won, nor could win, the War. The War had won, and would go on winning.'

Yet in his park, where he walked each day, so little had changed. The rhododendrons bloomed like pink crinolines and the swifts, noisy at dawn, toiled at their nests under the deep overhanging eaves of the cottages. Cherry's favourite refuge, after the pirouetting hut, was the old brick arbour at the foot of the bluebell dell. In the peaceful summer evenings, as the bells of St Helen's tolled faintly over generations of Garrards, the rooks returned to the tall elms, darkening the sky, and the stoaty smell of evening seeped from the wood. The water snails clung to the buttercups in the shallows of the Lea and the baby swallows hung on the twigs of the red willow. The buds swelled and opened and flowered and the leaves fell, and he was still there, doing nothing, while so many were doing so very much.

Towards the end of the war H. G. Wells wrote that for the first time in their lives the men of Cherry's generation 'had met direction that believed in itself . . . They were up against something that seemed to be Order and something that had an aim.' Many of those who had served felt, after the war, that the world had been everlastingly divided into those who had been there, and those who had not. To Cherry that binary vision had been cast before 1914, and the war only served to polarise it further: those who had been south, and those who had not. His psyche never fully engaged with the war. It was still in the Antarctic. 'Talk of ex-soldiers,' he wrote, 'give me ex-antarctics, unsoured and with their ideals intact. They could sweep the world.'

At least he had a new enemy to occupy him, and he was determined that there should be no surrender. The Bishop of Peterborough had appointed a new rector to the living of Wheathampstead after a two-year interval following the death of the last incumbent at the age of eighty-five. The new man, Canon Nance, was sixty-four. This, according to Cherry, was too old, and he informed the Bishop that unless he stopped using Wheathampstead 'as a dumping ground for his pensioners' he would be seeing the end of Cherry's tithe, which amounted to some £300 a year plus extras. The Bishop of St Albans weighed in to defend Peterborough and Nance, and excruciatingly polite acrimonious letters were exchanged.

Cherry did not attend church, but he paid his feudal dues, and that, he felt, gave him a proprietorial right to poke his nose in. He did not have faith in any formal sense; like many of his generation, it had vanished with his first pony. As he didn't feel remotely guilty about it he was able to blunder on, relentlessly beating the clergy on the head with his bank book. But in the secular field of public life he had inherited none of his paternal forbears' predilection for municipal responsibility, and he was never to develop the slightest leanings in that direction. He was a very private man, and civic duty bored him.

He lived a solitary life with few servants, though he had engaged a middle-aged spinster, Eliza Merchant, as his housekeeper. By the middle of September he was able to walk about 300 yards. The loyal Farrer took the train up from Euston, and once they had got their business out of the way they strolled in the park and talked things over in a more general way. It did Cherry good to hear about events beyond the house and garden from a living person rather than a newspaper. But when, the following spring, he suggested a little partridge and pheasant shooting, Farrer declined on moral grounds: it seemed obscene to go out shooting when young men were being shot by the thousand across the Channel.

An anti-aircraft detachment had appeared on Gustard Wood Common a mile away, the officers billeted in the Mid-Herts Golf Club and the men in the thatched cottages clustered nearby. Soon a smaller one sprang up in Ayot St Lawrence, the leafy hamlet north-east of Lamer. From his bedroom window Cherry watched the silvery rods of the searchlights roam, briefly freezing the gentle Hertfordshire hills in a cold, grey-white frame. That portion of the county was a popular destination for Zeppelins. One night in October his heart 'stood still for about half a minute' as one flew low above the house; it went on to drop more than thirty bombs before being shot down over a field. Cherry got a good view, 'so vivid that I fancied I could feel the heat coming from her'. The next day, a rainy one, the bodies of the crew were laid out in a barn, and crowds pressed in on the police cordon to catch a glimpse of a genuine dead German. The tallest man had the best view. His name was George Bernard Shaw.

GBS was thirty years Cherry's senior. He was the most famous author in the world, and had been a household name for half a generation. He had married Charlotte Payne-Townshend in 1896, and a decade later, while Cherry was at Christ Church, they had rented the rectory in Ayot, once described by Shaw as 'a village where nobody dreams of dressing'. Shortly after the war they bought the house, and it became known as 'Shaw's

Corner'. Compared to Lamer it was a mean little Victorian dwelling (actually it was built in 1902), but it had eight bedrooms, and a revolving hut of its own at the bottom of the garden to which the master could escape to work.* The Shaws kept a flat in London and flitted between town and country. They were committed travellers, both in the UK and abroad, and Ayot was their bolt-hole away from the glare of public attention and the wearisome business of packing and repacking. *Au fond*, Shaw liked his own company, and at Ayot, more than anywhere else, he got it.

One day during Cherry's long convalescence, Charlotte Shaw had appeared at the house to ask if there was anything she or her husband could do to help. The rectory was only a quarter of a mile from Lamer, and the Shaws' land abutted the park. Cherry didn't need help, but he needed company, and as soon as he was able to walk properly he got into the habit of strolling down the avenue of lime trees and over the footpaths to Ayot.

Cherry and the Shaws became intimate friends, in touch weekly and often daily until GBS died in 1950. The mundane detail of everyday living was the glue of their long relationship. They discussed fences and birds' nests and what was to be done about rubbish collection, ate each other's leftovers and took up the threads of each other's conversation. The Shaws' West Highland terrier, Kim, shrank at the approach of Kris, and the vegetarian GBS raised his exflorescent eyebrows in mock horror as Cherry turned up at the back door with a dead rabbit in one hand and a gun in the other. They colluded over local affairs, campaigning jointly against municipal neglect and doubling then quadrupling charitable collections raised by pious villagers. (Cherry was unwilling to take on civic responsibility, but willing to complain if he felt aggrieved.) When one or the other was away, they corresponded. Shaw had bought his first car in 1908, thereby imperilling the hapless villagers on a regular basis, and he was always on hand to advise Cherry on the purchase and maintenance of his own vehicles, a subject about which neither of them knew anything, or to take him on a spin through the previously quiet lanes around Ayot. The villagers did not know what to make of either man.

At first glance there was much that separated them. GBS thrived on public attention, and Cherry recoiled from it. Shaw's Fabian instincts revolted at the sight of landowners like Cherry raking in unearned income and, as Shaw perceived it, exploiting the working classes. But their

---

* After Shaw's death Harold Nicolson advised the National Trust that it was morally obliged to accept the house for the nation and to keep it exactly as Shaw left it, 'as an example of the nadir of taste to which a distinguished writer could sink'.

friendship was profound and lasting, despite their ideological differences. GBS instinctively questioned the orthodox, and that appealed to Cherry. Neither had much interest in God; both responded deeply to literature. Both naturally rebelled against the idea and the reality of war, and both badly wanted peace (when Shaw visited the front he said that Sir Douglas Haig, commander of the British forces, was a very chivalrous man who made him feel that the war would last thirty years). Both were qualified cynics. Above all, the mix of seriousness and frivolity that was the essence of GBS was exactly what Cherry sought from a companion. Shaw never disappointed him.

Shaw towed many in his glittering wake who became regulars at Lamer during these later war years. One was Arnold Bennett, already a grand old man of letters but provincial in his heart, as Cherry was in his. He too toured the front, a companion of the war correspondent George Mair, Cherry's brilliant Christ Church friend, and went on to occupy a senior post at the Ministry of Information. Bennett was an innately good, honourable man entirely without pretension, and Cherry admired him. (He liked his books, too: he had taken some of them to the Antarctic.) Another Shavian visitor who was a frequent house guest at Lamer for a short period was J. M. Barrie, the strange little man in whom Scott had found an unlikely friend. Although Barrie's *Peter Pan* had confirmed his position as the most commercially successful dramatist alive, he was shy, like Cherry, and in the case of emotional matters both found writing easier than speaking.

As the autumn advanced Cherry was well enough to acquire a girlfriend, the mysterious* Christine Davis, and to take the train down to London to complain to anyone who would listen about his tax bills. But his colitis continued to flare up periodically, and by the middle of October a navy doctor had found him unfit for further service. His commission was terminated, and he was thanked for his contribution to the war effort.

Shortly after his discharge, his doctor despatched him to a nursing home in the north of Scotland. At Duff House in Banff Cherry lived on a diet of Presbyterian severity and took walks along the banks of the Deveron in the perishing autumnal cold that crept off the North Sea. His life of lone splendour set him thinking about the point of having such a vast estate. The first thing he did on his return was to sell an outlying farm called Kimpton Bottom. 'It is right out of the estate,' he wrote to Farrer, who dealt with the transaction, 'and it seemed unwise to go on paying out money in tithes,

---

* Mysterious to me, I mean.

rates, property tax, insurance and management to a limitless degree. I live in solitary grandeur here. It's a pity it isn't someone who enjoys grandeur more!' Cherry was to see less and less point in owning so much land and property; he had started the process which was going to end, thirty years later, in his owning no land at all.

Stalemate and attrition characterised the war at the end of 1916. At home, Asquith resigned as prime minister, the coalition goverment broke down and Lloyd George took over at Downing Street. Food shortages, rising costs and servant problems had become the norm in country houses. The war had seeped so deeply into daily life that it seemed it had always been there. When Cherry came back from Banff for his first Christmas at Lamer without his mother, he fortunately had Kathleen to jolly him through the cheerless dawn of 1917. She had responded to the war with her usual energy and independence. At first she had organised the transportation of cars and ambulances to France, and had even stayed on the Continent for a time to help set up a French hospital. Then, back in England, she had joined the production line at a Vickers factory that made electrical coils. At the end of 1916 she took up an office job at the Ministry of Pensions. She and the eight-year-old Peter spent that Christmas at Lamer. They all tried to make the most of it: Peter took a stocking into Cherry's room on Christmas morning, Shaw read them a play about the Kaiser on Boxing Day afternoon, and several guns went shooting. Cherry was an excellent shot, reputedly one of the best in the county, and he always took trouble to ensure that the game coverts in the woods were well stocked.

After Christmas, Kathleen took him back to London with her, 'for I diagnose cheerful forgetfulness as the quickest cure for him . . . He wants a dose of hilarity or intense interest in something to be quite cured.' But there was no prospect of cheerfulness: only more sorrow.

On 26 December 1916, Reggie threw himself out of a fourth-floor window at Green Street. He had been seriously depressed for weeks, and was known to be suicidal. It was not the first time he had been ill; he had almost had a breakdown in 1913. Nurses had been placed on round-the-clock duty, but in an unguarded moment poor Reggie had hurled himself out of the sash window in his pyjamas. Cherry had been close to him all his life, and Reggie had shared his Antarctic experience, good and bad, more intimately than anyone who was not actually there. Green Street had been Cherry's second home. Most importantly of all, Reggie had been a link with Wilson, who still lived in Cherry's fantasy life. 'I want to say,' the dying Wilson had written to the Smiths from the last tent, 'how I have valued your friendship and your example, and how I and my beloved wife have loved you both from first to last.'

The funeral took place in London on 29 December. 'We saw Mrs Wilson there,' noted Kathleen. 'She's an absurd prig.'

His health more or less restored, in 1917 Cherry began to make fuller use of the house. Visitors colonised the spare bedrooms: Kathleen and Peter took the train up at least once a month, and when GBS and Charlotte were in Hertfordshire they used to walk over for lunch and invite everyone back to Ayot for tea. Peter caught newts, Kathleen sculpted, and in the season some of them shot. The whole party would then stroll back down the avenue of limes for dinner at Lamer, followed by a play-reading by GBS (occasionally he even banged out a song on the old silk-backed piano). When the weather was mild, people slept outside, and Kathleen danced barefoot in the moonlight in her nightie. Cherry knew that GBS was the draw: 'It's much better fun . . . when he's here,' he wrote to Christabel McLaren when she was planning her own visit.* He relished his lesser role, while chuckling over the star attraction.

Meanwhile Cherry had got himself into a jam with Christine Davis. She was putting pressure on him to get engaged. 'He was he says bounced into it by an old woman who said Christine was making herself ill wanting to know the situation,' Kathleen reported to her diary after Cherry had stayed the night with her in London. Christine had also complained that he wasn't passionate enough. But as many girlfriends were to discover, he was not given to external passions; they embarrassed him. At the end of May, to his immense relief, he divested himself of Christine, and she disappeared leaving no trace. By then, another young woman had begun to appear regularly at Lamer. Pussy Russell Cooke was a swan-like creature with a slender figure, crinkly dark hair she wore parted in the middle, and piercing brown eyes. She was classically English in appearance, with a creamy porcelain complexion and a becoming diffidence. Pussy had a handy chaperone in her brother Sydney, who went everywhere with her, and at the end of June Kathleen arrived at Lamer to find Cherry and Pussy 'most intimate and cordial friends'. The pair of them slept on a bed of hay outside the revolving summer house, the spell of romance shattered only by Cherry's old sleeptalking tricks and a stertorous Kathleen in the shelter (obviously Sydney wasn't a very effective chaperone). Soon Charlotte

* Christabel McLaren (later Lady Aberconway) was a fashionable society hostess and art collector who married Lloyd George's private secretary. Cherry touched the edges of 'Society' through acquaintances like McLaren, but he never entered the fold.

Shaw was announcing conspiratorially to Kathleen that it could only be a matter of days before Cherry proposed to Pussy, and that she was sure Pussy would accept – though, personally, Charlotte had preferred Christine Davis.

Towards the end of a wet July the gang decamped to the Isle of Wight, where the Russell Cookes had a home near Newport. Cherry was to be a regular visitor at this house, which was called 'Bellecroft'; it was there that he forged a friendship with the young Stephen Roskill, the son of Pussy's half-sister and later a distinguished naval historian. That weekend in July 1917 Cherry and Pussy gazed lovingly at each other, but no proposal was forthcoming. A few days after they crossed the Solent and returned to Portsmouth, the assault on Passchendaele began to the north-east of Ypres.

Cherry saw Kathleen regularly throughout that year. She opened her London home to him as he opened Lamer to her. He confided in her, they read each other poetry, and she sent him warm, affectionate letters. He was fond of her son, Peter, who sometimes stayed on at Lamer when his mother had to return to her job at the Ministry of Pensions, and bought him a special junior bed at Heal's. In London he took the boy to pantomimes and dined at Claridge's with Kathleen, well aware of his position in the hierarchy: once, visiting for tea in 1915, Cherry was hastily shoved out of the door as Asquith – admittedly the prime minister – was about to arrive. If she rented a holiday cottage Cherry would often turn up, usually on Shaw's coat-tails. Yet her diary reveals a cooler attitude. He rarely has more than a walk-on part in its discursive entries, the speaking roles being allocated to brighter stars such as GBS. Kathleen adored Shaw, and he was a large part of the attraction of Lamer (unusually, she also liked Charlotte). The feeling was mutual. Some years later Shaw told Kathleen that she was so like a man (this was meant to be a compliment) that his affection for her was 'the nearest I ever came to homosexuality'. Kathleen's romantic admirers were legion. Cherry was one of the few men on the planet to meet her without falling hopelessly in love; perhaps this lapse on his part explains her condescension. 'He is coming on in intelligence,' she wrote in her diary, 'but it's acquired. He is very easily influenced. He is echoing Shaw . . . Are all young things like that?'

However undemonstrative and curmudgeonly he might be, Cherry was also capable of sustained support for a good cause. He leapt to the defence of the King penguins and other beasts that were allegedly being boiled alive for their oil on the Australian-owned Macquarie Island, out in the Southern Ocean 900 miles from Tasmania. Wilson had agitated against this barbaric practice after the *Discovery* expedition, and in 1917 Cherry once again took up his baton. The Yorkshire-born Australian explorer Sir Douglas Mawson was also campaigning for the penguins. Cherry knew and admired Mawson, and while he was in England they swapped notes on Macquarie Island and lobbied the Zoological Society. The value of each bird's oil, minus freight, was about a farthing, but the voracious wartime demand for fats and oils meant that the King penguin was in danger of extinction. Cherry roped various famous friends into signing letters of protest, and even wrote to *The Times* supporting his enemy Sidney Harmer's arguments against the slaughter.

Although he was now active and well, Cherry was still subject to moods. Bleak fogs descended on him intermittently throughout his adult life. At the beginning of May, during dinner at Lamer with Kathleen, GBS and Harley Granville Barker, he said almost nothing throughout the meal. It was partly his silence that appealed to Barker, a refugee from a failing marriage who was a frequent guest at Lamer that year. An actor, director, dramatist and poet of dazzling talent and unspeakable handwriting, Barker was twenty-one years younger than Shaw and the pair enjoyed a successful collaboration which resulted in the introduction of repertory to the London theatre.* Barker had been using the Shaws' Ayot house as a second home throughout the war (according to GBS he was 'a regular domestic institution'), and, when they were away, he took to staying at Lamer instead. Although he was a heartbreakingly handsome man who could turn on the charm of Adonis himself, Barker also exuded a certain *froideur*, and it suited him to lose himself at Lamer during the day and join Cherry for dinner ('If you happen to have other people coming or want to have them say no to me, for quite brutally I am bad company for strangers and casual acquaintances just now'). Besides that he was a glutton for luxury and appreciated the art and furniture that made Lamer such an endlessly beguiling house. Barker fulfilled a filial role for the childless Shaw, one which, to a certain extent, Cherry took over when Barker withdrew to Devon with his second wife.

Cherry's real friends, however, were still mostly ex-Antarcticans. In the difficult middle war years, when it seemed as if the fighting would never end, he grew close to Denis Lillie, the sandy-haired, blue-eyed biologist who thought he had been a Persian in a previous existence. Like Cherry, Lillie could not fight. He was a conscientious objector.

---

* 'The two most brilliant theatre geniuses of the first years of this century,' wrote Sir John Gielgud, 'were undoubtedly Edward Gordon Craig and Harley Granville Barker.'

Lillie had been a popular figure on board the *Terra Nova*, especially when he produced his excellent caricatures, though he had always seemed out of place in the rowdy wardroom. He was a thoughtful man, even a dreamer; the life of the spirit meant more to him than any other kind of life, and he did not fit into any of the readily available moulds. He discussed philosophical theory with Cherry, and they exchanged books on the subject. Cherry was not much of a mould man himself, and Lillie's restless quest for something more than material satisfaction and conventional success reflected his own aspirations. Both men were searching for pattern and meaning. Currently working as a bacteriologist for the military, Lillie had been one of the few visitors at Lamer during the bad months in the middle of 1916. They became unusually intimate ('I should love to see your chubby cheeks again'), and after one weekend Lillie scrawled with typical irreverence in his note of thanks that, 'It was only my body which left you, for my ultimate Reality still walks behind your Bath chair and meditates about the many paths of your lovely garden. With love.' He described his work as 'examining military shit for three pounds a week' (this was quite literally what he did), and was relieved that he didn't have children, as it meant he would not have to answer the question currently screaming from the recruiting posters, 'Daddy, what did YOU do in the Great War?'

Lillie had decided that he was not the marrying type, claiming that he had evolved beyond it. In later years Scott's young Norwegian skiing expert Tryggve Gran recounted that as they crossed the Equator on the *Terra Nova* Lillie had revealed that he was a woman trapped in a man's body. 'When I see a naked man I blush,' he allegedly said as the others sprawled shirtless on the deck in tropical sunshine, 'I am split and I can't help it. Luckily I understand myself and have the control to avoid doing anything wrong.' Gran was a notoriously unreliable source, and it is hard to imagine anyone having the courage to say that under those circumstances; but perhaps Lillie did. In September 1916 he had been transferred to the pathology lab of a military hospital in Bournemouth, which he loathed ('no nice cliffs or sea birds, only sand banks and orange peel'), and was appalled to learn the next year that Cherry was poised to become engaged to Christine Davis ('being unconventional and as near to nature as I can get, it seems all wrong to me that you should have to tie yourself up for the sake of Society'), but he strove, generally, to be optimistic, whereas Cherry was permanently resigned to his destiny. In August 1917 Lillie returned to Lamer for a week. Writing in advance with details of his train to Hatfield, he concluded that, 'if a motor does not turn up the wings of joy will waft me those four-and-a-half miles bag included. So don't worry.' They had a wonderful time together. 'I do hope,' Lillie wrote when he was back in horrible Bournemouth, 'your throat and the rest of you continues to get well and worthy of the sunny spirit which I see under the label ACG.' He was full of beans, and plans to go to East Africa.

In the spring of 1917 Cherry abandoned his attempt at writing a report for the museum based on his penguin notes and decided to concentrate on the official narrative. He sat at his father's old desk in the library, endlessly drafting and redrafting pages. Alone at Lamer, his life ran on two tracks, the writing all too frequently derailed by the demands of the estate. When an odd-job boy was summoned from the village Cherry would turn over a discarded page of typescript and set down a list of tasks to keep him busy for the day ('Clean all boots in boot room'). He broke for lunch at 12.30, when Miss Merchant served up a plate of rabbit stew or, on an exceptionally good day, a portion of pheasant. If the Shaws were not at Ayot he worked through the afternoon until the colours drained from the room, and when he was tired of ice and snow he sat in an armchair by the fire and read about the war in *Blackwood's*.

By the middle of 1917 he had finished several chapters. He sent one of them off to Admiral Sir Lewis Beaumont, an august and friendly Arctic hand whom he had sought out when he embarked on the project, and himself a writer of elegant prose. Cherry was still muddled about what kind of book he wanted to write, and was struggling to find the confidence to escape the limitations of a handy factual guide for future explorers. Somewhere in his subconscious he knew that he wanted to paint a landscape rather than draw a map, but it was several years before this realisation floated to the surface. He clung to his lists and tables and appendices of hard facts while more important subjects remained tangled in skeins of desires that he did not fully understand. In the meantime he had been requesting accounts of specific activities from other *Terra Nova* men. Lashly, the stoker who had tended the scurvy-ridden Teddy Evans, sent him his field notes ('I know you would like a bit of shooting,' wrote the seaman on his return from the Dardanelles and the Adriatic, where he had been serving with the Italian fleet, 'but not at Germans'). Deb, newly married (according to Kathleen to a 'very ordinary, middle-class girl with no sort of personality'), also sent material. He ended one of his cheery letters with typical sturdy candour: 'I have seen Lyons and he is a blighter.' This struck a chord with Cherry. As the architecture of the book took shape and he wrote and crossed out and rewrote the chapter breakdown on old expedition notepaper, he began to doubt that what was gestating in his mind could ever be compatible with the expectations of the dreaded committee. The small worm of anxiety wriggled away.

Food rationing, fuel shortages and air raids were sapping morale at home, and on the Continent, after the failed offensive known as Third Ypres and the unwritable horrors of Passchendaele, long trains were trundling across Europe transferring hundreds of thousands of German troops from the Eastern Front. 'I see no end whatever of the whole beastly show,' Cherry wrote to Emily Bowers in December 1917, 'nor, I think, does anybody else.' The gloom thickened into the black days of the last German offensive at the beginning of 1918. Defeats on the Western Front in March catapulted the nation into shock. *The Times* rallied as usual to shore up public confidence, issuing advice on all fronts, including the stern 'Don't think you know better than Haig', even though most people over the age of ten probably did.

At Lamer, Kris the Beautiful went down with incurable tetanus, and one morning, shortly before the Bolsheviks came to power in Russia, Cherry went out in his dressing-gown and shot him. It was an awful business. Everyone missed Kris. It had been Miss Merchant's job to walk him, and, being inexperienced with huskies, she never quite mastered the task. Two decades later GBS still remembered the sight of her flying through the air on one end of Kris's lead. Cherry was upset about the dog. He was also bored, and on the look-out for targets for his frustration.

At about this time Canon Nance, the pensioner Cherry had so warmly welcomed by telling the Bishop he was too antiquated, began to solicit opinion as to the form and location of a village war memorial. 'If it be admitted that we want any reminder of the war beyond that of the national debt,' Cherry began his letter on the subject waspishly, 'I am entirely in sympathy with the general idea.' He then took the opportunity to deliver a sermon of his own:

If it is to be in church it should be to the memory of those who have suffered and died for the principles of Christ. Personally, I think these principles are wrong: it is obvious that the bulk of the nation and also the clergy thinks so too: I believe that if A. wants to hit you on the head you had better hit him first, that you don't do to others what you would wish to have done to you, in fact that the more Huns we can kill the better.

He really wanted to berate Nance about the plight of conscientious objectors. 'At the same time there are some 900 men still left, men such as Clifford Allen and Stephen Hobhouse,* whose professions before this war were those of true saints, who are such good Christians that they have refused to act against their faith, and such brave men that they have faced persecution every whit as bad as that meted out to the Protestants of old: and some of them have suffered death.' He was referring to the sentences handed out by the tribunals set up in the wake of the Military Service Act to deal with conscientious objectors. Though nominally permitted to exercise their conscience, the men who went before the tribunals were frequently used as whipping boys: a primitive way of expiating the horror of the front. As always in Britain, the moral majority leapt into action to denounce conscientious objectors. Even Lloyd George promised that he would make their path as hard as he could.

'I have neither their convictions, nor, if I had them, should I have the courage,' Cherry continued, 'to face their illegal persecution (for it should not be unknown to you that such men were given total exemption by act of parliament). At the same time I have at least the decency to recognise their worth and to try and better their illegal treatment. It should of course be the first act of every official conscientious objector, namely the clergy, to publicly condemn the treatment of their universal brethren, but I gather that all they have done is sign a protest . . .'

Cherry instinctively identified with the intelligent misfit. It was, in part, what drew him so powerfully to Lillie, a conscientious objector himself. As for the ethics of war and the practices of the armed services, the cream of his idealism had soured into the curds of disillusion. He no longer believed that war was intrinsically noble. Britain had entered this one, at least in some measure, to refute militarism, so conscription seemed contrary. But did Nance deserve such a battering? Cherry was not really attacking him, of course; he was grappling with the response of organised religion in general to the war, as were many others. Sassoon conjured the hopeless inefficacy of the Church of England amid the carnage when he described a Forces chaplain delivering a pep talk to the latest batch of canon fodder as they were about to leave for France. 'And now God go with you,' concluded the padre. 'I will go with you as far as the station.'

Cherry had continued to see a good deal of the swan-like Pussy, both in London and at Lamer. In October 1917 she had told Kathleen that she

---

* Shaw, who also spoke out against the maltreatment of conscientious objectors, had cited these two men in an article in the *Nation*.

loved him more than anyone else in the world. ('How amazing,' noted Kathleen. 'How could anyone love Cherry – like that?') But by the following January Pussy had begun to complain ominously to Kathleen of 'a slight waning in the Cherry love passages'. In middle-age Cherry said he was afraid of women. He once told Lillie that a happy married life was impossible for him, a claim that reflected his solipsistic confusion and sense of alienation, and not one that stood the test of time. Besides a superficial fear of feline gold-diggers, he had sufficient self-knowledge to see that he would not be able to make the compromises that children bring to their parents' lives.

Coming down the stairs one fine day in May, he was pleased to see an envelope in Lillie's hand on the hall table. But it was not from the hated Bournemouth, or from a new billet in some East African military headquarters. Lillie was in Bethlem mental hospital in south-east London following a severe nervous breakdown. 'If you have a job on one of your farms I should like to lend a hand and live on a farm,' Lillie wrote, 'and really do some work. Also I should like to see you and have a talk.'

There had been no warning signs. Lillie had not been mentally ill before. He was neurotic, and profoundly restless, but he had seemed so full of spirit and plans. Cherry was horrified, and wrote immediately asking when he could visit. He suggested that Lillie come to Lamer and be nursed. A physician superintendent replied instead of his friend, saying that Lillie was neither well enough to have visitors, nor to leave the hospital. Cherry wrote again, impotent and desperate. On 3 August the Orwellian physician superintendent informed him categorically that 'visiting is contra-indicated'. Lillie had been 'frequently relapsing', and visiting disturbed him greatly.

Lillie was in Bethlem for three years. When he was discharged, Cherry took him to the Berkeley Hotel and offered practical help, but Lillie never got over his breakdown. He eventually entered an asylum in Exeter, not far from his brother's home. There he lived on and on, lost to the world. Both Cherry and Deb wrote to the asylum, asking if anything could be done for their old shipmate. They were told he had all the interests he could manage, and that although he was perfectly happy, 'it was an incurable case'. Cherry never saw him again. Lillie died in Exeter in 1963. He was seventy-eight.

By October 1918 the pages on Cherry's desk had grown into a pile several inches high. He discussed the material frequently with both Shaws, usually in the afternoon as teacakes disappeared into the wilderness of the Shavian beard. He even read some passages aloud to Kathleen, who noted, 'I think it is not at all bad', not the view she was to hold of the final version. He was fidgeting, of course, over the business of the dogs and Scott's instructions for them, and he wrote to the dog-handler Cecil Meares, pressing him to reveal his exact orders. 'I think you may make trouble,' Atch warned. They were both adamant that Meares 'disobeyed orders' by not laying the depôt, but the allegation could not be backed up in writing. Cherry had to keep it to himself for another thirty years, until it all came out (or almost all) in a little-read postscript to his masterpiece.

The Allies advanced steadily through the autumn, and the killing continued. A tide of German prisoners appeared to work the farms on and around Lamer, and more wounded soldiers languished outside the Cricketer's Arms. Columns listing a different kind of death sprang up in *The Times*: in October 2,225 Londoners died of flu. But on 11 November, at eleven o'clock on a lugubrious grey morning, Lloyd George announced the Armistice to the House, hoping that it brought an end to 'all wars'. When the news reached Wheathampstead shopkeepers emerged onto the High Street to ring handbells, schoolchildren ran around waving flags, the policeman blew his whistle and everyone else banged tin trays. The masks came off the few streetlights, licensing restrictions were forgotten and men spilled from the Bull onto the street in a palpable release of tension. The fifteenth was designated Victory Day, and a celebratory beanfeast was hastily arranged in the meadow at Marford. Cherry saw little to celebrate. Worldwide, more than eight million men had died; the fighting might have ended, but the grief would never end. As the flags fluttered up and down the High Street and the bells of St Helen's pealed jubilantly, he shared in an indeterminate sense of depletion. Vera Brittain spoke for many of Cherry's generation when she described the desolation the war had left behind. 'My mind,' she wrote, 'groped in a dark foggy confusion, uncertain of what had happened to it or what was going to happen.'

10

The Most Wonderful Story
in the World

'Though the old forms continue,' Stephen McKenna wrote little more than a decade after he and Cherry had gone down from Christ Church, 'the life that inspires them is new: the schools and universities, the learned professions and public services, the government itself are manned from a different class and activated by different ideals.' The Versailles Peace Treaty was finally signed on 28 June 1919, but in Britain a numbed nation emerged from the war in bewildered confusion. Kipling summed it up as 'waking from dreams'. The economic consequences of the slaughter (and the peace) included unemployment, widespread poverty and stagnant industry. The collective emotional consequences were harder to define.

Cherry shared the general disillusion that swelled through 1919. After Kimpton Bottom he had sold other farms on the estate, as well as cottages and chunks of land. Ever since he had returned from the Antarctic he had been moaning obsessively to Farrer about the punitive duties being imposed on landowners. 'The country cannot tax the agricultural landlord out of existence,' he thundered, 'and expect him (as landlord) to carry on on the same generous terms as he has done in the past.' To occupy himself while the sales were proceeding he began to weed the Lamer silver and jewellery. But it was not enough to satisfy his restless urges, and as the year wore on he decided to dispose of more significant manor-house properties. He was even thinking of getting rid of Lamer itself. It was primarily an agricultural estate, and farming had never interested him. He relied on his land agents Rumball & Edwards of St Albans to handle the bulk of his farm management, and perhaps because of that he was generally perceived as a benign employer and landlord who more or less kept to himself. He seldom went into the village; when he did he drove down the High Street in his open-topped car, honking his horn to alert loiterers (if he honked as he zoomed down to the station, the station-master held the train). Even his housekeeper rarely shopped locally, as provisions came rumbling up the drive in the large Shoolbreds lorry that made a loop of all the big houses.

He had the idea that he might move to Wittenham Wood, part of the Cherry estate in north-east Berkshire. A pre-Roman fortified camp loomed over nearby Shillingford, and the intermingling of history and landscape appealed to him. He had sold off some of his holdings at Little Wittenham, but still owned a sizeable piece of land there which abutted the Thames on the north side. He knew the area well, having undertaken many tours of inspection, and he hoped to build a small house in the wood, overlooking the river at the top of a slope called Trotman's Stairs. The centrepiece of the estate was Wittenham Clumps, two breast-like hills north-west of Wallingford in the Sinodun range, each topped with a strangely symmetrical sculpted cluster of trees. The Clumps had recently inspired the young modernist artist Paul Nash, who described the country round them as 'grey hollowed (or hallowed) hills crowned by old trees of Pan-ish places down by the river . . . full of strange enchantment. On every hand it seemed a beautiful legendary country haunted by old gods long forgotten.' The dense wood where Cherry planned to build his house lay at the base of these hills. According to Nash it was 'part of the early forest where the polecat still yelled in the night hours'. Nash first painted the Clumps in 1912 – calm, stylised landscapes in robust reds and blues – and he returned to them thirty-five years later, towards the end of his life.

Cherry was casting around for a project that would engage his creative energies. His rancour over the government's land-taxing measures was to a large extent a symptom of a more general dissatisfaction. For a time the idea of building a home on new territory absorbed his attention. In the end, it was his book, not a house, that was to satisfy his creative longings, and as his plans to sell up were overshadowed by his increasing preoccupation with his manuscript, anxieties over authorial independence replaced land tax as his major obsession. Having reopened negotiations with Lyons, he sought legal advice to establish whether he could legitimately remove his book from the committee and publish it independently. He was ready to take the plunge. Counsel concluded that he would be free to publish as long as he first made separate copyright arrangements for the material he had obtained from other members of the expedition. This he did. But he made a meal of what followed. Having informed Lyons at the beginning of the year that the book 'approaches completion', he waited until the autumn to send him a 1,200-page bound typescript, insisting that he was offering it 'as a completed work and not as a draft for recasting or unlimited amendment'. He was trying to goad Lyons into provoking the break.

It was not *The Worst Journey in the World* that he parcelled up for Lyons. Certain sections, polished up, would appear in the book he finally published three years later, but the architecture of this 1919 typescript was quite different. It included numerous lists of clothing and equipment, as well as separate articles on Antarctic cooking and other weighty topics. Furthermore, it had not yet acquired its title. It was called *Never Again: Scott, Some Penguins and the Pole.*

Lyons, who worked at the Meteorological Office, read the work during one of the proliferating strikes, and immediately wrote to congratulate its author. But when he raised specific points – in particular he wanted more details of stores and weather separate from the personal matter – Cherry pounced. 'The refusal of my book does not come entirely as a surprise to me,' he annnounced with lordly pomposity, 'nor is it, as a matter of fact, entirely unwelcome. I will now proceed to make arrangements to publish it in the ordinary course of business, concerning which I anticipate no difficulty.' A baffled Lyons replied that to his recollection the book had not been refused at all. 'Am I to understand that you wish to withdraw from your preparation of a volume for the committee?' he asked, genuinely perplexed.

Cherry knew he would have to proceed carefully if he was to ensure that the committee did not have the legal right to prevent him from going ahead with his own book. Grasping Lyons' letter, he set off down the avenue of limes and through the rectory and down the garden path to GBS, who was contentedly spinning in his hut. Always willing to dispense detailed advice on any topic, GBS drafted a conciliatory reply ('My dear Lyons'). The conflict ostensibly hinged on whether the book was to be a personal narrative or a kind of almanac for future explorers. The two, after all, were quite different, and Lyons had put forward the sensible suggestion that the distinction be made clear by a physical separation of material into two volumes. Cherry was not keen on this plan. He was concerned that the committee would treat any book he produced in the same way they had dealt with the expedition's scientific reports (Lyons had told him they planned a print run of only 500 copies) and consign it to the dusty bookshelves of the universities. 'I want it read,' he told Lyons, 'because I want the public to know to whom the credit of the work was due . . . If the book I have written is too readable, I am extremely sorry.' The truth was that Cherry had not resolved the conflict in his own mind about what kind of book he wanted to write, and had not yet garnered the confidence to jettison the tedious lists and interminable appendices. His impatience and confusion found an outlet in the bitterness and intemperance of his attitude towards Lyons.

As 1919 progressed, Cherry tugged and tugged until he had his book back. The loyal Atch, anxious to avoid trouble, warned him that if anything displeased Evans he would certainly take action. 'Teddy Evans is probably suffering from too many medals,' Cherry reassured him breezily (after his dazzling performance commanding the *Broke*, Evans had featured regularly in the newspapers and had emerged as a classic war hero). Anyway, Cherry had been careful. 'He comes out of my book,' he told Atch, 'far better than I desire or he deserves.' It was true. Evans came out all right. Cherry had determined to be royally diplomatic. There was to be no criticism of Evans, none of the tortuous saga triggered by Scott's decision to take the dogs further than planned, and no suggestion – though this remained in the book until a late draft – that the dual goals of science and the Pole had exposed the expedition to fatal pressure.

The Antarcticans' widespread distrust of Evans came to a head in December. Teddy delivered a lecture at the Queen's Hall in London chaired by Sir Eric Geddes, transport minister and former First Lord of the Admiralty, and the bones of the proceedings were subsequently published in *The Times*. In his unctuous paean to Teddy, the minister described him as 'the right-hand man to Captain Scott'. This was too much for Ponting. He sent a long letter to all the morning newspapers 'in the hope of correcting an erroneous impression that has been current for too long'. Rising majestically to the occasion, Ponting informed his readers, 'without in any way detracting from the record of a brave sailor', that Wilson was Scott's right-hand man. Emphasising the vital roles of Atch and others, he went on to clarify the limited part played by Evans, who had not even been present for a large chunk of the expedition: he had 'unfortunately' been invalided home. *The Times* ran the letter, and Cherry wrote to thank Ponting, as did many others including Atch and Ory ('Bill used to say that Evans was surprisingly stupid'). Further difficulties arose in the spring of 1921 when Evans' book *South With Scott* was published. Determined to secure his footing, Cherry had bludgeoned Emily Bowers into accepting £100 in return for a written agreement to surrender copyright in the extracts he planned to use from Birdie's diary. Evans had taken no such precaution, freely reprinting some of the same extracts for which Cherry had gone to such trouble to obtain exclusive copyright. A befuddled Mrs Bowers forgot that she had shown Evans the diary back in 1913. Leaning heavily on Shaw for advice on copyright law, Cherry despatched a strong letter to Collins, Evans' publisher. The firm took cover behind its author, and Evans eventually replied personally from HMS *Carlisle* in Hong Kong. 'I don't like the tone of your letter,' he wrote, 'with its insinuated threat of process legal.' The matter fizzled out, but Cherry had made his point.

By the start of 1920, Cherry's professional relations with the committee had been severed. 'You are now utterly untrammelled,' Kathleen had written pointedly when she heard the news, 'an estate which is always essential for your happiness, I know. Come and have lunch.' Cherry summed up the events in the introduction to the book that was eventually published as *The Worst Journey*. 'Unfortunately I could not reconcile a sincere personal confession with the decorous obliquity of an Official Narrative; and I found that I had put the Antarctic Committee in a difficulty from which I could rescue them only by taking the book off their hands.' The kind of official narrative required by a committee would not, he continued with an honesty he had not felt able to show to Lyons, effect 'any catharsis of the writer's conscience'. Cherry knew that he had behaved badly towards Lyons. 'In a most ruthless and high-handed way,' he wrote in an unpublished paragraph, 'I took [this book] out of the hands of the committee. No doubt they think me an unprincipled bounder. I am.'

The labour unrest that seethed through the summer of 1919 finally paralysed the country on 27 September, when the railway workers came out in a national stoppage. Food rationing was introduced, the government bared its teeth, and although the strike was settled in the first week of October, the industrial troubles spilled over into 1920 and permeated the nation with gloom.

Cherry shared the outrage of most of his class when he contemplated the horrible spectacle of working men asking for higher wages. He retreated to Lamer, where the Shaws eased him out of his black moods. The three of them strolled over his footpaths after lunching on eggs hollandaise and gooseberry tart, busily comparing blooms and harvests with those of the year before and the year before that. In the spring they admired the daffodils and cherry blossom, took notes on the cuckoo population and waited – with disapproval, in GBS's case – for the shots of the woodmen culling the rooks. When it grew hotter they took lunch outside (Cherry loved picnics) and watched the harvest landscape swell and the stooks of corn multiply. In the autumn they contemplated the dripping elms from the warmer side of the window as the branches of the Norwegian maples swayed against heavy November skies.

In the cosy quietude between Christmas and New Year, folded into an armchair at Lamer, GBS set down a half-page Rules of Punctuation, explaining, with muscular examples of Shavian vigour, the usage of the semi-colon and colon. Cherry soon became a rabid deployer of both. But the Shaws did more than punctuate. Both picked over the typescript during the long months that Cherry spent reworking it, offering more felicitous phrasing, rearranging clauses or simply making suggestions ('Good literary criticism has been passed as it was written, word by word and chapter by chapter', Cherry noted). GBS was a gifted interpreter of unformed thoughts. He could also see where a phrase or a new idea needed elaborating, and many of his questions ended up in the text as rhetorical devices ('What is pack?' Cherry wrote to introduce his disquisition on pack ice). The adamantine clarity of *The Worst Journey* owes much to Shaw's questions and responses as he strolled with Cherry through the spinneys, reliving, in gentle Hertfordshire, the cold and exhaustion, the exhilaration and wonder, the anxiety and grief. Looking back from a distance of almost thirty years, GBS claimed that the whole book had been his wife's idea. 'Charlotte told him he must write it, and promised to read his proofs and help him in every possible way. He had not thought of this, and still retained his boyish notions of Scott and the expedition. To him Amundsen was a lubberly candle-eating Swedish second-mate, who had meanly stolen a march on the heroic Scott . . .' This was a typically Shavian misrepresentation of events, but the role of the Shaws was unquestionably crucial. From the beginning GBS was certain that if the book were to be worth anything, it had to address the relative merits of the protagonists with a mature eye. 'I said to Cherry one day that international courtesy and sportsmanship made it advisable to be scrupulously just and polite to Amundsen. I suspect that this was the hardest pill for him to swallow; for the moment that he went into the question he had to admit that Amundsen was no scallawag, but a very great explorer.' But when Cherry asked if he should acknowledge his editorial role, GBS was quick to dissuade him. In a letter from Wales, he wrote:

It would be fatal to make any suggestion of collaboration on my part . . . As my experience on the ice dates from the great frost of 1878 (or thereabouts) when I skated on the Serpentine, my intrusion into the Antarctic Circle would be extraordinarily ridiculous. Besides, the suggestion would be misleading . . . You need not be at all uneasy as to the integrity of your authorship. All books that deal with facts and public controversies are modified by consultation, mostly to a much greater extent than this one. It is only in pure fiction that the author takes no counsel.

While continuing to accumulate material for the lists of equipment that were still to append the second volume, Cherry experimented with character sketches and psychological analysis and began to craft a story that took into account not just the length of the sledge runners but also the motivation and personality of its protagonists. It was a daring approach: biography was only just then stirring from its Victorian cocoon of deference. Cherry knew enough about literature to see for himself that the real interest of the story lay in the men. Like most good writers, he had a visceral sense of his book before he put it into words. But without the Shaws' encouragement, *The Worst Journey* may have remained an official narrative; and perhaps the dullest story in the world.

The romance with Pussy slowed to a terminal halt early in 1919, and once it was over she and Cherry became firmer friends. The following year he spent Christmas at Bellecroft with all the Russell Cookes, enjoying tramps over the windy Isle of Wight hills in the afternoon and listening to the gramophone during the long evenings in front of the fire. Pussy went on to get engaged to a bright young man called Jasper Harker, whose widowed mother Lizzie was the author of popular novels. Cherry remained intimate with both Jasper and Pussy for the rest of their lives, and Jasper in particular was to prove a steadfast supporter in the terrible times that lay ahead.

Cherry, meanwhile, began dallying in London with an art student called Thelma. He spent a lot of time in the capital in the years following the war, usually staying at the Berkeley Hotel, a grand, roomy old palace in Piccadilly where he felt at home. Thelma did not prove as lasting in his life as this august institution, and he was spotted abroad with other *belles*: the young Malcolm Sargent, then an organist but about to turn himself into a conductor, once arrived at Kathleen's breathless with gossip about Cherry and a creature called Gladys Orr. He was obviously coping manfully with the rising tides of flapperdom that startled his conventional soul.

When he wasn't labouring at his book or enjoying bouts of the high life, he began to experiment with short forms of writing. He made his journalistic debut in several magazines in 1919, often celebrating the appearance of his first piece by despatching an angry letter to the editor complaining about typographical errors. He wrote a dazzling review of Shackleton's *South* for H. M. Massingham's weekly, the *Nation*, displaying the flair and rhetorical flourish which was to come to maturity in *The Worst Journey*. 'Some centuries ago, it seems,' the review began, 'when Scott was in the Antarctic . . .' Cherry was critical of certain decisions, but overall he paid tribute to Shackleton. 'Now I know,' he wrote, 'why it is that every man who has served under Shackleton swears by him.' The piece ended with a vignette of three battered little boats and their exhausted, frostbitten crews. 'Darkness is coming on,' Cherry wrote,

> the sea is heavy, it is decided to lie off the cliffs and glaciers of Elephant Island and try and find a landing with the light. Heavy snow squalls and a cross sea – and both the wind and the sea rising. Many would have tried to get a little rest in preparation for the coming struggle. But Shackleton is afraid the boat made fast to his own may break adrift. She is hidden by the darkness, but a breaking wave reveals her presence every now and then. All night long he sits with his hand on the painter, which grows heavier and heavier with ice as the unseen seas urge by, and as the rope tightens and drops under his hand his thoughts are busy with future plans.

Cherry had not given up his campaign to end the penguin slaughter on Macquarie Island. At the beginning of April he wrote to *The Times* to tell its readers that the stories coming from that island 'make the atrocities of Belgium sound like a Sunday School treat'. Appealing for parliamentary intervention, he ended with a paean to the birds themselves. 'The penguin has won a little bit of affection from all of us because he is entirely lovable, and because he snaps his flippers at the worst conditions in the world. If we do not help him now we can never look him straight in the eyes again. Poor penguins, but poorer we.' In the same month he wrote a piece for the *Spectator* appealing for government control over the killing of Antarctic fauna. The punch came in the last line. Having listed measures that should be taken to safeguard southern species, he concluded, 'Otherwise the penguins will call us Huns, and we shall deserve every bit of it.' He was so pleased with his Hun joke that when news came through in December that the killings were to stop he produced it again in another letter to *The Times*. While he was about it, he publicly thanked H. G. Wells, whose support he had co-opted. ' "There are some Huns among them", the penguins say, "but the nice people, like *The Times* and Mr Wells, and others not so well known (but just as nice) have been too much for them" . . . When the frost is in the trees and the snow is on the ground you will hear them [the penguins] say "thank you", and so does yours sincerely, Apsley Cherry-Garrard.'*

Shortly before the end of the war Shaw had introduced Cherry to Wells. It was difficult to see what they had in common. They were different in background, political instinct and temperament, and Wells, who plotted schemes to tax the rich with his friend Arnold Bennett, never really liked humanity much. But he and Cherry found common ground, and they met and corresponded occasionally for three decades. Wells was attracted to the potential for scientific investigation in the Antarctic and seized any opportunity to quiz Cherry on polar matters, whether in an armchair at Ayot, at a first-night drinks party in the Shaws' London flat, or under a tree at Lamer. He had smuggled the Macquarie penguins into his 1919 novel *The Undying Fire*, a heavy-going twentieth-century rendition of the allegory of Job. (Wells must have had Cherry on his mind when he toiled over his book, as he also tossed in a reference to a parasitical liver disease in China.)

The penguins had offered Cherry the chance to expatiate on the Antarctic, and he was always on the look-out for other opportunities to refer to his favourite topic. In October 1919 he seized his pen in response to a long article in *The Times* on the efficacy of that new weapon of mechanised war, the tank. Pointing out that Scott had used a forerunner of the tank in the Antarctic, he disingenuously described the 'considerable success' of the motor sledges on the ice, going on to claim, with the deft, polished style that was becoming his trademark, 'Fetch one of these two derelicts off the Barrier, and case it in armour, and you would have something very like the modern tank, which is largely an imitation of our old friends. With Churchill at the Admiralty and Scott still alive tanks would have been in action long before September 1915.' This was demonstrably untrue, but it sounded nice, and it expressed the mood of elegiac melancholy that was to characterise his best writing.

He was also quietly building up a small art collection. His first major acquisition was Rodin's bronze skater, which he bought for £640. GBS had famously sat for Rodin, and he had also sat for the young American expatriate sculptor Jacob Epstein (though when Epstein's bust was finally completed Charlotte refused to let it into the house on the grounds that it made its subject look like a savage). Epstein's work, with its stylised figures and powerful sexual component, represented the new and iconoclastic in

---

* In 1933 Macquarie Island was formally declared a wildlife sanctuary by the Governor of Tasmania.

art, and as such it attracted controversy for years: in the summer of 1925 the sculptor's tribute to W. H. Hudson in Hyde Park, *Rima*, was to be tarred and feathered. In 1920 Epstein exhibited his first Christ at the Leicester Galleries in London. The *Risen Christ* was a startlingly beautiful bronze, a taller than life-size representation with enormously distended fingers raised, on the right hand, to display the open wound. The upright head was stern, dignified and quietly moving, though the features were hard, not crumpled like the faces of the standard nineteenth-century messiahs. Inevitably the conservative wing of public opinion weighed in with loud and warlike criticism of this outrageous strike at their securely held opinions. The ferocious Jesuit priest and social reformer Father Bernard Vaughan published his attack – 'Is it Really Christ?' – in the *Graphic* in February, objecting chiefly that the statue was not sufficiently English in appearance (it was more like an Asiatic, or a Hun, or, God forbid, '*an American*'). Shaw counter-attacked in the pages of the same magazine a month later with one of his most endearing pieces of polemic journalism. The operatic Christ favoured by Father Vaughan, he argued, had been invented by St Luke. 'All the Christs in art must stand or fall by the power of suggesting to the beholder the sort of soul that he thinks was Christ's soul.' Indeed.

Cherry bought the Christ. He walked into the gallery shortly before the exhibition closed and paid £2,100 (about £45,000 today). The controversy had appealed to his anti-establishment streak, Shaw had encouraged the purchase, and he could see for himself that it was a remarkable work. Besides that, it was bound to annoy Canon Nance. He put it in the garden, where the servants had much to say about it for many years.

In the winter of 1918/19 an argument over a pair of motor cars created a rift between Kathleen and Cherry that never quite closed. She had handed over two vehicles to Snowdon Hedley, a colleague of Cherry's from the squadron and now a captain; he was to organise repairs and sell the cars on her behalf. When no sale (or at least, no money) was forthcoming, Kathleen asked for the cars back. For months Cherry acted as intermediary, but finally a furious Kathleen, provoked by the sight of Hedley quaffing cocktails in Regent Street with ladies in silver dresses, put the matter into Farrer's hands, and Cherry was summoned to Lincoln's Inn Fields for a series of formal interviews. He simmered with rage and frustration for weeks. 'My natural kindness of heart,' he wrote in a letter to Kathleen that was never sent, 'of which I am daily reminded that I have too large a share, has placed me, all unwilling, between two of my friends in this matter . . . This has already meant at least four special journeys to London, telephones, telegrams and postage innumerable, at least a year off my life in mental distress [here he crossed out, 'As well as lunches at the Café Royal which I shudder to contemplate'].'

The matter was settled without recourse to the courts, and Kathleen and Cherry tried to remain friends despite the chilly air that had descended. She continued to bring admirers to Lamer, among them the tall Norwegian explorer, oceanographer and statesman Fridtjof Nansen, whom Cherry considered the father of all modern sledge travel. Nansen stayed at Lamer for what he described as 'two unforgettable days' when the bluebells were out in the dell and daffodils covered the park. His exploits in the Arctic were legendary, and Cherry pumped him for details about sledge runners which he might include in the appendices to his double-decker book (the typescript was becoming more unwieldy as each month expired).

In 1921 Cherry saw much less of Kathleen. She had fallen in love with Hilton Young, a distinguished junior minister, and in March 1922 they married. Kathleen's life was increasingly taken up with politics, and as Young had a house in the country she no longer needed Lamer. But more than a husband had come between Kathleen and Cherry. Even without the business of the cars, their friendship would inevitably have cooled. Cherry was distancing himself from the official side of the expedition. His attitude to Scott was maturing, and he needed to draw apart from his widow in order to see and write clearly.

In his search for a publisher it was to Shaw, of course, that Cherry turned. Smith, Elder were too close to the committee; and anyway Reggie was dead. Cherry had decided to get *Never Again: Scott, Some Penguins and the Pole* typeset and printed at his own expense, thereby retaining editorial control. It was a similar system to the one used by Shaw, who had begun publishing his work himself with *Man and Superman* in 1903, establishing a distribution arrangement with the firm of Constable that worked satisfactorily for almost half a century. In the middle of February 1920 Cherry approached Shaw's printer, R. & R. Clark in Edinburgh, for a price for 240,000 words, in two volumes, with appendices totalling 72,000 words. He asked to be quoted on 1,000 and 1,500 copies. The matter was handled by Clarks' director William Maxwell, who looked after Shaw's voluminous oeuvre for many years. As the first chapters went up for setting straight into page proof, Cherry opened negotiations with the eminent fine-art publisher Emery Walker, whose offices were in Fleet Street. Besides being a friend of Shaw's, Walker had known Scott and Wilson, and his company had worked on Scott's *Voyage of the 'Discovery'*. He was to undertake the reproduction of the illustrations in *Never Again*.

Finishing a book is largely a matter of stamina. Cherry sat it out in the library, writing sections or isolated paragraphs in longhand on separate sheets and arranging them for the typist who arrived from an agency and sat clacking in an upstairs room. When the typed pages came back downstairs he snipped them up and reordered the pieces. Although the recent glut of books on the expedition put him, in one sense, at a psychological disadvantage, a consideration of their contents helped focus his mind on the kind of book he had to write.

Scott's executors had been first off the mark only months after the *Terra Nova* docked. The two volumes of *Scott's Last Expedition*, edited by Leonard Huxley, went through half a dozen reprints in less than a year. Besides that, five of Cherry's surviving shipmates had got their books out before him. Ray Priestley's enchanting *Antarctic Adventure* had been published in 1914, though stocks had been destroyed in the war and the book was hard to obtain. Two years after Priestley, Griff had produced his breezy and agreeable *With Scott: the Silver Lining* (in a letter to Cherry he referred to it as 'Ortobiogriffie'). The two books concentrated largely on parts of the expedition at which Cherry had not been present, and he praised them both in *The Worst Journey*, describing *The Silver Lining* as a book which offered 'a true glimpse into the more boisterous side of our life'. Evans' stiff and uninspiring *South with Scott* appeared in 1921, followed later the same year by Ponting's equally wooden *The Great White South*. This last pair went on selling for many years, and although they were frequently offered as Sunday School prizes in the hope that the recipients would absorb some of their heroic spirit, they had little literary merit and made no serious attempt at critical analysis of motivation and personality. Finally Cherry had taken much delight in George Murray Levick's *Antarctic Penguins* (1914). Dr Levick's book is almost entirely about Adélies, amongst which he had spent much time (he was one of Campbell's Northern Party). 'If you think your own life hard,' Cherry wrote, 'and would like to leave it for a short hour I recommend you to beg, borrow or steal this tale, and read it and see how the penguins live.'

So he struggled on, hunched over the old desk, stirring only when the housemaid crept in to lay more logs on the fire or when Miss Hill, the suitably antediluvian spinster who had replaced Miss Merchant, announced that luncheon was served. As the war receded and the book finally began to take shape, he experienced a sense of purpose that was to coalesce into one of wellbeing. He tipped back his chair and looked out at the lawny vista unfurling beyond the window, or at the friendly books populating the old glass-fronted bookcases on either side, and at last he saw very clearly that he hadn't slogged up the Beardmore in order to compile appendices listing the weight of pony fodder.

Battling to subdue his monstrous regiments of material, Cherry learned that his most faithful ally was the waste-paper basket. After weeks of work on a chapter he had called 'Science', out it all went. He also jettisoned the rambling, repetitive chapter on Antarctic psychology which he had planned to begin with a eulogy to Bill. In fact, the psychology section had some fresh and touching paragraphs. 'Why do men who have returned [from the Antarctic] always wish to go back again to that hard and simple life?' Cherry wondered.

What is it that we wish to gain? I believe it to be this. A man on such an expedition lives so close to nature, in whom he realises a giant force which is visibly, before his eyes, carving out the world, and he lives sometimes so close to the bedrock of existence, that it seems to him on his return to be almost impossible to live comfortably in England because life there is so complicated. To mention a small instance, it struck me as absurd that hundreds of men should be rushing to catch trains at big London termini. Why this waste of energy when there were other trains in less than an hour? . . . This, then, is what I believe has something to do with the call of the south.

It was also something to do with his own restless longings. He had never recaptured the fulfilment he had experienced during that first year on the ice.

In these pages he elaborated on 'the bondage of possessions', a state he perceived as the antithesis of the Antarctic experience ('the Polar Party stands out as the negation of materialism'), and mused on the 'mystical and invisible something which has been the object of all religions'. He had been deeply influenced by Lillie, a dedicated student of mysticism. In Cherry's mind the rejection of materialism was an essential corollary to the pursuit of knowledge for its own sake, an idea which, as he perceived it, was slipping out of fashion with disastrous consequences. The importance of the endless search for truth became one of his favourite themes.

He left some surprising embryonic essays among the abandoned material. One was written in response to a tub-thumping address by the Bishop of London, who wished to expunge the stain of prostitution from the streets of the capital. 'Have you ever starved and had no means to get a bed from the frost?' Cherry raged. Another essay, a long, reasoned account which reveals the breadth of his scientific reading, was a kind of thinking-man's history of the planet. In this heady mix of geological theory and philosophical speculation Cherry strikes a peculiarly modern note. In a section on the function of carbon dioxide in climate change he shows that he knew all about the greenhouse effect. He discusses the role of thermohaline circulation in the oceans (without using the term) as well as the part played by changing polar oceanic currents in the growth of ice sheets – both topics keenly pursued by 21st-century scientists. While he recognised that in many areas 'we are in guess land, but not in fairy land', he believed there was no limit to what science could achieve. 'We shall visit the moon now before very long,' he prophesied, 'probably within the next thousand years.' He was less than 950 years out.

There was a kind of redemption in the act of writing. In the stillness of his library Cherry returned to the landscape where life had made sense. In his mind's eye he saw the coast of Ross Island where land met solid sea in the pleated cliff of a glacier or a tangle of blue-shadowed pressure ridges. He imagined sitting up again in a heavy reindeer-pelt bag, pushing back a gritty cambric tent flap and looking out over bloodless snowfields while ice crystals skittered through the blistering air and into his eyes. 'Even now,' he wrote,

the Antarctic is to the rest of the earth as the Abode of the Gods was to the ancient Chaldees, a precipitous and mammoth land lying far beyond the seas which encircled man's habitation, and nothing is more striking about the exploration of the Southern Polar regions than its absence, for when King Alfred reigned in England the Vikings were navigating the icefields of the north; yet when Wellington fought the battle of Waterloo there was still an undiscovered continent in the south.

He travelled far back through time and space to the small hut, where a single shaft of light from the midnight sun cut above the mound of snow piled against the window and fell on the jar of paint brushes on Bill's small table, casting distorted shadows on the far wall. At the end of the evening Bill liked to stand there next to the table in his pyjamas, listening to Clara Butt singing 'Abide with Me' on the gramophone. 'It is hard,' Cherry wrote, 'that often such men must go first when others far less worthy remain.'

He described standing at Hut Point watching the sun set behind the Western Mountains with Scott and the others in 1911, and then again a year later. The second time he was alone. He was on his hands and knees in the doorway of the hut after collapsing at the end of the journey to One Ton with Dimitri and the dogs, knowing that five men were slogging back across the Barrier and six more stranded somewhere up the coast. He would never forget those days, 'Yet time will slowly but surely cause these dark memories to become as shadows, from which – and because of which – stand out in happy contrast the beauty, the simplicity, the good comradeship of it all. And the good times were such as the Gods might have envied us . . .' Much of *The Worst Journey* sings faintly with the unquiet dissatisfactions of a man approaching middle-age. Its depictions of carefree days at Cape Evans read like a lament for lost innocence, and it is this that frees the book from the shackles of its time and place. Through his story Cherry reached out to something universal: the eclipse of youth, and the realm of abandoned dreams and narrowing choices that is the future.

The structure of the finished book is chronological, beginning with a historical introduction to Antarctic discovery and thereafter following the progress of the expedition. But the narrative is artfully interleaved with analysis and reflection. Within a single paragraph Cherry can range from historical disquisition through personal narrative and on to polemic. As he wrote ruefully of the *Terra Nova*:

> People talk of the niggardly equipment of Columbus when he sailed west from the Canaries to try a short-cut to an inhabited continent of magnificent empires, as he thought; but his three ships were, relatively to the resources of that time, much better than the old tramp in which we sailed for a desert of ice in which the evening and the morning are the year and not the day, and in which not even polar bears and reindeers can live. Amundsen had the *Fram*, built for polar exploration *ad hoc*. Scott had the *Discovery*. But when one thinks of these *Nimrod*s and *Terra Nova*s, picked up second-hand in the wooden-ship market, and faked up for the transport of ponies, dogs, motors, and all the impedimenta of a polar expedition, to say nothing of the men who have to try and do scientific work inside them, one feels disposed to clamour for a Polar Factory Act making it a crime to ship men for the ice in vessels more fit to ply between London Bridge and Ramsgate.

The mood of poetic musing mingled with practical explanation builds to a final meditation on the tawdry world to which the survivors came home. This counterpoint between the nobility of the spirit in which the expedition was undertaken and the grasping materialism of the post-war era, most clearly expressed in the plangent last page, reflected Cherry's inner life more clearly than anything else he wrote. Besides his private griefs, the general feeling of decay and punctured ideals that he observed all around him had fuelled his disillusion. Most of the contemplative passages of *The Worst Journey* were written in 1921, when Britain was experiencing one of the most severe depressions since the industrial revolution. In March the government declared a state of emergency following critical labour disputes in the mines, and the following month coal was rationed. In June, unemployment passed two million.

As the years of writing painfully unfolded, Cherry had risen above his pessimism and by sleight of hand turned the kernel of his story into a kind of parable. 'And I tell you,' he concluded,

> if you have the desire for knowledge and the power to give it physical expression, go out and explore. If you are a brave man you will do nothing: if you are fearful you may do much, for none but cowards have need to prove their bravery. Some will tell you that you are mad, and nearly all will say, 'What is the use?' For we are a nation of shopkeepers, and no shopkeeper will look at research which does not promise him a financial return within a year. And so you will sledge nearly alone, but those with whom you sledge will not be shopkeepers: that is worth a good deal.

It was the dislocation between the lushness of his Antarctic experience and the aridity of the present that formed his powerful sense of irony. From then on, irony became his dominant mode of expression. It suited him: it was as English as Kipling.

Cherry did not place himself at the centre of the stage; he was too modest. It was this that enabled him to write with such candour about his companions. The perspective of detached remembering that characterises so much of his account is most evident in his analysis of Scott. His thoughts on the man had matured, once the initial shock had subsided into a far-reaching, background grief. Scott himself had written about his conquest of his weaker nature, and Cherry deeply admired it. 'Naturally so peevish,' he wrote, 'highly strung, irritable, depressed and moody . . . His triumphs are many – but the Pole was not by any means the greatest of them. Surely the greatest was that by which he conquered his weaker self and became the strong leader whom we went to follow and came to love.' He admired Scott hugely, but he was angry at him for the mistakes he had made, and struggled not to blame him for the deaths of Wilson and Birdie. The frank admission and exploration of an unheroic side to Scott's character helped Cherry reconcile the bitterness he felt towards the man; temporarily, at least.

Schooled by Shaw, Cherry had developed a sensitive awareness of the rhythm of his material. Seeing that the last chapter was tending to the apocalyptic, he leavened it with an account of the life of penguins, who function as a kind of group fool to his Lear. ('We *must* admire them,' he concludes, 'if only because they are so much nicer than ourselves.') He finessed the extracts he quoted from his own diary, and from the diaries and field notes of Birdie and Lashly, in order to vary the tone and pace of his narrative and provide the immediacy of a close-up shot. And he husbanded his reflections, allowing only the most potent to survive. Although he recalled the bad times – the resentment, sickness and crucifying cold – he also acknowledged the treachery by which the mind can create a paradise of the past. 'So much of the trouble of this world is caused by memories, for we only remember half.'

He had been worried about the book's unwieldy title, and now it too was among the casualties. Talking over the winter journey with Shaw one day, Cherry concluded that he supposed it had indeed been 'the worst journey in the world'. He was thinking of Scott's comment when Cherry, Birdie and Bill staggered back into the hut encased in iron-hard windproofs and hollow-cheeked with tension and exhaustion. 'You know,' Scott had exclaimed, 'this is the hardest journey ever made.' A decade later, in the shadow of a chestnut tree, Shaw blinked. 'There's your title,' he said.

Cherry is a master of the short sentence, and as a counterweight to his often abrupt style, he addresses the reader directly. Like many shy writers, he loved to do this on the page, because he could not do it in the drawing room. 'A favourite pastime was the making of knots,' he wrote of the weeks spent waiting at Hut Point. 'Could you make a clove hitch with one hand?' His prose is lean and supple, an almost classical model of the virtues of clarity. In a few brush strokes he conjures the troglodytic existence of Campbell's Northern Party. 'But they also had their good, or less bad days; such was midwinter night when they held their food in their hands and did not want to eat it, for they were full; or when they got through the *Te Deum* without a hitch; or when they killed some penguins; or got a ration of mustard plaster from the medical stores.' The war seeped into the book, as it was bound to do (there is a blinded soldier crawling about in no man's land in the Dardanelles, among other references), and infused the story with riper significance. Scott and the expedition came to represent the last flowering of an ideal before the blight set in.

Shaw had put Cherry in touch with Otto Kyllmann, his publisher at Constable, and in June 1922 Cherry signed a publicity and distribution contract with the firm. He went back to his printer – two years after the first pages of the manuscript had been typeset – and ordered a first run of 1,500 two-volume boxed sets. The books were to be produced with two different bindings: an expensive creamy white Morris which Cherry preferred, and a blue cloth which was put out at three guineas. Even that was a small fortune, but Cherry was determined to produce a sumptuous book with fold-out maps and colour illustrations.

Constable published on 4 December, and the reviews began appearing immediately. The *Daily News* headlined its piece 'A Glorious Narrative', and the deputy editor of the *Nation*, literary man-about-town H. M. Tomlinson, reassured the reader that 'the man of taste and conscience would willingly forgo a weekend in Brighton [the same cost as the two volumes] in order to buy Mr Cherry-Garrard's story'. One of the best notices, in the *Evening Standard*, was written by Cherry's Christ Church contemporary George Mair, and it was this long, considered piece that attracted the most attention. 'I should call the book,' wrote Mair, 'the most wonderful story in the world. I do not think that in the whole of the collections of Hakluyt and his successors, or even in the great modern travel books like those of Stanley and of Scott and Shackleton themselves, you will find anything so impelling and authentic in its appeal or any record so noble of a noble event.' Mair was not the only critic who drew attention to Cherry's thoughtful analysis of Scott's character, which for the first time acknowledged dark as well as light. 'The real value of the book is as a contribution to polar psychology,' wrote the Antarctic historian Hugh Robert Mill in *Nature*. He judged it 'in some ways the most remarkable' of the six books that had appeared on the expedition. 'The iron of his [Cherry's] sufferings,' Mill wrote with bombastic eloquence, 'has entered into his soul and imparted a ferric quality to his recollections.' The *Bookman* critic thought it scarcely decent even to review the work. 'It would be more seemly to salute such a book with the ancient greeting of the Roman, standing with outstretched, uplifted arm in silent admiration of the great men and great deeds recorded.' Cherry was ecstatic. 'I'm having the time of my life,' he revealed jubilantly to Kyllmann on 8 December. Several weeks later he reported gleefully, 'Galsworthy has gone cracked about my book;

says it is the best of all polar books.'* This was what Scott had wanted: the tale had not been lost in the telling.

Not all the reviews were positive. The *Manchester Guardian*'s man objected to being labelled a shopkeeper, and thought some of Cherry's philosophising amounted to 'slipshod thinking'. The unattributed review in *The Times* was sour. (Cherry had shamelessly suggested to *The Times* that Shaw review the book and, equally shamelessly, GBS had offered to do so. But he didn't.) *The Worst Journey* would have been better, the reviewer thought, 'if the personal element had been more concentrated. It contains much which has been told elsewhere in the same words.' The dead hand of the committee was plainly visible in this piece. 'He has evidently,' the reviewer sniffed on, 'quite in the post-war manner, resolved to say what he thinks and emphasise the "heroism" of the story as little as possible.'

Several readers objected vociferously to *The Worst Journey*. Kathleen was furious that her first husband had been portrayed in less than godlike terms ('He has criticised Con in the most appalling fashion'). Cherry had sent her a boxed set inscribed 'with very grateful thanks'; she quickly added a few 'Rots!' in the margins. Shaw wrote to her joking feebly that she'd better not come to Ayot as she might murder Cherry if she saw him. Her friends attacked the book in public and private, homing in on what they perceived as its rank disloyalty. Barrie went hurrying round to Kathleen's house in Buckingham Palace Road and pointed out that, knowing both parties, Cherry's contention that Scott lacked humour was rich. (Knowing a little about Barrie, his own observation is richer still.) He decided against impugning Cherry in print on the grounds that his action would only serve to publicise the offending volume. Shaw, as usual, had hurled himself into the conflict. Hearing of Kathleen's anger, he sent her a long, typewritten apologia for Cherry and his book, scribbling at the top, 'Keep this for a quiet hour: it is about Cherry and old times and sorrows.' In this laborious and counter-productive letter he asked Kathleen to take *The Worst Journey* seriously, for Cherry, 'always a case of suppressed ability, has found an outlet for it in this book . . . and . . . bringing a hero to life always involves exhibiting his faults as well as his qualities'. It might have been common sense, but Kathleen did not want to hear it. Shaw, she thought privately, seemed unconsciously determined to make her resent the author of *The Worst Journey*. 'I have never admired Cherry,' she wrote in her diary, 'but I am very fond of him and don't want to have to cease to be.' Further

---

* Cherry admired Galsworthy's work immensely. 'I'm afraid I'm taking a larger hat,' he wrote to the author of the Forsyte chronicles after he had praised *The Worst Journey* in print.

comment came issuing from the Shavian oracle. Having cheerfully analysed 'Con' as if he had known him all his life, GBS warned Kathleen of the dangers her friends were running when they denounced Cherry and his book: 'The other day Cherry said to me quite spontaneously, "I had, as you know, the greatest admiration for Scott; but these people will end by hardening me against him: they will not listen to reason; and they know nothing about it."'

Kathleen's doctor confirmed that she was pregnant at about this time, so she had other things on her mind. But Shaw's words had not persuaded her. Five years later she tried to get Cherry's description of Scott being 'weak' and 'peevish' removed from *The Worst Journey*. When that strategy failed she took a different tack, sanctioning her erstwhile admirer Stephen Gwynn, an Irish journalist and former MP, to write a hagiography of Scott in the hope that it would obliterate Cherry's account in the manner of a palimpsest. But few read Stephen Gwynn now.

The mandarins at the Natural History Museum were also displeased. Cherry had flamboyantly exposed the indifference with which the museum had received the Emperor penguin eggs back in 1913. The exchange, skilfully presented as a comedy of manners ('This ain't an egg shop . . . Do you want me to put the police on to you?'), furnished Cherry with a striking contrast to the moral value of the winter journey and the spirit in which it was carried out ('We did not forget the Please and Thank you . . .'). Scenting a good story, the press picked it up, and a purple-faced Harmer, now the dignified Sir Sidney, complained indignantly to both the *Daily News* and Cherry, insisting that his staff had been gravely maligned ('the story seems devoid of any semblance to the truth'). Cherry drafted in the help of GBS (by post, inconveniently, as the Shaws were in London), and the pair of them tormented Harmer with courteous, clever letters that were impossible to refute. The main culprit at the museum was dead, but Cherry had a witness up his sleeve, as Scott's sister Grace, who had accompanied him on one visit to the Cromwell Road, confirmed his account of events in writing. For a week or two rants from both sides enlivened the pages of several newspapers including *The Times Literary Supplement*, Harmer sending forth a stream of denials and Cherry noting that 'the manners of the Natural History Museum have not changed for the better since 1913'.

Complaints notwithstanding, Shaw announced that the book's success 'has exceeded all expectations'. He considered that the reviews, 'favourable or not, all show that he has impressed his vision of the expedition irresistibly on his readers'. 'The book does seem to have made a hit,'

Cherry wrote to Emery Walker. 'It has done what I specifically wanted it to do – get the business into some kind of perspective and proportion.' Constable reported brisk sales, despite the high cover price, and a fortnight after publication a reprint was mooted. Soon a second edition was rolling off the Edinburgh presses with a short new preface, fewer plates (the stock of some of the panoramas had been exhausted) and some minor corrections. Buoyed up by his success, Cherry felt the deep sense of satisfaction that came from having achieved exactly what he had intended. 'This post-war business is inartistic,' he had written in his preface, 'for it is seldom that anyone does anything well for the sake of doing it well.' It had been a great relief, he said, to wander back into the past, a place which was so foreign that it seemed to him 'an age in geological time'. After paying tribute to the contribution both Shaws had made to the development of his writing, he concluded: 'At an advanced age, I am delighted to acknowledge that my education has at last begun.'

11

The Chaos which Threatens

*T*he *Worst Journey* had established Cherry's reputation, and in 1923 he entered the sacred pages of *Who's Who*. Despite his ambivalent attitude towards the establishment, a part of him yearned to belong, as parts of most of us do. He relished the social prestige conferred by his literary success. Through his book he had found a place in the world, and now he trotted zestfully round the country on social visits, accepting invitations to Emery Walker's house in Gloucestershire, to Donegal, and to Devonshire, where, in the summer of 1923, he fell eighty feet down a cliff. Nothing was broken, but he could not sit down comfortably for weeks. He was also still a regular guest at Bellecroft, the Russell Cookes' house on the Isle of Wight. Half a century later, Pussy's nephew Stephen Roskill remembered those times. 'I suppose,' he wrote, 'many of my happiest days were spent at Bellecroft in the 1920s when the house always seemed to be full of young, lively and intelligent people.' Roskill was often at Lamer too. He remembered a goat there which always turned its back when people approached: Cherry had named it Evans. Roskill knew Evans the man as well, and remarked that he was 'exactly the opposite to Cherry in being very self-advertising and flashy'.

Personal success notwithstanding, Cherry still fidgeted ceaselessly over the direction in which the country was heading, especially after January 1924 when Ramsay MacDonald became the first Labour prime minister. (MacDonald was to hold office for just ten months, though he would be back.) Cherry's political views changed little with the years. He had a visceral loathing of socialism but despised most politicians, whatever their allegiance, and shunned any involvement in party politics. In a description of the horse in *The Worst Journey* he wrote that the beast 'rivals our politicians in that he has little real intellect'.

He still fretted relentlessly over his finances. The high rates of income tax and other duties imposed during the war had never been brought back down to pre-war levels, and Cherry's response was to dispose of further assets. He was not alone: after 1918 a whole generation experienced a feeling of *après nous le déluge* that was to extend beyond the next war. In a famous *Encounter* article Nancy Mitford called it 'the spirit of divest, divest'. Cherry put the remaining rump of the Wittenham estate on the market: the wood where he had considered building the house of his dreams, the Clumps that had inspired Nash, the ancient camp on Sinodun Hill. Rumours of the possible destruction of the camp incited a howl of protest on the Letters page of the *Sunday Times*, among other places, and eventually His Majesty's Office of Works listed the site under the Ancient Monuments Act. Farrer tiptoed round a suggestion that Cherry might like to give a bit of it to the National Trust ('Do not think I have turned socialist,' he added hastily at the foot of his letter). 'I have always admired Charles and his courteous end,' Cherry replied tartly, 'but even a king was not expected to pay his executioners.'

With Wittenham sold, he decreed that Denford had to go. 'The country estate in my opinion is as out of date as foxhunting,' he wrote to the long-serving (and long-suffering) Farrer. 'It is a matter of opinion, but mine is a very clear one – we ought to get out.' He was over-optimistic about the price he would get for Denford. After consulting with his mother, a reserve of £28,000 was agreed. But the business dragged on, and the estate remained his.

In the summer, the Denford furniture was auctioned in anticipation of a sale. The candlestick that had lit the way up the curling stairs, the grained tray-top washstand at which four generations of Cherrys had faced their day, the japanned coal scuttle that had frightened the little boy in the night nursery: it all went, all except the carpet in the library, which Evelyn wanted. Finally, the freehold and 785 acres were sold for £20,000. The money was invested to provide an income for Evelyn, as she was a life tenant of Denford under the terms of the General's will. 'My mother and I are both extremely glad to be out of Denford,' Cherry informed Farrer in August, 'and our disappointment at the price realised is compensated a good deal, I think, by our pleasure at shedding one more liability. I imagine the next step will be Bride Hall house and land here, and finally perhaps, if one can shed one's taxation by so selling, Lamer.'

★　★　★

The Shaws were a permanent fixture in Cherry's social life as girlfriends came and went. He got to know many of their huge cast of theatrical acquaintances: in the winter of 1923 he heard Sybil Thorndike read *Saint Joan* in the rectory sitting room. (Not long afterwards he watched her star in the première.) At about the same time both GBS and Cherry acquired giant four-valve wireless sets, and they spent hours keenly fiddling with the buttons and pontificating on the changes this startling new technology would bring as waves of indecipherable crackle broke over their bent heads. As the years passed, age yielded material for a far more gripping topic, their health, or, more precisely, their ailments. Eagerly exchanging symptoms along with names and addresses of specialist doctors, when one or the other was away they continued the debate on paper. 'My bowels refused to act in the smallest degree,' GBS revealed conspiratorially in a bulletin from Birmingham in October 1923, 'though my digestion and appetite were as healthy as possible. In desperation I resorted to senna tea and paraffin oil . . .' If a particularly exciting condition manifested itself while they were apart, the patient hurried home to report his symptoms. 'We must compare damages when I return to Ayot,' GBS wrote from Malvern after having his ribs X-rayed. On the rare occasions when neither had any difficulties they turned to Charlotte and her state of health, and in an emergency they furrowed their brows over the diseases of the servants.

Besides the vagaries of physical wellbeing, they also colluded on matters of municipal concern. They both campaigned vigorously against an odiferous rubbish dump a mile south of Ayot. This strange place, embroidered with flowers in spring and colonised by rats in every season, consisted of a cluster of gravel pits packed with refuse sent up from London by the ponging trainload. 'My famous neighbour Mr Cherry-Garrard,' Shaw confided to the local press, 'sole survivor of "the worst journey in the world", after the horrors of which one would suppose that no discomfort possible in these latitudes could seem to him worth mentioning, has written a letter implying plainly that there is little to choose between midwinter at the South Pole and midsummer at Lamer Park when the dump is in eruption.' The unhealthy aspect of the dump, and the limitless range of illnesses for which it might be responsible, were of special concern to the two complainants when they did not have bigger fish to fry. 'I was ulcerating somewhere,' GBS reported eagerly from Boar's Hill in May 1926, 'and I take in and put out unnatural volumes of fluid.' His receipt of the Nobel Prize for Literature did nothing to stem the flow of medical data.

Cherry had been among the first in the county both to acquire a motor car and to install a coal-fired electricity generator. Yet he had an ambiguous attitude to change. For a decade he had been fretting about the bewildering shifts he observed in the world around him, and in the twenties he witnessed a rush of progress in sleepy villages around Lamer which had altered little in centuries. Although horses were still being shod in Wheathampstead at the forge behind the Swan, and one of them still pulled the pump for the municipal sewerage system, vehicles were gaining ground, and the furious honk of the horn on Cherry's open-topped silver Vauxhall as he sped down to the station had been downgraded to a minor event in the village day. Soon the first petrol pump was exhaling its fumes outside the Abbot John pub, Wren's wheelwright shop was replaced by a garage, and in 1925 the High Street was tarred. Gas had made its appearance in 1922 when forty lamps were purchased to replace the old oil ones, though they were turned off at ten o'clock each night on the basis that nothing ever happened after that hour.

Not far off, the pioneering new towns of Welwyn and Letchworth were burgeoning, and Wheathampstead labourers took the omnibus to the building sites during the increasingly frequent periods in which there were no jobs on the farms. These were the original garden cities, conceived at the turn of the century as a solution to urban overcrowding and designed to combine the best of town and country, with no pubs to distract the happy populace from gardening. GBS began to joke that Cherry's estate would end up as Lamer Garden City.

The sodden summers of 1925 and 1926 drove several tenant farmers around Ayot and Wheathampstead to the edge, and over it, especially when the closure of the railway during the General Strike meant they couldn't send their produce down to London. As small-scale agriculture continued its inexorable decline, light industry appeared in the form of Murphy & Son, an agrochemical factory that was almost as smelly as the dump. The Batford amalgam rubber plant which came soon afterwards was the first to install a hooter summoning the workers to their posts, and for many years it blared magnificently at 7.55 each morning. Murphy and the others strengthened the link, previously so frail, between Wheathampstead and the outside world. It was a connection that became steadily stronger during Cherry's lifetime, until the village was just another small part of a deafening and homogeneous universe.

The brand of heroic melancholy spawned by the news of Scott's death was out of place amid the languid sophistication of the twenties. It had more or less died in the trenches, or at least when the truth about the trenches was known. In the summer of 1924 it raised its head for a last Lazarus-like spasm when George Mallory and his youthful companion Sandy Irvine vanished on the summit ridge of Everest, 'going strong for the top'.

Like Scott, Mallory was compared to Sir Galahad; like Scott, his failure on this earth was transmogrified into success in the world beyond. The Bishop of Chester, mourning the mountaineers at their memorial service at St Paul's Cathedral, referred to their last climb as 'the ascent by which the kingly spirit goes up to the house of the Lord'. 'The real value [of the expedition] is moral and spiritual,' *The Times* had written after the *Terra Nova* reached New Zealand. Cherry had known Mallory at Winchester, and after his death he likened him to Bill, his hero. 'In a way,' he wrote, 'he who lies in the snow of the Barrier was like Mallory who lies on the snow of Mount Everest.' But the days of heroic innocence were gone, and while the country was prepared to indulge in one last spree, for Cherry there was no return. In his memory, his dead friends stood alone. 'Mallory was burning with a kind of fire, an ardent, impatient soul, winding himself up to a passion of effort the higher he got,' he concluded. 'Bill was not like that . . .' In the long, lonely years of anguished recollection, Cherry regretted that he hadn't asked Bill enough questions about himself, to learn what made him as he was. How many people have wished for their time again, once the beloved is gone? How little is learned from those lessons.

Cherry was now considered an authority, or at least an urbane commentator, on travel to remote regions, and in June 1926 the *Daily News* asked him to contribute to a debate on the future of exploration. Noting first the speed with which the world was shrinking (in the previous three months Alan Cobham had flown from London to Cape Town and back, and Amundsen, taking off from Spitsbergen in an airship, had flown over the North Pole and on to Alaska), Cherry developed a theme he had raised in *The Worst Journey* by suggesting that the future of polar exploration was in the air. 'When an airship can be used like a motor-car,' he suggested, 'there will be no more blank spaces in the world.' He predicted that large government-funded scientific stations would be built in the Antarctic, specifying Ross Island as a probable site.* But it didn't much interest him. The virgin territories of Asia, he reckoned, were more appealing: 'Rather pick primulas in Szechwan than lava on the Beardmore now.' Via this circuitous Chinese route he steered his argument round to the familiar comparison between the noble purity of the true expedition and the tawdry materialism of the modern world. 'England has a genius for

---

* The largest base in the Antarctic, America's McMurdo Station, is situated on Ross Island, adjacent to the *Discovery* hut. The summer population of the base can reach 1,500.

compromise, and in this dreadfully civilised world, with so many people and so many interests, compromise pays: a limited Monarchy, a limited Democracy, a limited Socialism, and now perhaps a limited Trade Unionism – and quite time too.' (The TUC had called off the General Strike* six weeks previously, leaving the striking miners to battle on alone.) A few of his father's ideals of Englishness had survived in the toxic soil of his disillusion. 'For the English do not really like compromise,' he informed the confused readers of the *Daily News*, 'and God, as I believe, does not want compromise. He wants people to have strong beliefs and to go all out for them.' For the last fifty years of his life, Cherry believed the present to be all wrong. Like many in Britain, he looked back with Chekhovian longing to an imaginary pre-war society (more accurately pre-Antarctic, in his case), and as the distance from that halcyon time lengthened, so his dissaffection with the present intensified. Most people live in the past when they reach old age; by his early forties, Cherry already saw the present in black and white and looked backwards to a lost youth that glowed in glorious colours.

Evelyn had moved out of her rented house in Southampton with the long-suffering Peggy in tow and bought a property on a hill near Godalming in order to be near Mildred, her third daughter, who was living in Reigate in Surrey with her young family. The West House remained Evelyn's home for over a quarter of a century. Cherry visited her occasionally, and they exchanged telephone conversations in which each shouted at the other before being cut off. He also saw Lassie and her brood in St Albans, where Lassie's husband, now a canon, held a diocesan office, but otherwise he was growing distant from his family. Edith, having recovered from her childhood invalidity to conquer the Matterhorn, had continued upwards and embraced religion, hopping cheerily from church to church and giving away all her money. Cherry saw little of her, and disapproved of her financial piety. The rituals of birth and death meant nothing to him, and he refused to turn up for relatives' funerals, staying away from Bedford in August 1927 when his uncle Colby Sharpin was buried. Colby had been a distinguished doctor as well as a carnation- and picotee-fancier of national standing. He died at 11 Lansdowne Road, two doors away from the red-brick house where Cherry was born. But Cherry was more self-absorbed

---

* During the General Strike – class war by any other name – Cherry was astonished to read in *The Times* that the descendants of his armoured cars were patrolling the streets of London, mobilised by their old ally Churchill to keep law and order.

than most, and his far-off, unremembered beginnings were irrelevant to him. He went through life apparently unconscious of the random stroke of fate that had led him to acquire his riches, and it never occurred to him that only an arbitrary set of events had separated him from a lifetime in a red-brick house in Lansdowne Road like his Uncle Colby.

As for the villagers, he was wholly indifferent to them. He paid his tithes, made his squirely contributions to hospital funds, complained occasionally and otherwise maintained a dignified distance – as long as people kept off his land. He chased away boys he caught bird-nesting in the spinneys, took the names of the girls who gathered bluebells in the dell by the ice house and banned the collection of firewood on the grounds that people were taking too much. Despite all that, his policy of non-intervention was popular with his tenant farmers. But if Cherry ever felt exploited, he showed immense determination.

His most protracted dispute in the mid twenties was with George Seabrook, the tenant of Lamer Farm, at 350 acres the largest on the estate.* Seabrook, whose family had worked the land there for generations, kept eighty ewes, thirty steers and three milking cows, as well as a flock of turkeys and a hundred head of poultry which, being truly free range, often popped up in unexpected places. For years Cherry had been asking him to refrain from grazing his horses in parkland near the house as they were gnawing the elm trees. Despite heavy expenditure on fencing and tree guards, the elms continued to sustain damage. 'Legally I believe I can put machinery in motion,' Cherry had written in an impassioned letter to Seabrook in May 1923, 'but that kind of thing leaves bitter feelings . . . I care far more for these trees which are sometimes hundreds of years old than I do about rents: I care so much that I do not think I can discuss the matter personally with calmness.'

The machinery, however, was the only solution. After two more years of demands and conciliatory gestures, Farrer was instructed and, incredibly, in December 1926 *Cherry-Garrard* v. *Seabrook* was heard in front of Justice Tomlin in the High Court. Affidavits were read from the bemused gardener Hyde, as well as Currell the woodman, and the judge gravely leafed through lists of numbered trees defaced with 'slight patches', 'severe patches' or 'very severe patches'. After an interim injunction ordering Seabrook to refrain from permitting his horses to eat the trees, the proceedings staggered to a botched settlement at the beginning of 1927. It was a Pyrrhic victory for Cherry. As he had predicted, there were bitter

---

* Now part of the Lamerwood Golf Course, where hole 10 is 'Garrard's Trek'.

feelings. The Farmers' Union insinuated that they might blacklist him. Not that he cared about that: he was determined to get out of agricultural land.

He had fallen into a depression towards the end of the case, and found it difficult to keep the trees and their horsey teeth marks in proportion. On bad days he couldn't get out of bed, and when he thought of Reggie, he was afraid. This was ominous. 'No man is greater than the man who can conquer himself,' he had written in a discarded description of Scott. But here he was, unable to conquer his own disposition. His failure to overcome his black mood trapped him in a wretched cycle of despair, and as the daffodils nodded behind the summer house and the May blossom cheered the park, Cherry retreated into autumnal gloom.

On good days he came down to breakfast when the factory hooter sounded, and as he tackled cook's coddled eggs and dark coffee under the eyes of his ancestors he asked himself how much longer he was prepared to struggle to keep Lamer going. Would he be the one to let it out of the family? The estate had already shrunk to 900 acres, of which 143 were parkland. He seemed to think that if things continued as they were, he would be ruined. The reality was that he was still very wealthy indeed. His capital had recently swollen by £18,000 (around half a million pounds in today's terms) when he had been paid the final tranche of the mortgage on Upper Forest Estate near Swansea. It was a great relief, and an end at last to the torrents of correspondence spewing out of Glamorgan almost daily.

Despite his lack of interest in land, Cherry was devoted to his trees, as Seabrook had discovered, and he planted 300 acres of larch and beech, most of which replaced cornfields. The planting was not simply inspired by dendrophilous tendencies: he did it to avoid land tax, which woodland did not attract. But he cherished his trees as if they were people, and when the Hertfordshire Hunt persisted in riding over the young plantations, Cherry angrily banned hunting at Lamer for the first time in the history of the estate.* Huntsmen do not easily break their habits, and in 1929 Cherry brought an action for trespass and damage. In court, the defendants' counsel tried gamely to elicit a motive. 'Was it hurt pride? A taste for litigation? A crank's distaste for good old-fashioned British blood sports? Mr Cherry-Garrard is a famous explorer, as everyone knows; why make a mountain out of a mole hill?' 'I have brought this as a test-case,' Cherry replied with his characteristic inscrutability. 'I am here for a decision.' When he got one, he smiled inside. He had won again.

---

* Glancing from his bedroom window on the eve of a meet, Cherry often glimpsed the flash of a hurricane lamp as the spotter, who lived in a cottage at Lamer Farm, stole through the woods with his brushing hook to block the entrance to the fox earths.

When he had no troublesome farmers or huntsmen to pursue, the chaos of Cherry's inner life manifested itself in a steady war of attrition against his old enemies, the tax commissioners and the clergy. In his fantasy life the country was led by a benign despot who ruled according to a strict policy of laissez-faire, levied income tax at a discretionary rate and administered a sharp kicking to any representative of the Church of England who raised his voice in protest. In October 1929 his natural pessimism was painfully gratified when the collapse of the New York stock market precipitated global economic depression. British exports were paralysed, unemployment rose dramatically and in his 1930 budget Philip Snowden, the chancellor who smoked Turkish cigarettes in an ivory holder, raised income tax and surtax and, to Cherry's rage, revived proposals for a tax on land value.

Throughout these years, Cherry remained obsessed with the burden of the property owner. The estate contracted in violent spurts, and in some corner of his mind he associated the final sale – the sale of Lamer – with the final casting-off of anxieties. He loved Lamer deeply; every yard of the park had its associations. Each day he saw his father's waxed moustache in the large oil on the dining-room wall, and the recriminations stalked his imagination. The tension between his ancestral duty, his attachment to his estate and the desire to liberate himself from the responsibilities of the landlord tightened as each year progressed. But for all his talk, he could not yet sell Lamer.

In 1925, through the Shaws, Cherry had met the gnome-like T. E. Lawrence. Already a national hero widely known as the uncrowned king of Arabia, Lawrence had enlisted in the air force under the assumed name of Ross, ostensibly to escape his own legend. When the story got out he was forced to leave. He changed his name again, this time to Shaw, and after a stint in the Tank Corps was transferred to the RAF Cadet College at Cranwell in Lincolnshire. To get there from London he had to drive near Wheathampstead, and he was in the habit of stopping off at the Shaws for the weekend. Once installed, he accompanied his hosts to Lamer for lunch. Charlotte especially was fond of Lawrence: she was thirty years his senior, yet they were remarkably intimate. GBS had tinkered away at the flabby typescript of *Seven Pillars of Wisdom* for two years, and both Shaws inevitably drew comparisons between that book and *The Worst Journey*. When Lawrence told them, with typically ostentatious self-deprecation, that nobody would be interested in the subject matter of his unpublished volume, GBS, citing the success of Cherry's book, asked why sand should not have the same appeal as snow.

Lawrence was two years younger than Cherry. He was a small man with engaging eyes and a cupid-bow mouth, and looked boyish into his forties. With sly contrivance he had manipulated the facts of his life and stoked the legend that blazed around him. He was more intellectually magnetic than Cherry, and more dazzling. Shaw was effusive in his praise of *Seven Pillars*, but it has none of *The Worst Journey*'s artful spontaneity: its prose is convoluted, its imagery overburdened. Lawrence's letters are much better; in them he becomes lovable. As for his relationship with Cherry: although they were never particularly close, their inner lives were more similar than their public personas suggested. Both men fought long and terrible battles with the masked enemies of fear, doubt and introspection. Both were frequently unhappy. Lawrence explained to Charlotte that he had no faith in himself as a writer and so had 'backed out of the race'. Frustrated by the tensions between literature and action, he claimed he no longer wished to be 'a half and half: a Cherry-Garrard'. Yet for all his pseudonyms and flights to the ranks, Lawrence was a more public man than Cherry.

Lawrence admired *The Worst Journey* ('one of the great travel books') and adored Lamer ('It has an astonishing feeling of being intact and undisturbed'). When Cherry subscribed thirty guineas to the private, slimmed-down edition of *Seven Pillars*, Lawrence signed his copy, 'A. C-G. from T. E. Shaw . . . shamefacedly, for I feel that my bad journey is so much worse told than his.' For once, he was right. In his *Spectator* review of *Revolt in the Desert* (the anorectically abridged version of the edited *Seven Pillars*), GBS linked Cherry and Lawrence ('Do tell me that his praise scares you, also,' Lawrence wrote girlishly to Cherry). It was astonishing, reckoned Shaw the elder, to find such a superlative synthesis of literature and action in two young men of the same generation. Commenting on this privately to Cherry, Lawrence suggested, 'If our sexes had been different (one of us, I mean) we could have pulled off a eugenicist's dream.' The thought beggars the imagination.

Lawrence inhabited a twilit zone between reality and fantasy. He had a passion for concealment, and cultivated his own image with relentless intensity. This was foreign to Cherry's mental world. In the end, Charlotte grew apart from Lawrence. 'He's such a liar,' she told Cherry, and soon he too drifted out of touch with Lawrence (the weekend visits to Ayot had ceased at the end of 1926, when Lawrence was posted abroad). After Lawrence was killed in a motorcycle accident in 1935, his brother Arnold asked Cherry to contribute to a collection of essays. *T. E. Lawrence by his Friends*, published by Jonathan Cape in 1937, included a short analytical piece by Cherry in which he wrote of his friend's crucifying anxieties from a very near perspective. 'Experiences such as Lawrence had been through,' he said, 'do not drop you: they torture you.' He knew all about that. 'To go through a terrible time of mental and physical stress,' wrote Cherry, 'and to write it down as honestly as possible is a good way of getting some of it off your nerves. I write from personal experience.' But only 'some' of this stress was removable: later, in Lawrence's case, 'Having been knocked about so much, all these troubles and primitive and subconscious fears began to come to the surface.' This was plainly Cherry's case also. 'In the long run,' he stated bleakly, 'no man can escape himself.'

The Worst Journey had drifted out of print, and in 1929, seven years after its first appearance, it was reissued by Constable. Shaw provided a 200-word publicity blurb ('It was perhaps the only real stroke of luck in Scott's ill-fated expedition that Cherry-Garrard, the one survivor of the winter journey, happened to be able to describe it so effectively') which was printed prominently on the dust jacket. From an Italian hotel where he was on holiday GBS also dispatched advice on obtaining the best deal in America, where the Dial Press were also to publish a new edition.

Otto Kyllmann at Constable had proposed a scheme for an American edition back in October 1922, and Cherry had engaged Shaw's lawyer in New York to register copyright in *The Worst Journey in the World*. Constable duly secured a deal with the well-known firm of George H. Doran, and a small run of specially printed copies was imported into the United States at the end of February 1923. The book failed to make an impact, though a lone reviewer compared Cherry to Teddy Roosevelt ('He is a man after Roosevelt's own heart. His refusal to allow his near-sightedness to interfere with his exploration was especially Rooseveltian').

Doran allowed the book to go out of print, and now the Lincoln MacVeagh imprint at the Dial Press was about to have another go with a single-volume edition printed in the US and priced at five dollars.* This time, the book had a chance. Antarctica had rarely been off the front pages in the months prior to publication: the young Virginian naval pilot Richard Byrd claimed to have flown over the South Pole in an aluminium Ford trimotor – the first man at ninety south since Scott. Three years previously Byrd, an outstanding egotist even by the demanding standards of polar explorers, had become the first man to fly over the North Pole (or so it was

---

* Doran merged with Doubleday in 1927, making Doubleday Doran the largest publishing concern in the English-speaking world. Almost fifty years later Dial was also acquired by Doubleday.

believed at the time: Byrd has since been discredited). In 1928, already famous and sponsored in part by the *New York Times*, he had sailed down to the Antarctic with three aircraft on board his ship and established a base called Little America on the Ross Ice Shelf. With the benefit of radio technology and a *Times* journalist on the team, Byrd was able to thrill the public with his adventures on a daily basis, and his exploits received the kind of attention lavished on the moon landings forty years later. On 29 November 1929, the very day that Byrd peered down at the awful South Pole through the pebble-glass window of the Ford, Cherry signed a five-year agreement with Dial. In the week the book was published Byrd returned to a hero's welcome which included a ticker-tape parade and a speech by the Mayor of New York in which the deeply unattractive Byrd, with pleasing American understatement, was called 'one of the finest human beings ever born into the world throughout its fine history'. Medals and banquets were lavished upon him, followed by receptions at the White House and promotion to rear-admiral by means of a special bill rushed through Congress by President Hoover. Furthermore, although only Americans could afford such fabulously equipped expeditions in the twenties, Byrd did not have the Antarctic to himself. In 1928 the Australian Hubert Wilkins had made the first powered flight over the continent (with a news contract with Hearst in his pocket) and he had gone on to discover new land by air and to map vast tracts of Graham Land on what is now known to be the Antarctic Peninsula. Douglas Mawson had recently returned to the south leading a joint British, Australian and New Zealand research expedition which was cruising between King George V Land and Enderby Land and exploring inland by air, and the Norwegian Hjalmar Riiser-Larsen was charting another segment of the coast by seaplane from a whaler. So when, in the spring of 1930, *The Worst Journey* was at last widely available to American readers, the time was ripe.

The critics loved it. The *Bookman* said it was 'one of the most thrilling and absorbing narratives in modern literature, and makes Byrd's journey by airplane to the Pole seem no more harassing than a train trip from Albany to Troy. It is as packed with suspense as a mystery story, as tragic as a Russian novel . . .' The man at the *Nation* judged it one of the most interesting books he had ever read, and the long, glowing piece in the *New York Times Book Review* praised Cherry's 'remarkable descriptive powers', claimed that not a paragraph was laboured and asked its readers, 'Where shall the like of it be read for sheer strength, clarity and beauty of phrase in the literature of polar exploration?' There were caveats. The *New York World* found the book thrilling and 'very splendid', but was annoyed by

Cherry's claim that Scott 'cared nothing about being first' at the Pole. 'Why English writers,' the reviewer concluded testily, 'should be so set on proving this one point is something of an enigma.' The *Saturday Review of Literature* welcomed the book as a 'fine, thrilling' literary record that had 'long been regarded as a classic', but objected to Cherry's blanket statement about the miseries of polar exploration, pointing out that Eskimos got on all right and so had a lot of other explorers. But the plum review was by H. L. Mencken in the *American Mercury*. The influential, Baltimore-born Mencken, a beer and cigar man, was famed for his fierce satires on philistines of all kinds, especially if they played golf (he was also a rabid Kipling fan). According to his chum Edmund Wilson, he was 'our greatest practising literary journalist'. Revealing his European roots by hailing Cherry's use of irony, Mencken praised *The Worst Journey* without equivocation. '[It] is very well-written,' he decided, 'and makes capital reading. He is plainly far more intelligent than most explorers. He has a gorgeous story to tell, and he tells it without heroics and with enough quiet waggishness to make it very unusual.' Mencken seized the opportunity to puncture a few myths. The scientific value of polar exploration, he argued, was greatly exaggerated.

> The thing that takes men on such hazardous trips is really not any thirst for knowledge, but simply a yearning for adventure. But just as an American businessman, having amassed a fortune, always tries to make it appear that he never had any desire for money, but only wanted to set up an orphan asylum or get time to study golf, so a Polar explorer always talks grandly of sacrificing his fingers and toes to science. I daresay Admiral Byrd will be doing it before these lines get into print.

Glowing notices notwithstanding, within three years *The Worst Journey* was again unavailable in the United States. 'They [Americans],' Cherry concluded, 'seem difficult people to deal with.' He had sent Doran twenty-five boxed sets of review copies free of charge and was never shown a single review. Dial had not bothered to communicate with him, and Constable told him that the firm had sold some of its edition in the UK, which was outside its copyright territory. Though keen for his book to be read in America, Cherry could never take his New York publishers seriously. He had inherited from his father, who spent his life buttressing the Empire, the belief that the Englishman was superior to the foreigner, and he could not accept that an American might be able to publish and sell his book with the smallest degree of efficiency. Much later, after US copyright law was modified at the Havana Convention, he encouraged Allen Lane to import the legal limit of 1,500 copies of the Penguin edition into the States ('I don't want to be a lost cause'); but he never established a satisfactory working arrangement with a foreign firm. Americans in general, he felt, were unreliable, a view shared by most of the Conservative Party at that time, and he endorsed his hero Kipling's opinion of the country as 'one big, uneasy refugee camp'. Unsurprisingly, he was consistently dismissive of American endeavour in the Antarctic. He received new polar titles by post from a bookshop where he kept an account (the postman had a hook instead of a hand at the end of one arm, and he hung the book parcels from the hook as he bicycled up the drive). When an account of Byrd's expedition swung its way up to the front door it came in for an especially savage beating. 'Bow wow', Cherry noted in the margin of a purple passage, and he judged the Admiral's comment, 'What a disheartening sight is the Fokker', to be 'more bow wow'. The claim that 'Seldom have men undertaken so difficult a trail journey for purely scientific investigation' provoked an indignant 'Rot!'

One of Cherry's former shipmates was still deeply involved with the Antarctic. For more than a decade Frank 'Deb' Debenham, now a lecturer at Cambridge, had devoted much of his considerable energy to a polar research institute he had founded in 1920 as a memorial to Scott and his party. It was a project conceived one stormy afternoon on the ice when Deb was trapped in Shackleton's hut by a blizzard. 'Exploring the many boxes and cupboards inside the hut,' he recalled years later, 'I came upon some blue-lined foolscap in Shackleton's cubicle, so heavy in quality and smooth of surface that it positively invited me to write. Accordingly I spent the morning writing down on this noble stationery an outline of the idea.' After the war he had campaigned sturdily to secure cash from the fund raised in honour of the polar party, and despite difficult periods when little money was forthcoming, he never lost faith in the project. For the first five years his institute was housed in an attic loaned by the university at the Sedgwick Museum. Deb had pressed Cherry to endow a memorial to Bill ('The most minor member of the expedition would couple Bill and Cherry together in their minds'). Cherry perceived the whole project as a gift to the government, and as the government was the enemy of the landowner, he refused. But the friendly institute was a congenial refuge. It had a growing collection of memorabilia as well as a first-rate polar library, and it quickly became a meeting point for all those with an interest in the Arctic and the Antarctic. When it moved to larger premises at Lensfield House in

1927 Cherry often motored over to take Deb and his assistant, Miss W. 'Francis' Drake, out for gammon steaks at the University Arms. He was still pursuing his apprenticeship as a water-colourist, and in later years spent many hours in front of the Wilson landscapes hung on the institute's walls, making copies in his artist's sketchbook. 'How they bring it all back,' he wrote. 'Better than all the photographs in the world.'*

Back at Lamer, he had acquired several of Wilson's paintings for himself and he hung them on the drawing-room wall. Other purchases included a ten-foot-square unframed oil of a dog tethered to a red post. It was in the hall next to the frowning ancestors, the crowd of them towering over a pair of Emperor penguins in a glass case. Cherry also bought another Epstein, this time a bust. In his literary tastes, he was less adventurous. Always a reader, he remained loyal to Trollope, Jane Austen, Kipling, Conrad and Galsworthy. Among new writers he read only those who were old at heart, like P. G. Wodehouse (of course) and Agatha Christie. He was never exposed to avant-garde literature and the great works of the modern movement in the way he had been exposed to Rodin (yet both *The Waste Land* and *Ulysses* were published in the same year as *The Worst Journey*); and he was never curious enough to try them for himself. But he did read widely. Besides fiction, he immersed himself in philosophy and religious theory, and kept up with the classics. When he was depressed he sat in the library and sought help from the volumes ranked behind the glass cases. Although he had lost his own faith many years before, he was drawn to the teachings of the Christian mystics. 'All is not lost,' he underlined in a chapter of Thomas à Kempis, 'even though again and again thou feel thyself broken or well-nigh spent.' It was only institutionalised religion that repelled him. He did not deny the existence of the transcendental; he reached out to it, and the spiritual dimension was as real to him as the oaks in the park. In a sense, his vision was pantheistic. He admired Spinoza's concept of the 'intellectual love of God', and recognised that the sacred should be honoured. He believed, like Bill (and Spinoza), that man attained perfect happiness by goodness and piety, and that virtue was its own reward.

In February 1929 Atch suddenly died on a navy ship on his way home from India, and was buried at sea. He had never fully recovered from the

---

* Emerson said that an institution is the lengthened shadow of a man. The Scott Polar Research Institute, now an internationally renowned centre and the heart of British polar studies, lies in Deb's friendly shadow. After Cherry died, Deb wrote to his widow, 'Though I called the work I did over the PRI "in memory of the Pole Party", it was really in memory of Bill.' So it should be renamed the Wilson Polar Research Institute.

horrific incident in Dover Harbour just over a decade earlier in which he
had been burned and partially blinded. After the death of his wife in 1928,
he had had a breakdown. He told Cherry that he was going to leave the
service and, incarcerated in a naval hospital, expressed the hope that he
might soon join his dead wife. One of his sisters wrote to Cherry in despair,
asking him to help: she was afraid her brother was going to drink himself to
death. It was a curious reversal of roles. But Atch rallied. Within the year
he had been promoted, married his first wife's cousin, moved to Glasgow
and sailed to India with the navy. Everything had seemed so promising;
now, just months after his recovery, Atch was dead. Cherry was deeply
moved. Eight years later he published a tribute to his friend in the preface
to a new edition of *The Worst Journey*. 'His voice has been with me often
since those days,' he wrote after revealing what a 'rock' Atch had been in
the last terrible year in the Antarctic. 'That gruffish deep affectionate
monosyllabic way he used to talk to you when he knew you were ill and
perhaps feeling pretty rotten. Not but that he was abrupt at times. It was of
the manner of the man to be so; it was his pose. The funny thing was that
he could not prevent the tenderness poking through, despite himself.' He
ended his testimonial by expressing regret that Atch's death had passed
almost unnoticed. 'I am glad,' he recorded, 'to have this opportunity to
witness something of what we owe him.'

That last February of the twenties was bitter. At Lamer, just as a black
frost killed the winter oats and turned the cornfields to yellow charlock,
Cherry met George Seaver, an intelligent polar enthusiast who was
planning to write a biography of Wilson. They had been introduced by
Ory, who was quick to reassure Cherry that although Seaver was a priest,
he was 'not of the usual type'. Seaver wanted to discuss the expedition, and
so Cherry invited him to luncheon.

Four years younger than Cherry and born, like Wilson, in Cheltenham,
Seaver had served in the war and then spent five years as a commissioner in
Northern Rhodesia. A bachelor living with his elderly father, he was a
gentle, thoughtful and exceptionally well-read man with a finely tuned
understanding of the vagaries of human nature. Ory had warned him in
advance of Cherry's Voltairesque dislike of clergymen; but Seaver was
game for a challenge. (He was not very keen on parsons himself. 'I
sympathise with you in the Church's efforts to relieve you of some money,
and hope you may frustrate them. The Church has got quite enough
money as it is.')

When Seaver's taxi drew up outside the porch at Lamer the long arms of
the sweet chestnuts were bare and spindly in the pale wintry light and the

wind was tormenting the yew hedge in the walled garden. Having been shown in by the housekeeper, the reverend waited in the drawing room, which already smelt faintly of boiled greens, and warmed his feet in front of a deep coal fire. Cherry was in the garage, fiddling under the bonnet of the Vauxhall (an electric heater had failed, and the car was iced up). Eventually he appeared, tense and rigid, apologising for the delay and rubbing his hands. But for once, Cherry relaxed. He had much in common with Seaver. Both were old-fashioned sceptics. Both loathed what Seaver robustly called 'those post-war productions that masquerade as works of art and reflect the malaise of a diseased sensibility'. Epstein was one thing; but to men of their generation the rise of truly radical avant-garde art movements symbolised the destruction of settled pre-war values, and modernism was regarded, like the war itself, as a perilous destructive force.

Over a plate of stewed rabbit, brown potatoes, sprouts and gravy Cherry opened up to the sympathetic Seaver's questions about the expedition. Besides reeling off factual details about sledges and rations, he ruminated frankly over less tangible issues. It had been a mistake to take five men to the Pole instead of four; the polar party 'finally starved' as a result of 'lack of vitamins';* Taff Evans had collapsed mentally first, before his physical decline. Seaver noted that his host seemed troubled. 'I often wonder,' Cherry said, when the maid had cleared away the milk-pudding plates and left a silver jug of dark coffee, 'whether if I had plugged on from One Ton after that Blizzard, killing dogs for food as necessary, I might have reached them.' Seaver pointed out gently that the distances and dates showed that this would have been impossible. Cherry was unconvinced. Long spells of illness since those days had made a wreck of him, he said, puffing thoughtfully on a Russian Gold cigarette. 'But surely you are the same man that went on the winter journey?' Seaver asked. 'Am I?' asked Cherry in return. 'I wonder.' 'But he was,' Seaver wrote privately. 'The heroic spirit was still there, though its over-taxed earthly vehicle could no longer respond to it as it did in youth.'

Cherry continued to meet or correspond with GBS several times a week, despite Shaw's raving evangelism for Soviet Communism. In May 1930 GBS had sent bulletins from his hotel in Buxton, Derbyshire, on Charlotte's latest illness, scarlet fever. 'The doctor says,' he revealed, 'the

---

* Atch had researched the subject, and shared his conclusions with Cherry. In a draft of *The Worst Journey* Cherry wrote that the polar party had starved, but in the end he held this bald statement back from the public.

streptococcus is not virulent enough to infect anyone over the age of five. I am more concerned with what happens over the age of seventy.' When everyone was well, Cherry was invited to performances of Shaw's plays in London. At a lunch party at the Shaws' flat he was introduced to Amy Johnson, who had recently hogged the headlines when she became the first woman to make a solo flight from Britain to Australia. More excitingly for Cherry, he met Charlie Chaplin, whom he greatly admired. Chaplin was in town for the British première of his smash hit *City Lights* – still silent, despite the arrival of the talkies.

Although in his cheerful spells he enjoyed socialising with the stars, most of all Cherry relished the homely intimacy he shared with the Shaws. It was a relief to stroll down the avenue of limes, stretch his legs in front of their fire and allow himself to be infected with GBS's many enthusiasms. One of these was the composition of doggerel. Extolling the village cemetery one dark autumnal afternoon, GBS was inspired to write the verse 'Here Ayot's deaders/Into eternity take headers', which tickled Cherry. He was soon at it himself, one year composing this verse to accompany the image of an Emperor penguin on his Christmas card: 'While elsewhere I might be cosier/The living's cheaper at Cape Crozier.' In his dotage Shaw published a volume of his locally inspired poetry illustrated with his own photographs, and underneath a snap of Cherry sprawled in a garden chair, knickerbockered legs splayed, he wrote a caption ending, 'Young Cherry-Garrard soon became/Our neighbour of the greatest fame.' Not Nobel material, perhaps; but an endearing record of a true friendship.

Apart from the Shaws, as he entered the thirties and his own mid forties Cherry led a solitary life. His main hobby was bird-watching. His two-volume *Birds of the British Isles* by T. A. Coward was permanently at hand on a low table in the library, battered and bulging with newspaper cuttings reporting rare sightings. He went shooting, attended to his young trees and was permanently vexed by the moods of his temperamental coal-fired generator. When he needed company he whizzed over to Cambridge in the Vauxhall's successor, a primrose Rolls convertible known as the 'yellow peril'. He had commissioned a personalised model from the well-known firm of Mulliner's, and, in an uncharacteristic display of vulgarity, had the family crest mounted in the centre of the doors. In Cambridge he remorselessly cultivated Frankie Drake and other bright young women on the staff of Deb's research institute, taking one out for lunch and another out for dinner on the same day. He was well, physically and emotionally, for much of 1930 and 1931. But even in his bright periods he could turn sour. When he went to assist the sculptor C. S. Jagger with his Shackleton statue, commissioned for the new Royal Geographical Society building, the episode ended badly. Cherry had agreed to lend his polar mitts and lanyards, even though he claimed that he still wore them ('I will freeze in the meantime'), because he admired Jagger's work. He trekked down to the sculptor's studio in the wilds of Battersea in south London, took one look at the preliminary sketches and told the baffled Jagger what he thought, which was not wholly complimentary. 'A wasted afternoon,' Cherry tartly informed poor Frankie Drake, who had organised the whole thing.

The economic and political crisis in the middle of 1931 that culminated in the end of the gold standard was potentially calamitous for investors like Cherry. Now the Depression bit, and although Wheathampstead, like most of the south-east, was not especially affected by the recession, it was not immune. The village was still reliant on agriculture, and farmers were suddenly even more hard pressed than they had been in the twenties. Casual work on the farms dropped off altogether, and in the mornings a gaggle of men queued outside the little forge behind the High Street, looking for work which was rarely offered. Elsewhere, even in the relatively prosperous south, ordinary people began to register their frustration with riots and hunger marches. Cherry prophesied darkly that graver disasters lay ahead.

In the spring of 1932 the Shaws brought Sidney and Beatrice Webb over to Lamer for lunch. The dining room was bright with May sunshine, the bronze figurines gleamed on the enamelled sideboard and a vase of freshly picked gold roses stood in the centre of the mahogany dining table. Sidney, the ugly and astonishingly brilliant son of a hairdresser,* had gone to the Lords as Passfield after the May 1929 general election, combining the posts of Dominions and Colonial Secretary. Beatrice, the daughter of a plutocrat, had spent much of her adult life working for an improvement in the lot of the labouring classes. Shaw had recently inflamed her with his fanatical talk of the Soviet Paradise, and the pair of them, both in their seventies, were about to leave for Moscow to study the co-operative movement.

Despite sharing a birthday and a depressive tendency with Cherry, as a committed Fabian socialist and reformer Beatrice was an unlikely ally. The visit was a disaster. Beatrice recorded in her diary that Cherry, 'ruined' by the slump, 'has become a semi-maniac in his hatred of the working class'. According to her, he had fallen out with neighbours, tenants and servants

---

* Charles Webb was a Pooterish figure who for a period ran his wife's hairdressing shop. He described himself as a hairdresser on Sidney's birth certificate.

and spent his time raving apocalyptically. 'In nine months' time we shall all be starved,' he told her as she sat on his Chippendale chair and sipped his wine. He was, she concluded, 'a victim of his evil environment of irresponsible wealth and unmerited social prestige'. Can it really have been that simple? In Beatrice's world, it was. 'Years ago he [Cherry] was a personally attractive . . . rather distinguished youth with artistic and intellectual gifts, today he is drab and desolate, looks as if he were drinking and drugging as well as hating. I should not be surprised to hear that a revolver shot had solved his problem.'

It was true that Cherry had lost money in the Depression. He had invested in a range of foreign stocks, including South American and African railways, and much of that money had melted away. Yet he was very far from being ruined. His capacity for gloom was a facet of his Englishness, and he shared the unattractive upper-class habit of complaining about being 'poor'. (In E. M. Forster's novel *Howards End*, Margaret Schlegel declares, 'I'm tired of these rich people who pretend to be poor.') But Beatrice Webb was a bad judge of character.* There was something dimly recognisable in her caricature of Cherry, but when she reported his claim to have sacked 1,300 men, and his thanks to God that those men would starve, she undermined her credibility. And it was unlikely that he spoke highly of her.

In 1933, George Seaver's biography of Wilson was published. Cherry contributed an introduction. Bill's courage, he wrote, was especially poignant in an age when 'ideals have been smashed by the million and disillusion has won the temporary day'. Cherry set Bill's faith against a darkly pessimistic vision of the future ('the chaos which threatens'), harking back to the happy days on the sunlit snow so many worlds before. 'What they did,' he wrote of the polar party, 'has become part of the history of England, perhaps of the human race, as much as Columbus or the Elizabethans, David, Hector or Ulysses. They are an epic.' He dictated the introduction to Betty Creswick, who had replaced Frankie Drake as Deb's secretary at the institute. 'There were moments,' Creswick recalled, 'when, as he paced up and down, and his inimitable prose poured from him in effortless perfection, emotion tightened his throat and he was hard put to it to keep his voice level.'

---

* Professor Norman MacKenzie, who edited a selection of her letters, concluded, 'For a well-read and highly intelligent woman the psychological assumptions which underlie her social analysis are astonishingly naïve.'

The process of writing *The Worst Journey* had provided Cherry with a definite purpose that nothing could replace. He had seriously considered writing a full-length book about Campbell's Northern Party, but his passions were not engaged by the story, gripping and heroic though it was. He had said all he really wanted to say, and the truth was that he didn't have another book in him. What more was there to add?

Instead, he returned again and again to the *Terra Nova* years. In middle age Cherry became more negative about Scott. The reconciliation he had effected between his bitterness at the death of his friends and his admiration for Scott had proved a temporary truce. He re-read accounts of the expedition, and exercised his spleen in the margins: 'Scott was playing about with sea ice and running quite useless risks'; 'Scott was extraordinarily ignorant of the physical condition of his men'; 'Scott gave Seaman Evans, Birdie and Wilson a rotten time.' 'Scott was obsessed,' he wrote angrily on the page of his journal describing their battle across the Plateau. He was poorly placed to talk about obsession. He made himself cross reading new books that rehashed the expedition, and on cruising holidays sat in a deck-chair with a pencil in his hand irritably scribbling 'WJ' in the margins to indicate that the writer had plundered his own book. At Antarctic reunion dinners he collared colleagues to quiz them on exactly what had happened at three o'clock on a particular afternoon two decades previously. Some of them didn't like it. Over poached halibut and carrots at the Athenaeum during the hot, droughty summer of 1933, Cherry interrogated Sunny Jim, the meteorologist nicknamed after a cartoon character with a quiff. In the two decades since the expedition George Simpson (his real name) had risen to the rank of director at the Meteorological Office, and he now lived in Highgate in north London with his young family. He was much the same, though he had lost his quiff to the advancing years. He told Cherry bluntly that he didn't want his feelings harrowed any more. Like Sunny Jim, most of the other Antarcticans had flourishing careers and families to occupy them, whereas Cherry had a superfluity of time in which to dwell on the past. But after Seaver's biography of Wilson was published, Simpson wrote to congratulate Cherry on his introduction. 'It was just what I would have wanted to say,' he said. 'I wish I could write.'

Cherry continued to pursue his conspiracy theories, compulsively working out who typed Scott's journals and when, and harping on about Teddy (groaning under the weight of his medals and recently knighted to boot, Evans would be an admiral before the decade was out). Sitting at his desk in the library, a solitary, greying figure surrounded by old books behind glass on beeswaxed shelves, Cherry listed letters in his possession from Scott, Wilson and Pennell showing that 'Bowers and I were supposed to be the great successes of the expedition'. And when he made a fresh list of sledging distances, he found that he still topped the table.

The conflict between grief, recrimination and loyalty splintered something inside Cherry. In the lengthening autumn days he contemplated the good gone times, and the house closed in around him. The years of Depression were permeated with hopelessness for many people, but to a man already struggling under a burden of far-reaching sorrow it was a crushing time. The outlook was equally forbidding abroad. There had been much talk of world peace, and disarmament, but Cherry was sceptical. On the day the German people voted in the summer of 1932, foreign correspondent Randolph Churchill filed copy from Berlin predicting that, 'The success of the Nazi party sooner or later means war.' The following year, Hitler became chancellor.

12

Danced with AC-G

In the mid 1930s, as he approached fifty, Cherry regularly took two cruises a year. One was always scheduled to avoid Christmas, a festivity he disliked so vehemently that he talked about founding a society dedicated to its abolition (this was also a popular Shavian theme). Despite the explosion of commercial air travel, he was never tempted to fly to a fixed holiday destination. Cruising suited a single man like Cherry: everything was laid on, and it was easy to find a dinner companion in the smoking lounge or over a friendly game of deck quoits. His favoured route was through the Mediterranean. He would disembark in Marseilles or Palermo and walk over the ridges of sand and among the fish goggling on the early morning slabs along the jetty, or sketch the milky sea at sunset from under a plane tree. But mostly he liked to be on board. Surrounded by the sea, that most ancient symbol of the unconscious, he was able to make peace with himself, and with the ageless dead friends embalmed in his memory. When he walked the decks at night and held up his binoculars to look at Jupiter, he saw the familiar guide that had shown the way to Crozier. On a more practical level, he enjoyed retaining his creature comforts while marooned. Most Englishmen are obsessed with their bowels, and one who has suffered an acute and prolonged disease of those parts might be expected to be more than usually obsessed. On a P. & O. liner you knew where you were as far as lavatories were concerned, and that was worth a lot.

Back at home, Cherry's Antarctic friends were pressing on with their careers. In 1934 Silas was appointed director of scientific research at the Admiralty, and the following year Sunny Jim was knighted for services to meteorology. Deb had become the first professor of Geography at

Cambridge, and he was combining his duties at the faculty with his responsibilities as head of the research institute. Cherry often turned to Deb when he needed a confidant in the thirties, and he always found a steady, sturdy friend who responded with a genial mix of brisk practical advice and warm sensitivity. When he was well – his colitis still flared up occasionally, and he also had arthritis – Cherry would spend contented hours sketching at the institute (he sent postcards ahead, 'Will be with you Thursday, heaven and housekeeper permitting') and take Deb and Betty Creswick out for lunch at the University Arms. The menu now extended to extra-hot curries which Deb consumed until tears ran down his cheeks.

In February 1935 Ponting died, aged sixty-four. He had always been a figure of fun, ever since he took a case of cayenne pepper to the Antarctic to keep his feet warm, and he had not advanced his case in recent years when, desperate for funds as usual, he had patented a stuffed, fluffy penguin toy called a Ponko.* Looking back to the far-off *Terra Nova* days, Silas, Deb and Cherry often chuckled privately when they thought of Ponting. Something calamitous always happened when he was in the vicinity, and if he was not there in person, his camera had the same effect. But the last two decades had been desperately sad ones for Ponting, characterised by a succession of business failures, ill health and depression. Cherry experienced an odd sense of loss when he died, as he left a hole nobody could fill. He was always whining about the small sums of money he had made from his Antarctic work, yet he was deeply committed to the memory of his dead friends, and he saw Cherry, whose book he admired hugely, as an eerie living link to Bill and the others. 'Do you know,' he once wrote to Seaver, 'that whenever I see Cherry I find it difficult to find words. He wears that smile always, but I simply cannot help thinking back to that night when the three of them returned to the Hut looking like . . . beings from another planet . . . I have the feeling when in the presence of Cherry that he is almost of another world.' It was this supernatural apparition who wrote Ponting's obituary for the Royal Geographical Society's journal. The Antarctic, Cherry stated, 'is the most beautiful place in the world', and he paid generous and sincere tribute to the man who 'has enabled the world to share that beauty'. It is an exquisite piece of writing, building to a climax that conjures worlds in a single lapidary sentence: 'Here in these pictures is beauty linked to tragedy – one of the great tragedies – and the beauty is inconceivable for it is endless and runs through eternity.'

---

* One of these amiable Ponkos turned up at Christie's recently.

For the rest of that year Cherry pondered the question of rearmament which was so exercising the politicians and the leader writers of *The Times*. He was minded to agree with Churchill, who was calling for a higher defence budget in the face of a horrifyingly militarised Germany. Cherry was not a warmonger. He hated war, but as a pragmatist he saw the prudence of heading it off. Mostly, however, he sheltered from his fears in the sanctuary of his park.

In an attempt to chivvy him out of his gloom Sunny Jim put him up for the Athenaeum. Conveniently situated on Pall Mall in the heart of St James's, it was a popular club for established writers of the old-fashioned variety (including the sainted Kipling), a feature which appealed to Cherry, who continued to describe himself as an 'author and explorer' when required to state his occupation. In the elegant, somnolent rooms of the Athenaeum, where cigar smoke clung to the velvet curtains and antediluvian Tories wheezed through the swing doors for a spot of serious snoozing behind the ample pages of *The Times*, Cherry found the traditional atmosphere deeply reassuring – a semi-literal manifestation of the deep, deep sleep of England commemorated by Orwell. When the statutory two-year period had elapsed and his name came up for election, his candidate's sheet was displayed as usual in the drawing room. It attracted a pleasing mix of supporters from both arts and sciences, the former led by the distinguished painter and principal of the Royal College of Art, Sir William Rothenstein. (The medic John Conybeare was so keen for Cherry to join that he signed the form twice.) Cherry was duly elected in November 1937, and often sauntered along to Pall Mall when he was in London, sinking into a horsehair armchair on a Saturday afternoon to talk about Mallory with his fellow climber Tom Longstaff, or eating Brown Windsor soup and stale bread rolls on a Monday evening with his Oxford contemporary Henry – now Sir Henry – Tizard, who was busy developing radar.

The Worst Journey, meanwhile, had acquired the status of a minor classic, and was beginning to pop up in antiquarian catalogues for upwards of ten guineas, an astonishing sum for a book published not much more than a decade previously. But it had again slipped out of print. Cherry determined that he would produce an affordable, one-volume edition to suit the times. He had approached the affable Otto Kyllmann at Constable with the idea back in September 1934, but they had failed to agree terms. Cherry abruptly terminated the long and successful partnership they had enjoyed, leaving Kyllmann to wonder what he had done wrong.

Having arranged to use Clarks' to print the text again and Emery Walker the colour plates, Cherry came to a publicity and distribution arrangement with Chatto & Windus by which the firm would take fifteen per cent of net receipts. Shaw acted as unofficial literary agent for Cherry just as he had for Lawrence, and in December 1936 he drafted a fresh contract a few days before Cherry left on his Christmas cruise. At the Chatto offices tucked behind Trafalgar Square, Cherry established a working relationship with director Harold Raymond which was to flourish for many years. Raymond was a sensitive publisher, and consistently handled Cherry – not the easiest of authors – with tact and intelligence.

In April 1937 *The Worst Journey* appeared for the first time in a single volume. The text was reproduced in full, as were four of the five original maps, but all the colour plates had to go, as did most of the black and white illustrations. The short new preface was essentially a tribute to Atch. At the end of it, Cherry made a political appeal. After alluding to the horrors of the Great War, he averred, 'War is out of date; yet between jealousy and fear we are heading into another . . . The destruction caused by a major war between equally matched opponents will leave both of them down and out. Surely England should arm and remain outside unless she is attacked: she can dictate her terms when the others have finished.' By now, this argument was raging in clubs and drawing rooms all over the country. Cherry did not share the view that rearmament would incite war. He believed that the country could only avoid conflict by rearming and regularly shook his head with exasperation over *The Times*'s editorials, as under Geoffrey Dawson the paper supported appeasement. When the reedy-voiced Neville Chamberlain replaced Baldwin as prime minister in May, Cherry was sceptical of his widely supported view that reconciliation was the best policy for bringing Germany into line. Despite himself, Cherry was at some level engaged with the most vigorous and modern aspects of the period. An anachronistic old grouch in so many ways, he was in touch, in this case, with what history would judge to be the right position, and was more 'modern' in his outlook than the wing-collared statesman on the tarmac. In this, as in his views on the social and individual fragmentation towed in the wake of twentieth-century progress, Cherry was not as out of step with *The Waste Land* and *Ulysses* as he thought he was.

The modest first printing of a thousand copies of *The Worst Journey*, priced at 7s 6d, quickly sold out. 'I hope you will not grow weary of well doing,' wrote Raymond, following two hasty reprints. But well doing was coming at Cherry from all quarters. He was about to benefit handsomely from the publishing revolution that had begun two years previously when Allen Lane produced the first Penguin. According to book-trade legend,

Lane, a publisher at the Bodley Head, invented the paperback while waiting for a train at Exeter railway station. Searching the stalls for a good book to read on his journey and failing to find anything suitable, he had the idea of reprinting a series of hardback classics in cheaper editions between paper covers. It was a brilliant plan, but Lane met with stiff resistance. When he wrote around canvassing support, Harold Raymond at Chatto informed him that, 'The steady cheapening of books is in my opinion a great danger in the trade at present.' Lane was not discouraged, and launched his series, which he called Penguin, in 1935. It was an immediate success. In August 1936 GBS sent the visionary publisher a postcard suggesting that he might add *The Worst Journey* to his distinguished list. Lane was happy to oblige. (A lively opportunist, in his reply thanking Shaw for the suggestion, Lane added a postscript saying he'd like to issue Shaw's *The Intelligent Woman's Guide to Socialism* in paperback, too. GBS agreed, and the book appeared as the first Pelican.)

Penguin published *The Worst Journey* in two sixpenny volumes in June 1937. As they were numbers ninety-nine and one hundred in the series a poster was printed depicting a penguin with a cricket bat tucked under one flipper bowing to a distant crowd. 'We celebrate our centenary,' read the caption, 'with Mr Cherry-Garrard's Worst Journey in the World.' Both volumes reprinted three times inside eighteen months. Cherry thought Penguin had pulled off 'a wonderful bit of production', and was thrilled with sales. He dealt mainly with Eunice Frost, a key member of the early Penguin staff and a rare woman in the clubbish world of bookmen. He admired her, but barriers took a long time to fall in Cherry's mental world – he continued to write to Frost as 'Dear Sir' until 1943.*

The middle months of 1937 were good ones for Cherry. He felt well, buoyed up by the renewed popularity of his book. His illnesses, mostly nervous insurrections, had been treated by seventeen doctors over the past two years, and a course of injections for his arthritis finally seemed to have done some good. He even agreed to participate in a live televised talk on the Antarctic at the Alexandra Palace in the northern outskirts of London. The BBC had transmitted the first talking pictures from the same studios only a year before, and the whole idea of television was still a novelty. It was an ordeal to perform under the hot, flaring lights, hemmed in by steel

---

* The hard-working Frost was relentlessly determined. Working with the American arm of Penguin in the fifties on a new edition of A. J. A. Symons' classic biography of Frederick Rolfe, she wrote, 'Even more important than *The Quest for Corvo* is the quest for my stockings and I confirm nine and a half is my size.' She was later awarded an OBE for services to literature.

cables and pressed upon by men in overalls sweating against heavy rolling cameras. When Cherry was told off for swaying during the rehearsal, Deb, a sturdier participant, offered to hold him up. Cherry's attitude to television reveals his paradoxical response to the more modern manifestations of the world around him. He was fascinated by the mechanics of transmission and sought to understand them, but instinctively mistrusted television as a medium and never owned a set. Furthermore, he was too shy ever to step before the cameras again. He even recoiled at the idea of being snapped by a stills photographer for Penguin, acquiescing only by extracting the counterproductive assurance that the pictures would not be used in the press.

That summer, Cherry sailed to the Norwegian fjords on an Orient Line cruise. In order to meet the SS *Orion* at Immingham docks he took a train up to Lincolnshire from London's Marylebone station. It was a familiar rail journey past dull villages and dreary towns, punctuated only by a light luncheon in the first-class restaurant car and a nodding snooze. Later, Cherry called it the best journey in the world.

The *Orion* steamed across the silvery North Sea and slipped between Norway and Denmark while passengers eddied around the top deck in the mellow sunshine of a northern summer. As the lumbering liner bore down upon the waterways around Oslo, Cherry was leaning over the rail, clutching his binoculars and peering out at a gull perched on a distant rock. The bird rose into the tepid draughts of sea air, and Cherry turned to the young woman next to him. They had noticed each other more than once over the preceding days. Now, for the first time, they spoke.

Twenty-year-old Angela Turner was travelling with her parents and younger brother. She was slim, with thick, deep caramel hair, bright blue eyes, clear skin and a beguiling smile. Cherry liked her straightaway, and she was thrilled to find herself talking to a dashing explorer. Before she went to sleep that night she noted in a neat and tiny hand in her diary, 'Danced with AC-G.'

Born six weeks after her father had had his leg blown off on the Somme, Angela had spent much of her childhood at her paternal grandparents' home in Bentley, a village near the Suffolk–Essex border. At seventeen she had left school and studied domestic science in Ipswich for a year. At that time one of her friends was nursing at St Thomas's in London, and the job appealed to Angela, who was sociable, patient and naturally sensitive to other people's needs. Her mother had other ideas.

Clara Turner was a difficult character. Through a confused mixture of deluded grandeur and a naïve desire to keep her offspring at home, she put a stop to her daughter's plans to nurse, and shortly before the cruise even broke up her romance with a local boy. Kenneth Turner, on the other hand, was a most agreeable character, and from the start Cherry enjoyed his company. They were about the same age, and both concealed an emotional centre under a calm, controlled surface. From solid Suffolk stock, Kenneth worked as a land agent and surveyor, and he and his family lived comfortably in a modest house, with a maid, on the edge of Ipswich. As for the Turners' adored son Noël: he was immensely likeable. Fifteen months younger than his sibling, the pair were united victims of Clara's volatile temperament, and they remained close all their lives. Noël lived in London during the week, training to be a land agent like his father at the College of Estate Management in Lincoln's Inn Fields. He was a keen reader, and when he returned home to Ipswich at weekends he brought back the latest Penguins. Both he and Angela knew Cherry's name, and they had seen the cricketing penguin posters pasted in tube stations all over and under London.

Cherry was soon sitting with the Turners at dinner and taking regular turns with Angela on deck. When the *Orion* steamed up to Bergen and docked at the inner harbour of Vågen, all five went for their first walk on shore ('We always move in fours,' Clara announced when someone suggested the family might split up). But Cherry and Angela did manage to shake the others off, and they strolled together past the narrow wooden warehouses squeezed onto the old Bryggen wharf, enjoying the salty, oily smell, the firm ground, and the very unfirm feelings that were creeping upon them both. When they stopped to sit on a bench near the Bergenhus, Cherry bent down to pick up a small piece of quartz and offer it to his new friend. Years later, when she had become an Antarctic expert, Angela discovered that the courtship ritual of the penguin centres around stone-giving, stones being a vital commodity for the construction of the nest.

Pausing later outside a bookshop on the harbour, Cherry was astonished to see displayed in the window a pair of handsome, cherry-red Penguin *Worst Journeys* with a Norwegian sticker in the corner of the covers. Fiddling in the pocket of his tweed jacket for some kroner, he went in and bought the volumes. Outside, he handed them to Angela, his second gift. How could any woman not fall in love with a man who did that?

After the cruise, Cherry wrote to Angela as soon as he arrived home. A fortnight later she visited Lamer, met at the station by Cherry, the Rolls and a picnic. For her twenty-first birthday a month later he took her for another picnic on the grass verge under the Welwyn Viaduct. Like his father, Cherry enjoyed watching trains, especially fast ones, and at Welwyn he loved to hear the blustery roar of the *Jubilee* and *Coronation* engines as they whistled towards the dark brick piers. The viaduct was a magnificent forty-arched creation over the valley of the Mimram, a characteristically brooding piece of Victorian civil engineering that reared a hundred feet above the river at the highest point. Sitting on a plaid blanket in the pearly autumn sunshine, Cherry spread out egg mayonnaise sandwiches, apples and a flask of coffee. For her birthday gift he produced a copy of the new one-volume Chatto hardback, continuing the theme he had begun on their first outing on land.

Cherry had built up an aversion to the institution of marriage. 'It sometimes seems that there is not one completely happy home,' he once wrote, going on to lament 'the everlasting friction of it all'. It was an odd opinion for a man from an indubitably happy home. It was true that he had witnessed several bitter divorces (Granville Barker's, for example). But his swaggering generalisations protected him from his own vulnerability. He was afraid of exposing his raw inner self (who isn't?) and afraid that he too might fail. His father's stiff, bulky figure, quite literally towering over the breakfast marmalade, still cast a long shadow.

He told Angela that women frightened him, but she, with her gentle good nature, damped down his fears. Years before, he had said that a happy married life was impossible for him. Now he saw in Angela the ideal companion; the friend to fill the void; the figure from his fantasy life whom he had never dared dream might materialise. Although it was not outwardly obvious, Cherry's sensibilities were deeply romantic. He was easily moved, especially by literature, and valued feeling and content above order and form despite his Victorian worship of Duty. He was practical, and a vocal pessimist, but he believed in the power of the imagination to lift the human spirit from its trough, and in the deeper levels of his consciousness he believed in human perfectibility.

The thirty years between them did not seem much to Angela. Besides being an engaging romantic, Cherry was handsome, had impeccable manners, and could be very amusing; altogether, she found him a deeply appealing mixture. But she didn't tell her mother.

Cherry was too prudent to abandon his bachelor habits prematurely. He said nothing to Evelyn when he motored down to the West House on one of his filial visits. At Christmas, he disappeared on a cruise. His mail was forwarded to ports where the ship was to dock, and he kept up with his business as he went round, sneaking in cablegrams to Angela while he was about it. Much of his correspondence concerned *The Worst Journey*.

Cherry's complicated publishing arrangements reflected his tortuously obsessive nature. Somewhere in his psyche he was determined to occupy himself as fully as possible with administrative detail, and wherever he was – on board, in port, away visiting – he kept a sharp eye on Chatto and its accounts department. The firm had agreed to pay him quarterly, and if a cheque was not forthcoming a letter was soon despatched enquiring politely after its whereabouts.

Following the success of his Wilson book, the likeable George Seaver had been commissioned by John Murray to write a biography of Birdie Bowers. It was scheduled to appear in the autumn of 1938, and Cherry agreed to supply another introduction. He had written little in recent years, but his gift for the winning one-liner had not deserted him. When Lord Dulverton asked, on the Letters page of *The Times*, if any reader had ever observed the phenomenon of a ground rainbow, which he had just witnessed on Tadmarton Heath golf course, Cherry took up his pen. He had seen one of these on the Barrier almost exactly twenty-six years before, and had pointed it out to Bill, who painted it and named it the Garrard halo. 'It is the only one I shall ever have,' Cherry concluded his letter, 'but it is most beautiful.'

The introduction was delayed by an attack of backache that struck soon after the winter cruise, and he finally tackled the job in the spring, producing another fine essay of crafted prose far superior to the limp biographical narrative that followed it. The piece spoke, inevitably, of its times. The next war, Cherry wrote parenthetically following a reference to the last one, which had settled nothing, 'will settle everything – and everybody'. Appeasement had begun in earnest the previous November when Chamberlain sent the gaunt Lord Halifax to see Hitler, and Cherry took the opportunity to give it a sound kicking. 'If the politicians get you into another war (in order to keep the peace) . . .' he wrote, 'pray to God to let you die or for a man like Birdie to lead you out.' His light touch did not fail him. The barbed political comments were concealed within a sustained and lyrical appreciation of a man he had loved deeply. Birdie, 'a tiger for work', was an ugly little fellow all right, but, after all, 'this civilisation is a funny business; the shop window is very different from the shop'. Cherry wanted to point out the universal appeal of a good, humble man who did not fail. '[His] story does not die . . . It is a spirit without boundaries . . . he and his companions have left something behind in men's minds; it is shadowy and intangible and perhaps a little fanciful, but it is something greater than all the pyramids in the world, and much more important.'

He used the introduction to say something else that had been preoccupying him. The building boom of the thirties had altered the appearance of Hertfordshire, and to Cherry the countryside around Wheathampstead was becoming increasingly unrecognisable. There were more houses, more cinemas and more tarmacked roads as well as more light industry, the latter proliferating as heavy industry shrank elsewhere. 'It has been my happiness,' Cherry wrote,

> to see two of the most beautiful parts of the world. The one was England. [The other was the Antarctic.] In its domestic way pre-war England was perhaps the most beautiful thing the world has ever seen. It took at least fifteen hundred years of thought, and fighting and courage and love to make that beautiful thing; it has taken about twenty years to ruin a very large part of it. One hundred years hence men will do anything to get it back to what it was: and they will not be able.

It was true that the countryside had taken a battering. The cressy shallows of the Lea where the General and Evelyn had held their crayfishing parties had been polluted by the advent of both industrial and domestic ribbon development, and the crayfish had disappeared. A rural way of life that had taken hundreds of years to evolve was vanishing, apparently in a matter of decades. And the urbanisation of Hertfordshire was about to speed up. In 1946, the year the New Towns Act was passed, E. M. Forster broadcast an impassioned talk in defence of a county and district he still believed was the loveliest in England. He had learned that Stevenage New Town, a satellite for 60,000 inhabitants, was to be built near his old home. 'The people now living and working there are doomed,' Forster prophesied. 'It is death in life for them and they move in a nightmare.' Like the counties on the other sides of London, Hertfordshire was beginning to melt into the capital. To Cherry, the bleak rows of factories and the aeroplanes droning overhead were tangible symbols of the progress that threatened to overwhelm him.

Many things were changing along with the pastoral landscape of Cherry's youth. The position of the gentry was being eroded by the newly rich who moved into the manor houses previously occupied by generations of the same family. Harpenden to the north-east of Wheathampstead had been attracting new money ever since absentee landlords had sold off land to allow the railway to develop in the last quarter of the nineteenth century. Now there was new money everywhere, and the working people of Wheathampstead didn't like it. 'There was a wrong spirit in the new rich,' an elderly villager recalled in the 1960s, 'something quite different. With the old gentry you could talk to them man to man, but you couldn't with these others.' Cherry may not have been universally popular, but at least he was bona fide gentry. Everyone felt happy with that; they fretted when the village hierarchy was disrupted. A newcomer living in one of the manors Cherry had sold was definitely not sufficiently aristocratic: 'She *dinks* into church,' it was whispered, 'and sits in the Lamer chapel!' People filed into St Helen's to worship the established social order as much as God. As for the Brockets at Brocket Hall near Shaw's village at Ayot St Lawrence, why, they were *northern brewers*.*

As 1938 advanced, Cherry grew familiar with the seventy-mile drive up through north-east Essex and into Suffolk to collect Angela in the yellow peril (she was faintly embarrassed by the crests). From Ipswich they would set off for the windy Suffolk coast with a picnic provided by Clara. Angela introduced Cherry to the salt and freshwater marshes, to Southwold and Aldeburgh and, nearer home, the Stour valley and the watermills around Flatford and Dedham commemorated by Constable. Cherry loved it all, especially the wading birds in the estuaries that curled inland from the North Sea. In between his visits they met at the Berkeley for lunch followed by an exhibition and tea at the Savoy. Sometimes Angela went to stay at Lamer. Clara didn't approve, but her daughter was determined not to allow her to break up another friendship. Ensconced in Hertfordshire, Cherry and Angela fell into a comfortable, easy rhythm. When he went shooting, she went with him, not wielding a gun but walking in the line holding the cartridges, and when the weather was bad they took the train to London to see a film and catch up with the newsreels. The housekeeper was frenzied with excitement at the faint prospect that there might at last be a lady at Lamer, and she and the three Swiss maids kept everyone in the village informed.

Pussy Harker, Cherry's old girlfriend, and her amiable husband Jasper, who worked for the government intelligence services,† were regular house guests at Lamer in the late thirties, and so was Cherry's niece Susan, Lassie's daughter. All got on famously with Angela. As for GBS and Charlotte, they both adored her, and she in turn became immensely fond of them. While

---

* The second Lord Brocket did little to improve his image when Ribbentrop turned up as a house guest.

† Jasper Harker became Director-General of M.I.5. Pussy's brother Sydney Russell Cooke had also worked for the security services. In 1930 he was found dead in mysterious circumstances in his flat in King's Bench Walk. Russian involvement was widely suspected.

Charlotte was a mother figure, with GBS, a man sixty years her senior, Angela shared a girlish sense of humour. When she revealed how much she admired Wells, she and Cherry were immediately invited to a luncheon party at Whitehall Court, the Shaws' London flat, at which the great man was to be present. Wells was writing *All Aboard for Ararat*, the protagonist of which, Noah Lammock, is a modern incarnation of his Old Testament namesake. Over lunch Angela was teased for failing to answer some biblical questions. Taking the ribbing in the spirit in which it was intended, she rounded on Wells. 'All right,' she said. 'What kind of wood was the ark made of?' He didn't know – but she did. (It was gopher wood.)

After lunch Cherry and Angela were parting on separate errands and Wells, an enthusiastic adulterer, was on his way to a lecture. He offered Angela a lift in his taxi. Cherry looked down at them from the Shaws' window. 'I watched with misgivings,' he reported later, 'as Angela climbed into a car with Wells.'

It was an odd time to be happy. Most people in the country were now as fatalistic about the advent of war as Cherry, who had been forecasting Armageddon for some time. Snouty, fish-eyed gas masks were hanging in the halls at Lamer and Ipswich, and two days before Angela's twenty-second birthday Chamberlain recalled the House of Commons from holiday. Kathleen Scott, married to her politician, recorded in her diary that evening, 'Things look very dark in England. Everyone is in complete despair. Trenches are being feverishly dug in the park. There are guns upon Marble Arch.' But the next day she was celebrating her friend Chamberlain's third departure to negotiate with Hitler, and soon the 69-year-old Prime Minister was waving his piece of paper from the steps of his plane at Heston Aerodrome, infecting the country with euphoria over the 'peace agreement' he had concluded at the expense of the Czechs.

Cherry now employed a chauffeur for long journeys, mainly because of the vertiginous rise in the number of motor vehicles on the road. Ownership of private cars increased ninefold between the wars (though as taxation was based on horsepower, few drivers had a Rolls, crested or otherwise). He had an account with Cecil Allen, a Wheathampstead coal merchant who had a taxi firm on the side (this meant he had one car, which he drove as a taxi). Together Cherry and Allen motored off to the Henley Regatta and other sporting events. The outings were islands on which to shelter, briefly, from the swelling storm. Cherry liked to mingle with the public instead of buying access to the privileged enclosures. It was easier to lose yourself in a crowd, and he relished the anonymity of the throng. It was a kind of liberation.

In June 1939 Cherry invited Angela to join them for the Derby. It was a brilliant summer day, the flowers were out on Epsom Downs, and after a picnic the three of them worked their way to the front of the crowd and stood together on Tattenham Corner to see Blue Peter gallop first past the post. On the way back up to Lamer, the placards outside the newsagents' shops shouted joyfully, 'BLUE SKIES, BLUEBELLS, BLUE PETER'.

Raymond had told Cherry that the Penguin edition was denting Chatto's hardback sales, but in fact the single-volume *Worst Journey* continued to sell steadily. In May 1939, when stocks were low, Raymond suggested a reprint. (In normal circumstances a publisher will order a reprint without consulting the author, but in the case of *The Worst Journey*, Cherry was his own publisher, and Chatto were only his distributor.) Cherry was staying with friends in a small hotel in the north Norfolk marshes when he received Raymond's letter. He wrote back to say that he was all for reprinting, but he wanted to wait to see 'how things turn out in Europe, and what expenditure I have to put into land'. Back at home in July he informed Raymond that 'if these blasted and never to be cursed sufficiently politicians haven't knocked the world to bits, I will then go into another printing'. There was something here beyond the scowling ill-temper of the crosspatch. In the midst of crisis Cherry listened to the radio and heard politicians trying to pass themselves off as leaders, only to remember what men like Bill had done. It was no wonder that he hit out in exasperation.

He decided to get another cruise in before the world was destroyed, and at the beginning of August he boarded SS *Orion* again at Immingham with all four Turners. They were to visit Iceland, the Baltic and the fjords. It was not the most auspicious month in human history to be loitering in the North Sea. Danzig (now Gdansk), a Free City on the Baltic supposedly protected by a League of Nations' mandate, had to be hurriedly struck off the itinerary as news came over the wireless of mounting hostilities. Having been the object of secret negotiations between the Poles and the Nazis, and before that a pawn in Halifax's appeals to Hitler, Danzig was teetering towards German control. To buy time, the harried captain of the *Orion* first made an unscheduled stop at Kirkwall – the Orkneys at least were not yet featuring in Hitler's plans. Cherry loved the saffron moors and purple mists of the bleak Orkney landscape, and after visiting the tomb of the Arctic explorer John Rae in the cathedral, he and Angela eagerly set off on foot towards the colonies of puffins and eider ducks.

After peaceful visits to Reykjavik and the fjords they stopped in Oslo and, with special permission, visited Amundsen's ship the *Fram* (they had done the same thing on their previous cruise to Norway). Cherry was delighted to step on the smooth decks, as he had begun to see Amundsen as the brilliantly gifted explorer that he was. But his mood darkened with the ship when, on her return passage across the North Sea, the *Orion* had to be blacked out. Tension, insecurity and rumour swirled around the ballroom as Cherry and Angela stumbled round the dance floor, he in a white tie and she in an evening gown, falling towards each other as the *Orion* headed to the uncertainty waiting on Humberside. A man's mind might easily turn to making big decisions while he was still free to do so.

Three days after the *Orion* docked, Ribbentrop and Molotov signed the Nazi–Soviet pact while Angela was having lunch with Cherry at the Berkeley. A week later, on Friday 1 September, Cherry telephoned and asked her to marry him.

He suggested she think about it, and told her he would call back later for an answer. She didn't need to think about it. 'I had fallen in love with him,' she remembered, 'and I never thought he was going to ask.' Her mother was upstairs, and Angela determined to go up and tell her straightaway. She took one step up, hesitated and returned to ground level. The stepping up and down continued for some minutes until she abandoned the project and went into the garden to tell Noël, who was filling sandbags which would in due course guard Ipswich against marauding Germans.

When they heard the news, the Turners were shocked and pleased – even Clara was pleased. Shocked, because they hadn't been aware of how serious the relationship had become. Pleased, because they liked Cherry, and of course because he was wealthy: no parent could deny being pleased about that. The age difference didn't concern them very much. In those days it wasn't uncommon for a man to marry a woman a generation younger than himself.

When Cherry telephoned again after a few hours' anxious striding among the sweet chestnuts, Angela accepted. 'I'm so thankful I don't know what to say,' he murmured. Referring years later to one of her copies of *The Worst Journey*, Angela noted that these were almost exactly the words Cherry had used to describe the moment when Birdie found the tent at Cape Crozier: 'We were so thankful we said nothing.' He had found a more permanent refuge.

They decided to marry immediately, before gas masks were permanently strapped to their faces. Angela rushed into Ipswich with Noël to buy a platinum wedding ring. Cherry made a hasty trip to Godalming, feeling that it wouldn't be right to announce the news to his unsuspecting mother on the telephone, particularly as she had a weak heart. Evelyn was thrilled, despite the fact that she had never met her future daughter-in-law. Apsley, as he was still called by his family, was settling down at last, and that, in Evelyn's world, was the important thing. In the middle of it all, Britain declared war on Nazi Germany.

Cherry had booked Allen to drive him to Ipswich and back on Wednesday 6 September. 'I am to be married,' he announced after the car had crunched up the gravel at first light. 'To whom?' replied the astounded chauffeur. 'You know,' said Cherry, 'that young lady we took to the Derby.' On the three-hour journey to Ipswich they stopped the car so that Cherry could practise his lines.

Like many couples at that difficult time, Cherry and Angela had obtained an instant special licence allowing them to marry in a church. The short ceremony took place at St Margaret's, near the Turners' home, witnessed only by Angela's parents, two of her uncles, Noël and Allen, who doubled up as best man. None of Cherry's family were present. Hasty arrangements were commonplace in those early days of the war. 'We all thought we were going to be gassed at any moment,' Angela recalled. She wore a light silk calf-length dress which buttoned all the way down the front, and a fox fur stole with the head still attached. He wore a light suit and a pale tie, and carried his hat. His hair was neatly parted in the centre, and he looked relaxed and happy. On the marriage certificate, under rank or profession, he wrote, 'of independent means'. He must have been too bashful to write 'explorer', at his age, in such an intimate company. He was fifty-three (just a year older than his father had been when he married), while his wife was coming up to twenty-three.

The reception back at the Turners' house featured a cold roast chicken and salad (lettuce, tomato, hard-boiled eggs and Heinz salad cream) served with white wine and followed by sherry trifle and Bird's custard. Once the maid had cleared away the plates Cherry produced a single-sided, ready-printed will form from his inside pocket. He had already filled it in, leaving everything to Angela, and now he signed it, handing it to the maid and Allen to be witnessed. (His executors were Sunny Jim and Farrer – not Arthur, but Hugh, his son, who had taken over at Lincoln's Inn Fields.) As for maintenance, it was agreed that both Cherry and Angela's father Kenneth would provide the bride with £100 a year. With the formalities out of the way, Cherry, Angela and Allen left for Hertfordshire. Cherry was anxious to get back before dark as headlights had been banned in the interests of national security, resulting in a huge leap in fatalities. Masked versions were not yet widely available.

After an uneventful run home they motored up the gravel drive to find the rooks returning to the elms and the housekeeper and maids waiting on the porch, wreathed in smiles. There were to be no honeymoon rituals. There was a war on.

To announce their marriage they had tiny cards printed with the words '*with Mr and Mrs Apsley Cherry-Garrard's compliments*', and in the top right-hand corner '*Angela Turner*' appeared, pierced with an arrow. These were sent out without the customary slice of crumbling wedding cake, as nobody's mind was on cake. On the High Street, where the news was billed above troop crossings to France, shoppers expressed astonishment and surprise that the old curmudgeon had gone and done it at last.

Three days after they were married Lassie came to lunch, and a few days after that Allen drove them to Godalming. Evelyn's heart problems had confined her to bed at the West House. She ruled her small empire in good spirits from a reclining position, waited on by Peggy and a lady's maid. Evelyn adored her new daughter-in-law. For the next seven years Cherry and Angela visited her regularly (she never got up again), and Peggy and Angela became great friends. Peggy played the violin in the Charterhouse choir but was otherwise more or less imprisoned in the West House, nursing her mother. Like Cherry and Reggie, she was prone to depression, and in the early forties she had a breakdown.

Everyone liked Angela. She was perennially good-natured (Seaver said her name was her nature) and cheerfully tolerant of Cherry's foibles. Deb, who was her friend for thirty years and adored her, eventually said she was like a member of the expedition. She dealt with the dramatic transformation from aspiring student nurse to lady of the manor with dignity and warm good humour. Within weeks of her marriage she was more involved in village life than her husband had ever been. She bicycled down to the High Street and shopped in person, and on Sunday attended morning service at St Helen's alone, sitting quietly at the end of a pew in the Lamer chapel alongside several centuries of dead Garrards. The villagers were thrilled. George Seabrook, the son of the man Cherry had taken to court and himself a tenant farmer, was so fond of her that when his daughter was born he called her Angela. Soon little Angelas were proliferating all over Wheathampstead.

As for Cherry, he followed the progress of the war through the BBC's special wireless reports and settled down to the deep, deep peace of conjugal pottering. He continued to take the train down to London, either to keep appointments with one of his squadron of doctors or to see a film with Angela. In the autumn of 1939 the capital was pleasantly empty, with less traffic on the streets and fewer people in the shops and parks. The bombs were not falling after all. But it was impossible not to feel the war all around. Gaggles of small, white-faced children with numbers on their backs vanished into tube stations on their way to the strange countryside and stranger families. In the new year butter and bacon were rationed, followed shortly by other essential foodstuffs. Worse, Cherry's Russian Gold cigarettes disappeared from the shelves. The yellow peril was put on bricks in a gesture to conserve petrol for the war effort, and Cherry bought a Baby Austin. It might have guzzled less petrol, but it was not a Rolls-Royce, and the air inside it thickened with swear words as Cherry vainly pressed his foot to the floor.

The question of a hardback reprint was raised again in October 1939. During the August cruise Cherry had written to Raymond to say he would consider another printing 'if there are no panics [when we get back]'. Now Raymond saw his chance. 'One can't exactly say that there have been no panics,' he wrote, 'but before long a good deal of money will be spent by various organisations on books suitable for troops, hospitals and so on, and *The Worst Journey* would certainly be in demand in directions like that.' Before the month had expired the title had indeed appeared on the National Book Council's list of suitable reading material for the forces. Scott had been fed to the troops in the first war, and now he was being cooked up again for the second.

Cherry couldn't make his mind up about the reprint, and fidgeted about how much the war was going to cost him and what the government would make him do with his land. When he decided not to go ahead, Raymond, keen to exploit the emerging heroism market, suggested that Chatto might take on the burden, and the risk, of publication. It was a sensible idea, as publishing had become a far more taxing business. Raw materials were in desperately short supply, and the government told the paper mills it intended to commandeer all production. When paper was available for civilians, stringent quotas were imposed based on pre-war usage. Inevitably, prices rose sharply, sometimes every fortnight. In addition, Cherry's printer, Clarks' of Edinburgh, was regularly disrupted by air-raid warnings. During an acute food shortage in the capital, Clarks' director William Maxwell was so sorry for Raymond that with a quotation for printing *The Worst Journey* he included a packet of Dunbar kippers. Nobody seemed able to commit to anything, and every transaction was subject to long delays. It made it awfully difficult to get a book out. 'If a manufacturer is neither in a position to say when he can deliver goods,' Raymond wrote to Maxwell in exasperation at the beginning of November, 'nor how much they will cost when delivered, we had all better shut up our shops and play shove ha'penny until the end of the war.' But he had enjoyed the kippers.

The Worst Journey was eventually reprinted in December 1939 on a slightly different basis, with Chatto taking on most of the production arrangements. It had gone up to 8s 6d, and to Cherry's regret the exigencies of wartime meant that the colour jacket had to be abandoned. At about the same time Allen Lane approached Cherry to see if he could rescue the American rights from the Dial Press. Lane had just opened an American branch of his firm and was working hard to build the list. The rights had indeed lapsed, but nothing ever came of Lane's idea. As Cherry was indifferent to foreign editions he did little to encourage any of them. Polish publishers asked many times in the thirties if they might buy the rights, but Cherry refused. Following another feverish request from Warsaw in the summer of 1939, a time when most people might have been inclined to show the Poles some sympathy, Cherry told Penguin bleakly, 'I do not think there is much point in its being translated into Polish.'

At the beginning of December, Cherry was ill. The medical repertoire of his middle age included arthritis, rheumatism, backache, bronchial congestion and a chronic sensitivity of the bowel, the latter a relic of his colitis. In addition, his teeth often needed attention: the few that had survived the Antarctic had to be regularly maintained by a dentist from Harpenden, as did his top and bottom sets of dentures. Angela accompanied him up and down to London to see doctors, chased around for his prescriptions and indulged his many whims. She had become a nurse after all. But whether he was ill or not, Cherry spent an increasing amount of time worrying about his health. Most of his obsessional concern over physical ailments was a manifestation of anxiety transferred from mental distress. That, of course, was more difficult to identify, let alone address; but it was becoming increasingly hard to ignore.

13

A Darker Continent

In the dying days of summer 1940 the evening air over the estate thickened with the sweet smell of harvest dust, and Cherry, sweating into his hairy tweed jacket, chugged along the pale horizon in a tractor, his silhouette vanishing into the feather-branched elms.

The demands of war had compelled Cherry to turn himself into a farmer, and once he got started, he enjoyed it: it gave him a sense of purpose. He conferred earnestly with representatives of the War Agricultural Committee, and to comply with new regulations ordered hundreds of acres of Lamer parkland and pasture to be ploughed up and sown with corn and wheat. He bought fertiliser and seed, organised the boys who walked over to shock and sheave after school, and supervised the driver and feeder of the clanking threshing machine that was hired by all the farmers in turn. As he tended his fields and marshalled his workers, he became attuned to the rhythm of the seasons.

Both house and park had grown shabby. The brickwork was mottled and dusted with a powdery grey film of lichen, the mechanism that allowed the summer house to revolve was seized with rust, the grass was shaggy and many of the hedges were overgrown, spoiling Repton's lines. Now, as the war advanced, the house decayed and the estate turned yellow with rippling corn. Cherry and Angela withdrew to the library, while the other rooms were shrouded in dust sheets and shut up. In the musty specimen room on the ground floor where Cherry's oars hung in parallel on the west wall, a furry lid of dust closed over the glass cases that billeted armies of pinioned moths, and thin bluish mildew crept over yak-tail brushes and Zulu shields from the far-off days of the General's soldiering. Coal was short, especially in the bitter winter of 1939/40 when the Hertfordshire roads were often silent with snow. They kept the fire going in the library and ate at the small mahogany table underneath a large oil painting of a gloomy morning on Loch Tulla. In the evening they drank their gin ration with an orange beverage made from swede, and ate mashed potato, beetroot and rabbits that Cherry shot flat-eared in the standing corn. Angela kept two hen-houses on the rough ground at the back of the house, and poached eggs made a frequent appearance, served with maize and cabbage or marrows grown on frames in the kitchen garden.

The war took over. The villagers closed the High Street for fundraising days, the Wheathampstead Youth Service collected conkers for the Macleans factory to turn into toothpaste, and the Women's Voluntary Service made pasties for the gangs of recently recruited agricultural workers. In June 1940 the fighting came closer when a bomb killed nine people in Cambridge. Tin-hatted women from the Wheathampstead Air Raid Precautions service began to clamber onto village roofs in their belted mackintoshes, scanning the skies for German aircraft. The road signs at the station crossroads were removed to fox the invaders, now expected hourly.

Fighter Command outgunned the Luftwaffe in the Battle of Britain that summer, but the bombs didn't stop falling. Wheathampstead took hits earmarked for the Hatfield aerodrome. A tall brown flower of earth blossomed next to the broach spire of St Helen's, the blast shattering a stained-glass image of a genuflecting St John. In November, a bad month, a storm of shrapnel hailed down on the Shaws' roof, and in December a 2,000-pound bomb detonated at the dump cracked fourteen windows at Lamer and twisted the front door. The air-raid siren squealed remorselessly from Ayot, and from his bedroom window Cherry followed the criss-crossing beams of the searchlights as they roamed the sky, freezing the same grey vistas of gentle Hertfordshire hills as they had in the other war, twenty-four years before. During the Blitz the villagers could hear the dull rumbling from London, and on the porch roof, dawn after dawn, Cherry watched the luminous glow of fires roaring through the bombed-out buildings of the capital.

Before the war he had been against Churchill, though they were on the same side over appeasement and shared the same romantic respect for the monarchy and august institutions such as the House of Lords. But when Churchill dramatically replaced the aldermanic Chamberlain as prime minister in May 1940 and began assuring everyone over the wireless that their little island would be defended whatever the cost might be, like hundreds of thousands of others Cherry's patriotic instinct was stirred. After the fall of France and the poignant, plucky heroism of Dunkirk he signed up with the Local Defence Volunteers. This well-intentioned auxiliary force, soon renamed the Home Guard, was chronically short of weapons, which was perhaps a good thing as its men were more of a danger to themselves than to the enemy. Cherry was having trouble with his feet at the time, and he obtained permission to parade in his house slippers. The sergeant in charge of Cherry's section was called Hall, and he was also the baker. With the chaff still prickly under his shirt, Cherry presented himself at platoon headquarters every evening to be marched down the High Street by Hall, the entire straggling body wheeling to the left to collect a batch of doughnuts before proceeding to guarantee the safety of the crossroads.

Many of the big Hertfordshire houses were requisitioned. Brocket Hall near Ayot was colonised by pasty-faced nursing mothers from the East End and Canadian soldiers who carved their names, numbers and home addresses inches deep on the James Paine bridge. Bride Hall, which had been part of the Lamer estate until Cherry sold it, was occupied by officers of the Special Operations Executive, set up in July 1940 as part of the Secret Service. The friendly SOE men made regular social calls at Lamer. They appreciated Cherry's restrained, affable hospitality, informed conversation and well-stocked library, and their host in turn enjoyed their company immensely. As for Lamer itself, the authorities had their eye on it. A group of men in brown pork pie hats came to size it up.

The Shaws retreated to Ayot for most of the war, accompanied for long stretches by GBS's secretary Blanche Patch, who knitted for the soldiers and complained about the cold. They lunched with Cherry and Angela on Sunday and Wednesday, alternating between Ayot and Lamer. After Charlotte was diagnosed with Paget's disease she would arrive up the drive by car while GBS was still marching down the footpaths and under the lime trees. He remained as sprightly as ever, and rose to greet the war with stoic good humour. When he heard the siren wail, he would hurry to the piano and begin hammering out jolly operatic tunes, and when he discovered a new barber in Welwyn he sent Cherry a postcard raving, 'he wields a new electric automatic hair mower with extraordinary dexterity'.

The war cut them off, but it brought them closer to their neighbours. Geoffrey de Havilland became a favourite at Lamer. Cherry knew his father, Geoffrey senior, the aviation pioneer and test pilot who had moved his company to nearby Hatfield in 1920. The younger Geoffrey was the firm's chief test pilot, and he used to telephone from the aerodrome to say he was going up for a spin in the latest Dragonfly or Flamingo, if Cherry and Angela would care to join him. Cherry approached aeroplane flights with the same quizzical detachment that he brought to all new experiences.

But he loved to see Lamer from the air. At ground level, de Havilland kept a model railway, and its tiny sidings and miniature level crossing captivated Cherry almost as much as his dizzying ascensions.

At the beginning of the war Cherry's publishers forwarded a fan letter from Ettie Desborough. An Edwardian hostess of the powdered footman school, in her dazzling youth Ettie had been painted by Sargent. Now, in her dotage, she had become an Antarctic devotee and a passionate admirer of *The Worst Journey*, and she was thrilled to learn that Cherry lived in the same county. He and Angela were soon invited over to the crenellated vastness of Panshanger Hall near Hertford where Ettie and her husband, the first and last Lord Desborough, were living in splendid decrepitude, shrunk into one small room and attended by an aged butler (they had recently been joined by a dead German pilot whose plane was brought down on the lawn). Lord Desborough, once a great athlete, took Angela punting on the section of the Mimram that flowed through the Panshanger grounds, and the two couples continued to exchange visits till the late forties. When petrol rationing kept them at home, Ettie wrote instead, ending her increasingly spidery letters, *To strive, to seek, to find and not to yield*.

The Antarcticans who had survived the first war were too old to serve again, but most played their part on the home front. Murray Levick, author of the book about Adélie penguins that Cherry admired so much, trained commandos in extreme-environment survival. Silas worked on the development of radar at the Admiralty and served in the Home Guard. Initially a sergeant, with characteristic irreverence he demoted himself gradually to lance-corporal by snipping off his stripes one by one. At his day job he occupied the post of director of scientific research throughout the war, and was knighted for his services in 1946. Together with his wife Edith, he often met Cherry and Angela at the Berkeley, along with Sunny Jim and Dorothy, Lady Simpson. As for Deb, the institute was taken over by a section of the Naval Intelligence Division, so he made himself useful teaching RAF officer cadets the theory of navigation. Teddy Evans, now an Admiralty grandee, had another fine war. Churchill sent him on a secret mission to Norway before that country fell, and Evans met the beleaguered King Haakon on the run, in the bedroom of a small hillside farmhouse. Back at home Teddy was loaned to the Ministry of Aircraft Production, and during the Blitz he toured the air-raid shelters of the capital, medals flashing, to stiffen morale.

William Lashly, the man who had nursed a failing Evans back to life almost three decades previously, saw little of the war: he died in 1940. Although in recent years Cherry had seen him only at smoky reunion dinners at the Café Royal, in the period following their return from the south the two had been close; as close, at least, as a quasi-officer and a seaman could be (in 1916 Cherry wrote to say how much he would like 'to have a yarn' with his old sledging mate). After the first war, in which he had served in the Naval Reserve, Lashly was demobilised at the age of fifty-one. He returned to his pre-war work as a customs officer at the Board of Trade in Cardiff, and remained in Wales until he retired, whereupon he moved back to Hambledon, the Hampshire village of his birth. He called his last home Minna Bluff after an Antarctic headland not far from Hut Point. Lashly had been to Lamer, and had collaborated on *The Worst Journey* by sending Cherry a set of his field notes which he had copied out specially. When Cherry instructed Hatchards, one of the bookshops where he kept an account, to send him Shackleton's *South*, Lashly wrote that the gift 'came from one who do not forget we were once plodding over the snow to try to reach our goal, I don't think we shall ever forget those times . . .' He was a sober, solid stoker whom Cherry admired immensely: he considered that Lashly would have made a fine fourth man for the polar party, with Scott, Wilson and Bowers. Cherry submitted a touching obituary to the journal *Polar Record*. 'So now he lies at peace,' he concluded after an appreciation of Lashly's considerable achievements. 'No more facing the utmost physical toil, starvation and death together: no more knowing you can't go on and going on all the same: no more continual hunger awake or asleep; just peace.'

Nine months of Blitz ended in May 1941, leaving 30,000 British civilians dead. But what Churchill called the Battle of the Atlantic ground desperately on, followed in the summer by widespread discouragement at home over events in the Mediterranean and Middle East. Nobody really believed Britain could win the war. Cherry certainly didn't. Bombs, blockade and the strain on the railways brought accumulating shortages, clothes rationing was introduced (until new ration books were printed, margarine coupons had to be used) and only a siege economy kept the country alive. When Angela's mother sent a basket of oranges to the Shaws from Ipswich, Charlotte wrote to her, 'I think the only really great pleasure in this terrible time is seeing Angela's sweet face sometimes. She is the one bright spot. And it *is* bright.'

War stimulated the public appetite for adventure tales dignified by noble purpose, as Raymond had predicted, and the blackout hours were long. *The Worst Journey* flourished. The Chatto hardback sold well, requests for translation rights arrived from locations as exotic as Burma, and Penguin reprinted their two volumes as well as a special Forces Book Club edition. Nancy Mitford gave sales an extra push when she wrote a long, lively piece for the *New Statesman* in which she called *The Worst Journey* 'the best book in the world on that particular subject'. Like Ettie Desborough, she had become obsessed with the expedition (she could remember hearing the news of Scott's death as a girl of eight). She even called her draughty upstairs lavatory 'the Beardmore'.*

After a large batch of unbound copies was destroyed in the Blitz, Cherry was furious to discover that His Majesty's Inspector of Taxes planned to include the lost stock as a credit item on the grounds that Cherry would at some point receive monies for the bombed goods when he made a claim to the War Damage Commission. The interminable correspondence between him, his private bankers, the tax people and Raymond began to wear him down.

One day towards the end of 1941 Angela returned from a trip to London to find the staff in a flap. Mr Cherry-Garrard, the kitchen maid revealed in low and urgent tones, had been standing guard all day in the warren of servants' rooms at the back of the house, proclaiming with ringing confidence that robbers were about to strike. He had also telephoned his neighbour Dick Oakley, asking him, in a whisper, to hurry over as a clutch of Germans were hiding in the rhododendron bushes. Soon he was telling the SOE officers that there were 'people' in the house, as well as machines in the attics sending messages over the roofs.

Cherry was not depressed. He was cheery and busy and full of the war effort. Quietly delusional, he was experiencing a psychotic episode, almost certainly a manifestation of a pathological anxiety. (Like nightmares, delusions usually involve predators and persecutors such as Cherry's Germans.) His imagination had become so overloaded that he could no longer protect himself from his fears. But the episodes quickly passed. The friendly SOE officers toured the attic with Cherry before they left each night, confirming that there were no people up there, or machines: just a

---

* Twenty years later she wrote about Scott in greater detail in *The Water Beetle*, drawing heavily on *The Worst Journey* and referring to Cherry as 'the only one [on the expedition] who could be called an intellectual'. But she also wrote privately on the subject to Evelyn Waugh. 'If Cherry-Garrard had been more of a chap,' she told him, 'he would have rescued them [the polar party], but nobody has ever said so . . . Scott or Amundsen would have tried, no doubt.' Fortunately Cherry was not alive to read this: it was the accusation he most feared. Mitford could conceivably have been right on this occasion, but in general she and Waugh were fond of launching duff opinions on matters of which they knew little. In his reply to 'Darling Nancy', Waugh cheerfully announced that Scott had probably eaten Oates' body.

lot of dust-choked boxes. The delusional phase would have passed without fuss if Cherry hadn't told William Pope Genge about the people hiding in the house. Genge was an employee of Rumball & Edwards, the St Albans firm that had managed the Lamer estate for more than a generation, and he passed the news on to an alarmed Lassie, who in turn telephoned Mildred's husband Peter Ashton.

Ashton habitually played the role of man of the family. The canon was dead, and except for Mildred, Peter's wife, the sisters were husbandless. (Until Cherry married, Ashton's son, also Peter, was the heir to Lamer.) On hearing the news, he announced authoritatively that his brother-in-law should be in a mental home. Soon he was crunching up the drive with Mr Webb, a solicitor at Farrers', and Dr Henry Yellowlees, OBE, physician for mental diseases at St Thomas's Hospital in London, lecturer in psychological medicine and Harley Street consultant.

The grim little group gathered under Loch Tulla, sipping tea and waiting for Yellowlees to pronounce while Ashton, his jaw set, jabbed the fire with the poker and sized up the furniture. The identification of neurophysiological and neurochemical factors in psychotic disorders was a long way off. Diagnosis depended not on science but on handwriting. Yellowlees gravely asked the patient if he would care to write a line or two. The gently sloping hand with which Cherry contentedly obliged was all the evidence Yellowlees needed to diagnose 'general paralysis of the insane'. Antipsychotic medication did not yet exist, and the three visitors agreed that immediate incarceration was the only solution. Yellowlees already had a mental hospital in mind. It was The Retreat in distant York, a pre-Victorian asylum where he had served as physician superintendent.*

Angela, intimidated and afraid, felt certain that the harmless delusions would pass without intervention, but after another visit from the tyrannical Webb she understood that she was in danger of being overpowered. In desperation she set out down the avenue of limes and hurried over to the old rectory, where an appalled Charlotte propelled her along the garden path to the revolving hut, where they found the master sitting in his wicker chair at his flap-top table in the glow of the electric heater, fingering his portable typewriter. He had never heard such rot. Inserting a fresh sheet into the portable, he clacked off a sharp letter to Webb and Yellowlees for Angela to copy out. After insisting that Cherry was not mental-hospital

* Virginia Woolf's 1925 novel *Mrs Dalloway* satirised an eminent Harley Street specialist who incarcerated his mental patients willy-nilly. Woolf was familiar with The Retreat as Roger Fry's wife Helen had been locked up there. Of course, Woolf also knew all about mental illness from the inside. But even she would not have dared invent the name Yellowlees.

fodder, the letter ended, 'Please stop coming here.' When he had whipped out the sheet he looked up at Angela. 'I'm going to add a PS saying Yellowlees is a bloody fool!' he said with a glint in his eye. It was the only time she ever heard him swear.

'The Shaws were wonderful,' Angela remembered. 'They turned it from something nightmarish into something quite manageable. They were so normal and nice.'

A week later she went to London for a meeting with Webb, Ashton and Yellowlees, accompanied, for moral support, by her father and Noël, who first took her for a fortifying lunch at Marshall and Snelgrove's department store. On Christmas Eve she rang Yellowlees and told him she didn't want to see him again. 'You may think you are doing the best thing for your husband,' he retorted, 'but in fact you are doing the worst.' Soon afterwards she received a letter from Webb that ended, 'We should be so upset if anything were to happen to you', implying that Cherry might murder her.

Webb continued to telephone, Ashton to insist and Yellowlees to send in his bills, and then they all gave up. As for Cherry, he quickly recovered. He never knew about the intervention of the Shaws, and had a memory blackout covering the whole delusional period. Some months later, when someone mentioned Pearl Harbor, he was amazed to hear of it.

The live-in staff disappeared, called elsewhere by the remorseless demands of war, and the Cherry-Garrards were left with only a daily. Angela mastered the solid fuel Aga, learned to operate the water pump and made her own butter, a quarter of a pound at a time. They both liked it when the daily went home and they were alone. Evelyn was baffled at the idea of surviving at Lamer without the platoon of servants she had deployed. 'But who brings you your tea in the morning?' she wrote incredulously to Angela. 'We think you are a very wonderful person,' she wrote again when she heard that Angela had helped with the fundraising for 'Wings for Victory' week and joined the village branch of the Women's Volunteer Service, 'and how you get through that amount of work I cannot imagine.'

The winter of 1941/2 was another severe one, and Cherry had trouble with his hip. He had been prescribed poultices, which had to be scooped from the tin, heated and applied with a spatula. This, like everything else, was Angela's job, and the wretched poultice was always either too hot or too cold. 'We think he [Apsley] is very lucky to have you,' wrote Evelyn, though she had no idea just how lucky. Besides his hip, for months he could hardly write because of the arthritis in his fingers. His spirits lowered.

Angela would lure him into the village with promises of something interesting to see, but he had never enjoyed playing lord of the manor and was increasingly uncomfortable in the role. His waistline had thickened, his skin was a matt grey and he began to shamble. Still only in his late fifties, he behaved like an old man, and looked like one too, though his hair, distinguished now with grey wings, remained thick and full for many years. In his dealings with Raymond he was markedly less in control, and when the publisher suggested another edition, Cherry wrote wanly, 'I have thought it over carefully and feel that it is best to leave it. I am sorry.'

He went down to London each week to be treated at a Harley Street practice with radiant heat massage, another course of injections and physiotherapy from a woman who kept bees on the roof. After an especially bad bout of arthritis he took to carrying a hot-water bottle around with him, and this was soon followed by an inflatable rubber ring which enabled him to sit without discomfort.

They were not permitted to stay at the Berkeley for more than a week, as wartime regulations forbade it, so Cherry decided to rent a flat near Harley Street, despite the fact that most people were trying to move out of London, not into it. On a damp and sooty autumn afternoon in 1942 he and Angela looked at several possibilities in the nine-storey Dorset House in Gloucester Place, on the southern edge of Regent's Park and the northern edge of the West End. A colossal structure built on an acre of the Portman estate, Dorset House was like a liner sailing magisterially north, its geometric, blocky façade and banked curves the epitome of thirties chic. The main entrance was dominated by two large carved stone reliefs called *Eating* and *Washing*, which depicted stylised figures engaged in those domestic activities. They were the work of Eric Gill, one of the finest English craftsmen of the twentieth century. The Dorset House board of directors had vetoed Gill's other two suggestions, *Sleeping* and *Drinking*, on the grounds that the images might be morally suspect.

Small, modern flats were in fashion in the thirties. A survey in the *Financial Times* which featured Dorset House began, 'The large private house in the West End has seen its day', and went on to assert that these flats reflected 'a new mode of living'. Built by the famous property man Claude Leigh and opened in 1935, Dorset House had been marketed as 'London's most up-to-date block'. The 185 flats were aimed at wealthy types who had better things to do than eat in, and as a result they all had poky little kitchens. 'Optional Service will solve all your servant and entertaining problems', ran the advertisements. Despite a trace of snobbery over its unfortunate location north of the park (Hyde, of course), Dorset

House still attracted theatrical people and minor members of the royal family. One day a year or two later, as Cherry and Angela waited on a couch in the hall for Shaw to arrive, King George and Queen Elizabeth marched in. Cherry leapt to his feet, shoving his rubber ring down into the couch. The royal couple sailed past and entered the lift, on their way to dinner with a cousin who lived on the ninth floor.

The vast building was empty. Because of its multitudinous wings and winglets it did not have miles of institutional corridors smelling of Jeyes cleaning fluid. It was a friendly place, with attractive modern features such as central heating and letter chutes in which tenants could deposit their mail. The Cherry-Garrards chose No. 23 East, a sixth-floor, one-bedroom flat underneath Bertrand Russell, his third wife Patricia Spence, known as 'Peter', and their small son Conrad. It was going at the controlled rent of £220 a year. The small living room had two sets of floor-to-ceiling bay windows, one set looking out onto Gloucester Place, then a two-way street. Outside, an ornamental balcony with green metal railings overlooked the roof terrace of the first-floor flats, Dorset Square and the increasingly skeletal London skyline beyond. The other windows faced Melcombe Street and the grey rooftops to the north, including that of the Alliance Française, under which the exiled de Gaulle was making his wartime broadcasts.

Like a cruise ship, the building was self-contained. The ground floor was encircled by small shops that included a newsagent, a fishmonger, a chemist and a grocer with a dairy to which milk was delivered by pony and cart. On the other side of Gill's figures, porters sat in a cubby-hole adjacent to a spacious art deco entrance hall lined with couches, and glass double doors opened onto a restaurant with murals of rural scenes under which a bridge club met on Thursdays. Cherry liked it all very much. At last he had another little hut, without any responsibilities.

So they started a new life in London in a harsh year on the home front. Cherry's Winchester contemporary Stafford Cripps, recently promoted to the War Cabinet, banned motoring for pleasure. A limit of five shillings was imposed on restaurant meals (though this was frequently evaded), sporting events were curtailed, soap was rationed to a bar a month and the icing of cakes was forbidden. But the hotels, swarming with American soldiers, still held dances, and Londoners queued outside cinemas to watch *Casablanca* or Noël Coward's *In Which We Serve*. Cherry perked up. On Saturday afternoons he went to the Athenaeum and sat among the purple faces and salt-and-pepper suits. In the unaccustomed darkness of the blackout he and Angela walked gingerly through the quiet West End streets to literary events with Harold and Vera Raymond, and on Sunday afternoons they went to concerts at the Wigmore Hall. They watched the restricted wartime cricket at Lord's, just a few minutes' walk from Dorset House, and took the tube to Wimbledon for the odd tennis match: 'He loved showing me things he had seen alone before he met me,' Angela remembered. 'It was fun being married to him. Between his illnesses he really enjoyed life. He could be such a happy person.' With Pussy and Jasper Harker, their most faithful visitors, they strolled up Gloucester Place and, slipping through the circle of white stuccoed Nash terraces, into Regent's Park and over the footbridge to the rose bushes of Queen Mary's Garden. There, all through the war, they watched short-trousered boys playing at rescuing their mothers from burning houses. In the evenings they sat by the Bertrand Russells under the restaurant's friezes, eating tinned sausages and swimmy vegetables followed by dry pastry tarts with ersatz cream.

Angela went to Soho on the underground, the tunnelled walls of the stations plastered with imitation Cubist advertisements, and queued for the dark coffee Cherry liked. GBS walked across town for tea when he came out of hiding in Ayot; the porters loved to see his loping figure at their cubby-hole. When there was no butter to be found, which was often, Angela made him macaroons from unrationed peanut butter, and they soon became a leitmotif with GBS, permanently on the lookout for a target for his merciless jokes, although he always ate the macaroons. The three of them sat around the wireless to hear the latest news from the front. The reports had become part of the fabric of their lives, and so had Tommy Handley's breathless slapstick *ITMA* (*It's That Man Again*).

They spent increasingly long periods in London, returning rarely to Lamer, where the estate staff thought they must have gone quite mad. Jim Hyde had taken over from his father as gardener and handyman, and he went down to London by train to deliver fruit, vegetables and pheasants to flat 23. Angela missed Lamer. She would casually mention that the rhododendron that flowered like a crinoline must be in bloom, or wonder if the woodpecker was loitering by the summer house, trying to tempt Cherry back to Hertfordshire. It seldom worked.

When the sirens went off they heard the clicking footsteps of the woman in the flat opposite as she fled to Baker Street tube station in her high heels, but they sat it out. A few small incendiary bombs fell on the roof, though they caused only a small amount of damage. Dorset House was a steel-framed building promoted for its safety ('*WARTIME WORRIES SOLVED*'), and Cherry was quite unconcerned about the planes that throbbed overhead. He was much too preoccupied by his injections and, at a more profound level, by the inner battlefield. That held greater terrors than all the bombs in the world. What else would have induced him to move to the capital at a time when every other free man in the country was doing all he could to get out of it? He picked his way to Harley Street among shards of glass and clouds of brick dust, past Queen Anne houses with the walls ripped off that boldly displayed their private life to a distracted world. The row of cottages opposite Dorset House had been bombed in the Blitz, and the workmen setting up a water supply in the ruins found a cat living in the rubbly sockets. Lazarus, as he was named, would cross Gloucester Place and stroll into Dorset House to mew outside the doors of the flats. He soon became the tyrant of No. 23. At night, sprawled on the carpet, he made protesting noises when the gas fire became too hot for him, and Angela was obliged to get up and turn it down.

The difficulties of wartime travelling gave Cherry the perfect excuse to avoid family events. Of his five sisters he saw least of Edith, who continued to flit between churches, handing out money and accosting strangers to ask if they had been saved. The second eldest of the sisters, Elsie, a devoted employee of the Church Army, was at least staunchly Anglican. To general astonishment, when she was well into her fifties she announced that she was to be married. Like Lassie thirty years before her, she wed a vicar (Peter Ashton gave her away), and she settled down with her Fred to a happy old age in a cottage in Bramley in Surrey, he doing the cooking and she the gardening. Cherry was surprised to discover that he liked his new brother-in-law.

The five sisters had turned out to be remarkably unenthusiastic reproducers, only managing four children between them. Cherry took little interest even in those four, at least until they had ceased to be children. Although he enjoyed seeing Lassie, and sometimes, when he could get to Surrey, Elsie and Fred, on the whole he was more interested in his health than in his siblings. He didn't try to cover it up, and the family no longer expected him to turn up at weddings or funerals. Angela went to them all in his place. She was a more active member of his family than he had ever been.

As for old friends: Cherry had seen little of Kathleen in the two decades that followed publication of *The Worst Journey*. Its frank portrait of Scott still rankled, and she told anyone who would listen that Cherry had only been taken on the expedition because of his subscription. The feline diarist and architectural historian James Lees-Milne was one of those who did not believe her. She told him, while she was on the subject, that Cherry had been 'a poor creature, an ugly youth', and that it was she who had introduced him to GBS. Shackleton was rotten, Wilson a prig, Ory drab, Ponting just out for money.* Now, in the early forties, Cherry ran into her by accident. He and Angela were having tea at the Berkeley during a rare meeting with Edith, at that time an enthusiastic Baptist. As the piano tinkled and the china clinked and the fans wafted the smell of golden syrup around the large room, Kathleen entered with her husband and one of her sons. 'Now, Cherry, don't pretend you don't know me,' she hooted. Cherry, flustered and terrified that Edith was about to leap up and ask Kathleen if she were saved, stood to shake hands. 'This must be Wayland,' he stammered. (Wayland was Kathleen's son by her second marriage.) 'It's Peter,' replied Kathleen with a glare.

Kathleen died two years after the war ended. In many ways she was a heroine. She had an enviable ability to grasp the good in her life and rise above her sorrows. She asked to have the words 'Kathleen. No happier woman ever lived' engraved on her tombstone. What could be more heroic? Her biographer wrote of her that, 'She took hold of her life with rare glee, and raced through it without shame, without fear and with scarcely a backward look.' It would be difficult to imagine a better description of what Cherry was not. She continued to irritate him from beyond the grave when Seaver revealed her view that 'Bill had very little character'. It was bitter to hear such things.

In September 1943 Charlotte died. A postcard arrived from GBS to say that her last hours were happy, and the end 'not what I had feared'. A few days later he walked over to Dorset House in the autumn drizzle, ate a large tea, this time with jam, which he said he never got, and told them all about it. She had been in great pain for some time, but the day before she died the furrows disappeared from above her eyes and she looked quite young again – like the woman he had met in 1896. He told her she was perfectly beautiful, and although he could not understand what she said, she was 'quite happy'. She died in the night.

Not long afterwards, Angela's father died too. Cherry avoided the funeral, and Angela had the good sense not to try to talk him into it. From then on she had to negotiate maternal visits, though Cherry was polite to his mother-in-law to the point of oriental inscrutability. At least at Dorset House they could put her in one of the serviced guest rooms where

---

* Lees-Milne recorded that Kathleen was the worst-dressed woman he knew, which was one of the nicest things anyone ever said about her.

breakfast was provided. But they had to spend Christmas at Lamer with Clara. Cherry was still implacably opposed to the festivities. He wouldn't have a tree and never bought anyone a present, including Angela, though he loved the stocking she gave him. (He never gave her a birthday gift either; he never even remembered it was her birthday. But he didn't remember his own birthday.) She accepted his foibles and learned to love the lovable bits of him. It was a lonely life for her, in many ways, but not a bleak one. 'We were very happy,' she remembered. 'It was one of those things that grew. I was very lucky. Cherry was a romantic at heart.' He had quickly become dependent on her. When she was ill, he noted in his small engagement diary, 'A. has flu. I had a great deal of work to do.' He, too, learned to adapt, though he did very much less adapting than she did. He had at least abandoned the strict financial demarcation he had imposed in the first year or two of their marriage. Under those early rules Angela had been obliged to pay for half of every journey they made. When she took Cherry's book of coupons to London to shop for his socks and pyjamas, she paid for Allen's taxi rides from the station. She had even paid for her own telephone calls. Cherry was not mean, but he had a fear of being fleeced that was part of a larger, unformed paranoia. He had never understood how difficult it was for Angela to play the role of lady of the manor on two hundred a year.

The war continued. Dead Americans rotting under distant palm trees; mass hangings in Ukrainian village squares; the hollow-eyed ghetto in Warsaw; blindfolded resistance fighters queuing to be shot; gangrenous Tommies writhing in the desert sand; distended merchant seamen floating eyeless in the Atlantic; angular mountains of bones in the camps; motionless children, everywhere; Stalingrad. It was difficult for the living to stay sane. Tilbury, head gardener at Lamer for more than thirty years, lost his two sons. Deb's eldest son, Barry, was killed flying over the Mediterranean. Cherry remembered all three running through the Lamer elms, brandishing sticks and capturing butterflies. In the summer of 1943 the tide turned for the Allies, but the weariness at home was bone-deep.

Cherry had good days, even good weeks and months. But his illnesses never quite disappeared in those years, and the dark periods hovered above him like clouds heavy with rain. When they came low, he lived in their shadow. With his remaining friends from the *Terra Nova* he talked obsessively about the expedition, but at other times he was too involved in his interior world to speak about it at all, even when he had an eager audience. Bertrand Russell's small son Conrad was consistently disconcerted at his famous neighbour's refusal to talk about the Antarctic. By handing over responsibility to Angela for the daily practicalities of his life, and releasing himself from the grind of running his estate, Cherry had exposed a whole layer of emotional experience that had been more or less submerged. The irony was that the peaceful relief of his happy marriage allowed his anxieties to take hold.

Early in 1944 a rumour spread through Wheathampstead that an heir was to be born at Lamer. The war-weary villagers were hungry for cheery news as one gloomy year toppled into the next, but there was to be no baby at the big house. Cherry had no affinity with children; more significantly, he was too enmeshed in the present (and the past) to care about the future, and too fearful of what lay in the shadows. His imagination was already buckling with exhaustion: he could not conjure the joy a child might bring. His attitude hardened when Pussy and Jasper experienced the agony of a stillborn baby. He and Angela saw more of the Harkers than anyone, and had watched with horror as the once swan-like Pussy sank into ill-health. She had a kidney removed, looked permanently ravaged and finally had a stroke during dinner at Dorset House. She died a few days later.

Cherry was ill himself: a new kind of bronchial trouble had joined the litany of his complaints. On top of everything else he found it difficult to sleep. Doodle-bugs and rockets were not designed to alleviate insomnia. The low drone of the pilotless doodle-bugs and the hanging silence as they fell dominated the summer, and once again the station platforms were crowded with whey-faced Londoners evacuating to the country. Once again, too, Cherry and Angela set their jaws firm, even when fresh terror arrived in September in the shape of V-2 rockets that made a peculiar tearing sound as they hurtled vertically to ground. The air in Gloucester Place was permanently tinged with the bitter smell of magnesium and charred wood, and on his daily outings to Harley Street or the West End Cherry stepped round craters layered with silvery ash.

Shortly before peace was at last declared, Ory died in a nursing home in Hampstead. She had been ill for several years. Cherry had never lost touch with her; she was always protective of him, as Bill had been. She had led a full and active life, returning often to New Zealand, which she knew so well. During the First World War she had been awarded a CBE for her voluntary work with the New Zealand Red Cross. The cool, aloof Ory had never remarried. Her few close friends thought it would have been out of the question: 'the loss of him clung to her'. Although she enjoyed hearing news of the surviving Antarcticans, she saw little of them. A deeply private person, she was determined not to allow future generations of polar enthusiasts to pick over her relationship with Bill. As a result, she burnt most of his letters. She had lost her faith, and no longer believed they were to meet again. Before she died she left instructions that the green leather volume of Tennyson's *In Memoriam* which Cherry had lent Bill, and which he had found on his hard body, should be returned to its first owner. Cherry was deeply moved to see it again, the faded marker between the same cracked pages. He wrote to *The Times*, so that the return of the book should be noted, and the letter was published.

The week after VE Day Cherry and Angela joined record crowds at Lord's for an unofficial 'Victory' test match, swept along in the foamy tidal wave of national relief. Like most places in the capital, Dorset House altered dramatically in the summer of 1945. Fresh tenants arrived and the art deco entrance hall was crowded with light grey chalk-striped demob suits. Cherry and Angela, now virtually permanent residents, were bursting out of No. 23, so when the flat next door came up they rented that too, and began making them into one. Like everyone else who voted Tory, Cherry was aghast at the Labour landslide that followed the outbreak of peace. He did not rush to the Post Office to withdraw his savings, but he retreated further into demoralised isolation. When he turned sixty London was still in the pincers of wartime austerity: in February 1946 it was announced that there was only one week's coal left. Later in the year bread was rationed, which it had never been during the war, and even the small loaves that were doled out were made with reduced wheat. The Ministry of Food issued a recipe for squirrel pie.

On 25 June 1946 Cherry woke in such pain that he tugged up the sheet and stayed in bed. He had been complaining of rheumatism and indeterminate aching for several weeks, and had been reluctant to leave the flat, claiming that it would be too painful for him to stand up. On 29 June, in the morning, Angela went into his bedroom to wake him as usual, pleased to see that he was enjoying a sound sleep. But he was not asleep. He was unconscious. His regular doctor was hastily summoned, and he in turn called in Dr John Forest Smith, who at first announced that Cherry must have accidentally taken an overdose. To ascertain just how unconscious he was, Forest Smith lit a cigarette and burnt the tip of his left ear. The absence of response led to a diagnosis of 'cataleptic stroke'. Two days later Cherry began to move, and on 3 July he regained full consciousness. Thereafter he remained virtually immobilised for a year, locked into a private world of distant despair.

This was complete nervous breakdown. The golden purpose of the brief weeks slogging over the ice ridges to Cape Crozier had dimmed and vanished as Cherry spiralled down through the decades. In the Antarctic he had lived so close to what he called 'the bedrock of existence' that the complicated, crowded and corrupt world he occupied at home seemed to him now to be worth nothing at all.

He had been displaying classic symptoms of severe depression intermittently for years: self-absorption, loss of interest in the outside world and general joylessness, accompanied by a range of physical illnesses. Profound depression frequently manifests itself in ostensibly unconnected physical complaints, and severe cases are known to extend to the semi-paralysis experienced by the disintegrating Cherry in the summer of 1946.

Depression is not a bad case of the blues. It is a frightening, disabling pathological condition, and in the 1940s it came with a hefty stigma attached. Was the aetiology of Cherry's illness a question of his genes, of biological changes in the brain, or of what psychiatrists now call life events? The untidy answer is that it was probably a combination of all three.

His genetic inheritance predisposed him to depression. Peggy had a breakdown; Reggie, his cousin, had intermittently suffered from the disease for many years, and ultimately took his own life. But genes offer only a partial explanation. Changes in brain chemistry can be a major factor in an individual's vulnerability to depression, as the success of modern drugs has confirmed. These changes can be linked to external events, and in Cherry's case it seems likely that what happened in the Antarctic activated a biological process which culminated in breakdown. In other words, his depression was in some part reactive. Loss is the most significant of the grim roster of depressogenic life events; it has been called the touchstone of depression. Cherry's failure to adapt to the loss of Bill, and his unformed sense of guilt that he could have prevented his death, guided him down the dark path to breakdown. The decades in between were years of accumulating strain. The disease had progressed from its unfocused stirrings in the Antarctic, through the disabling years of ulcerative colitis (a recognised psychosomatic disorder) and inexorably onwards to the psychotic period of Lamer five years before total collapse.

Almost a decade after Cherry's breakdown his friend and former shipmate Sir Raymond Priestley, recently retired as vice-chancellor of Birmingham University, delivered a lecture on 'The Polar Expedition as a Psychological Study'. He spoke of 'the trail of broken men that polar exploration has always left in its wake', citing factors such as the difficulties of readjusting to normal life and the stark contrast between a long period of isolation and intense public attention. 'Polar madness', he said, was a characteristic symptom of exploration work, usually (but not always) after the expedition had returned to civilisation. 'There are many cases of polar madness of which the world does not hear,' he suggested darkly. Priestley was much too discreet to name names, but he could have been thinking of Amundsen's and Nansen's colleague Hjalmar Johansen, who shot himself; Abbott, the wrestler who broke down on the way home after his experiences with Campbell on Inexpressible Island; or indeed Cherry himself, though no other explorer had taken quite so long to go mad.

For Angela, there was no question of hospitalisation. Cherry had a horror of hospitals. A day nurse and a night nurse were engaged instead, though Peter Ashton launched a renewed campaign for incarceration. For months Cherry barely improved. He was permanently numb, as if he had been filled to the brim with cold liquid lead. Suspended between dread and alienation, his mood beyond the reach of the mediating intellect, he found it almost impossible to achieve any kind of mental focus. He lost several stones in weight and looked shabby and buffeted, his shoulders stooped and his eyes pouched. When he stood at the window and saw ordinary men and women strolling up Gloucester Place, he turned to Angela and said, 'Aren't some people lucky? They can go to the park.'

He was reluctant to let her out of his sight. She had to telephone the loyal Jasper and ask him to sit with Cherry when she needed to shop or take the laundry to the blanchisserie in Mayfair. Peggy also came, and so did Isabel, Reggie's widow, who would arrive early wearing a large hat and take Angela for a drive round the park. But she had little respite. Two days before her thirtieth birthday, they heard on the wireless that Geoffrey de Havilland's aircraft had exploded during a test flight. His obituary in *The Times* described him as one of the best demonstration pilots in the Empire.

Cherry had entered a dark world in which the dominant emotion was anxiety, and he focused it on his physical ailments. The bodily symptoms of a depressed patient are not imagined: they are as real as broken bones, and Cherry's went on and on. The link between mental and physical illness is one of the murkier areas of medicine.* Cherry was reluctant to acknowledge that his physical problems had anything to do with his state of mind, even when all of them improved at the same time. Few severely depressed people can make the connection. A generation on, the American author William Styron also experienced catastrophic nervous breakdown at

---

* There is evidence that severe depression suppresses the immune system. Furthermore, it is clinically proven that whatever physical illnesses a patient might have, depression makes the prognosis worse.

the relatively advanced age of sixty. He wrote powerfully about the tortures of depression-induced hypochondria. 'It is easy,' Styron thought, 'to see how this condition [preoccupation with bodily ills] is part of the psyche's apparatus of defence: unwilling to accept its own gathering deterioration, the mind announces to its indwelling consciousness that it is the body with its perhaps correctable defects – not the precious and irreplaceable mind – that is going haywire.'*

Cut off now almost entirely from the world beyond Dorset House, Cherry became hypersensitive to noise. When the Bertrand Russells played music in their flat Cherry sent Angela upstairs to tell them to stop. Quailing at the prospect of issuing orders to one of the towering intellects of the Western world, she havered. 'I'd do it for you,' Cherry persisted innocently, as if that situation would have been remotely comparable. During the winter of 1946/7, the coldest in both their lifetimes, black ice closed Baker Street for weeks, and traffic was diverted up Gloucester Place, hiking the decibel level. Falling temperatures and fuel shortages proved a devastating combination for London that winter, and both the big freeze and the power crisis dragged on into March. Transport strikes made everything worse. Further austerity measures were introduced as Britain counted the cost of the war, television broadcasting was suspended for a month to conserve fuel, and everyone ate corned beef.

Cherry was beyond the reach of his multitudinous doctors, his small band of loyal friends, and his wife. Six months into his illness his long-serving arthritis specialist recommended yet another doctor, a distinguished Harley Street neurologist called Rupert Reynell. Cherry was prejudiced against psychiatrists, afraid of the stigma their attentions attracted. But though the genial, Australian-born Reynell was in practice a psychiatrist, his neurological label made him acceptable.

The staple pharmacological remedies for depression were still bromides, paraldehyde, barbiturates and amphetamines, all unsatisfactory in different ways. Instead of dishing out pills, Reynell talked to Cherry and encouraged him to talk back. For many months, in sessions at the flat, Cherry talked about his Antarctic experiences in minute detail. Reynell hazarded medical opinions (it was he who diagnosed Dimitri as suffering from 'hysterical hemiplegia', for example). More often, he tossed in general comments. 'Of

---

* Sylvia Plath, another victim of depression, ascribed exactly the same need to discover a physical illness to the protagonist of her novel *The Bell Jar*. 'I would rather,' says Esther Greenwood, splayed in a psychiatric ward in the wake of a nervous breakdown and compulsively taking her temperature, 'have anything wrong with my body than something wrong with my mind.'

course, she was an artist and she may have had a twist,' he offered vaguely on Kathleen. As Cherry worked through his preoccupations Reynell tried to alter his thought processes and teach him new ways of thinking. Today it would be called cognitive therapy.

Quite literally, Reynell got him on his feet. He showed Cherry that he could rebuild his self-esteem, take control of his mind and restore his grip on reality. But Cherry's recovery did not come in time for him to see his mother again. Evelyn died in Godalming on a freezing December day in 1946 at the age of eighty-nine. Angela went to the funeral at St Helen's alone. 'Cherry v. upset,' she noted in her diary. He mourned in some far-off private place, his pain silent and unfathomable.

Then, in 1947, triumphs piled up. First, Angela got him into the hall. By February his arthritis was improving, though he began to get painful muscular spasms if he tried to do anything with his hands. By May he was able to write a short note thanking Hugh Farrer for his work on his stock portfolio. Soon Angela got him into the street, where he shuffled falteringly up and down past Gill's eating and washing figures accompanied by the languid Lazarus, who eyed the smoking nostrils of the pony delivering the milk. Then she got him to lift his foot onto a kerb, and then into a taxi. By September he was walking twenty steps almost every day; he even made it to Lincoln's Inn Fields to sign some papers (first making sure that the right kind of chair was available). His treatment, he said, 'was almost like a miracle'. The mists had dissolved.

14

A Winter Journey Indeed

In July 1947, as Repton's sweet chestnuts bloomed over the park, Sir Nicholas Cayzer, chairman of the Clan Line shipping firm, purchased Lamer for £45,000. The outdoor staff watched in bewilderment as a procession of removal men sweated on the gravel, bent under dark portraits in gilt frames, glazed cases of stuffed eagles and four-poster beds with fluted mahogany pillars.

Reynell believed that if Cherry were to stay well, he must cast off all responsibilities: he had therefore recommended the sale of Lamer. Cherry had accepted the suggestion calmly. He spoke of letting Lamer go with regret, as if someone else was making him do it. 'He did love Lamer desperately,' Angela reflected. 'But he also wanted to get away from things.' The literal shedding of responsibility mirrored an emotional equivalent, and somewhere in his psychic life the sale symbolised the renunciation of his past, a casting aside of the influence and expectations of his father and, more significantly, of the burden of his neuroses.

Angela was horrified. Who wouldn't be, faced with the prospect of exchanging a lovely country house for a city shoebox? Shaw, now ninety-one, tried manfully to help her through it. 'You will outlive Cherry,' he wrote to her in August, 'and he could not leave you with a white elephant like Lamer instead of a gilt-edged annuity.' Shaw was putting a gloss on it. Lamer was not a white elephant; not to Angela. She was only thirty, and still hoped to overcome her husband's resistance to children. But she had been boxed in. 'Reynell was a miracle worker,' she concluded ruefully. 'How could I contradict him?'

Cherry never returned to Lamer. The furniture was auctioned without delay and the books put into the London salerooms. Six Chippendale armchairs with figured silk velvet seats went to a manufacturing tycoon in St Albans for £130. Local people who bought old mahogany pieces were astonished to find, when they got the booty home, that the drawers were stuffed with family documents. Angela tried to secrete away the most treasured items, knowing that Cherry would regret their loss. She saved the Wilson watercolours, and sneaked some of the furniture into the Harrods depository on the Thames, where it duly rotted. A polar sledge and cooker were hastily donated to Deb's institute. Esptein's *Louise*, a fine bust, was sold at auction for £110, but the sculptor's long-fingered Christ rose from its packing case and was not sold, despite a peripatetic jaunt back to Epstein's studio and a mooted sale at the Leicester Galleries.*

Reynell recommended a break in Eastbourne, the quiet Sussex resort renowned for its sunshine and sheltered from the prevailing south-westerlies by the chalky bulk of Beachy Head. In the autumn Cherry and Angela dutifully swayed down to the south coast on the Southern Railway, newly nationalised by Attlee's Labour government. Following Reynell's suggestion, they booked into a suite at the Grand Hotel, a splendid old monster on the seafront that harked back to the Victorian era.

Just sixty-five miles from France, Eastbourne was still emerging from the tunnel of war. Rolls of Dannert wire lolled alongside the bathing huts, anti-tank concrete blocks called Dragon's Teeth lay beached on the grassy verges of the backstreets, and from his hotel window Cherry watched the old Martello tower disgorging weapons. He felt really well. Armed with notebook and binoculars, he and Angela took the little bus that climbed out of Eastbourne and dipped up and down the hollows of the South Downs along narrow roads shadowed by oak and beech. It was good birding country, and after lamb sandwiches and shandy in Alfriston they walked along the banks of the winding Cuckmere as it bent towards the shallow blue trapezium of sea at the Haven. At night, after dinner in their sitting room, they even foxtrotted round the Grand's chandeliered ballroom. Angela had her husband back.

'You really are a most satisfactory patient,' wrote Reynell on receipt of a jolly note from Eastbourne. 'I wish that all were as self-helpful. Sixty is generally considered too old for psychological treatment, but you have been a brilliant and heartening exception. Now I know that all that is necessary in such cases is that they shall have been trained in the Antarctic; have been on the "Worst Journey"; shall be very intelligent and still

---

* It can now be seen in the Scottish National Gallery of Modern Art in Edinburgh.

receptive, and lastly and very important, that they shall have a wife who is, amongst other things, courageous, cheerful and above all, selfless.

'Having ensured the above trifles, I will know that the rest is easy.'

'He has recovered his health rather miraculously,' GBS wrote after his former neighbours turned up unannounced in the unseasonably warm March of 1948. Cherry had put on weight and was thriving. That year he bounced off to Epsom and Henley with a picnic stowed in the boot of a hired car, watched scullers training on the Thames at Mortlake, and spent lazy days at Bramley with gardening Elsie and cooking Fred. 'The depressions lasted months,' Angela recalled when she looked back on those years, 'but they don't seem much now.' When Penguin proposed a single-volume, unabridged paperback of *The Worst Journey*, Cherry encouraged the project with zest. More than 165,000 copies of the two-volume edition had been sold, and in the summer Penguin duly ordered a first printing of 100,000 double-deckers.

When Reynell died suddenly of cancer Angela feared Cherry would relapse. But he didn't. He was very happy. Sometimes, as she watched him bending to smell a rose in Queen Mary's Gardens, she saw the tiny scar on the tip of his left ear where Dr Forest Smith had burnt him. He never even knew he had it.

Returned to the familiar territory of his right mind, he decided that he didn't want to lose his books after all, so he went down to the Hodgson's saleroom in Chancery Lane and bought some of them back. He also began appearing at the Hodgson's office asking for books to be removed from sale just as the catalogues describing them were half-way through production. (On recapturing his 1713 edition of *Paradise Regained*, he inscribed the title page, 'This is the Lamer copy saved by me.') The rescue operation stimulated a serious interest in book-collecting, and Cherry's raincoated form became a familiar landmark at the back of the salerooms on New Bond Street and Chancery Lane. Overhanging spires of volumes soon dominated even the large two-in-one flat, and he had to have a special library built in what had been the dining room – though the rarest volumes went straight into the vaults of Hoare's bank. The jewel of his collection, acquired at Sotheby's, was a flawless fourteenth-century missal from Paris, probably written for the private chapel of a member of the French royal family.* In 1952 he was guest of honour at the Antiquarian Booksellers'

---

* Cherry's investments were shrewd. His collection of illuminated manuscripts, printed books and Americana was sold at Sotheby's in 1961, in separate lots, for £64,215 (about £829,000 today). The missal fetched £22,000 (£284,000).

Association dinner at the Mayfair Hotel. He gave a magisterial speech, ranging from the subject of reading and writing in the Antarctic to the value of books in general. 'I think they are ultimately important,' he told the audience, 'as a record of conflict, between wisdom and human folly, between good and sheer human infamy, between light and darkness; and because the best of them include truth and beauty . . . The best stories are not what people do, but why they do it.' In his saner moments Cherry saw that his greatest achievement had been to write a book unlike any other that did reveal the truth and beauty he sought so earnestly. Many adventurers write books, but Cherry's transformation of a journey that was almost superhuman into a book that approached poetic genius was unique. Thirty years later a guest at the booksellers' dinner recalled 'the generosity, clarity and conviction of all that he said'.

Just as his chronic arthritis had been a manifestation of his debilitating depression, his energetic pursuit of his hobby was a symptom of his rebuilt self-esteem. But book-collecting ran counter to the claustrophobic culture of shortages and dock strikes. The London Olympics of 1948, the first for twelve years, became known as the austerity games, though in fact the adjective was applied to every aspect of British life in the pinched and colourless post-war years, the birth of the welfare state notwithstanding. Clothes rationing was about to be abolished after eight years, but Britain was broke, and soon the sugar ration was reduced again and sweets (much loved by Cherry, along with good chocolate and ice-cream) were brought back onto the ration books only three months after restrictions were lifted. In September 1949 Sir Stafford Cripps, Chancellor of the Exchequer and prince of austerity, devalued the pound by thirty per cent. Whale meat, which people were already eating in the form of fresh steaks, appeared in tins, as if Spam had not been testing enough.

Money, as always, helped lighten the grey, and with Lamer sold and most of his investments holding up well, Cherry had more cash than at any other time in his life. Following the general trend to take up what had been left off in 1939, he and Angela booked a cabin on one of the first post-war cruises to Athens. Always content at sea, Cherry again prowled the deck with his sketch book in his pocket, rising before the sun and tracking the stars after it disappeared again. When they disembarked they had their picture taken at an ancient amphitheatre, both smiling in the diaphanous Greek sunshine, he enthroned in a stone priest's seat, she standing in a full-skirted cotton frock with a nipped-in waist and an Audrey Hepburn headscarf tied under her chin.

In 1948 Sir Michael Balcon's and Charles Frend's Technicolor feature film *Scott of the Antarctic* was shown in London by royal command, with John Mills in the title role. Mills was already well established on the large screen as the star of numerous war films, and the story of the expedition was presented as a noble fable of class integration. Soon audiences up and down the country were marvelling at this iconic display of British heroism, a commodity that was in perilously short supply in the constipated late forties. While the feature was in production Cherry was asked to sign a form permitting the film-makers to change his character into anything they liked, and he replied by giving the studio bosses a good telling-off. Most of the 'survivors', as the press called them, were initially opposed to the project. 'Besides a general aversion to the idea of yet more money being made out of the tragedy,' Deb wrote, 'the one common dread among us was that the story would be tampered with to suit the ends of Drama, a fear which found its extreme expression in wondering how the film people were going to introduce glamorous blondes into a polar hut.' But Deb was won over, as most of them were, and some of the men even went onto the set at Ealing Studios and met the actors playing them. After watching the film at the command performance they crowded into the smoky foyer of the West End cinema as the flashbulbs popped and cast their votes in favour of Frend's interpretation. Cherry stayed away, implacable.* He never saw the film, though hostilities did not extend to the actors – he subsequently sat next to John Mills at dinner at Deb and Dorothy's. It was a pity that he couldn't allow himself to share in something that had given the others so much pleasure.

Cherry never saw a piece written by Frend after he had shot the film, citing as his formative influence *The Worst Journey in the World*. 'The more I read [of *The Worst Journey*],' wrote the director, 'the more I felt that a film could be made of Scott's last expedition.' So Cherry couldn't really complain. He had started it.

He was still obsessed, despite the passing years, and returned to the old Antarctic questions with renewed zeal, seizing every opportunity to interrogate his weary former shipmates ('Try and throw your mind

---

* Barry Letts was the actor who played Cherry. As it turned out, most of his important scenes ended up on the cutting-room floor, including Cape Crozier and the dog journey to One Ton.

A generation later, Cherry was again portrayed on film, this time on the small screen. In the 1985 television series *The Last Place on Earth*, based on Roland Huntford's joint biography of Scott and Amundsen, he was played by an unknown English actor called Hugh Grant.

back . . .'). Deb, Silas and an increasingly deaf Sunny Jim bore the brunt of it, though Silas retired back to Canada and saw little of Cherry from 1949 onwards. Once again Cherry dwelt on Scott's decision to take the dogs on further than he had planned, and on the repercussions of that decision. 'Of course, it is this dog biscuit which is the crux of the whole problem,' he wrote in the margin of his Antarctic journal in 1948. Once again, as he absorbed himself in the past, his anger and resentment towards Scott swelled. 'Here was Scott,' he wrote in one of his well-thumbed expedition volumes,

> with a tremendous urge to carry out his depôt and polar journeys. He depended on ponies and manhauling. What was it in Scott which prevented him from having good ponies and good manhaulers? Somewhere it is his own weakness. Why was he so easily persuaded by Kathleen and Teddy Evans? His bad ponies and bad manhaulers led to inevitable strains on himself and others. The polar party died and he left us in the power of Kathleen Scott and Teddy Evans and tragedy after tragedy has followed for forty years.

This was an exaggerated version of reality. Cherry's tendency to explain his own behaviour in terms of external events, and other people's in terms of their personalities, was a self-deluding habit that trapped him in a painful negative loop. Underneath the barrage of explanations his self-recrimination was Johnsonian in its magnitude; but this he could not put into words. Perhaps if he had been able to do so, he could have saved himself.

He decided to write a frank postscript to a new hardback library edition of *The Worst Journey*, a kind of ironic meditation that would reveal facts he had been obliged to leave out of the other versions. The single-volume paperback was selling well, but Cherry wanted to put certain things on record between hard covers. 'It may be historically important,' he told Allen Lane at Penguin. After years of silence he contacted Harold Raymond at Chatto, and was advised to make his own application for paper, which was still in short supply, although Chatto were again to handle distribution. When eventually he succeeded in getting the paper in his own name, he wrote triumphantly to Raymond, 'I am now a publisher and can meet you on equal terms.'

He wrote the postscript in the small back room on the sixth floor of Dorset House, looking out over the gleaming slate roofs, sooty chimney-stacks and muggy London fogs. The hum of engines floated up from Gloucester Place, still punctuated by the cry of the dairyman's boy as he brought the horse to the kerb. Cherry's essay included new information about Scott's orders to Meares, quoted within a painstaking but measured reappraisal of the crucial sledging journeys towards the end of the 1911/12 austral summer. Cherry had also found a solution to his dilemma over where to place the blame for the disaster. Scott was not at fault ('in this sort of life orders have to be elastic'); it was the lack of vitamins that did it. 'I feel more and more,' he wrote, 'that a ration free of, or seriously deficient in, vitamins played a leading part in this tragedy.' Atch had given him the idea, and Reynell had endorsed it. As an explanation it attracted Cherry as it exonerated everyone from responsibility: vitamins had not been discovered when the *Terra Nova* sailed. His public reassessment of Scott was positive and considered ('he viewed life as the struggle which it is'). It was followed by a hymn to Wilson and his 'forgetfulness of self', an ideal that Cherry deeply admired, though his own tragedy was that he was unable to participate in its wonder. He longed to cast off selfhood, as Wilson had, but his inner burdens weighed too heavily. It is impossible to understand the true nature of Cherry's neuroses, and to feel how hard they pressed down; but from what he did reveal of his torments, it is clear that he did remarkably well to travel with them as far as he did.

Above all, he used the postscript to praise Wilson's belief in the importance of 'the response of the spirit'. 'Wilson was working in a world which, I believe, was losing its ancient faiths without having much to put in their place. The rumblings of the storms to come reached us from the outside world when the ship came down.' In a violent, angry and tired world, he continued, 'Wilson sets a standard of faith and work . . . We have missed him ever since he died. But you must find him: his voice, it is a quiet voice, is for those who listen . . . and he will live, in many hearts.'

The postscript is a confused essay which adds little to the general reader's understanding of what had unfolded. It wanders amiably away from the Pole to consider the regrettable dismantling of the empire and to wonder at the noble fighting spirit that saw England through two wars ('a winter journey indeed'). Seaver called it 'a somewhat tortuous document'; it was certainly eccentric. But Cherry's passionate and sane appeal for the responsible use of knowledge rings true. Writing as atomic clouds rose on distant islands and hydrogen bombs took shape in labs on two continents, he noted, 'We cannot stop knowledge: we must use it well or perish . . . Those who guide the world now may think they are doing quite well: so perhaps did the dodo. Man, having destroyed the whales, may end up by destroying himself.' It was a prescient suggestion.

In the end he hauled himself above his obsessions and the clutter of the days and years and found that he could still touch his ideals. He cleared his mind, picked up his pen and wrote down what mattered – to him, and to anyone with half a heart. 'To me, and perhaps to you, the interest in this story is the men, and it is the spirit of the men, "the response of the spirit", which is interesting rather than what they did or failed to do: except in a superficial sense they never failed. That is how I see it, and I knew them pretty well.'

The Cherry-Garrards continued to enjoy Eastbourne, though not at the Grand. The hotel was a popular conference venue, and, even worse, the plain-speaking Foreign Secretary, Ernie Bevin, took holidays there until shortly before his death in the wet spring of 1951. Cherry was irritated when the public rooms swarmed with Labour Party officials and their wives and security men, and resented eating (as he perceived it) food left over by the roly-poly Bevin and his party. The rock-quarried Foreign Secretary was not only a Labour minister but a solid union man to boot. Cherry snorted at him, and at Britain's socialist experiment and nationalisation programme. Like many of his class he felt that the vaunted 'new equality' discriminated against him; that, of course, was the point of it. In protest he moved from the Grand to the gabled brick and pebble-dash Hydro, a hotel at the far end of the front. On high ground and surrounded by a garden, the smaller, family-run Hydro became a second home to Cherry and Angela, and throughout the early fifties they decamped there for four or five weeks at a time, settling into a routine that revolved around concerts under the turquoise doughnut domes of the bandstand and grilled sole in the high-ceilinged dining room. Cherry loved pottering round the South Downs with his deerstalker and birding notebook, the latter stored in a cloth envelope that had been part of his Antarctic kit. The quintessential Englishness of the landscape appealed to him: purple hollyhocks in the garden of the thatched Clergy House at Alfriston, yellow wagtails dipping over the Pevensey marshes and the smell of drying grass at haymaking. He studied the birds that bobbed in the reeds of the chalky wetlands and hovered in the wrinkled air over the wheatfields. ('Mottled on top of head and back. Lot of white in tail when spread. Nest exactly like a chaffinch. Chack-chack-chack.') The landscape was so emblematic that during the war a painting of the Downs had appeared on morale-boosting posters above the slogan, *Your Britain, Fight for It Now*. But in 1950 a colder war crept over Beachy Head when a convoy of lorries trundled towards it loaded with materials for an underground radar bunker opposite the winking lighthouse. As Cherry had written, 'We cannot stop knowledge.'

★ ★ ★

Shaw missed them; he complained that since they had left, there was only one couple in the village he could talk to. He remained a keen correspondent, and colluded enthusiastically in the quest to acquire rare books. When he put part of his own library up for sale at Sotheby's Cherry snapped up several volumes, including a valuable Dante and the rather less valuable 1937 *Oxford Companion to English Literature* which he took with him on a visit to Ayot. 'I never opened this book,' GBS wrote on the flyleaf in a shaky hand, 'and am astonished to find that I ever possessed it. Companions are no use to me. But it is a pleasant surprise to find that it has passed on to so valued a friend as Apsley Cherry-Garrard.' When Angela had an operation for varicose veins in the spring of 1950 Cherry seized on the opportunity to return to their favourite topic. 'The nursing home,' he wrote to Shaw in disbelief, 'said to be the best in London, was like the Crimea before Florence Nightingale went out.'

Five months later, Shaw died. In his ninetieth year he had cited Cherry in a letter to *The Freethinker*. He had found in his young neighbour an example of the evolutionary appetite for power and knowledge that characterised the 'Life Force', the atheist's substitute for the soul. ('The squire abandons his comfortable country house, and undertakes "the worst journey in the world" to gather an egg or two of the Emperor penguin because it is a missing link in genetic theory.') This, he claimed in triumph, was surely evidence that a godless world was not a world without meaning or purpose. It was an encouraging thought, and a touching epitaph to a true friendship.

In the same year, Cherry's third sister, Mildred, died. She was followed ten days later by Isabel, Reggie's widow, who was found dead at the age of eighty-seven at 11 Green Street, the elegant Mayfair house that had been a refuge to Cherry in his youth. She and Cherry had kept close; he thought she had 'quite the best brain of any woman whom I have met'. She had seen, all too painfully, her husband's depressive tendencies replicate themselves in his younger cousin. 'Poor boy,' she commented on Cherry before his marriage. 'I wish he could have a happier outlook on life.' She left him her collection of Wilson's pencil drawings and water-colours, and Scott's letters to Reggie. The house was turned into offices.

His losses did not drag him down, at least externally. He rejoiced heartily when Attlee's government fell and the 77-year-old Churchill was returned as head of the 'New Look' Tory party. It was at the end of that year – perhaps to celebrate – that Cherry designed his own block-printed Christmas card from a sketch he had made of an Emperor in front of a smoking Erebus. He sent it out inscribed with a verse that rivalled Shaw's in its appallingness ('I come to you by Cherry drawn/To wish you joy this Christmas morn'). It was part of Shaw's legacy.

Cherry still felt close to the Antarctic, and he was pleased when two members of Expéditions Polaires Françaises wrote to ask if they might present him with an egg from an Emperor colony they had reached by tractor. When the pair turned up Cherry and Angela took them to the Trocadero restaurant for dinner (whale meat was served) and were duly presented with the egg in a green box. But when he heard the Frenchmen's stories Cherry did not wish that he had been able to do it their way. He agreed with Deb, who wrote in 1959 that present explorers 'won't believe it when one assures them that we were contented to be without wireless and aeroplanes and tractors, and that the only thing we could really envy them for is their ability to carry plenty of fuel so as to dry clothes in the tent and get better sleep'.

The Cherry-Garrards visited Wheathampstead occasionally in the middle fifties, despite the hole left by Shaw. Anti-aircraft posts still stood in the cornfields, banked with split sandbags. They avoided Lamer. The news of it was too terrible. Cayzer had instructed the Portmeirion architect Sir Clough Williams-Ellis to remodel the dilapidated house. But in those grim post-war years property owners were required to obtain permission before spending more than £100 on improvements, and Cayzer was unable to procure any of the licences he needed. He quickly sold Lamer on to Grenville Hill, an unpopular local insurance broker and a former tenant of Cherry's. Hill began to strip the estate of its assets, selling off the remaining outlying properties and plots of land and generally annoying everyone. After attempting to sell the house itself for conversion into a 'school, country club or institution', in 1949 he demolished most of it (licences not being required for that) and flogged everything saleable, including chimney-pieces. He began to build an ugly new property on the site using parts of the old exterior walls and some of the oak beams. Before he finished, he went bankrupt. Then died. The unfinished new house and 600 acres were purchased in 1953 by George Seabrook, the son of the man Cherry had taken to the High Court. Seabrook farmed the land and thinned the woods Cherry had planted, then he sold the house to Fred Drake, who was no relation to the earlier Drakes who had married into the Garrard family. It was no longer Lamer; but an experienced eye could still see Repton's lines, and his sweet chestnuts still flowered in July.*

★　★　★

* And still do.

It was still a bleak time to be living in London. Most useful things remained in short supply, and the white stuccoed terraces circling Regent's Park were peeling after years of neglect. Edmund Wilson observed: 'There is about London a certain flavor of Soviet Moscow.' In 1952, Angela and Cherry fled to the Mediterranean three times.

In the new year he had congestion of the lungs. The smog in the capital didn't help. The previous December had brought the worst pea-souper in living memory, and Dorset House had disappeared in a murky gulp, with visibility on Gloucester Place down to five yards. A performance of *La Traviata* at Sadler's Wells had to be called off when smog crept indoors and the audience could no longer see the stage. Now Cherry went off to the Hydro to recuperate, and in June he and Angela escaped the rain which unseasonably soaked the crowds on the day Elizabeth II was crowned by sailing off to Venice. While they were at sea the thrilling news came over the ship's wireless that the third Pole had been conquered: Edmund Hillary and Tenzing Norgay had reached the summit of Everest. Cherry was immensely moved. Tenzing described the wind on the last reaches of the South Col as 'roaring like a thousand tigers'. Like the Antarcticans, the climbers on Everest had a vision of another world. ('I have never heard or felt or seen a wind like this,' Cherry had written at Cape Crozier. 'I wondered why it did not carry away the earth.') Less than five years after his triumph, Hillary and a small party became the first men since Scott to reach the South Pole overland. It was no longer quite such an awful place: the Americans had built a scientific station there, and the Stars and Stripes was flapping merrily on the hard ice. As a young man Hillary had been inspired by *The Worst Journey* ('I read it time and again,' he wrote in his autobiography). On his own Antarctic expedition he and his British partner Vivian 'Bunny' Fuchs used orange tracked vehicles (one of which was named 'Rock'n'Roll') that were descendants of the motors Scott had taken south. Four men, led by Hillary, also drove tractors to Cape Crozier and found the remains of the stone 'igloo' that had saved Cherry, Bill and Birdie. They dug out some of Bill's pencil drawings, as well as the blubber stove and other relics, 'chafed by nearly half a century of wind and drift but . . . in excellent condition'. A second party found the Emperor colony, still thriving.

Shortly after their return to London Cherry and Angela decided to take a more ambitious trip to Australia in the autumn. They were full of plans. Then quite suddenly, he broke down again. The familiar symptoms queued for recognition: dramatic weight loss, lack of interest in the outside world and a crushing listlessness which extended to a partial inability to move. It was a heavy blow to Angela. Seven years had gone by since the last breakdown, and they had been such happy ones, with no indication that another collapse was lurking.

He was incapacitated for months, and the Australian holiday was cancelled. The therapeutic sessions seven years previously had not resolved the fundamental conflict playing itself out in Cherry's psyche. But despite the painful absence of Reynell, the breakdown was not terminal. By the end of the year Cherry was beginning to emerge from the tunnel. Once again Angela counted the number of steps he took each day, and the cold winter weeks were marked by small triumphs as he tottered to the end of the corridor, then down to the foyer, and finally all the way to the frosty lawns of Regent's Park, where they watched out for the first crocus or a new family of mallards on the lake. He continued to be plagued with neuralgia and other physical ailments, obsessively consulting a dermato-logist about a persistent rash and an eminent ear, nose and throat specialist about problems with his sinuses. His sensitivity to noise worsened; the growl of motors had become louder when traffic lights were installed on Gloucester Place directly under their sixth-floor windows, and workmen hammering down the corridors brought on a stomach upset. But by the late spring of 1954 he was well enough to return to the Mediterranean, sending a special Fortnum's deck-chair to the ship ahead of time. Although he rarely disembarked, the long cruise did him good, and at the end of it they both felt confident about rebooking the Australian cruise for the autumn.

The six-month 'ordinary run' to Australia and back included a hugely long extra leg across the Pacific and down the coast of North America. But first, to get to Western Australia, the sparkling Orient Line ship *Oronsay* followed the route Cherry had taken on the *Ormuz* forty-five years earlier, when a passenger on another liner in the Suez Canal had shouted over to ask who had won the Derby. From Fremantle she proceeded round to the east coast. Angela was busy organising her husband's medicines ('I was haunted by his prescriptions'), and if the ship's doctor couldn't oblige, excursions were often arranged around the location of the pharmacy. In Auckland Cherry was pleased to see a copy of *The Worst Journey* displayed in a bookshop window. For the rest of the holiday he rarely went ashore, preferring to remain on deck, observing the teeming wharves through his field glasses or simply sitting in a deck-chair, a cup of tea in his hand. Angela usually disembarked on her own ('Don't be long'), and she fell in love with Suva in Fiji, returning to the cabin with pungent armfuls of tropical fruit. But at the next stop, Honolulu, uniformed men came on board to sniff out foreign foodstuffs (Hawaii was not yet an American state, but it had long been annexed, and American officials had a firm grip on the islands) and most of the fruit had to be thrown overboard. The *Oronsay* continued across to a bitterly cold Vancouver, and by 9 December she was off San Francisco. Cherry recognised the rocks beyond the harbour where he had watched seals playing in 1910, a young man full of hope, returning home to sign up for the adventure of a lifetime. On the way back, they went to all the same places in reverse order, meeting up in Sydney with Griffith Taylor and his wife Doris. Griff had recently retired to the Sydney suburb of Seaforth after a distinguished and often controversial career as a geographer. The 'halo of good fellowship' that Cherry had described so warmly in *The Worst Journey* was still hovering over his head.

The shops filled up with newer and better things as the decade wore on, and to Cherry's delight ice-cream trolleys reappeared in Regent's Park. But the growing affluence of the fifties was shadowed by poor industrial relations, and one of Sir Anthony Eden's first acts as prime minister when Churchill at last retired was to declare a state of emergency after 60,000 dockers came out on strike. The country was becoming a bewildering place for a man imbued in his youth with the spirit of the Victorian age. 'He was still trying to live up to his father's ideals,' Angela remembered. Day after day *The Times* reported the dying spasms of imperialism alongside startling accounts of a young American singer called Elvis Presley, and the West End streets that radiated south from Gloucester Place began to look increasingly unfamiliar, peopled with Teddy boys, angry young men and women wearing tight jeans. Cherry had little contact with these baffling changes. Several months after the cruise, he once again broke down.

Back came the heavy numbness and the sense that his body was filled with cold liquid lead. But just when the prognosis was at its most gloomy, his sinus specialist recommended a new doctor called Gordon Mathias. He was a Welshman with an Antarctic link, having trained at the London Hospital under the auspices of a sponsorship programme set up by Wilson's sisters, and he had known both Ory and Isabel Smith. The connection created an immediate bond between doctor and patient, and it enabled Cherry to open up. Mathias specialised in psychiatry, and besides offering therapeutic sessions in which he encouraged Cherry to talk, he suggested a course of electroplexy, now known as electroconvulsive therapy (ECT) in the UK and electro-shock therapy (EST) in the United States, of which he was a pioneering practitioner.

Cherry had already taken barbiturates to little or no effect, and by this stage, lost in his private darkness, he was willing to try anything. ECT had been practised in Europe since the late thirties. It has had a controversial history and continues to stimulate fear, but correctly deployed, it has relieved many thousands of depressive mood disorders. Cherry's sessions duly took place at Dorset House, closely monitored by Mathias and an anaesthetist. Cherry was put under for the duration of a therapeutic seizure that was caused by the application of electrodes on either side of his head. The effect was immediate. Cherry felt better after the first treatment and continued to improve as the course progressed until he was completely well.

Once again, Angela had her husband back. Years later, she reflected simply, 'There were two Cherrys, you see.' This was true throughout Cherry's life, and he acknowledged it in his 1951 postscript. 'Know yourself,' he wrote. 'Accept yourself: be yourself. That seems a good rule. But which self? Even the simplest of us are complicated enough.' As he turned into an old man he found it increasingly difficult to engage in the present. Like Robert Graves' cabbage-white butterfly, he had never quite mastered the art of flying straight, but lurched 'here and here by guess/And God and hope and hopelessness'. Externally, his life had been haphazard (whose isn't?). Internally, he had fought his private wars and come out just about all right, true to an ideal or two, and still believing in 'the response of the spirit', despite everything.

In the spring of 1958 the Gothic chapel hidden among the beech trees at Denford was demolished. Five years previously the vicar of Hungerford, by default responsible, had tracked Cherry down through the pages of *Who's Who* and asked what he wanted to do about the building: his grandfather, grandmother, uncle and aunt were after all buried beneath it. But the contact fizzled out, and after a small local controversy in which the Georgian Group attempted to save the pinnacled chapel (Betjeman described it as 'charming and lacelike'), it was pulled down and the bodies forgotten.* It was a lugubrious finale for the Cherrys of Denford.

Their representative on earth had turned seventy more or less in sound mental health, but he was becoming frail, and was now permanently obsessed with noise. He insisted on moving into the Berkeley for months at a time, taking one of the quieter rooms overlooking the well at the back.

---

* The last private owners of Denford bequeathed the estate to an order of Catholic nuns who ran it as a prep school until 1967, when it became Norland College, a training institute for nannies. The ruins of the chapel are visible among the beech trees, if you look hard, but nobody at the college is aware of the quartet of rotting Victorians that lies close by the children's playground.

Angela would return to Dorset House to wash their smalls and cook Cherry's favourite food, which she ferried back to the hotel in covered basins. It was an unnatural life, but she had to go along with it, as she had gone along with so much. He did not think of her needs. It was a personal failure.

There were pleasurable outings. A car and driver would be summoned to the hotel to take them over to Kew Gardens or up to Ken Wood on Hampstead Heath, where the neo-classical villa had a handsome Adam south front that was reminiscent of Lamer (Repton's hand was visible there, too). On a good day they took a boat down the Thames and had a picnic, or walked along the towpath at Putney. But these were secluded years.

The world spun away from Cherry. In October 1957 the Soviets launched Sputnik 1, and a month later they shot a dog into orbit. Cherry had always felt that space was the next frontier, after the Antarctic. 'We shall visit the moon now before very long,' he had once written. 'Perhaps within the next thousand years.' In 1959 the unmanned Lunik 2 crash-landed on the moon, and only ten years after that Neil Armstrong wobbled about on its craterous surface. Cherry was out of step with the times, as usual, but *The Worst Journey* continued to win all hearts, and requests for translation rights still arrived from distant corners of the world, thirty-seven years after first publication. It was a source of deep satisfaction to him. The Antarctic had both redeemed and destroyed his life. Redeemed, because it produced *The Worst Journey*, a superlative piece of art that vaults above the human experience which gave it form. Destroyed, because it fatally engaged his anxieties. His life was proof that emotion has its own chronology.

In the middle of May 1959 they had a peaceful, happy day at Ken Wood. The daffodils were blazing on the landscaped slopes in front of the house and the first summer sunshine glanced off the ponds puddled next to the trees. Two days later Cherry slipped over in the Berkeley and broke his arm. An X-ray machine was brought to the hotel, and Mathias, wanting a second opinion, called in the specialist Sir Horace Evans. But on 18 May Cherry died of congestive heart failure and bronchopneumonia. He was seventy-three. 'Men do not fear death,' he once wrote. 'They fear the pain of dying.' There had been no pain at the end, and nothing to fear.

He was buried in St Helen's churchyard, with his secrets.

Guide to Notes

All books published in London, unless otherwise indicated.

Correspondence, diaries and unpublished material are held at the Scott Polar Research Institute, unless otherwise indicated.

Abbreviations

AC	Apsley Cherry	EW	Edward Wilson (Bill)
ACG	Apsley Cherry-Garrard	FD	Frank Debenham
AF	Arthur Farrer	GBS	George Bernard Shaw
AM	Angela Mathias	HB	Henry Bowers (Birdie)
CS	Charlotte Shaw	KS	Kathleen Scott
EA	Edward Atkinson (Atch)	LO	Lawrence (Titus) Oates
ECG	Evelyn Cherry-Garrard	RFS	Robert Falcon Scott
ES	Ernest Shackleton	RS	Reginald Smith

Journal/Annotated journal   Apsley Cherry-Garrard's polar journals, held at SPRI.

BSCL III Dan Laurence, ed., *Bernard Shaw: Collected Letters* III (1911–1925), 1985.

SLE   Robert Falcon Scott, *et al.*, *Scott's Last Expedition*, arranged Leonard Huxley, 2 vols., 1913. (Scott's diary was published under the title *Scott's Last Expedition*. Material was excised from the first published version, and has remained excised from subsequent published versions. The full text can be found in the facsimile edition: University Microfilms Ltd, Tylers Green, 1968. To avoid confusion among editions, I have given the date of entry as the reference in all extracts from Scott's diary. In all other published diaries, I have used the edition cited in the bibliography.)

WJ   Apsley Cherry-Garrard, *The Worst Journey in the World*, 1922. Page numbers refer to the 1994 Picador edition, which is currently available.

Archival sources used in notes

BL	British Library
Bristol	Penguin Archive, University of Bristol
BRO	Cherry-Garrard Papers, Berkshire Record Office, Reading
Hertford	Garrard Papers, Hertfordshire Archives & Local Studies, Hertford
Kennet Papers	Kennet Papers, Cambridge University Library
Oslo	National Library of Norway, Oslo
PRO	Public Record Office, Kew
Reading University	Chatto & Windus Archive, University of Reading
SPRI	Scott Polar Research Institute, Cambridge
Temple	Constable & Co. Directors' Files, Special Collections Department, Temple University Libraries, Philadelphia
Texas	Harry Ransom Humanities Research Center, University of Texas at Austin

Notes

Introduction

2 **God in his Heaven** Siegfried Sassoon, *The Old Century*, 1938, p. 153.
2 **was losing its ancient** Postscript to *WJ*, 1951, p. 599.
4 **To me, and perhaps . . . It is a story** *ibid.*, pp. 602–3.

Chapter 1: Ancestral Voices

5 **All Scott's orders had** Annotated journal. The comment appears alongside entries for December 1911 & April 1912. In all subsequent notes, the location of the comment is indicated in square brackets. Researchers should note that this material, stored at SPRI, is restricted access.
5 **Those first days of** *WJ*, p. 110.
5 **Can we ever forget** Draft material, *WJ*.
6 **In this sort of** Postscript, p. 589.
6 **If you knew him** *WJ*, p. 207.
6 **My relief was so** Annotated journal [May 1912].
6 **it was [is] a grave** Journal, 12 November 1912.
6 **If we had travelled . . . But we never dreamed** *ibid.*, 'Written on the Barrier after finding the remains of the Southern Party', n.d.
7 **I am almost afraid** *ibid.*, 12 November 1912.
7 **We did not forget** *WJ*, p. 302.
7 **If you march your** *ibid.*, p. 598.
8 **The sepoys have kicked** AC to Charlotte Cherry, 18 July 1857,

300

family collection. I am grateful to John Gott for making this material available to me.

8 **Send this please to** AC to Charlotte Cherry, 7 January 1858, family collection.

8 **I don't think you** AC to Charlotte Cherry, 5 February 1858, family collection.

9 **I can fancy you** AC to Charlotte Cherry, 16 July 1858, family collection.

9 **Mind you give me . . . It seems to be** AC to George Cherry, n.d., family collection.

9 **during an interval in** AC to Charlotte Cherry, 7 January 1858, family collection.

9 **I thank you exceedingly** AC to George Cherry, n.d., family collection.

9 **All the morning I** AC to George Cherry, 1 May 1878, family collection.

9 **If you have to** AC to Alfred Welby, 29 March 1879, family collection.

9 **What a fearful mistake** AC to George Cherry, 9 February 1879, family collection.

10 **Between you and me** AC to Alfred Welby, Easter Sunday 1879, family collection.

10 **Bedford** For an account of the period, *see* C. D. Linnell, 'Late Victorian Bedford', *Bedfordshire Magazine* VII (1959–60).

11 **dresses of braided cream** *Newbury Weekly News*, 12 February 1885.

11 fn. **In nearly all serious** *Bedfordshire Mercury*, 24 April 1908.

14 **one of those men** Harriet Loyd-Lindsay, Lady Wantage, *Lord Wantage VC KCB: A Memoir by his Wife*, 1908, p. 164.

16 **LADDIES BEST LOVE BABYS** *and all other childhood notes* Family collection.

17 **I belong to the** E. M. Forster, *Two Cheers for Democracy*, 1951, p. 67.

Chapter 2: Lamer

20 **the balcony opening out** Carola Oman, *Ayot Rectory*, 1965, p. 157.

21 **Dearest Mother, The hounds** *and all other childhood letters* Family collection.

22 **We knew him best** Wheathampstead Church Magazine XXIV (December 1907).

26 **The young master did** Mary Amy Coburn, *George and Henry*, Wheathampstead, 1992, p. 47.

26 **Lo, all our pomp** Rudyard Kipling, 'Recessional', 1897.

28 **For five years at** Arnold Toynbee, *Experiences*, Oxford, 1969, p. 6.

28 **Except in the Army . . . we were hardly aware** *ibid.*, p. 11.

29 **Under the system then** D. N. Pritt, *From Right to Left*, 1965, p. 254.

33 **In other colleges the** S. P. B. Mais, *All the Days of My Life*, 1937, p. 29.

33 **It may be of** John Jolliffe, *Raymond Asquith: Life and Letters*, 1980, p. 29.

33 **Show me a researcher** Ronald Clark, *Tizard*, 1965, p. 12.

34 **content to live like** *ibid.*

34 **Nothing anywhere seemed as** Compton Mackenzie, *Sinister Street*, 1913, p. 542.

35 **many who had been** Stephen McKenna, *While I Remember*, 1921, p. 61.

35 **a dark, lean, rather . . . Otherwise he was remarkable** *Evening Standard*, 6 December 1922.

35 **it was practically impossible** Kenneth Clark, *Another Part of the Wood*, 1974, p. 121.

35 **a life of familiarity** Raymond Asquith to Margot Asquith, [n.d.] October 1897, in Jolliffe, p. 33.

35 **How dense the barbaric** Leonard Woolf, *Sowing*, 1960, p. 82.

36 **In my time at** Mais, p. 32.

36 fn. **How long, O Lord** *New Statesman*, 8 July 1922.

38 **Father said he would** ACG to AF, 29 October 1906, Hertford.

38 **Sir Lander has just** ACG to AF, 1 November 1906, Hertford.

38 **showed promise** Oxford University Boat Club records.

39 **being very short in** *ibid.*

39 **I was very sorry** ACG to Henry Hobbs, 10 May 1907, private collection.

39 **I am very very** ACG to Henry Hobbs, 17 May 1907, private collection.

40 **The seeds of his** *Herts Advertiser*, 15 November 1907.

40 **In ever loving memory** Coburn, p. 49.

40 **as if it cannot** *ibid.*

40 **I had thought of** *ibid.*, p. 50.

41 **As a proof of** *St Albans Times*, 10 November 1907.

Chapter 3: Untrodden Fields

43 **new and untrodden fields** Winston Churchill, speech in Dundee, 10 October 1908; published in *The Times*.

43 **It was not a** Michael Holroyd, *Lytton Strachey* I: *The Unknown Years*, 1967, pp. 33–4.

45 **that fool of a** Virginia Stephen to Violet Dickinson, [n.d.] January 1905, in *The Letters of Virginia Woolf: The Flight of the Mind*, eds. Nigel Nicolson & Joanne Trautmann, 1975, p. 171.

45 **From now onward till** EW to RS, 18 April 1910.

46 **I have seen him** John Fraser, in George Seaver, *Edward Wilson of the Antarctic*, 1933, p. 20.

46 **and something must be** Seaver, *Wilson*, p. 170. Many of Seaver's primary sources were later destroyed by Wilson's widow. Seaver uses no notes, and should be treated with caution, as he was fond of conflating sources. Where Seaver is quoted as the source of correspondence, the letter is presumed destroyed.

46 **to let nothing stand** Address by George Seaver at the opening of Edward Wilson Memorial House, London, 5 July 1952. Transcript in private collection.

47 **Without a love for** Seaver, *Wilson*, p. 124.

47 **My dear Billy . . . it** ES to EW, 12 February 1907, in *ibid.*, p. 174.

48 **Of all the continents** Richard Byrd, *Antarctic Discovery*, 1936, p. 1.

48 **the exploration of the** Royal Geographical Society, *Report of 6th International Geographical Congress*, 1896.

49 **Beauty is still sleeping** Roald Amundsen, *The South Pole*, 1912, p. 194.

49 **The stark polar lands** ES, *The Heart of the Antarctic* I, 1909, p. 1.

49 fn. **The combined armies of** Frederick A. Cook, *Through the First Antarctic Night*, 1900, p. 468.

50 fn. **This is how it** Doris Lessing, Afterword to *The Making of the Representative for Planet 8*, 1982, p. 130.

52 **When I first knew** Introduction to Seaver, *Wilson*, p. xx.

53 **I shall be only** ECG to ACG, 11 December 1910, family collection.

54 **the greyhound of the** *The Times*, 11 January 1887.

55 **the Bishop is a** Harry Woollcombe, CEMS *Men's Magazine* (January 1910), Lambeth Palace Library.

56 **a very cultivated, capable** AF to Roland Farrer, 4 January 1910, BRO.

56 **My dear Cherry-Garrard** EW to ACG, 8 December 1909.

57 **I am biased in** EW to ACG, 18 April 1910.
57 **Dr Wilson is up** RS to ACG, 3 February 1910.
58 **Welcome home delighted see** EW to ACG, 7 April 1910.
58 **I have seen Wilson** RS to ACG, 18 April 1910.
59 **Putting it quite baldly** *ibid.*
59 **I am more sorry** EW to ACG, 20 April 1910.
59 **Captain Scott wants to** EW to ACG, 25 April 1910.
60 **as vague blobs walking . . . At that time I** *WJ*, p. 239.

Chapter 4: Winning All Hearts

61 **The *Discovery* was a** Seaver, *Wilson*, p. 198.
62 **I shall never forget** E. R. G. R. Evans, *South with Scott*, 1921, p. 6.
63 **The verb 'to wangle'** *ibid.*, p. 7.
63 **Every prospect of a** Journal, 21 June 1910.
64 **an ever-ready laugh** Charles Wright, *Silas: The Antarctic Diaries and Memoir of Charles S. Wright*, eds. Colin Bull & Pat F. Wright, Columbus, 1993, p. 28.
64 **excellent food – I had** Journal, 23 June 1910.
64 **This is always to** *ibid.*
64 **I really never have** EW to RS, 26 June 1910.
64 **And so with a** Fridjtof Nansen to Roald Amundsen, 2 April 1913, Oslo, trans. Roland Huntford.
65 **The pump is going** Journal, 23 June 1910.
65 **I think I shall** *ibid.*, 27 June 1910.
65 **as happy as the** *WJ*, p. 4.
65 **He was father and** Draft material, *WJ*.
65 **by far the most** EW, *Diary of the 'Terra Nova' Expedition to the Antarctic 1910–1912*, ed. H. G. R. King, 1972, 26 January 1911.
65 **He is only eighteen** HB to May Bowers, 22 August 1910.
66 **Enjoying myself greatly** Journal, 17 July 1910.
66 **I have been more** *ibid.*, 23 July 1910.
66 **the lack of something** *Silas*, p. 9.
66 **robust, willing and uncompromising** Draft material, *WJ*.
67 **good-hearted, strong, keen** *SLE*, 5 May 1911.
67 **though there was hardly** *WJ*, p. 10.
67 **Campbell, Cherry-Garrard and** EW, *Diary*, 11 August 1910.
68 **When we first got** *WJ*, p. 15.
68 **One of the days** Journal, 26 July 1910.

68 **Wilson took Cherry-Garrard** Evans, *South with Scott*, p. 15.

68 **We are [a] peaceloving party** HB to Emily Bowers, 23 August 1910.

68 **we usually hunt in** HB to May Bowers, 25 September 1910.

68 **Cherry-Garrard is a** *ibid.*

68 **our young millionaire . . . a** HB to Emily Bowers, 22 June 1910.

69 **There wasn't a twist** George Seaver, *Birdie Bowers of the Antarctic*, 1938, p. 72.

69 **I love my country** HB to May Bowers, 17 July 1907.

69 **Ever since I went** HB to Emily Bowers, 6 September 1907.

69 **If only they will** HB to Emily Bowers, 30 April 1909.

70 **Well, we're landed with** Elspeth Huxley, *Scott of the Antarctic*, 1977, p. 189.

70 **the wives are much** Journal, 16 August 1910.

70 **I glowed rather foolishly** Lady Kennet [KS], *Self-Portrait of an Artist*, 1949, p. 76.

71 **Darling, I will be** Louisa Young, *A Great Task of Happiness*, 1995, p. 93.

71 **little rippers and ladies** HB to May Bowers, 28 August 1910.

71 **with staid and proper** *et seq.* HB to May Bowers, 1 September 1910.

72 **I did a lot** Journal, 4 September 1910.

72 **It will be terrible** HB to May Bowers, 22 August 1910.

72 **It is delightful to** EW to RS, 10 September 1910.

73 **one of the landsmen** Thomas Griffith Taylor, *With Scott: the Silver Lining*, 1916, p. 13.

73 **as strong as a** EW to RS, 10 September 1910.

73 **takes no part in . . . has a taste for** *Silas*, p. 27.

73 **Evans is leader in** FD, *The Quiet Land: The Antarctic Diaries of Frank Debenham*, ed. June Debenham Back, Huntingdon, 1992, p. 24.

74 **To all his comrades** Raymond Priestley, 'Robert Falcon Scott', unpublished essay, 1960, p. 13.

74 **I hope it will** EW, *Diary*, 12 October 1910.

74 **Cherry-Garrard had a** W. H. Fitchett to RS, 17 October 1910.

74 **Mrs Wilson told me** *ibid.*

75 *Beg leave to inform* Original telegram lost.

76 **I shall be at** *WJ*, p. 41.

76 **We are all a** Journal, 24 October 1910.

76 **Among the executive officers** *WJ*, p. 43.

76 **I was very frightened** *ibid.*, p. 4.

76 **Campbell as the President** EW, *Diary*, 11 July 1910.

76 **Cherry-Garrard has won . . . You will be equally** RFS to RS, 18 November 1910, in *WJ*, p. lxi (original lost).

77 **minding his cakes at** RS to AF, 29 December 1910, BRO.

77 **We are all working** ECG to ACG, 20 November 1910, family collection.

77 **I feel you have** ECG to ACG, 11 December 1910, family collection.

77 **I am so very** *ibid.*

77 **in the night when** ECG to ACG, 27 November 1910, family collection.

77 **and hoped it would** ECG to ACG, 25 December 1910, family collection.

78 *Nobby*. **Aged. Goes with** LO, Diary (destroyed; partially copied out by his sister Violet and quoted in Sue Limb and Patrick Cordingley, *Captain Oates: Soldier and Explorer*, 1995, p. 122).

78 **There was more blood** LO to Caroline Oates, 23 November 1910.

78 **If ever Con has** KS, Diary, 28 November 1910, Kennet Papers.

78 **I don't know who** HB to May Bowers, 28 November 1910.

79 **wonderfully capable** *SLE*, 20 January 1911.

79 **was the last straw** HB to Emily Bowers, 7 December 1910.

79 **From the first I** Annotated journal [Sept–Oct 1910].

80 **May it never be** HB to Emily Bowers, 7 December 1910.

80 **In a quiet way** FD, *The Quiet Land*, p. 125.

80 fn. **to raise a mutiny . . . It seems incredible that** Marginalia, private collection.

82 **Dante tells us that** *WJ*, pp. 48–9.

82 **As I looked into** Raymond Priestley, 'The Polar Expedition as a Psychological Study', unpublished lecture transcript, July 1955.

82 **For sheer downright misery** *WJ*, p. 50.

83 **One scientist reverted to** Taylor, *With Scott*, p. 45.

83 **a halo of good** *WJ*, p. 318.

83 **Large iceberg ahead, sir** Herbert Ponting, *The Great White South*, 1921, p. 28.

83 **We are shaking down** Journal, 9 December 1910.

83 **One of the best** *ibid.*

83 **It was more than** *ibid.*, 10 December 1910.

84 **I have never thought** *ibid.*, 11 December 1910.

84 **to moon around with** *ibid.*, 15 December 1910.

84 **What an exasperating game** *SLE*, 18 December 1910.

85 **ignominiously called back . . . Felt a bit chippy** Journal, 21 December 1910.

85 **a general scrap . . . Titus dragged all Bill's** *ibid.*, 24 December 1910.

85 **the most Christmassy Christmas** *ibid.*, 25 December 1910.

85 **A most acceptable pair** Taylor, *With Scott*, p. 13.

85 **very pleasant but with** Thomas Griffith Taylor, Diary, 17 December 1910, in The Griffith Taylor Collection, ed. Wayne Hanley, unpublished, 1978.

85 **Cherry is very generous** HB to Emily Bowers, 23 August 1910.

85 **I do think in** FD, *The Quiet Land*, p. 37.

86 **Have you seen the . . . And there they were** *WJ*, p. 81.

86 **the very air permeated** HB to May Bowers, 1 January 1911.

86 **Our previous troubles seem** *ibid.*

86 **I have seen Fuji** *WJ*, p. 82.

87 **I made an awful** Journal, 4 January 1911.

87 **Many watched all night** *WJ*, p. 86.

87 **my private chapel** Seaver, *Wilson*, p. 213.

87 **These days are with** EW, *Diary*, 4 January 1911.

87 **There, if anywhere, is** Taylor, *With Scott*, p. 448.

87 **Antarctica reflects the mystery** Barry Lopez, 'The Gift of Good Land', *Antarctic Journal of the United States* XXVII, 2 (June 1992), p. 1.

Chapter 5: Out of the World

90 **It is wonderfully comfortable** Journal, 18 January 1911.

91 **This evening a variety** *ibid.*, 12 January 1911.

92 **ready for everything** RFS to RS, 1 February 1911.

92 **a second year has** ACG to AF, 19 January 1911, BRO.

92 **I am enjoying every** ACG to AF, 19 January 1911, BRO.

92 **I expect you are** ACG to AF, 2 January 1911, BRO.

92 **If we sat down** *WJ*, p. 107.

92 **We finally left camp** *ibid.*

92 fn. **It is a terrible** ECG to ACG, 14 May 1911, family collection.

93 **Every seal-hole was** *ibid.*, p. 110.

93 **As we came up** *ibid.*, p. 115.

93 **Cherry-Garrard is remarkable** SLE, 13 February 1911.

93 **It was surprising what** Evans, *South with Scott*, p. 75.

93 **He is excellent and** *SLE*, 19 February 1911.

94 **everybody as happy as** Journal, 19 February 1911.

94 **Cherry, you are going** *ibid.*, 20 February 1911.

94 **There is a pleasant air** *ibid.*, 21 February 1911.

94 **My companions today were** *SLE*, 21 February 1911.

94 **Up to this day** Annotated journal [February 1911].

95 **I never thought he . . . But above all and** *SLE*, 22 February 1911.

95 **The world will watch** Raymond Priestley, *Antarctic Adventure*, 1914, p. 40.

95 **For an hour or** *WJ*, p. 132.

95 **By Jove what a** Journal, 24 February 1911.

95 **Scott said we could . . . We had hours of** Annotated journal [February 1911].

96 **to go forward and** *SLE*, 22 February 1911.

96 **He said it was** Annotated journal [February 1911].

96 **Teddy a quitter** *Silas*, p. 117.

96 **almost in tears** Annotated journal [March 1911].

96 **a queer study – his** *SLE*, 5 May 1911 [1968 facsimile edition].

96 **He is the best** HB to Emily Bowers, 28 November 1910.

97 **He is a man** HB to Emily Bowers, [n.d.] July–August 1910.

97 **The tops of the . . . a dark streak of . . . Very little was said** HB, 'letter home' (copied out by his mother into an exercise book), n.d., pp. 32–5.

98 **utterly done. I remember** Journal, 1 March 1911.

98 **I suppose there is** *ibid*.

98 **It was not a . . . What about the ponies . . . I don't care a** HB, 'letter home', pp. 40–2.

98 **Between us and the** *WJ*, p. 158.

98 **This is the end** *ibid.*, p. 182.

98 **The others meanwhile, a** *SLE*, 3 March 1911.

98 **Scott was the man** Marginalia, private collection.

98 **Oh! Cherry, Cherry, why** Journal, 3 March 1911.

98 **The events of the** *SLE*, 2 March 1911.

99 **We spent . . . our evenings** *WJ*, p. 164.

99 **Perhaps this is not** *ibid*.

99 **Supper by candlelight in** *Silas*, p. 119.

100 **Bit by bit I** *SLE*, 17 March 1911.

100 **a very lazy and** Journal, 28 March 1911.

100 **contemporary to ten years** *Silas*, p. 120.

100 **Robinson Crusoe genius** E. R. G. R. Evans, 'My Recollections of a Gallant Comrade', *Strand Magazine*, December 1913.

100 **Those Hut Point days** *WJ*, p. 180.

100 **Today has been the** Journal, 23 April 1911.

101 **The sun rose for** *ibid*.

101 **regular hat racks** FD, *The Quiet Land*, p. 95.

101 **I feel very unsettled** Journal, 24 April 1911.

101 **Every morning now there** *ibid*., 25 April 1911.

102 **Wonder if any of** *Silas*, p. 170.

102 **showed merely a tourist's** Journal, 9 May 1911.

103 **Science – the rock foundation** *SLE*, 9 May 1911.

104 **It will be a** HB to KS, 27 October 1911, Kennet Papers.

104 **Scott took the British** Priestley, 'The Polar Expedition'.

104 **If we had a** Amundsen, p. 108.

104 **The fact of the** FD, *Antarctica: The Story of a Continent*, 1959, p. 183.

104 **He was eager to** *WJ*, p. 204.

105 **a subtle character, full** *ibid*., p. 205.

105 **nightmare** Draft material, *WJ*.

105 **Temperamentally . . . was a weak** *WJ*, p. 206.

105 **a lazy, posing fellow** *SLE*, 6 January 1911 [1968 facsimile edition].

105 **Meares hates exercise** *ibid*., 17 March 1911.

105 **cocksureness** *ibid*., 3 June 1911.

105 **a young man whose** *ibid*., 13 July 1911.

105 **there used to be . . . and the worst was** Noted by Caroline Oates, 28 April 1913, private collection.

105 **Captain Scott would be** Noted by Caroline Oates, 27 April 1913, private collection.

105 **not in the least** FD, *The Quiet Land*, p. 125.

106 **He is certainly a** George Simpson, Diary, 11 June 1911.

106 **I got badly ragged** Journal, 25 April 1911.

107 **Cape Crozier is a** EW, *National Antarctic Expedition 1901–1904: Natural History* II: *Zoology*, 1907, p. 31.

107 **The possibility that we** *ibid*.

107 **a bad needle about** Journal, 19 June 1911.

108 **a good bust out** *ibid*., 21 June 1911.

108 **O Blubber Lamp! O** *The South Polar Times* III (1911), Part I, facsimile edition, 1914.

108 **The funniest part now . . . it was very funny** Journal, 22 June 1911.

Chapter 6: Even with God

109 **on the weirdest bird's** *WJ*, p. 240.

109 **This winter travel is** *SLE*, 27 June 1911.

109 **a regular snorter** EW to Oriana Wilson, in Seaver, *Wilson*, p. 242.

109 **I was a fool** *WJ*, p. 241.

110 **must be sure not** Journal, 27 June 1911.

110 **It does not look** *ibid.*, 30 June 1911.

110 **They talk of chattering** *WJ*, p. 246.

110 **a mass of the** *ibid.*, p. 245.

111 **Generally we steered by** *WJ*, p. 245.

111 **a terrible day. I** Journal, 2 July 1911.

111 **it was difficult not . . . You've got it in** *WJ*, p. 247.

111 **The day lives in** *ibid.*, p. 253.

111 **I had to keep** EW, *Diary*, 4 July 1911.

111 **Bill had a tremendous** *WJ*, p. 255.

111 **Scott will never forgive . . . it is a principle** *WJ*, pp. 255–6.

111 **the temperature was down** ACG to ECG, 28 September 1911 & following days, private collection.

112 **or girls** *WJ*, p. 247.

112 **There is something after** Journal, 7 July 1911.

112 **If we had been** *WJ*, p. 259.

112 **My nerves were about** Journal, 14 July 1911.

112 **I for one had** *WJ*, p. 242.

112 **Do things slowly, always** *ibid.*, p. 246.

112 **Always patient, self-possessed** *ibid.*

113 **I think we are** *ibid.*

113 **I was quite sure** *ibid.*, p. 254.

113 **It is wonderful how** Journal, 15 July 1911.

113 **were a Sunday school** *WJ*, p. 259.

114 **After indescribable effort and** *ibid.*, p. 274.

114 **Cherry, you *must* learn** *ibid.*, p. 277.

114 **we were already beginning** *ibid.*, p. 278.

115 **I said my prayers** Journal, 3 August 1911. Cherry wrote up most of the Crozier journey on his return to the hut.

115 **I might have speculated . . . The road to Hell** *WJ*, p. 286.

115 **Yes, comfortable warm reader** *ibid.*, p. 287.

116 **Our lives had been** *ibid.*, p. 289.

116 **as if I should . . . I felt a brute** *ibid.*, p. 292.

116 **a masterpiece** George Simpson, in Seaver, *Bowers*, p. 209.

116 **He was up and** *WJ*, pp. 283–4.

116 **We're all right . . . Despite the fact that** *ibid.*, p. 284.

116 **I think he thought** HB, 'Account of Winter Journey, etc.', p. 11.

117 **The day's march was** *WJ*, p. 302.

117 **Antarctic exploration is seldom** *WJ*, p. 304.

117 **I saw self-sacrifice** *ibid.*, p. 302.

117 **In civilisation, men are** *ibid.*, p. 252.

117 **I think we reached** *ibid.*, p. 279.

117 **I was incapacitated for** EW, 'The Winter Journey to Cape Crozier', in *SLE* II, p. 42.

117 **few doubts and no** *WJ*, p. 214.

117 **He made life look** Introduction to Seaver, *Bowers*, p. xvi.

117 **Spread out well and** *WJ*, p. 304.

118 **By Jove! Here is** *ibid.*

118 **Cherry staggered in looking** Taylor, *With Scott*, p. 285.

118 **You know, this is** *WJ*, p. 311.

118 **I managed to keep . . . We slept ten thousand** *ibid.*

118 **We are looked upon** *ibid.*

118 **The result of this** *SLE*, 2 August 1911.

118 **I don't know . . . Probably Lashly would have** *WJ*, p. 239.

119 **his spirit never wavered** *SLE*, 2 August 1911.

119 **Wilson considers the journey** Tryggve Gran, *The Norwegian with Scott*, 1984, p. 114.

119 **We had attempted too** EW, 'The Winter Journey', in *SLE* II, p. 52.

119 **the response of the** This phrase appealed immensely to Cherry: it went to the heart of his beliefs. It was coined by Seaver in *The Faith of Edward Wilson*, 1948, p. 10.

119 **I'll swear there was** *WJ*, p. 302.

119 **a very eventful day** Gran, p. 111.

119 **Tempers are beginning to** FD, *The Quiet Land*, p. 117.

119 fn. **The marvellous part of** *ibid.*, p. 125.

120 **As I get more . . . Ever since we came** Journal, 10 August 1911.

120 **that really horrible** *ibid.*, 11 August 1911.

120 **We felt like boys** Ponting, p. 159.

120 **It seems very far** *SLE*, 18 August 1911.

120 **Poor Cherry perspired over** *SLE*, 10 September 1911.

120 **It's you or me** Annotated journal [April 1911].

120 **the cheerful and lovable** *WJ*, p. 222.

121 **I intended Oates to** *SLE*, 22 October 1911 [1968 facsimile edition].

121 **I personally don't see** LO to Caroline Oates, 23 November 1910.

121 **great string of rotten** in Seaver, *Wilson*, p. 263.

121 **He is spoken to** *ibid*.

121 **I dislike Scott intensely** LO to Caroline Oates, 24 October 1911.

121 **more than extra mouldy** Journal, 24 September 1911.

122 *to appeal to the* ACG to ECG, 28 September 1911 & following days, private collection.

122 **worried and unhappy** *WJ*, p. 319.

123 **I can't say I** William Lashly, Diary ('Southern Journey, Motors'), 1 November 1911.

123 **It reminded me of** *SLE*, 2 November 1911.

123 **At the back of** *WJ*, pp. 331–2.

123 **My personal impression of** *ibid.*, p. 333.

124 **it was about as** HB, Diary, 13 November 1911.

124 **a prolonged Council of . . . serio-comic** *WJ*, p. 338.

124 **I go all the** Journal, 29 November 1911.

125 **touch and go** *SLE*, 23 November 1911.

125 **Gallant little Michael** Journal, 4 December 1911.

125 **Oh! but this is** *SLE*, 6 December 1911.

126 **a perfect piece of** EW, *Diary*, 8 December 1911.

126 **This morning was just** Journal, 17 December 1911.

127 **though both put their** *SLE*, 14 December 1911.

127 **I had expected failure** *SLE*, 11 December 1911 [1968 facsimile edition].

127 **and a better march** Journal, 18 December 1911.

127 **but things being close** *ibid*.

127 **I'm afraid I have . . . No, no, no. At** Journal, 20 December 1911.

127 **the best man in** Clements Markham, *Antarctic Obsession*, Huntingdon, 1986, p. 96.

127 fn. **Wilson wrote that I** Marginalia, private collection.

128 **Please write to Mrs** EW to Oriana Wilson, 21 December 1911, in Seaver, *Wilson*, p. 275.

128 **He is the most** RFS to RS, in *WJ*, pp. lxiv–lxv.

128 **mournful air** Journal, 21 December 1911.

128 **pulling his guts out** *ibid*.

128 **Scott has only to** *ibid.*, 22 December 1911.

128 **With the depôt which** RFS to EA, in *WJ*, p. 426.

128 **Had a hell of** Pat Keohane, Diary, 22 December 1911.

128 **puddingy** Journal, 22 December 1911.

128 **a good whack of** *ibid.*, 24 December 1911.

128 **Had a bad bellyake** Keohane, Diary, 25 December 1911.

128 **I will take on** ACG to EW, 28 December 1911.

129 **I watched my companions** Postscript, p. 588.

129 **My birthday, and given** Journal, 2 January 1912.

129 **Within a yard of** *Silas*, p. 235.

129 **As I lay in** Keohane, Diary, 13 January 1912.

129 **I miss you horribly** ECG to ACG, 23 July 1911, family collection.

129 **I thought as I** ECG to ACG, 28 May 1911, family collection.

130 **absolutely bewildering. England seems** Journal, 3 February 1912.

130 **the rumblings of the** Postscript, p. 599.

130 **Personally I hope it** Harry Woollcombe to ACG, 18 October 1911.

130 **Scott a fool . . . Too** *Silas*, p. 221.

131 **as big as Regent** Evans, *South with Scott*, p. 198.

131 **I think the British** HB to Emily Bowers, 3 January 1912.

132 **too great a sacrifice** Evans, *South with Scott*, p. 208.

132 **he is turning black** *The Diary of William Lashly*, Reading, 1940, p. 21.

132 **I kissed his old** Evans, *South with Scott*, p. 225.

132 **How funny we should** *Lashly*, p. 37.

132 **I'm right in it** Journal, 24 February 1912.

132 fn. **as it would not** RFS to Joseph Kinsey, 28 October 1911, Alexander Turnbull Library, Wellington.

133 **It did not cross Cherry's mind to disobey those orders** After Cherry died, Deb wrote in his obituary in *Polar Record* X, 64 (1960, p. 93) that the fact that he disobeyed orders weighed on his mind for the rest of his life. (Deb did not mention this in his other, fuller obituary in *The Times*.) This inaccurate statement reflects the muddled understanding of Scott's orders on the expedition, and the lack of awareness over the changes Scott made on the march. Cherry did not think that he had disobeyed orders, and he had not. What weighed on him was the thought that he might have taken another decision at One Ton and pressed on in the blizzard. Deb was presumably referring to Scott's order to 'take the dogs as far as you can'; but this had been superseded by Atch's order on no account to risk the dogs.

Deb appeared to confirm that his friend was in no way guilty of disobeying orders in his *Times* obituary (19 May 1959) which refers to Cherry's depression in later years and his 'needlessly uneasy conscience about the part he played'.

133 **I had no reason** *WJ*, p. 434.

134 **We hope against hope** SLE, 7 March 1912.

134 **Dear Sir, We leave** ACG to RFS, 16 March 1912.

134 **Lately I have felt** Journal, 14 March 1912.

134 **Cherry-Garrard under the . . . Both men were in** EA, 'The Last Year at Cape Evans', in *SLE* II, p. 306.

134 fn. **It's a miserable jumble** *SLE*, 10 March 1912 [1968 facsimile edition].

134 fn. **At last we have** Ernest Joyce, Diary, 26 October 1915, Alexander Turnbull Library, Wellington.

135 **If the depôt had** GBS to ACG, 18 November 1948 (notes inserted in Journal).

Chapter 7: It is the Tent

136 **Is is sad that** Journal, 17 March 1912.

136 **hardly cared what happened** *ibid.*, 21–2 March 1912.

136 **What castles one builds** *SLE*, 5 January 1912.

137 **Atch and I look** Journal, 25 March 1912.

137 **Hullo! Cherry, they're in . . . Who's cook** *ibid.*, 26 March 1912.

137 **hope sprang up anew** *WJ*, p. 442.

137 **morally certain that the** EA, 'The Last Year', in *SLE* II, p. 309.

137 **I think I have** Journal, 2 April 1912.

137 **more or less an** *ibid.*, 1 May 1912.

138 **a garbled, disloyal account** *ibid.*, 3 April 1912.

138 **Evans has been the** ACG to RS, 15 July 1912.

139 **This winter is passing** Keohane, Diary, 21 July 1912.

139 **We usually wear our** Thomas Williamson, Diary, 11 July 1912.

139 **It is of some** Journal, 17 August 1912.

139 **that has been one** *ibid.*, 7 July 1912.

140 **Cherry was his usual** *Silas*, p. 300.

140 **a ghastly experience** *WJ*, p. 470.

140 **The scenery has lost** FD, *The Quiet Land*, p. 143.

140 **top dog** Journal, 9 September 1912.

140 **God knows I have** *ibid.*, 10 September 1912.

140 **It is all I . . . There is not a . . . And when we got** *ibid.*, 4 October 1912.

141 **others sit round the** *ibid.*

141 **forgetfulness of self** Postscript, p. 603.

142 **A vague kind of** *WJ*, p. 497.

142 **It is the tent** *ibid.*

142 **like old alabaster** The image is from Thomas Williamson's diary, 12 November 1912.

142 **That scene can never** *WJ*, p. 497.

142 **It was something breaking** Tryggve Gran, in *Scott's Last Journey*, BBC 2, 19 March 1972.

143 **All the day-dreams** *SLE*, 16 January 1912.

143 **It was a very** EW, *Diary*, 17 January 1912.

143 **our poor slighted Union** *SLE*, 18 January 1912.

143 **We are going like** Roald Amundsen, 'Sledging Diary', 8 November 1911, Oslo, trans. Roland Huntford.

143 **rather dull and incapable** *SLE*, 4 February 1912.

144 **We are in a** *ibid.*, 2 March 1912.

144 **living among the fleshpots** Amundsen, 'Sledging Diary', 7 January 1912, Oslo, trans. Roland Huntford.

144 **I am just going . . . Should this be found . . . and though we constantly** *SLE*, 16 or 17 March 1912.

144 **amputation is the least** *ibid.*, 19 March 1912.

144 **For God's sake look** *ibid.*, 'Last entry'.

144 **Death has no terrors** EW to E. T. Wilson and Mary Wilson, 21 or 22 March 1912.

144 **all is for the** EW to Oriana Wilson, 21 or 22 March 1912, in Seaver, *Wilson*, p. 293.

144 **Your ever loving Son** HB to Emily Bowers, n.d.

145 **He was one of** *WJ*, pp. 213–14

145 **How cold are your** *ibid.*, p. 298.

145 **We are weak, writing** *SLE*, 'Message to the Public', n.d.

145 **The Lord giveth and** *WJ*, p. 499.

145 **I do not know** *ibid.*

145 **They died having done** Huxley, p. 257.

146 **I for one shall . . . The question of what** Journal, 12–13 November 1912.

146 **Subsequent climate data reveals** Until recently little was known of the weather deep in the Barrier. But in the early 1980s American researchers positioned automatic weather stations at sites near Scott's route. Susan Solomon, a leading atmospheric scientist, analysed information yielded by these stations. She concluded that Simpson's prediction that in an average season Scott would have experienced temperatures of about minus 20 on his march back was correct – but 1912 was no average year out on the Barrier. Only one other year in the century was as cold. Scott was, in this respect, exceptionally unlucky. Solomon sets out her results in *The Coldest March* (New

Haven, 2001), and in her scholarly monograph, co-written with Charles R. Stearns, 'On the Role of the Weather in the Deaths of R. F. Scott and his Companions', *Proceedings of the National Academy of Sciences* (November 1999), pp. 13012–16.

146 **We were always careful** Journal, 12–13 November 1912.

146 **Hereabouts died a very** *ibid.*, 15 November 1912.

146 **his face transformed** EA, 'The Last Year', in *SLE* II, p. 349.

146 **It is the happiest** Journal, 26 November 1912.

147 **The road to hell** George Murray Levick, in *WJ*, p. xlv.

147 **Hope I have set** *Silas*, p. 355.

147 **a terrible fit of** Journal, 28 November 1912.

147 **Truly Shackleton's expedition must** *ibid.*, 5 December 1912.

148 **more like a steeplechase** *ibid.*, 25 December 1912.

149 **Are you all well . . . The Polar Party died** *WJ*, p. 584.

149 **The pleasant memories are** Journal, 19 January 1913.

149 **The last year has** *ibid.*, 18 January 1913.

149 **I do not believe** *ibid.*, 22 January 1913.

150 **I should like to . . . I wonder if all . . . It's fairly sickening and** *ibid.*, 26 January 1913.

150 **One started with such** *ibid.*, 3 February 1913.

151 **It seems to me . . . Their *biggest* day's march** E. R. G. R. Evans to Ralph, Silvia & Lal Gifford, 6 February 1913, private collection.

151 **Why should I be** Reginald Pound, *Evans of the Broke,* 1963, p. 157.

151 **I consider him to . . . I see he is** Journal, 25 January 1913.

151 **With what mixed feelings** *WJ*, p. 592.

151 **Come down here a . . . It's made a tremendous** *WJ*, p. 593.

152 **capable of maintaining the . . . moral and spiritual** *The Times*, 12 February 1913.

152 **She is as fine** Journal, 13 February 1913.

153 **I believe I am** *ibid.*

153 **the old, old story . . . quite hysterical . . . all that could be** *ibid.*, 14 February 1913.

153 **tapped** *The Times*, 12 February 1913.

153 **that relations between the** *Sydney Morning Herald*, 14 February 1913.

153 **All these questions and** Draft material, *WJ*.

153 **Do not worry about** ACG to ECG, 15 February 1913.

153 **congratulations . . . Longing to get you** ECG to ACG, 15 February 1913.

153 **All kinds of wild . . . I don't know that . . . Oh! She is**

wonderful . . . Beautiful table, good dinner Journal, 15 February 1913.

154 **It seems to be** Journal, 20 February 1913.

154 **a horrid day. Everybody** *ibid.*, 21 February 1913.

154 **He looks just a** Lilian Burton to ECG, 18 February 1913.

155 **It is a horrid** Journal, 3 March 1913.

155 **I know how splendidly** *ibid.*, 9 March 1913.

155 **You will pull the** RFS to Joseph Kinsey, 24 March 1912 (Kinsey photographed the letter. The print he gave Cherry is inserted in Cherry's journal).

155 **damned disgusted . . . that the men who** FD to ACG, 3 March 1913 (inserted in Journal).

Chapter 8: Kipling in Real Life

158 **Sometimes you seem a** Emily Bowers to ACG, 9 July 1913.

159 **Oh, he was just** Noted by Caroline Oates, 26 June 1913, private collection.

159 **disgusted with the way** *ibid.*, 27 April 1913.

160 **It is very undesirable** Francis Drake to ACG, 24 June 1913.

160 **Reginald Smith comes to** KS, Diary, 10 October 1913, Kennet Papers.

160 **gorgeous** RS to ACG, 12 June 1913.

160 **How stupid that minor** Grace Scott to ACG, 18 July 1922.

160 **The frosty reaction of the museum staff** Was Cherry unfair in his attack on the museum? Perhaps. After all, he did not have an appointment.

161 **neither has added greatly** C. W. Parsons, *British Antarctic ('Terra Nova') Expedition, 1910: Natural History Reports* IV: *Zoology*, 1935, p. 260.

161 **There is courage and** *Punch*, 12 November 1913.

161 **quite the nicest thing** ACG to AF, 21 July 1914, Hertford.

161 **They would not listen** Annotated journal [January 1913].

162 **The committee meant to** *ibid.*

163 **I feel how happy** Oriana Wilson to ACG, 8 July 1913.

164 **Lady Scott's possessive instinct** Annotated journal [October 1911].

166 **Dear Mr Garrad** H. G. Lyons to ACG, 15 February 1914.

167 **Among all the heroes** *The Times*, 24 February 1914.

167 **The country is in** ACG to AF, 31 March 1914, BRO.

168 **eye goggles, sledge, tapered . . . Find out the cause . . .** ACG, 'Notebook of suggestions for the official history'.

168 **Get details of acetylene . . . Plentiful supply of nails** *ibid.*

168 **I have missed you** EA to ACG, 23 May 1914.

169 **She asked me to** *ibid.*

169 **Some day you will** EA to ACG, [n.d.] May 1914.

170 **We never used snowshoes** ACG to Albert Hodge, 13 July 1914.

170 **I cannot read or** *Punch*, 29 July 1914.

170 **This is an interesting** *South Polar Times* III, Part II.

171 **I can say quite** ACG to Rudyard Kipling, 22 December 1913, the Kipling Collection, Wimpole Hall, Cambridgeshire. I am grateful to Andrew Lycett and George Potirakis for this information.

171 **My income seems to** ACG to AF, 21 July 1914, BRO.

172 **Now, God be thanked** Rupert Brooke, '1914', 1914.

172 **an awful wild goose . . . We might have as** ACG to AF, 23 August 1914, BRO.

173 **Here I am living . . . They are a splendid** ACG to AF, 23 September 1914, BRO.

173 **I am not sure** ACG to AF, n.d., BRO.

174 **The one thing which** *ibid.*

175 **They called it an** Josiah Wedgwood, *Essays and Adventures of a Labour MP*, 1924, p. 203.

175 **We shall be ready** ACG to AF, 16 December 1914, Hertford.

175 **this damn peninsula** Peter Ashton to ACG, 30 August 1915.

176 fn. **the stereotyped respectability of** Draft material, *WJ*.

177 **Tell them I die** *The Times*, 13 July 1915.

177 **the first mechanised cavalry** Josiah Wedgwood, *Memoirs of a Fighting Life*, 1941, p. 93.

177 **in trench warfare and** General de Lisle, Report to Admiralty, 27 May 1915, PRO.

177 **Thus at the very** Winston Churchill, Report to President of Royal Commission on War Inventions, September 1919, PRO.

178 **Remember the *Lusitania*** Pound, p. 154.

179 **At the end of June 1915** For further information on the demonstration at Wormwood Scrubbs, and on how the tank developed within the RNAS, *see* Rear-Admiral Sir Murray Sueter, *The Evolution of the Tank*, 1941 (revised edition).

179 **a pretty mechanical toy** Lord Kitchener, in Sueter, p. 91.

180 **contracted in his expedition** Admiralty service record, PRO.

180 **Before I had recovered** *WJ*, p. liii.

Chapter 9: The War had Won

182 **We all feel we** Ponting, p. 298.

182 **The war from a** Henry Pennell to ACG, 17 December 1915.

183 **We have had some** E. Snelling to ACG, 6 June 1916.

183 **I very much miss** A. L. Dykes to ACG, 17 September 1915.

184 **The intimate mental history** Siegfried Sassoon, *Memoirs of a Fox-hunting Man*, 1928, p. 335.

184 **Look here old chap . . . Please forgive any interference** EA to ACG, 1 February 1916.

184 **The public have not** EA to ACG, 1 January 1916.

184 **the constant poisoning from** ACG to AF, 11 March 1916, BRO.

184 **I don't think there** ACG to AF, 25 March 1916, BRO.

184 **I have written to** ACG to AF, 18 April 1916, Hertford.

185 **I am very gradually** ACG to AF, 12 June 1916, BRO.

185 **I shall be most** ACG to Sidney Harmer, 12 May 1916.

186 **that it is an . . . one example only. I** *ibid.*

186 **I don't want to** RFS to ES, 18 February 1907.

186 **I wish to God** EW to ES, n.d.

186 **Do you think he** ACG to KS, 8 July 1914.

187 **Darkness settled on six** Frank Worsley, *Shackleton's Boat Journey*, 1999, p. 161.

187 **Emerged from a war** Frank Hurley, *Argonauts of the South*, 1925, p. 290.

187 **We've had a hot** Tom Crean to ACG, 21 September 1917.

187 **desperate venture** Draft material, *WJ*.

187 **For a joint scientific** *WJ*, Preface [omitted from 1994 edition].

188 **When you have a** Draft material, *WJ*.

189 **neither race had won** Edmund Blunden, *The Mind's Eye*, 1934, p. 38.

189 **had met direction that** Introduction to *Keeling: Letters & Recollections*, ed. 'ET', 1918, p. xiii.

189 **Talk of ex-soldiers: give** *WJ*, Preface [omitted from 1994 edition].

189 **as a dumping ground** ACG to AF, 28 April 1916, BRO.

190 **stood still for about . . . so vivid that I** ACG to AF, 2 October 1916, BRO.

190 **a village where nobody** *Bernard Shaw's Letters to Siegfried Trebitsch*, ed. Samuel A. Weiss, Stanford, 1980, p. 243.

192 **It is right out** ACG to AF, 8 October 1916, Hertford.

193 **for I diagnose** KS, Diary, 28 December 1916, Kennet Papers.

193 **I want to say** EW to RS and Isabel Smith, 21 or 22 March 1912, in Seaver, *Wilson*, p. 293.

194 **We saw Mrs Wilson** KS, Diary, 29 December 1916, Kennet Papers.

194 **It's much better fun** ACG to Christabel McLaren, 30 March 1921, BL.

194 **He was he says** KS, Diary, 26 April 1917, Kennet Papers.

194 **most intimate and cordial** KS, Diary, 30 June 1917, Kennet Papers.

195 **the nearest I ever** Young, p. 175.

195 **He is coming on** KS, Diary, 10 June 1918, Kennet Papers.

196 **a regular domestic institution** GBS to Lillah McCarthy, 2 September 1917, in *BSCL III*, p. 503.

196 **If you happen to** Harley Granville Barker to ACG, 16 May 1917.

196 fn. **The two most brilliant** *Granville Barker and His Correspondents*, ed. Eric Salmon, Detroit, 1986, p. 9.

197 **I should love to** Denis Lillie to ACG, 7 July 1916.

197 **It was only my** Denis Lillie to ACG, 23 August 1916.

197 **examining military shit for** *ibid*.

197 **When I see a** Tryggve Gran to G. Evelyn Hutchinson, n.d. (*circa* July 1968).

197 **no nice cliffs or** Denis Lillie to ACG, 7 December 1916.

197 **being unconventional and as** Denis Lillie to ACG, 10 June 1917.

197 **if a motor does** Denis Lillie to ACG, 15 August 1917.

198 **I do hope your** Denis Lillie to ACG, n.d.

198 **Clean all boots in** Draft material, *WJ*.

198 **Lashly . . . sent him his field notes** Like most field diaries, Lashly's polar notebook consisted of brief notes written in extremely trying circumstances. When Cherry asked if he could meet him 'to have a yarn' (ACG to Lashly, 5 May 1916), Lashly was unable to get leave, so he copied the notebook out and probably at this point expanded his field jottings into the fuller account that Cherry duly had typed. The two versions of the diary do not differ in substance or interpretation. It is the fuller account that appears in *The Worst Journey*, and was later reprinted by the University of Reading in a limited edition with Lashly's co-operation (*The Diary of William Lashly*, Reading, 1940). 'It is the truth,' Lashly wrote when discussing the Reading edition (Lashly to Robert Gibbings, 4 October 1938). The original, much briefer version was partially reproduced in *Under Scott's Command: Lashly's Antarctic Diaries*, ed. A. R. Ellis, 1969. It was standard practice to expand field notes into a fuller diary when time allowed. Both versions of Keohane's diary, for example, can be read at SPRI.

198 **I know you would** William Lashly to ACG, 2 September 1916.

198 **very ordinary, middle-class** KS to ACG, n.d.

198 **I have seen Lyons** FD to ACG, 20 December 1918.

199 **I see no end** ACG to Emily Bowers, 14 December 1917.

199 **If it be admitted . . . If it is to** ACG to Canon Nance, 8 March 1918.

200 **At the same time . . . I have neither their** *ibid.*

200 **And now God go** Sassoon, *Memoirs*, p. 333.

201 **How amazing. How could** KS, Diary, 21 October 1917, Kennet Papers.

201 **a slight waning in** *ibid.*, 9 January 1918.

201 **If you have a** Denis Lillie to ACG, 28 May 1918.

201 **visiting is contra-indicated . . . frequently relapsing** Bethlem Royal Hospital to ACG, 3 August 1918.

201 **it was an incurable** FD to Angela Mathias, [n.d.] September 1959, family collection.

202 **I think it is** KS, Diary, 30 June 1918, Kennet Papers.

202 **I think you may** EA to ACG, 17 November 1918.

202 **disobeyed orders** *ibid.*, and elsewhere.

202 **My mind groped in** Vera Brittain, *Testament of Youth*, 1933, pp. 470–1.

Chapter 10: The Most Wonderful Story in the World

203 **Though the old forms** McKenna, p. 12.

203 **waking from dreams** Rudyard Kipling, *A Book of Words*, 1928, p. 217.

203 **The country cannot tax** ACG to AF, 22 May 1917, Hertford.

204 **grey hollowed (or hallowed)** Paul Nash to Mercia Oakley, 23 September 1911, Tate Gallery Archive.

204 **part of the early forest** Paul Nash, *Outline, An Autobiography & Other Writings*, 1949, p. 122.

204 **approaches completion** ACG to H. G. Lyons, [n.d.] January 1919.

205 **as a completed work** ACG to H. G. Lyons, 25 September 1919.

205 **The refusal of my** ACG to H. G. Lyons, 13 November 1919.

205 **Am I to understand** H. G. Lyons to ACG, 17 November 1919.

205 **My dear Lyons** ACG to H. G. Lyons, 22 November 1919.

205 **I want it read** ACG to H. G. Lyons, 2 December 1919.

206 **Teddy Evans is probably . . . He comes out of** ACG to EA, [n.d.] April 1919.

206 **the right-hand man** Sir Eric Geddes, *The Times*, 6 December 1919.

206 **in the hope of . . . without in any way . . . unfortunately** *The Times*, 11 December 1919.

206 **Bill used to say** Oriana Wilson to ACG, 26 December 1919.

207 **I don't like the** E. R. G. R. Evans to ACG, 12 January 1922.

207 **You are now utterly** KS to ACG, 24 November 1919.

207 **Unfortunately I could not . . . any catharsis of the** *WJ*, pp. lii–liii.

207 **In a most ruthless** Draft material, *WJ*.

208 **Good literary criticism has** ACG to EA, [n.d.] April 1919.

208 **What is pack** *WJ*, p. 59.

208 **Charlotte told him he** GBS to Lord Kennet, 21 February 1948, Kennet Papers.

208 **I said to Cherry** GBS to KS, 23 March 1923, in *BSCL III*, p. 816.

208 **It would be fatal** GBS to ACG, 26 April 1922, in *ibid.*, p. 768.

210 **Some centuries ago, it . . . Now I know why . . . Darkness is coming on** *Nation*, 13 December 1919.

210 **make the atrocities of . . . The penguin has won** *The Times*, 4 April 1919.

210 **Otherwise the penguins will** *Spectator*, 26 April 1919.

210 **There are some Huns** *The Times*, 29 December 1919.

211 **Wells** Two letters from the Cherry-Garrard–Wells correspondence have survived and can be seen at the University of Illinois Library at Urbana-Champaign.

211 **considerable success . . . Fetch one of these** *The Times*, 10 October 1919.

212 **Is it Really Christ** *Graphic*, 14 February 1920.

212 **All the Christs in** *ibid.*, 20 March 1920.

212 **My natural kindness of** ACG to KS (draft), 3 February 1919.

213 **two unforgettable days** Fridtjof Nansen, inscribed in a copy of *Farthest North* presented to ACG, family collection.

214 **Ortobiogriffie** Thomas Griffith Taylor to ACG, 17 November 1917.

214 **a true glimpse into** *WJ*, p. 1.

214 **If you think your** *ibid.*, pp. l–li.

215 **Why do men who . . . the bondage of possessions . . . the Polar Party stands . . . mystical and invisible something . . . Have you ever starved** Draft material, *WJ*.

216 **we are in guess . . . We shall visit the** *ibid.*

216 **Even now, the Antarctic** *WJ*, p. vii.

216 **It is hard that** *ibid.*, p. 252.

217 **Yet time will slowly** Draft material, *WJ*.

217 **People talk of the** *WJ*, p. 567.

218 **And I tell you** *ibid.*, pp. 597–8.

218 **Naturally so peevish, highly** *ibid.*, p. 206.

219 **We *must* admire them** *ibid.*, p. 584.

219 **So much of the** *ibid.*, p. 232.

219 **You know, this is** *ibid.*, p. 311.

219 **A favourite pastime was** *ibid.*, p. 168.

219 **But they also had** *ibid.*, p. xlvii.

220 **A Glorious Narrative** *Daily News*, 4 December 1922.

220 **the man of taste** *Nation*, 2 December 1922.

220 **I should call the** *Evening Standard*, 6 December 1922.

220 **The real value of** *Nature*, 24 March 1923.

220 **It would be more** *Bookman*, 19 July 1923.

220 **I'm having the time** ACG to Otto Kyllmann, 8 December 1922, Temple.

220 **Galsworthy has gone cracked** ACG to Otto Kyllmann, 2 January 1923, Temple.

221 **slipshod thinking** *Manchester Guardian*, 11 December 1922.

221 **if the personal element** *The Times*, 5 December 1922.

221 **He has criticised Con** KS, Diary, 7 December 1922, Kennet Papers.

221 **with very grateful thanks . . . Rots** Private collection.

221 **Keep this for a . . . always a case of** GBS to KS, 23 March 1923, in *BSCL III*, p. 815.

221 **I have never admired** Young, p. 214.

222 **The other day Cherry** GBS to KS, 6 April 1923, in *BSCL III*, p. 816.

222 **weak . . . peevish** *WJ*, p. 206.

222 **This ain't an egg** *ibid.*, p. 305.

222 **We did not forget** *ibid.*, p. 302.

222 **the story seems devoid** *Daily News*, 5 December 1922.

222 **the manners of the** *ibid.*, 6 December 1922.

222 **has exceeded all expectations** GBS to KS, 23 March 1923, in *BSCL III*, p. 815.

222 **The book does seem** ACG to Emery Walker, 10 April 1923, Texas.

223 **This post-war business . . . an age of geological . . . At an advanced age** *WJ*, Preface [omitted from 1994 edition].

Chapter 11: The Chaos which Threatens

224 **I suppose many of . . . exactly the opposite to** Stephen Roskill to AM, [n.d.] 1970, family collection.

225 **rivals our politicians in** *WJ*, p. 223.

225 **the spirit of divest** Nancy Mitford, 'The English Aristocracy', *Encounter*, September 1955.

225 **Do not think I** AF to ACG, 20 March 1924, Hertford.

225 **I have always admired** ACG to AF, 23 March 1924, Hertford.

225 **The country estate in** ACG to AF, 3 July 1924, Hertford.

225 **My mother and I** ACG to AF, 23 August 1924, Hertford.

226 **My bowels refused to** GBS to ACG, 8 October 1923, Texas.

226 **We must compare damages** GBS to ACG, 26 September 1923, Texas.

226 **My famous neighbour Mr** Allan Chappelow, ed., *Shaw the Villager and Human Being*, 1961, p. 177.

226 **I was ulcerating somewhere** GBS to ACG, 1 May 1926, Texas.

228 **going strong for the** Colonel E. F. Norton, despatch sent from Everest, 11 June 1924, published in *The Times*, 26 June 1924.

228 **the ascent by which** The Rt Rev. Henry Luke Paget, A.D., Lord Bishop of Chester, *The Alpine Journal* XXXVI, 229 (November 1924), p. 275.

228 **The real value is** *The Times*, 12 February 1913.

228 **In a way he . . . Mallory was burning with** Introduction to Seaver, *Wilson*, p. xvii.

228 **When an airship can** *et seq. Daily News*, 26 June 1926.

230 **Legally I believe I** ACG to George Seabrook, 12 May 1923, Hertford.

230 **slight patches . . . severe patches . . . very severe patches** Farrer & Co. legal papers, March 1925, Hertford.

231 **No man is greater** Draft material, *WJ*.

231 **Was it hurt pride** *WJ*, p. lxxvi.

233 **backed out of the race . . . a half and half** T. E. Lawrence to CS, 17 June 1926, in *The Letters of T. E. Lawrence*, ed. Malcolm Brown, Oxford, 1991, p. 303.

233 **one of the great** T. E. Lawrence to ACG, 4 April 1927, private collection.

233 **It has an astonishing** T. E. Lawrence to ACG, 11 April 1929, private collection; copy in BL.

233 **A. C-G. from T. E. Shaw** 1 December 1926, private collection.

233 **Do tell me that** T. E. Lawrence to ACG, 4 April 1927, private collection.

233 **If our sexes had** *ibid.*

233 **He's such a liar** AM, conversation with author.

234 **Experiences such as Lawrence . . . To go through a . . . some . . . Having been knocked about . . . In the long run** A. W. Lawrence, ed., *T. E. Lawrence by his Friends*, 1936, pp. 191–2.

234 **It was perhaps the** *WJ*, Jacket, 1929 edition.

234 **He is a man** *Literary Digest International Book Review*, March 1923.

235 **one of the finest** *New York Times*, 20 June 1930.

235 **one of the most** *Bookman*, August 1930.

235 **remarkable descriptive powers . . . Where shall the like** *New York Times Book Review*, 11 May 1930.

235 **very splendid** *New York World*, 11 May 1930.

236 **cared nothing about being . . . Why English writers should** *ibid.*

236 **fine, thrilling . . . long been** *Saturday Review of Literature*, 21 June 1930.

236 **our greatest practising literary** Jeffrey Meyers, *Edmund Wilson: A Biography*, Boston, 1995, p. 76.

236 **is very well written . . . The thing that takes** *American Mercury* XXI (1930), p. 123.

236 **They seem difficult people** ACG to Harold Raymond, 18 January 1938, Reading University.

237 **I don't want to** ACG to Allen Lane, 24 July 1950, Bristol.

237 **one big, uneasy refugee** Rudyard Kipling to André Chevrillon, 31 December 1921, Sussex University Library.

237 **Bow wow** *et seq.* W. L. G. Joerg, *The Work of the Byrd Antarctic Expedition 1928–1930*, New York, 1930; marginalia in ACG's copy, Mitchell Library, State Library of New South Wales.

237 **Exploring the many boxes** FD, *The Quiet Land*, p. 178.

237 **The most minor member** FD to ACG, 30 May 1920.

238 **How they bring it** Introduction to Seaver, *Wilson*, p. xxii.

238 **All is not lost** Family collection.

238 fn. **Though I called the** FD to AM (then Cherry-Garrard), [n.d.] September 1959, family collection.

239 **His voice has been** *WJ*, Preface to 1937 edition, pp. xi–xix.

239 **not of the usual** Oriana Wilson to ACG, 15 January 1929.

239 **I sympathise with you** George Seaver to ACG, 1 February 1929.

240 **those post-war productions** Introduction to *WJ*, p. lxix.

240 **finally starved . . . lack of vitamins** Seaver, quoting ACG, *ibid.*, p. lxxi.

240 **I often wonder whether . . . But surely you are . . . Am I? I wonder** *ibid.*, pp. lxxi–ii.

240 **But he was. The** George Seaver to AM (then Cherry-Garrard), 19 May 1959, family collection.

240 **The doctor says the** GBS to ACG, 6 May 1930, Texas.

241 **Here Ayot's deaders/Into** Note by ACG, n.d., family collection.

241 **While elsewhere I might** ACG to George Seaver, Christmas card, 1950.

241 **Young Cherry-Garrard soon** *Bernard Shaw's Rhyming Picture Guide to Ayot St Lawrence*, Luton, 1950, p. 31.

242 **I will freeze in** ACG to Francis Drake, 25 November 1930.

242 **A wasted afternoon** ACG to Francis Drake, 11 December 1930.

242 **ruined . . . has become a semi** *et seq.* Beatrice Webb, Diary XLVI, 4 May 1932, LSE.

243 **I'm tired of these** E. M. Forster, *Howards End*, 1910, p. 58.

243 **ideals have been smashed . . . the chaos which threatens . . . What they did has** Introduction to Seaver, *Wilson*, pp. xi–xix.

243 **There were moments when** FD, *The Quiet Land*, p. 188.

243 fn. **For a well-read** Norman MacKenzie, Introduction to *Index to the Diary of Beatrice Webb, 1873–1943*, Cambridge, 1978.

244 **Scott was playing about** Marginalia, private collection.

244 **Scott was obsessed** Annotated journal [December 1911].

244 **WJ** *See*, for example, Louis Bernacchi's biography of Oates, *A Very Gallant Gentleman*, 1933, family collection.

244 **It was just what** George Simpson to ACG, in Annotated journal [spring 1912].

245 **Bowers and I were** Annotated journal [December 1911–January 1912].

245 **The success of the** *Sunday Graphic*, 31 July 1932.

Chapter 12: Danced with AC-G

247 **Will be with you** FD, *The Quiet Land*, p. 187.

247 **Do you know that** Herbert Ponting to George Seaver, 12 October 1933.

247 **is the most beautiful . . . has enabled the world . . . Here in**

these pictures *Geographical Journal* LXXXV (January–June 1935), p. 391.

248 **author and explorer** 'Candidate for Election' form, The Athenaeum.

249 **War is out of** *WJ*, Preface to 1937 edition, p. xii.

249 **I hope you will** Harold Raymond to ACG, 9 April 1937, Reading University.

250 **The steady cheapening of** Harold Raymond to Allen Lane, 1 November 1934, Bristol.

250 **a wonderful bit of** ACG to Eunice Frost, 27 September 1937, Bristol.

250 **Dear Sir** Correspondence in Bristol.

250 fn. **Even more important than** Eunice Frost to Henry Paroissien, 29 April 1955, Bristol.

251 **Danced with AC-G** AM (then Turner), Diary, 13 August 1937, family collection.

252 **We always move in** *and all other direct speech* AM, conversation with author.

253 **It sometimes seems that** Draft material, *WJ*.

254 **It is the only** *The Times*, 18 November 1937.

254 **will settle everything – and** *et seq*. Introduction to Seaver, *Bowers*, pp. xi–xxi.

255 **The people now living** Forster, *Two Cheers*, p. 70.

255 **There was a wrong spirit** Unpublished collection of villagers' memories, recorded by Daphne Grierson, n.d., Chapter 9, p. 5, private collection.

256 **She *dinks* into church** Private conversation with author.

257 **Things look very dark** KS (then Young), Diary, 28 September 1938, Kennet Papers.

258 **BLUE SKIES, BLUEBELLS, BLUE** AM, conversation with author.

258 **how things turn out** ACG to Harold Raymond, 4 May 1939, Reading University.

258 **if these blasted and** ACG to Harold Raymond, 13 July 1939, Reading University.

259 **We were so thankful** *WJ*, p. 289.

262 **if there are no** ACG to Harold Raymond, 2 August 1939, Reading University.

262 **One can't exactly say** Harold Raymond to ACG, 13 October 1939, Reading University.

262 **If a manufacturer is** Harold Raymond to William Maxwell, 1 November 1939, Reading University.

263 **I do not think** ACG to Eunice Frost, 17 June 1939, Bristol.

Chapter 13: A Darker Continent

266 **he wields a new** GBS to ACG, 30 October 1940, Texas.

267 *To strive, to seek* Letters from Ettie Desborough to ACG, family collection.

268 **to have a yarn** ACG to William Lashly, 5 May 1916.

268 **came from one who** William Lashly to ACG, 31 January 1920.

268 **So now he lies** *Polar Record* III, 20 (July 1940), p. 331.

268 **I think the only** CS to Clara Turner, 30 October 1941, family collection.

269 **the best book in** *New Statesman and Nation*, 21 March 1942.

269 fn. **the only one who** Nancy Mitford, *The Water Beetle*, 1962, p. 18.

269 fn. **If Cherry-Garrard had** *The Letters of Nancy Mitford and Evelyn Waugh*, ed. Charlotte Mosley, 1996, pp. 465–6.

270 **general paralysis of the** AM, conversation with author.

271 **Please stop coming here . . . I'm going to add** *and all other direct speech* AM, *ibid.*

271 **We should be so** *ibid.*

271 **But who brings you** *ibid.*

271 **We think you are** ECG to AM (then Cherry-Garrard), 17 June [no year], family collection.

271 **We think he is** *ibid.*

272 **I have thought it** ACG to Harold Raymond, 2 July 1942, Reading University.

272 **The large private house** *Financial Times*, 15 October 1935.

272 **London's most up-to** *St Pancras Chronicle*, 25 October 1935.

272 **Optional Service will solve** Various adverts, 1940, Dorset House archive.

274 *Wartime Worries Solved* *ibid.*

276 **a poor creature, an** James Lees-Milne, *Ancestral Voices*, 1975, p. 31.

276 **Kathleen. No happier woman** Lady Kennet [KS], *Self-Portrait*, p. 361.

276 **She took hold of** Young, p. 272.

276 **Bill had very little** Annotated journal [September 1910].

276 **not what I had** GBS to ACG and AM (then Cherry-Garrard), 26 September 1943, family collection.

276 **quite happy** ACG, notes about Charlotte's death, 'about February 1944', family collection.

277 **A. has flu. I** AM, conversation with author.

278 **the loss of him** Evelyn Forbes, conversation with author.

279 **cataleptic stroke** AM, conversation with author.

280 **the bedrock of existence** Draft material, *WJ*.

280 **the trail of broken . . . Polar madness** Priestley, 'The Polar Expedition'.

281 **There are many cases** *ibid*.

282 **It is easy to** William Styron, *Darkness Visible*, 1991, p. 44.

282 **hysterical hemiplegia** Annotated journal [March 1912].

282 **Of course, she was** *ibid*. [September 1910].

282 fn. **I would rather have** Sylvia Plath (first published under pseudonym 'Victoria Lucas'), *The Bell Jar*, 1963, p. 193.

283 **Cherry v. upset** AM (then Cherry-Garrard), Diary, 22 December 1946, family collection.

283 **was almost like a** ACG to Hugh Farrer, 27 September 1947, Hertford.

Chapter 14: A Winter Journey Indeed

284 **He did love Lamer** *and all other direct speech* AM, conversation with author.

284 **You will outlive Cherry** GBS to AM (then Cherry-Garrard), 12 August 1947, family collection.

285 **You really are a** Rupert Reynell to ACG, 30 October 1947, family collection.

286 **He has recovered his** GBS to Hilton Young, 2 March 1948, Kennet Papers.

286 **This is the Lamer** Family collection.

287 **I think they are** *The Clique*, 7 June 1952.

287 **the generosity, clarity and** Private correspondence, 10 September 1983.

288 **Besides a general aversion** FD, '*Scott of the Antarctic*: A Personal Opinion', *Polar Record* V, 37 & 38 (January–July 1949), p. 311.

288 **The more I read** David James, *Scott of the Antarctic*, 1948, p. 136.

288 **Try and throw your** ACG, 'Notes on conversation with Wright', 26 October 1948 (notes inserted in Annotated journal).

289 **Of course, it is** Annotated journal ['Note written on the Barrier'].

289 **Here was Scott with** Marginalia, private collection.

289 **He decided to write a frank postscript** In 1948 GBS drafted a short postscript which Cherry eventually rejected in favour of his own, much longer version. Shaw's shorthand copy of his suggested postscript can be seen at the Carl A. Kroch Library, Cornell University.

289 **It may be historically** ACG to Allen Lane, 24 July 1950, Bristol.

289 **I am now a** ACG to Harold Raymond, 9 July 1948, Reading University.

290 **in this sort of** *et seq.* Postscript, pp. 589–600.

290 **a winter journey indeed** *ibid.*, p. 603.

290 **a somewhat tortuous document** Introduction to *WJ*, p. lxxvii.

290 **We cannot stop knowledge** Postscript, p. 602.

291 **To me, and perhaps** *ibid.*, p. 603.

291 **Mottled on top of** Birding notes, n.d., family collection.

292 **I never opened this** Family collection.

292 **The nursing home, said** ACG to GBS, 8 June 1950, Texas.

292 **The squire abandons his** *The Freethinker*, 30 June 1946.

292 **quite the best brain** Annotated journal [September 1910].

292 **Poor boy. I wish** Isabel Smith to George Seaver, 7 January 1934.

293 **I come to you** ACG to George Seaver, Christmas card, 1950.

293 **won't believe it when** FD to AM (then Cherry-Garrard), [n.d.] October 1959, family collection.

293 **school, country club or** Particulars, Frederick Reeks & Goode, Auctioneers, July 1948, private collection.

294 **There is about London**, Edmund Wilson, *Europe without Baedecker*, 1948, p. 5.

294 **roaring like a thousand** *Man of Everest: The Autobiography of Tenzing told to James Ramsey Ullman*, 1955, p. 255.

294 **I have never heard** *WJ*, p. 288.

294 **I read it time** Edmund Hillary, *View from the Summit*, 1999, p. 124.

294 **chafed by nearly half** Vivian Fuchs & Edmund Hillary, *The Crossing of Antarctica*, 1958, p. 96.

296 **halo of good fellowship** *WJ*, p. 318.

297 **Know yourself. Accept yourself** Postscript, p. 593.

297 **here and here by** Robert Graves, 'Flying Crooked', in *Poems 1926–1930*, 1931.

297 **charming and lacelike** Oxford Diocesan Papers, Oxfordshire County Archives.

298 **We shall visit the** Draft material, *WJ*.

298 **Men do not fear** *WJ*, p. 287.

Select Bibliography

All books published in London unless otherwise stated.

Amundsen, Roald, *The South Pole*, 2 vols., 1912

Arnold, H. J. P., *Photographer of the World: A Biography of Herbert Ponting*, 1969

Brendon, Piers, *The Dark Valley: A Panorama of the 1930s*, 2000

Campbell, Victor, *The Wicked Mate: the Antarctic Diary of Victor Campbell*, ed. H. G. R. King, Huntingdon, 1988

Cherry-Garrard, Apsley, *The Worst Journey in the World*, 1922

——, *The Worst Journey in the World, with Postscript*, 1951

——, Untitled biographical essay in *T. E. Lawrence by his Friends*, ed. A. W. Lawrence, 1936

Clark, Kenneth, *Another Part of the Wood*, 1974

Dangerfield, George, *The Strange Death of Liberal England*, New York, 1935

Debenham, Frank, *The Quiet Land: The Antarctic Diaries of Frank Debenham*, ed. June Debenham Back, Huntingdon, 1992

Evans, E. R. G. R., *South with Scott*, 1921

Fussell, Paul, *The Great War and Modern Memory*, Oxford, 1975

Girouard, Mark, *The Return to Camelot*, New Haven, 1981

Gran, Tryggve, *The Norwegian with Scott*, 1984

Jones, Steve, *Almost Like a Whale: The Origin of Species Updated*, 1999

Holroyd, Michael, *Bernard Shaw*, vols. I–V, 1988–92

——, *Lytton Strachey*, 1967

Huntford, Roland, *Scott and Amundsen*, 1979

——, *Shackleton*, 1985

——, *Nansen*, 1997

Select Bibliography

Huxley, Elspeth, *Scott of the Antarctic*, 1977

Kennet, Lady Kathleen (Kathleen Scott), *Self-Portrait of an Artist*, 1949

Lashly, William, *The Diary of William Lashly*, Reading, 1940

Laurence, Dan H. (ed.), *Bernard Shaw: Collected Letters* III (1911–1925), 1985

Lawrence, T. E., *Letters, Vol I: Correspondence with Bernard and Charlotte Shaw 1922–1926*, ed. Jeremy & Nicole Wilson, Woodgreen Common, 2000

——, *The Letters of T. E. Lawrence*, ed. Malcolm Brown, Oxford, 1991

Lees-Milne, James, *Ancestral Voices*, 1975

Levick, G. Murray, *Antarctic Penguins: a Study of their Social Habits*, 1914

Limb, Sue & Cordingley, Patrick, *Captain Oates: Soldier and Explorer*, 1995

Mackenzie, Compton, *Sinister Street*, 2 vols., 1913–14

Mais, S. P. B., *All the Days of My Life*, 1937

Manning, Frederic, *Her Privates We*, unexpurgated edition, 1999

Parker, Peter, *The Old Lie: the Great War and the Public School Ethos*, 1987

Ponting, Herbert, *The Great White South*, 1921

Pound, Reginald, *Evans of the Broke*, Oxford, 1963

Priestley, Raymond, *Antarctic Adventure*, 1914

Sassoon, Siegfried, *Memoirs of a Fox-hunting Man*, 1928

——, *The Old Century*, 1938

Scott, Robert Falcon, *The Voyage of the 'Discovery'*, 1905

——, (*et al.*), *Scott's Last Expedition*, arranged Leonard Huxley, 2 vols., 1913

——, *The Diaries of Captain Robert Scott*, 6 vols., facsimile edition, Tylers Green, 1968

Seaver, George, *Edward Wilson of the Antarctic*, 1933

——, *Edward Wilson, Nature Lover*, 1937

——, *Birdie Bowers of the Antarctic*, 1938

——, *The Faith of Edward Wilson*, 1948

Shackleton, Sir Ernest, *South*, 1919

Sissons, Michael & French, Philip (eds.), *Age of Austerity: 1945–51*, 1963

Smith, Michael, *An Unsung Hero: Tom Crean – Antarctic Survivor*, Cork, 2000

Solomon, Susan, *The Coldest March*, New Haven, 2001

The South Polar Times III (1911), facsimile edition, 1914

Styron, William, *Darkness Visible*, 1991

Symons, A. J. A., *The Quest for Corvo*, 1934

Taylor, Thomas Griffith, *With Scott: the Silver Lining*, 1916

Thomson, David, *Scott's Men*, 1977

Tuchman, Barbara, *The Proud Tower*, 1966

Wilson, D. M., & Elder, D. B., *Cheltenham in Antarctica: the Life of Edward Wilson*, Cheltenham, 2000

Wilson, Edward, *Diary of the Terra Nova Expedition to the Antarctic 1910–1912*, ed. H. G. R. King, 1972

Wolpert, Lewis, *Malignant Sadness: The Anatomy of Depression*, 1999

Wright, Charles, *Silas: The Antarctic Diaries and Memoir of Charles S. Wright*, ed. Colin Bull & Pat F. Wright, Columbus, 1993

Yelverton, David E., *Antarctica Unveiled*, Boulder, 2000

Young, Louisa, *A Great Task of Happiness: the Life of Kathleen Scott*, 1995

Selected Unpublished Sources

Bowers, Henry, Diary and Letters, various dates, SPRI

Chatto & Windus Archive, University of Reading

Cherry-Garrard, Miscellaneous Papers, Berkshire Record Office, Reading

Cherry-Garrard Archive, SPRI (includes Cherry's Antarctic journals, as well as correspondence with Atkinson, Lillie, Kathleen Scott, Oriana Wilson, Sidney Harmer and many others)

Constable & Co. Directors' Files, Special Collections Department, Temple University Libraries, Philadelphia

Emery Walker Collection, Harry Ransom Humanities Research Center, University of Texas at Austin

Garrard Papers, Hertfordshire Archives and Local Studies, Hertford

George Bernard Shaw Collection, Harry Ransom Humanities Research Center, University of Texas at Austin

Keohane, Patrick, Diary, 1911–12, SPRI

Oates, Lawrence, Letters to his mother, various dates, SPRI

Penguin Archive, University of Bristol

Simpson, George, Diary, 1910–12, SPRI

Scott, Kathleen, Diary, various dates (Kennet Papers, Cambridge University Library)

Williamson, Thomas, Diary, 1912–13, SPRI

Guide to Selected Antarcticans

Name	Title/Job	Nickname
E. R. Atkinson	Navy doctor & parasitologist	Atch
Henry Bowers	Lieutenant	Birdie
Victor Campbell	Lieutenant	The Wicked Mate
Tom Crean	Petty Officer	
Frank Debenham	Geologist	Deb
Edgar Evans	Petty Officer	Taff
Edward R. G. R. Evans	Lieutenant	Teddy
Dimitri Gerof	Dog-handler	
Tryggve Gran	Sub-Lieutenant, Norwegian navy; skiing expert	
William Lashly	Leading Stoker	
Denis Lillie	Ship's biologist	
Cecil Meares	In charge of dogs	
Edward Nelson	Biologist	Marie
Lawrence Oates	Army Captain	Titus
Harry Pennell	Lieutenant & navigator	Penelope
Herbert Ponting	Camera Artist	
Raymond Priestley	Geologist	
Robert Falcon Scott	Captain	The Owner
George Simpson	Meteorologist	Sunny Jim
Thomas Griffith Taylor	Geologist & physiographer	Griff
Edward Wilson	Chief of scientific staff & zoologist	Uncle Bill; Bill
Charles Wright	Physicist	Silas

Acknowledgements

The mystery and opacity of much of Cherry's long life meant that I often had to turn to others for advice, and I would like to acknowledge with gratitude the debts that I owe to the following individuals: John Allen; Allan Ashworth; Steve Blake at the Cheltenham Museum and Art Gallery; Malcolm Burr; Peter Clarkson; Amy Coburn; Trevor Cornford; Judith Curthoys at Christ Church, Oxford; Alison Edmonds; Ann L. Ferguson at Cornell; Evelyn Forbes; Steve Forbes; Oliver Garnett; Dave and Angela Gifford; John Gott; Bob Headland, Lucy Martin, Shirley Sawtell and the other staff of the Scott Polar Research Institute, Cambridge; Michael Holroyd; Simon Houfe; Clifford H. Irwin; Andrew Isles; Ruth Jeavons; Harry King; Nick Lambourn; Andrew Lycett; Luke McKernan; Steve Martin at the Mitchell Library in Sydney; Bruno Pappalardo at the Public Record Office at Kew; the late Alan Ross; Steve Sinon; Ian Smith; Mick Smith; Lisa Spurrier at the Berkshire Record Office; Barry Stephenson at Bedford Central Library; Penny Stokes; Melinda Varcoe; David Wilson; and Peter Wordie. Like many authors before me I am immensely grateful to Douglas Matthews, who prepared the index. Churchill College gave me a temporary home in Cambridge, and I owe a particular debt to Andrew Tristram and other members of staff there.

I particularly want to thank Roland Huntford. He shared his material with unstinting generosity, compiled background reading lists and offered practical advice. I think, in the end, that we disagree about many important issues (and people); but that, of course, couldn't matter less. At the beginning he told me graciously that Cherry was a closed book to him, and that the subject needed a female biographer. I don't know if the latter is true, but it was typically generous of Roland to say it.

I owe much to my publisher Dan Franklin, my editor Tristan Jones and my agent Gillon Aitken, and also to my editor at Random House in New York, Joy de Menil. My former editor, Tony Colwell, who taught me so much, always wanted me to write Cherry's biography. He had the first draft at his bedside when he died. As the final script took shape I tried to imagine him at my side, like the old days. Jeremy Lewis and Lucinda Riches battled through early drafts, as always; I rely on them. Peter Graham, my editor of first resort, lived for years with Cherry as well as with me, and still he was an astute reader. As for Hugh Turner, who contributed so very much at the beginning and the end: somehow, he understood everything.

My largest debt, of course, is to Cherry's widow Angela Mathias. When she agreed to co-operate with a biographer for the first time she had little idea what lay on the road ahead. Nobody will ever know the journey that she and I made together. I want to say that for my part I am most glad that we did it; and that we kept going till the end. Thank you.

I am extremely grateful to the following for permission to quote from published and unpublished works: Berkshire Record Office (Cherry-Garrard Papers); Barbara Debenham and June Debenham Back (*The Quiet Land* and unpublished material by Frank Debenham); The Hon. Edward Broke Evans (*South with Scott* and unpublished material by E. R. G. R. Evans); Chatto & Windus and the University of Reading (Chatto & Windus Archive); Hertfordshire Archives and Local Studies (Garrard Papers); Harry Ransom Humanities Research Center, University of Texas at Austin (Emery Walker Collection and George Bernard Shaw Collection); Lord Kennet of the Dene (Kathleen Scott's diary); the London School of Economics (Beatrice Webb's diary); Angela Mathias (*The Worst Journey in the World* and unpublished material by Apsley Cherry-Garrard); Mitchell Library, State University of New South Wales (Cherry's marginalia); John Murray Ltd (*Edward Wilson of the Antarctic*, *Birdie Bowers of the Antarctic* and *The Faith of Edward Wilson* by George Seaver); Ohio State University Press (Silas Wright's diary); Penguin Ltd and the University of Bristol (Penguin Archive); Scott Polar Research Institute (unpublished material by Henry Bowers, Frank Debenham, Pat Keohane, Lawrence Oates, Raymond Priestley, Kathleen Scott, Robert Scott, George Simpson, Thomas Williamson, Edward and Oriana Wilson, and Cherry himself); the Society of Authors on behalf of the Estate of Bernard Shaw; Temple University Libraries, Pennsylvania (Constable & Co. Directors' Files); the Trustees of the Will of Mrs Bernard Shaw.

The author and publishers are grateful to the following for permission to reproduce illustrations: Cheltenham Art Gallery & Museum; Christ Church College, Oxford; Mr John Gott; Mrs Angela Mathias; Scott Polar Research Institute; Alexander Turnbull Library, National Library of New Zealand; Winchester College; and Mr Peter Wordie.

Every effort has been made to contact the owners of copyright material reproduced herein. The author and publishers apologise for any inadvertent omissions, and will be pleased to incorporate missing acknowledgements in any future editions.

Index